D1609640

Books of the Bible
Vol. 5

THE BOOK OF PSALMS

Garland Reference Library
of the Humanities
Vol. 1413

BOOKS OF THE BIBLE

HENRY O. THOMPSON
Series Editor

THE BOOK OF PSALMS
An Annotated Bibliography
Thorne Wittstruck

I CORINTHIANS
An Annotated Bibliography
Watson E. Mills

THE BOOK OF REVELATION
An Annotated Bibliography
Robert L. Muse

THE BOOK OF DANIEL
An Annotated Bibliography
Henry O. Thompson

THE BOOK OF RUTH
An Annotated Bibliography
Mishael Maswari Caspi

THE BOOK OF PSALMS

An Annotated Bibliography

VOLUME I

Thorne Wittstruck

GARLAND PUBLISHING, INC.
New York & London / 1994

Library of Congress Cataloging-in-Publication Data

Wittstruck, Thorne.
The Book of Psalms : an annotated bibliography / Thorne Wittstruck.
p. cm. — (Books of the Bible ; vol. 5) (Garland reference library of the humanities ; vol. 1413)
Includes bibliographical references.
ISBN 0-8240-4700-1
1. Bible. O.T. Psalms—Indexes. 2. Bible. O.T. Psalms—Bibliography. I. Title. II. Series. III. Series: Garland reference library of the humanities ; vol. 1413.
BS1430.2.B63 1994
016.223'2—dc20 94-20559
CIP

Printed on acid-free, 250-year-life paper
Manufactured in the United States of America

For

Linda Miller Wittstruck

"My heart overflows with a goodly theme."
Psalm 45:1

And

Christopher Thorne Wittstruck

Heather Lyn Wittstruck

Naomi Elizabeth Sea Young Wittstruck

"I will cause your name to be celebrated in all generations;
therefore the peoples will praise you forever and ever."
Psalm 45:17

Advisory Board

The Book of Psalms
An Annotated Bibliography

Series Preface

It is a great pleasure to commend this annotated bibliography to the public. The pleasure is personal and professional. The Psalms have meant so much to millions. They have been heard on the lips of children. They have helped people in trouble, depression, sorrow, doubt, sickness and health. They have provided words for the unspeakable joy of faith. These words have been read and memorized and above all, sung, through the ages. Psalm 23 has been heard at the bedside of the dying. Dr. Wittstruck's fine work will facilitate the study, understanding and appreciation of what is surely one of the great compilations of poetry, serving devotions, learning, art, music. The plan presented in the table of contents will guide users to the several approaches to the psalms and to individual psalms, for special study or just because they are favorites or especially meaningful.

This volume is one of a series of bibliographies on the books of the Bible. As a whole, these bibliographies should be of value to students and faculty, to laity and professional, to religious and academic groups, to undergraduate and to graduate study. They have a significant role as reference works in libraries for the public, the university and religious groups, as well as individuals.

The series includes the Hebrew Scriptures (canon, rule of faith), which Jews call the Tenak or Tanakh, after the opening letters of its divisions: Torah (Instruction or Law), Nabiim (Prophets) and Kethubim (Writings; from the Hebrew for "cut" as in preparing a reed or quill pen). Christians call these Scriptures the Old Testament (OT). The Christian Bible includes the New Testament (NT). For Jews and Protestant Christians the Tenak and the OT are the same, though they arrange the books in a different order. Roman Catholic and Eastern Orthodox Christians have fifteen (more or less) additional Writings in the OT. Some call these deuterocanonical, "second canon," others say Apocrypha ("Hidden"). The series will include the latter.

Authors come from across the Judeo-Christian perspective and across doctrinal perspectives. Each author or compiler has had freedom of selectivity under the general rubric that the final product should be representative and comprehensive for the last fifty years with greater selectivity prior to that. Comprehensive here does not mean every thing in print, exhaustive. In general, it does mean available, though a few may be known but not available to the compiler. These are normally noted. The annotation has also been selective though sufficient to be of service to the user. There are several ways in which users can be of service to the series. One is notice of the continuing appearance of materials after an individual bibliographical volume has gone into print. Another is correction of errors in fact. While every effort has been made for complete accuracy, in works of this kind perfection is an ideal dreamed of, striven for, but seldom attained. Thirdly, if a reader knows where any item marked "unseen" or unavailable may be found, that information will be appreciated.

It is a joy to thank those who are making the series possible. That includes Dr. Thorne Wittstruck, other authors and the editorial board. It includes Garland Publishing for their services in producing these volumes. A special thank you to Editor Phyllis Korper, for commissioning the series, for editorial advice and direction, for a listening ear, a friendly voice.

Henry O. Thompson
Series Editor

Preface

In a work such as this, I cannot claim to have introduced some startling new and creative approach to the study of the Psalms. An annotated bibliography reflects the work of many, most notably the original authors. What I can claim, however, is to have encountered some truly gifted and inspiring people, and to have been blessed through a deeper encounter with the psalms themselves. They speak profound truths with the most simple and beautiful images. They touch our souls and shape our spiritual journeys in ways not always apparent to the conscious mind and the feeling heart. How to convey the fullness of these psalms? That is the question. Our task should certainly be that of Gunkel's -- to bring them to speech, to allow the voice that is within them to be heard. Here I believe Lamparter is right. It is not enough to have an aesthetic appreciation of the psalms, for they claim to be talk about God. The psalmists cannot be understood as isolated individuals, alone and apart from the worshipping congregation, for these psalms reflect the corporate life of worship and the shared journey of fellow believers.

How wide to draw the circle, that is the basic question. In attempting to answer that most basic question, I took my cue from various commentaries. I made one significant change, though, in the listing for the individual psalms. The interpretation of the psalms belongs not simply to the scholars; it also belongs to the musicians and to the preachers. I have thus included representative work from these fields. As the project developed, I soon became aware that the projected 500 pages simply would not be adequate. Garland Publishing was kind enough to permit a 1000 page volume. Even so, the challenge was how to reduce a 3000 page manuscript down to a 1000 page book. The process was painful and the task was not unlike a **JEDP** series of redactions. It began with **J**ust what seemed necessary -- 3000 pages. That was too much so I began to **E**liminate. This redaction shortened the annotations and drew a tighter circle. The 1700 pages was still too much. Therefore came the **D**elete stage.

Delete, Delete, Delete. 1250 pages was still too much. Finally the **P**ainful **P**rinting of the 1000 page book. In the process some rather impractical ideas had to be given up -- such as including a 100 page English summary of Mowinckel's *Psalmenstudien* and a 70 page English summary of Gunkel's *Einleitung*. The music took a beating; in fact, there came a night when the music almost died. Psalm 23, for example, started with 338 musical entries and ended up with only 19; Psalm 46 went from 143 musical entries to 8; Psalm 100 from 311 musical entries to 13. Many of the German and French commentaries originally had 4-5 page English summaries. Other casualties were commentaries from the 15th-18th centuries, as well as articles written before 1940. The result is a much tighter circle than I had wished, but I believe that there is enough here to get one pointed in the right direction.

I want to thank Henry O. Thompson for inviting me to be part of this project and Thurman Coss for suggesting my name. The entire process has been an inspiring adventure. I have enjoyed using the facilities of Luther-Northwestern Seminary for several years and had a productive two weeks using the Harvard Libraries this past summer. HOLLIS was a major help. Thanks also to Randy, Shirlee, Mark, Matthew, and Karen Ferrara for housing me during my stay in Boston. Not only was I able to renew friendships; I was also able to meet sundry ice dancing pairs as they skated in and out of the house. I also want to thank the people of God known as Evangel United Methodist Church. It has been a blessing to share ministry with them and to be inspired and challenged each week by their music and their faith. I thank them for allowing me to participate in this project. I am glad when they say to me, "Let us go up to the house of the Lord."

World Communion Sunday — Thorne Wittstruck
October 3, 1993

1. General Surveys and Studies

A. General Surveys

1. Anderson, A.A. "Psalm Study between 1955-1969." *Baptist Quarterly* 23 (1969): 155-163.

2. Beaucamp, Évode. "Psaumes II. Le Psautier." In *Supplément au Dictionnaire de la Bible 9,* ed. H. Cazelles and A. Feuillet. Cols. 125-206. Paris: Letouzey et Ané, 1979.

3. Beauchamp, Paul. "Bulletin d'exégèse de l'Ancien Testament." *Recherches de science religieuse* 72 (1984): 85-96.

4. Becker, J. *Wege der Psalmenexegese.* Stuttgarter Bibelstudien 78. Stuttgart: Verlag Katholisches Bibelwerk, 1975.

   A discussion of the rise of form criticism with Gunkel, the cultic approach of Mowinckel and others, plus studies of other approaches to the psalms. The final chapter considers the meaning of the psalms in the New Testament and in the Catholic tradition.

5. Binnie, William. *The Psalms: Their History, Teachings, and Use.* London: T. Nelson and Sons, 1870. xvi+414p. New ed., 1886.

6. Bjørndalen, Anders Jørgen. "Selected Aspects of Nordic Traditio-Historical Psalm Research Since Engnell: Limitations and Possibilities." In *The Productions of Time. Tradition History in Old Testament Scholarship,* ed. Knud

Jeppesen and Benedikt Otzen. 107-125. Sheffield: Almond, 1984.

7. Childs, Brevard S. "Reflections on the Modern Study of the Psalms." In *Magnalia Dei: The Mighty Acts of God. Essays on the Bible and Archaeology in Memory of G. Ernest Wright*, ed. Frank Moore Cross, Jr., Werner E. Lemke and Patrick D. Miller, Jr. 377-388. Garden City, NY: Doubleday & Company, 1976.

Evaluates modern trends and developments in research. One of his main concerns is how the Psalter came to be Sacred Scripture, and what this means for Christians.

8. Claudel, Pierre. "Les Psaumes. Courants et problèmes actuels d'exégèse." L'*Ami du Clergé* 73 (1963): 65-77.

9. Clements, Ronald E. "Interpreting the Psalms." Chap. in *One Hundred Years of Old Testament Interpretation.* 76-98. Philadelphia: Westminster Press, 1976.

Focuses mainly on Gunkel and Mowinckel and reactions to their approaches.

10. Clines, D.J.A. "Psalm Research since 1955." *The Tyndale Bulletin* 18 (1967): 103-126; 20 (1969): 105-126.

11. Coppens, Joseph. "Le Psautier et ses Problèmes." *Analecta Lovaniensia Biblica et Orientalia* 3 (1960): 906-915.

12. ______. "Études Récentes sur le Psautier." In *Le Psautier: Ses origines. Ses problèmes littérraires. Son influence*, ed. Robert de Langhe. Orientalia et Biblica Lovaniensia IV. 1-71. Louvain: Publications Universitaires, 1962.

13. Cosgrave, F.H. "Recent Studies on the Psalms." *Canadian Society of Biblical Studies Bulletin* 5 (July, 1939): 3-15.

14. Descamps, A. "Les genres littéraires du Psautier. Un état de la question." In *Le Psautier: Ses origines. Ses problèmes littérraires. Son influence*, ed. Robert de Langhe. Orientalia et Biblica Lovaniensia, IV. 73-88. Louvain: Publications Universitaires, 1962.

15. Eaton, J.H. "The Psalms in Israelite Worship." In *Tradition and Interpretation*, ed. G.W. Anderson. 238-273. Oxford: At the Clarendon Press, 1979.

16. Engert, Thaddaeus. *Der betende Gerechte der Psalmen. Historisch-kritische Untersuchung als Beitrag zu einer Einleitung in den Psalter.* Würzburg: Göbel & Scherer, 1902. iv+134p.

17. Feininger, Bernd. "A Decade of German Psalm Criticism." *Journal for the Study of the Old Testament* 20 (1981): 91-103.

18. Fransen, Irénée. "Psaumes, Psautiers et Célébrations." *Bible et Vie Chrétienne* 43 (1962): 75-81.

19. Galling, Kurt. "Psalmen. I. Im AT." In *Die Religion in Geschichte und Gegenwart. Handwörterbuch für Theologie und Religionswissenschaft*, ed. K. Galling and Others. 3rd. ed. V: Cols. 672-684. Tübingen: J.C.B. Mohr (Paul Siebeck), 1961.

20. Gerstenberger, Erhard S. "Literatur zu den Psalmen." *Verkündigung und Forschung* 17 (1972): 82-99.

21. ______. "Zur Interpretation der Psalmen." *Verkündigung und Forschung* 19 (1974): 22-45.

22. ______. "Psalms." In *Old Testament Form Criticism*, ed. John H. Hayes. 179-223. San Antonio, TX: Trinity University Press, 1974.

Traces the history of psalm research and especially of the form-critical approach.

23. Goeke, Hugo. "Das fremde Gesangbuch. Hilfen zur Arbeit mit den Psalmen und zu ihrem Verständnis." *Bibel und Kirche* 26 (1971): 114-118.

24. Goy, William A. "Quatre ouvrages catholiques français sur les psaumes." *Revue de Théologie et de Philosophie,* Third Series, 2 (1952): 39-45.

25. Gunkel, Hermann. "Aeltere und neuere Psalmenforschungen." *Die Christliche Welt* 30 (1916): 142-151.

26. Halévy, J. *Recherches bibliques, notes pour l'interpretation des Psaumes.* Tome III. Paris: Leroux, 1905.

27. Haller, Max. "Ein Jahrzehnt Psalmenforschung." *Theologische Rundschau,* N.F., 1 (1929): 377-402.

28. Hauge, Martin Ravndal. "Sigmund Mowinckel and the Psalms -- A Query into His Concern." *Scandinavian Journal of the Old Testament* 2 (2,1988): 56-71.

29. Hauret, Charles. "L'interprétation des psaumes selon l'école 'Myth and Ritual.'" *Recherches des Sciences Religieuses* 33 (1959): 321-342; 34 (1960): 1-34.

30. ______. "Les Psaumes, études récentes état de la question." In *Où en sont les études bibliques? Les grands problèmes actuels de l'exégèse*, ed. J.J. Weber, J. Schmit and Others. 67-84. Paris: Éditions du Centurion, 1968.

31. Hempel, Johannes. "Neue Literatur zum Studium des Psalters." *Zeitschrift für die alttestamentliche Wissenschaft* 56 (1938): 171-174.

32. Holladay, William L. *The Psalms Through Three Thousand Years. Prayerbook of a Cloud of Witnesses.* Minneapolis, MN: Augsburg Fortress, 1993. 360p.

Combines treatment concerning the origins of the Psalms with attention to their Jewish and Christian use through history.

33. Hopkins, Denise Dombrowski. "New Directions in Psalms Research -- Good News for Theology and Church." *Saint Luke's Journal of Theology* 29 (1986): 271-283.

34. Hunt, Ignatius. "Recent Psalm Study." *Worship* 41 (1967): 85-98.; 47 (1973): 80-93; 49 (1975): 202-214; 49 (1975): 283-294; 51 (1977): 127-144; 52 (1978): 245-258; 53 (1979): 221-241.

35. Johnson, Aubrey R. "The Psalms." In *The Old Testament and Modern Study: A Generation of Discovery and Research. Essays by Members of the Society for Old Testament Study*, ed. H.H. Rowley. 162-209. Oxford: At the Clarendon Press, 1951; reprint, 1961.

Surveys significant work done on the Psalms during the past 30 years, focusing primarily on Gunkel and Mowinckel.

36. Kapelrud, A.S. "Scandinavian Research in the Psalms after Mowinckel." *Annual of the Swedish Theological Institute* 4 (1965): 74-90.

37. ______. "Die skandinavische Einleitungswissenschaft zu den Psalmen." *Verkündigung und Forschung* 11 (1966): 62-93.

38. Ker, John. *The Psalms in History and Biography.* Edinburgh: Andres Elliot, 1887. xvi+219p.

39. Kroeze, J.H. "Some Remarks on recent trends in the exegesis of the Psalms." In *Studies on the Psalms: Papers Read at the 6th Meeting of Die O.T. Werkgemeenskap in Siud-Afrika.* 40-47. Potchefstroom: Pro Rege, 1963.

40. Le Roux, J.H. "W.S. Prinsloo se immanente lees van die Psalms." *Nederduits Gereformeerde Teleogiese Tydskrif* 30 (1989): 383-391.

W.S. Prinsloo's Immanent Reading of the Psalms, focusing on the final form rather than the formation history of the individual psalms.

41. Leslie, Elmer A. "The Book of Psalms." *Interpretation* 4 (1950): 62-77.

42. Lipiński, Edward. "Psaumes. - I. Formes et genres littéraires." In *Dictionnaire de la Bible Supplément 9,* ed. H. Cazelles and A. Feuillet. Cols. 1-125. Paris: Letouzey & Ané, 1979.

43. Lods, A. "Recherches récentes sur le Livre des Psaumes. Les Idées de M. Mowinckel." *Revue de l'histoire des religions* 45 (1925): 15-34.

44. Miller, Patrick D., Jr. "Current Issues in Psalms Studies." *Word and World* 5 (1985): 132-143.

45. Montgomery, James A. "Recent Developments in the Study of the Psalms." *Anglican Theological Review* 16 (1934): 185-198.

46. Mowinckel, Sigmund. "Psalm Criticism between 1900 and 1935 (Ugarit and Psalm Exegesis)." *Vetus Testamentum* 5 (1955): 13-33. Translated into German by Hermann-Josef Dirksen and printed as "Psalmenkritik zwischen 1900 und 1935. Ugarit und die Psalmenexegese" in *Zur Neueren Psalmenforschung*, ed. Peter H.A. Neumann, 315-340; Darmstadt: Wissenschaftliche Buchgesellschaft, 1976.

47. Neumann, Peter H.A., ed. *Zur neueren Psalmenforschung.* Wege der Forschung 192. Darmstadt: Wissenschaftliche Buchgesellschaft, 1976. 484p.

An anthology of significant studies on the Psalms during the previous 75 years.

48. Ohlmeyer, Albert. *Reichtum der Psalmen. Erschlossen von Heiligen aller Christlicher Zeiten.* 2 vols. Frankfurt am Main: Verlag Josef Knecht, 1965. 566p.

A compilation of short studies and meditations by a variety of people representing a variety of historical periods. The volumes are arranged in a way to facilitate locating a particular author or verse.

49. Ploeg, J. van der. "L'étude du Psautier, 1960 à 1967." In *De Mari a Qumran. Donum Natalicium Iosepho Coppens,* ed. H. Cazelles. Vol. 1: *L'Ancien Testament. Son Milieu. Ses*

Ecrits. Ses relectures juives. 174-191. Paris: P. Lethiellieux, 1969; Gembloux: Duculot, 1969.

50. Prothero, Rowland E. Prothero (1851-1937) *The Psalms in Human Life.* New York: E.P. Dutton & Co., 1909. 301p.

The Psalms as they appear in the life and writings of people from early Christianity to 1900.

51. Rappoport, Angelo Solomon. *The Psalms in Life, Legend, and Literature.* London: The Centenary Press, 1935. 239p.

Jewish and Christian interpretations from all ages on the authorship, character and contents, moral teaching, and theodicy of the Psalms.

52. Ridderbos, Nic. H. "De huidige stand van het onderzoek de Psalmen." *Gereformeerd Teologisch Tijdschrift* 60 (1960): 8-14. Reprinted in *Psalmenstudie. Prof. Nic. H. Ridderbos en het boek der Psalmen. Opstellen van prof. dr. Nic. H. Ridderbos,* ed. C. Van Ginkel and P.J. van Midden. 79-85. Kampen: Kok, 1991.

53. Rose, André. *Psaumes et prière chrétienne. Essai sur la lecture de quelques psaumes dans la tradition chrétienne.* Paroisse et Liturgie Collection de Pastorale Liturgique 66. Bruges: La Colombe, 1965. 298p.

54. ______. "Publications sur Psautier." *La Maison-Dieu* 93 (1968): 152-156.

55. Rowley, H.H. "Twentieth Century Trends in Psalm Criticism." *The Bible and Modern Religious Thought* 18 (January, 1940): 8.

56. Saint-Arnaud, I. "Psaumes. IV. Les Psaumes dans la tradition chrétienne" In *Dictionnaire de la Bible Supplément 9,* ed. H. Cazelles and A. Feuillet. Cols. 206-214. Paris: Letouzey & Ané, 1979.

57. Scammon, J.H. "Changes in the Interpretation of the Psalms in One Man's Lifetime." *Andover Newton Quarterly* 12 (1971): 91-98.

58. Schildenberger, J. "Die Psalmen. Eine übersicht über einige Psalmenwerde der Gegenwart." *Bibel und Leben* 8 (1967): 220-231.

59. Schneider, Heinrich. "Psalmenfrömmigkeit einst und heute." *Geist und Leben* 33 (1960): 359-369.

The Psalms in the first five centuries, plus some comments on today's approach to the Psalms

60. Sellers, Ovid R. "The Status and Prospects of Research concerning the Psalms." In *The Study of the Bible Today and Tomorrow,* ed. Harold R. Willoughby. 129-143. Chicago: University of Chicago Press, 1947.

61. Seybold, Klaus. "Beiträge zur Psalmenforschung." *Theologische Rundschau* 46 (1981): 1-18.

62. Stamm, Johann Jakob. "Ein Viertel jahrhundert Psalmenforschung." *Theologische Rundschau,* N.F., 23 (1955): 1-68.

63. Steckelmacher, M. "Die Psalmen in der Bedeutung einiger ihrer älteren und neueren christlichen Interpreten." In

Judaica. Festschrift zu Hermann Cohens siebzigstem Geburtstage. 48-73. Berlin: B. Cassirer, 1912.

Discusses the views of Duhm and Gunkel and opposes them on the basis of pietistic and traditional Jewish exegesis.

64. Stendebach, Franz Josef. "Die Psalmen in der neueren Forschung." *Bibel und Kirche* 35 (1980): 60-70.

A survey of the past couple of decades of Psalm studies written in German.

65. Stensvaag, John M. "Recent Approaches to the Psalms." *Lutheran Quarterly* 9 (1957): 195-212.

66. Tate, Marvin E. "The Interpretation of the Psalms." *Review and Expositor* 81 (1984): 363-375.

67. Vermeylen, Jacques. "Où en est l'exégèse du psautier?" *Lumière et Vie* 40 (1991): 75-92.

Psalm exegesis of the last 100 years.

68. Weber, J.-J. *Le Psautier.* Résultat des 50 dernière années de la critique biblique. 2 vols. Rome: Vatican Library, 1968.

69. Weinrich, Franz Johannes. *Die Psalmen. Ihre tausendjährige Geschichte und immerwährende Bedeutung.* Buxheim: Martin Verlag, 1957. 43p.

70. Welch, Adam. *The Psalter in Life, Worship, and History.* Oxford: At the Clarendon Press, 1926.

B. General Studies

71. Ackroyd, Peter R. *Doors of Perception. A Guide to Reading the Psalms.* Foreword by the Archbishop of Canterbury. Leighton Buzzard: Faith Press, 1978; reprinted London: SCM Press, 1983. 95p.

72. Aletti, Jean-Noël, and Jacques Trublet. *Approche poétique et théologique des Psaumes: Analyses et méthodes.* Initiations. Paris: Éditions du Cerf, 1983. 297p.

A combination of rhetorical analysis of poetic biblical texts with the study of their literary forms. I. An analysis of structure in about 120 psalms. II. Literary forms, psalms of praise and supplication. III. "Codes and messages," a semantic approach.

73. Alter, Robert. "Psalms." In *The Literary Guide to the Bible,* ed. Robert Alter and Frank Kermode. 244-262. Cambridge, MA: The Belknap Press of Harvard University Press, 1987. 678p.

74. Anderson, Bernhard Word. *Out of the Depths: The Psalms Speak to Us Today.* New York: Board of Missions of the United Methodist Church, 1970. 191p. Revised and reprinted as *Out of the Depths: The Psalms Speak for Us Today* by Philadelphia: Westminster Press, 1983. 254p.

75. Barth, Christoph F. *Einführung in die Psalmen.* Biblische Studien 32. Neukirchen-Vluyn: Neukirchener Verlag, 1961. Translated into English by R.A. Wilson and published as *Introduction to the Psalms.* New York: Charles Scribner's Sons, 1966. 77p.

76. Becker, Joachim. *Israel deutet seine Psalmen: Urform und Neuinterpretation in den Psalmen.* Stuttgarter Bibelstudien 18. Stuttgart: Verlag Katholisches Bibelwerk, 1966; 2nd ed., 1967. 94p.

A number of Psalms have been reworked and given a new interpretation for a new time. Many Psalms, in the form in which they appear in the present Psalter, exhibit a sense which goes beyond that of the original setting. This process of revising and updating the psalms is called "*relecture,*" "rereading," or "*Neuinterpretation.*" It should not be confused with an "allegorical reading of the text." The "new interpretation" comes out of the intended literal sense of the text as recognized by the redactor.

77. Bellinger, W.H., Jr. *Psalms: Reading and Studying the Book of Praises.* Peabody, MA: Hendrickson Publishers, 1990. 166p.

"The Psalms function as pilgrimage songs of faith from the depths of human experience. As such, these songs sustain the pilgrim community, articulate its common life, and define its faith. The Psalter reveals much of prayer and the life of faith and beckons the contemporary worshipping community to enter its world, a world full of the divine gift of life."

78. Boer, P.A.H. de., ed. *Studies on Psalms.* Oudtestamentische Studiën 13. Leiden: E.J. Brill, 1963. 199p.

Includes "Gesinnungsethik im Psalter" by B. Gemser, "Die Rache- und Fluchpsalmen im Alten Testament" by H.A. Brongers, "The Psalms: Style-Figures and Structure" by Nic. H. Ridderbos, "Remarks on Various Passages of the Psalms" by G.J. Thierry, "Psalm XV - Eine königliche Einzugsliturgie?"

by J.L. Koole, "Psaume XXVI et l'innocence" by L.A. Snijders, "Zwei alte *cruces* im Psalter: Ps. XXXII 6 and Ps. LXXXIX 20" by A.S. van der Woude, "Notes sur le Psaume XLIX" by J. van der Ploeg, and "Confirmatum est cor meum. Remarks on the Old Latin Text of the Song of Hannah" by P.A.H. de Boer.

79. Bonnard, Pierre-E. *Psaumes Pour Vivre.* Avant-propos d'Henri Bourgeois. Les Cahiers de l'Institut Catholique de Lyon 4. Lyon: Association des Facultés Catholiques, 1980. 168p.

Collection of nine articles which originally appeared in *Esprit et Vie*, 1978-1979.

80. Brueggemann, Walter. "Psalms and the Life of Faith: A Suggested Typology of Function." *Journal for the Study of the Old Testament* 17 (1980): 3-32.

Paul Ricoeur's work on the role of language in the life of faith suggests a classification of the Psalms on an "orientation-disorientation-reorientation" grid.

81. _____. "Response to John Goldingay's 'The Dynamic Cycle of Praise and Prayer' (*JSOT* 20 [1981] 85-90)." *Journal for the Study of the Old Testament* 22 (1982): 141-142.

82. _____. *The Message of the Psalms: A Theological Commentary.* Augsburg Old Testament Studies. Minneapolis, MN: Augsburg, 1984. 205p.

The Psalms contain three general themes: poems of orientation, poems of disorientation, and poems of new orientation. Human life consists in 1) satisfied seasons of well-being, 2) anguished seasons of hurt, alienation, suffering and death, and 3) turns of surprise when joy breaks through the despair. The psalms of orientation correspond best to Westermann's "descriptive hymns." The psalms of disorientation correspond to the laments. The psalms of new orientation correspond to the thanksgiving songs and the enthronement songs.

83. ______. *Israel's Praise: Doxology against Idolatry and Ideology.* Philadelphia: Fortress Press, 1988. 191p.

The social reality of the Psalms and the social enactment of reality done by the pastoral office meet in the act of liturgy, an act of resymbolizing community experience known as "world-making." Israel's world-making was not always faithful. Central to this distortion was the figure of the king, who is more attached to order than transformation, more responsive to majesty than to mercy, and more concerned to maintain present power arrangements than to critique and alter those arrangements. Israel's hymns of praise shifted in order to reflect the "made" world of the king and his social interests. In this process, world-transforming doxology gives way to the idolatry of a god who will do nothing and has no story and to the ideology of a social order that is absolute and cannot be changed or criticized. Against the deathliness of idolatry and the falsehood of ideology, Israel sings another world to reality. It does so through remembering and reciting the credos, through speaking the pain of the lament psalms, and through singing the songs of thanksgiving, whose memory and hope always stay close to pain and rescue.

84. ______. *Abiding Astonishment: Psalms, Modernity, and the Making of History.* Literary Currents in Biblical

Interpretation, ed. Danna Nolan Fewell and David M. Gunn. Louisville, KY: Westminster/John Knox, 1991. 96p.

The "Psalms of Historical Recital" (Psalms 78, 105, 106, and 136) have a social-political intention. Taken together, these psalms "make a world" that is inter-generational, covenantly shaped, morally serious, dialogically open, and politically demanding. They protest against a world that is one-generational, devoid of authorative covenanting, morally indifferent, monologically closed, and politically indifferent. They thus both propose a world and articulate a counter-world to the dominant world that is. This "ingression of what is new" can only be received with "abiding astonishment" (Buber). The historical psalms seek to make available to subsequent generations the initial astonishment felt at such moments and to affirm the "astonished" way of looking at life and Yahweh as valid in all times.

85. Buit, F.M. du. "Les Psaumes." *Evidences* 81 (1971): 26-58.

86. Chalet, F. *Cris d'hommes. Les Psaumes. Essai d'adoption pour notre temps.* Paris: Éditions ouvrières, 1966. 143p.

87. Chase, Mary Ellen. *The Psalms for/and the Common Reader.* New York: W.W. Norton, 1962.

88. Craven, Toni. *Psalms.* Message of Biblical Spirituality 6. Collegeville, MN: Michael Glazier Books, 1992. 176p.

The "Message of Biblical Spirituality" series is intended to provide "ready access to the treasury of biblical faith, a rich resource for the variety of ways in which people have heard God's call to live a life of faith and fidelity." The insights gained into the Scriptures are aimed at helping and encouraging readers to become a prayerful, biblical people.

89. Cullinan, Thomas. "Opening Words on the Psalms." *Clergy Review* 63 (1978): 205-207.

90. Cuzzola, Theresa. "Appreciating the Psalms." *Emmanuel* 88 (1982): 222-228.

91. Daniel, Robert T. *How to Study the Psalms: Based on an Exposition of Twelve Favorite Psalms.* Westwood, NJ: Fleming H. Revell Co., 1953. 271p.

92. Day, John. *Psalms.* Old Testament Guides. Sheffield: JSOT Press, 1990. 159p.

93. Del Páramo, S. "Salmos." In *Enciclopedia de la Biblia*, ed. A. Diez Macho and S. Bartina. VI: 369-385. Barcelona: Garriga Impresores, 1965.

94. Drijvers, Pius. *Over de Psalmen.* Utrecht: Uitgeveri Het Spectrum, 1964. Translated into French and published as *Les Psaumes: Genres littéraires et thèmes doctrinaux.* Paris: Éditions du Cerf, 1958. 221p. Translated into English from the 5th Dutch edition and published as *The Psalms: Their Structure and Meaning.* New York: Herder and Herder, 1965. 269p.

If we Christians wish to understand the Psalms, we must bear in mind that the roots of their thought lie in the past, in the Old Testament, while their blossoming reaches out into the far future, to the end of the world, to heaven itself. This approach to the Psalms therefore divides the Psalms into various groups or types, elucidates the themes of these groups, and transposes these themes onto the Christian and liturgical plane. In this way, the Christian character is brought out in clear relief.

95. Eaton, J.H. *The Psalms Come Alive.* London: Mowbray, 1984.

96. Engnell, Ivan. "Psaltaren." In *Svenskt Bibliskt Uppslagsverk*, ed. Engnell and Fridrichsen. cols. 787-832. Uppsala, 1952. English Version: "The Book of Psalms." In *A Rigid Scrutiny. Critical Essays on the Old Testament.* Translated from the Swedish by John T. Willis, with the collaboration of Helmer Ringgren. 68-122. Nashville, TN: Vanderbilt University Press, 1969.

97. Farndale, W.E. *The Psalms in New Light.* London: Epworth Press, 1956. 115p.

98. Feulner, Floyd H. *What the Psalms Really Mean.* Sylmar, CA: By the Author, 13233 De Foe Avenue, 1980. 243p.

The Psalms are meditations of Christ on the day he died on the cross.

99. Ginkel, C. van, and P.J. Midden, eds. *Psalmenstudie. Prof. Nic. H. Ridderbos en het boek der Psalmen. Opstellen van prof. dr. Nic. H. Ridderbos.* Kampen: Kok, 1991. 208p.

Includes 13 articles on the Psalms by Ridderbos, all but one previously published. They are listed individually.

100. Goldingay, John. "The Dynamic Cycle of Praise and Prayer in the Psalms." *Journal for the Study of the Old Testament* 20 (1981): 85-90.

101. Griffith, Leonard. *God in Man's Experience: The Activity of God in the Psalms.* Waco, TX: Word Books, 1968. 192p.

102. Guardini, Romano. *The Wisdom of the Psalms.* Translated from the German edition of 1973 (Wurzburg: Werkbund-Verlag) by Stella Lange. Chicago: Henry Regnery Company, 1968. 168p.

The Psalms form the basic material for the prayer life of the church. What do they mean for us? Those who speak in the Psalms are not pagans. On the other hand, they have not yet become Christian. They are on the way. As such, the Psalms can speak to us because we are all on the way. As we pray them, we are revealed to ourselves.

103. Guichou, P. "Prières du peuple de Dieu." *La Vie Spirituelle* 431 (1957): 127-146.

The Psalms in the life of Israel, in the life of Christ, and as the prayers of Christ. Psalms 1, 2, and 18.

104. Gunkel, Hermann. "Die Psalmen." *Deutschen Rundschau* 38 (Nov/1911): 241-261. Reprinted with a conclusion appended in *Reden und Aufsätze.* 92-123. Göttingen: Vandenhoeck und Ruprecht, 1913; reprinted in *Zur Neueren Psalmenforschung,* ed. Peter H.A. Neumann, 19-54; Darmstadt: Wissenschaftliche Buchgesellschaft, 1976.

105. _____. "Psalmen." In *Die Religion in Geschichte und Gegenwart: Handwörterbuch in gemeinverständlicher Darstellung,* ed. Friedrich Michael Schiele and Leopold Zscharnack. Band 4: Cols. 1927-1949. Tübingen: J.C.B. Mohr (Paul Siebeck), 1913. Reprinted with minor revisions: "Psalmen." In *Die Religion in Geschichte und Gegenwart:*

Handwörterbuch für Theologie und Religionswissenschaft, ed. Hermann Gunkel and Leopold Zscharnack. 2nd ed. Vol. 4: Cols. 1609-1630. Tübingen: J.C.B. Mohr (Paul Siebeck), 1930; translated into English and reprinted as *The Psalms: A Form Critical Introduction.* Introduction by James Muilenburg. Translated from the German edition of 1930 by Thomas M. Horner. Facet Books; Biblical Series 19. Philadelphia: Fortress Press, 1967. 52p.

Some of the Psalms belong to poetry used in worship, while others do not presuppose the worship service. Those that were composed for the cultus are, on the whole, older than those which the pious poet composed for his own use. A cult song is one in which word and act are so closely bound together that one without the other is inconceivable. There are four main types of psalms: 1) hymns, 2) community laments, 3) songs of the individual, and 4) thanksgiving songs. Apart from a few isolated cases, the "I" in the psalms refers to the individual. Many of the Psalms do not belong to the poetry of the cult. These presuppose no particular cultic acts. Rather these "spiritual poems" have grown out of the cult songs, have freed themselves of all ceremonial connection, and express the religion of the heart. These spiritual poems developed through the influence of the prophetic spirit during the 7th century. Mixtures and inner transformations of psalm types developed as the original setting of the literary types was forgotten or no longer clear. Minor differences between the 1913 version and the 1930 version are noted in the Facet Books translation.

106. Gunn, George S. *Singers of Israel: The Book of Psalms.* Bible Guides, ed. William Barclay and F.F. Bruce, no. 10. New York: Abingdon, 1963. 95p.

Bible Guides are directed toward the "non-theologically equipped readers." General concerns are followed by specific comments on Psalms 23, 46, 121, and 139.

107. Guthrie, Harvey H. *Israel's Sacred Songs: A Study of Dominant Themes.* New York: The Seabury Press, 1966. 241p. Paperback Reprint: A Crossword Book (Seabury), 1978. xii+242p.

This book is "primarily concerned with the way in which Israel adopted certain cultural idioms as means of praising and addressing her God, and with how these idioms were transformed by the content they were made to carry."

108. Haag, H. *Gott und Mensch in den Psalmen.* Einsiedeln: Benziger Verlag, 1972.

109. Hargreaves, John. *A Guide to the Psalms.* Theological Education Fund Study Guide 6. London: SPCK, 1973.

The approach is thematic, with constant application to present-day situations. There are photographs, musical notation, and commentary. Twenty psalms are studied.

110. Harris, R. Laird. "Psalms." In *The Biblical Expositor*, ed. Carl F.H. Henry with an introduction by Billy Graham. 416-452. Philadelphia: A.J. Holmon Company (J.B. Lippincott), 1973.

The Biblical Expositor emphasizes the relevance of God's living word to our own time. It is thoroughly evangelical.

111. Hauret, Charles. *Notre Psautier.* Sources de Spiritualité. Colmar, France: Éditions Alsatia, 1964. Translated into English by John M. McConnell and published as *The Songs of the People of God.* Chicago: The Priory Press, 1965. 178p.

Although Christians have certain objections about the Psalms, the "fuller sense" of scripture allows Christians to read the Psalms as prayers of Christ, prayers about Christ, or prayers to Christ.

112. Hawkins, Thomas R. *The Unsuspected Power of the Psalms.* Nashville, TN: The Upper Room, 1985. 128p.

113. Hayes, John H. *Understanding the Psalms.* Valley Forge, PA: Judson Press, 1976. 128p.

Reviewed by E.S. Gerstenberger in *JBL* 98 (1979): 295-296.

114. Hempel, Johannes. "Psalms, Book of." In *The Interpreter's Dictionary of the Bible,* ed. George Arthur Buttrick and Others. Vol. 3: 942-958. New York: Abingdon, 1962.

The origin and divisions of the Psalms, poetic forms and the religion and piety of the Psalms.

115. Henn, T.R. "A Note on the Psalms." Chap. in *The Bible as Literature.* 123-142. New York: Oxford University Press, 1970.

116. Hogan, Frances. *Psalms of Praise: Words of Life.* San Francisco: Collins (Harpers), 1990.

Practical, Bible-based spiritual counsel, along with an indepth exploration of the Psalms' important themes and a commentary on more than one third of the Psalms.

117. Hopkins, Denise Dombkowski. *Journey Through the Psalms: A Path to Wholeness.* Kaleidoscope Series. New York: United Church Press, 1990. 136p.

"Kaleidoscope is a series of adult enrichment resources for persons in the church, developed for Christians who want serious study and dialogue on contemporary issues of the Christian faith and life."

118. Kaltenbach, J. *Le Livre qui chante la Gloire de Dieu. Etudes sur les Psaumes.* Strasbourg: Editions Oberlin, 1949. 303p.

The Psalter is "the book that sings the glory of God." A general introduction to the psalms discusses the role of the psalms in the religious life of the people of Israel and of the Christian church, the formation of the collection, and the language of the psalmists. Various psalms are studied in groups according to content.

119. Keesecker, William F. *The Wisdom of the Psalms.* New York: The World Publishing Co., 1970.

Psalms or parts of psalms are selected and used for reflections on the Christian life. Many of the remarks are based on Calvin's commentary.

120. Kittel, Gisela. *Die Sprache der Psalmen: Zur Erschliessung der Psalmen im Unterricht.* Göttingen: Vandenhoeck und Ruprecht, 1973. 164p.

The Psalms should serve as the starting point in the instruction of children and young people in the Christian faith.

Reviewed by H.C. White in *JBL* 93 (1974): 452-454; also reviewed in *CBQ* 36 (1974): 601.

121. Kroll, Woodrow Michael. *Psalms. The Poetry of Palestine.* Lanham: University Press of America, 1987.

122. Kugel, James L. "Psalms, The." In *Harper's Bible Dictionary*, ed. Paul J. Achtemeier and Others with the Society of Biblical Literature. San Francisco: Harper and Row, 1985.

123. ______. "Topics in the History of the Spirituality of the Psalms." In *Jewish Spirituality I: From the Bible Through the Middle Ages*, ed. Arthur Green. World Spirituality: An Encyclopedic History of the Religious Quest 13. 113-144. London: Routledge & Kegan, 1986; New York: Crossroad, 1986.

The spirituality of the psalms, as they move from the cultic use to the subject of study ("scripturalization of the Psalms")

124. Lewis, C.S. (Clive Staples). *Reflections on the Psalms.* New York: Harcourt, Brace and Company, 1958. 148p.

A thinking aloud about the style and meaning of the Psalms and their relevance for contemporary life.

125. Limburg, James. *Psalms for Sojourners.* Minneapolis, MN: Augsburg Publishing House, 1986. 112p.

126. Lindblom, Johannes. "Bemerkungen zu den Psalmen I." *Zeitschrift für die alttestamentliche Wissenschaft* 59 (1942-1943): 1-13.

127. Longman, Tremper III. *How to Read the Psalms.* Leicester, Eng/Downers Grove, IL: InterVarsity Press, 1988. 166p.

128. Lubienska de Lenval, Hélène. *Pour lire les psaumes en hébreu.* Tourney: Casterman, 1966.

129. McEleney, Neil J. *The Melody of Israel. Introduction to the Psalms.* Pamphlet Bible Series, no. 42. New York: Paulist Press, 1968.

Reviewed in *CBQ* 30 (1968): 627.

130. MacKenzie, Roderick A.F. *The Psalms -- A Selection.* The Old Testament Reading Guide Series 23. Collegeville, MN: Liturgical Press, 1967.

Reviewed in *CBQ* 31 (1969): 86-87.

131. Martin-Achard, Robert. *Approche des Psaumes.* Cahiers Théologiques 60. Neuchatel: Delachaux et Niestlé, 1969. 109p.

132. Martindale, Cyril Charlie (1879-1963). *Towards Loving the Psalms.* New York: Sheed & Ward, 1940. 308p.

Reviewed by T.J. Kelly in *CBQ* 3 (1941): 88.

133. Merton, Thomas. *Bread in the Wilderness.* New York: New Directions Books (James Laughlin), 1953; reprint Collegeville, MN: The Liturgical Press, 1971. 179p.

A collection of personal notes on the Psalter, written in the monastic tradition.

134. _____. *On the Psalms.* London: Sheldon Press, 1977.

135. Miller, Patrick D., Jr. *Interpreting the Psalms.* Philadelphia: Fortress Press, 1986. 159p.

I. A discussion of the current issues in the interpretation of the psalms. II. An exposition of selected Psalms -- 1, 2, 14, 22, 23, 82, 90, 127, 130, and 139.

136. _____. "Psalms." In *The Books of the Bible*, ed. Bernhard Word Anderson. 203-220. New York: Charles Scribner's Sons, 1989.

137. Milton, John P. *The Psalms.* Rock Island, IL: Augustana Book Concern, 1954. 252p.

138. Murphy, Roland E. *Backgrounds to Both Psalms and Job.* Philadelphia: Fortress Press, 1977.

139. _____. "Israel's Prayer -- The Psalms." Chap. in *Wisdom Literature and Psalms.* Interpreting Biblical Texts Series. 110-149. Nashville, TN: Abingdon Press, 1983. 158p.

1) The titles of the various Psalms are at least as old as the Septuagint; the references to authorship are unverifiable. 2) Most of the Psalms were composed in the first instance for liturgical celebration. 3) The so-called messianic Psalms deal with the currently reigning king; later they were reinterpreted as referring to a future messiah. 4) The Psalms form the heart of Israel's prayer. In fact they are a "school of prayer" in the sense that they teach us how to pray. 5) Because the prayers of the Psalms were written over a period of some seven centuries, they constitute a profile of biblical theology. Psalms 1, 15, 22, 23, 30, 48, 117, 74, 89, 130, 37, and 73.

140. ______. "The Psalms in Modern Life." *The Bible Today* 25 (1987): 231-239.

141. Ormseth, Dennis H. "The Psalms and the Rule of God." *Word and World* 5 (1985): 119-121.

142. Parkander, Dorothy J. "'Exalted Manna': The Psalms as Literature." *Word and World* 5 (1985): 122-131.

143. Paterson, John. *The Praises of Israel: Studies Literary and Religious in the Psalms.* New York: Charles Scribner's Sons, 1950. 256p.

The main purpose is to show the enduring vitality of the praises of Israel. I. The Psalter grew like a living thing and from the beginning it was closely entwined with the life of the worshiping community. The Psalms spring from life and speak to us. II. Expository studies illustrating the main types of song in the Psalter. III. Doctrinal in character, setting forth the deep spiritual insights of the Psalms in regard to God, Man, Nature, Sin, Grace and the Life Hereafter.

144. Pidoux, Georges. *Du portique à l'autel. Introduction aux Psaumes.* Neuchâtel: Éditions Delachaux & Niestlé, 1959. 148p.

145. Poethig, Eunice Blanchard. *Sing, Shout, and Clap for Joy: A Study of Psalms in Worship.* New York: The Women's Division of the General Board of Global Ministries of the United Methodist Church, 1989.

146. Ravasi, G. *I Salmi.* Milan: Editrice Àncora, 1985. 246p.

An introductory account of the Psalms, assuming familiarity on the part of the reader with the content of the Bible as a whole, but no technical theological knowledge.

147. Ridderbos, Nic. H. *Die Psalmen -- Stilistischen Verfahren und Aufbau mit besonderer Berücksichtigung von Ps 1-41* Beihefte zur Zeitschrift für die alttestamentliche Wissenschaft 117. Berlin: Walter de Gruyter, 1972.

148. Ringgren, Helmer. *Psaltarens Fromhet.* Stockholm, Sweden: Svenska Kyrkans Diakonistyrelses Bokförlag, 1957. English version: *The Faith of the Psalmists.* London: SCM Press, 1963; Philadelphia: Fortress Press, 1963. xxii+138p.

149. ______. *Psalmen.* Stuttgart: Kohlhammer, 1971. 130p.

Although the psalms are used in worship, they focus on the personal religious life and experience. The community is the normal matrix of the piety of the psalmists.

150. Roguet, A.M. *Le miel du rocher ou la douceur des Psaumes.* L'esprit liturgique 27. Paris: Éditions du Cerf, 1967. 234p.

"The Honey of the Rock or the Sweetness of the Psalms." In order to be truly appreciated the Psalms must become more visceral and less cerebral. Suggestions are therefore offered for interpreting the Psalms most frequently encountered in the Breviary.

Reviewed in *CBQ* 30 (1968): 286.

151. Routley, Erik. *Exploring the Psalms.* Philadelphia: Westminster Press, 1975. 172p.

The purpose of this study is to introduce readers to the psalms as a basis for their devotions and as a door through which they will come to a special kind of understanding of the Old Testament and of our Lord's teaching. The psalms are grouped around thirteen subject areas: Suffering, Victory, Covenant, Praise, Pilgrimage, Royalty, Nature, Care, The City, Faith, Life's Stress, Wisdom, and Character. An introduction gives the background of the psalms in Old Testament history; a epilogue discusses the use of psalms in worship.

152. Sarna, Nahum M., and Others, "Book of Psalms." In *Encyclopaedia Judaica,* ed. Cecil Roth and Geoffrey Wigoder. Vol. 13: 1303-1334. Jerusalem: Keter Publishing House, 1972.

In the Bible (Sarna), in the Talmud and Midrash and in the liturgy (L.I. Rabinowitz), in the arts (B. Bayer), and musical renditions in Jewish tradition (A. Herzog).

153. Scamman, John H. *Living with the Psalms.* Valley Forge, PA: Judson Press, 1967.

154. Seidel, Hans. *Auf den Spuren der Beter. Einführung in die Psalmen.* Berlin: Evangelische Verlaganstalt, 1980. 180p.

155. Seybold, Klaus. *Die Psalmen. Eine Einführung.* Urban-Taschenbücher 382. Stuttgart: Kohlhammer, 1986. 215p. 2nd ed., 1991; 216p. Translated from the first German edition of 1986 into English by R. Graeme Dunphy and published as *Introducing the Psalms.* Edinburgh: T & T Clark, 1990. xii+260p.

156. Slack, Kenneth. *New Light on Old Songs. Studies in the psalms in the light of the new translations.* London: SCM Press, 1975. 116p.

157. Smith, Mark S. *Psalms: The Divine Journey.* New York/Mahwah, NJ: Paulist Press, 1987. 85p.

158. Snaith, Norman H. *The Psalms: A Short Introduction.* London: The Epworth Press, 1945. 40p.

159. Stedman, Ray C. *Folk Psalms of Faith: A Bible Commentary for Laymen.* Glendale, CA: Regal Books (G/L Publications), 1973. 321p.

Folk songs are the history of humankind set to music. The Psalms are rich in human experience, divine love and the drama of lives lived before God and with one another. They relate the experiences of believers of the past, reflecting the emotional upsets, problems, and disturbances which the saints of old have gone through. As such, they are "folk psalms."

160. Steinmann, J. *Les Psaumes.* Paris: Librairie Lecoffre, 1951. 187p.

The mirror of biblical piety, form-critical classification of psalms, and theology of the psalms.
Reviewed by J. Paterson in *JBL* 72 (1953): 269.

161. Taylor, Charles L. *Let the Psalms Speak.* New York: Seabury, 1961.

162. Terrien, Samuel. *The Psalms and Their Meaning for Today.* Indianapolis, IN: Bobbs-Merrill Company, 1951. 278p.

163. Thoben, J.A.H. *De liederen van Gods volk. Een studie over milieu, theologie en literaire vorm van de psalmen.* Nijmegen: Thoben, 1961. 381p.

164. Wevers, John Wm. "The Psalms." Chap. in *The Way of the Righteous: Psalms and the Books of Wisdom.* Westminster Guides to the Bible, ed. Edwin M. Good. 9-59. Philadelphia: Westminster Press, 1961.

The various categories of the psalms -- complaint, confession, thanksgiving, trust, dedication, intercession, and adoration.

165. Wilkinson, Violet. *Israel's Praise. A Study of the Psalms.* London: Oxford University Press, 1967. 96p.

2. Commentaries

A. Before 500 A.D.

166. Allegro, J.M. "Fragments of a Qumran Scroll of Eschatological Midrašim." *Journal of Biblical Literature* 77 (1958): 350-354.

On 4QFlorilegium, a midrash on 2 Samuel 7 and Psalms 1-2.

167. Allenbach, J., and Others. *Biblia Patristica. Index des citations et allusions dans la littérature patristique.* Vol. 1: *Des origenes à Clément d'Alexandrié et Tertullien.* Vol. 2: *Le troisième siècle (Origène excepté).* Paris: Centre National de la Recherche Scientifique, 1975, 1977. Vol. 1, 546p; Vol. 2, 468p.

An attempt to provide an exhaustive index of biblical material contained in early Christian literature. Volume one covers the period up to Clement of Alexandria and Tertullian.

Volumes one and two reviewed by C.D. Osburn in *JBL* 98 (1979): 469-470.

168. Alonso Schökel, Luis. "Interpretación de los Salmos hasta Casiodoro: Sintesis histórica." *Estudios Biblicos* 47 (1989): 5-26.

There is a rich variety of approaches to the Psalms from the NT authors through Cassiodorus, including historical, prophetic, typological, and allegorical. The commentators discussed include Origen, Eusebius, Athanasius, and Theodore of Mopsuestia.

169. Altaner, Berthold. "Wann schrieb Hieronymus seine Ep 106 *Ad Sunniam et Fretelam de Psalterio?*" *Vigiliae Christianae: A Review of Early Christian Life and Language* 4 (1950): 246-248.

170. Ambrose of Milan (340?-397). *Expositio psalmi CXVIII.* In *Corpus scriptorum ecclesiasticorum latinorum* 62, ed. M. Petschenig. Leipzig: G. Freytag, 1913.

171. _____. *Enarrationes in XII Psalmos.* In *Corpus scriptorum ecclesiasticorum latinorum* 64, ed. M. Petschenig. Leipzig: G. Freytag, 1919.

Ambrose's interpretation of twelve Psalms: Psalms 1, 35-40, 43, 47, 48, and 61. Drawn partly from dictation, partly from notes of sermons, full of warmth, enthusiasm and vivacity.

172. Apollinarius of Laodicea (?310-?). ΜΕΤΑΦΡΑΣΙΣ ΕΙΣ ΤΟΝ ΨΑΛΤΗΡΑ/Interpretatio in Psaltem. *Patrologia Cursus Completus, Series Graeca,* ed. J.P. Migne. Vol. 33: 1313-1538. Paris: J.P. Migne, 1857.

173. Arnobius Junior (5th cent.). *Commentarii in Psalmos. Patrologia Cursus Completus, Series Latina,* ed. J.P. Migne. Vol. 53: 327-570. Paris: J.P. Migne, 1847. Reprint, Turnhout, Belgium: Brepols, 1980. Also in Corpus Christianorum, Series Latina 25. Turhout, Belgium: Brepols, 1990.

His biblical works were allegorical commentaries on the Psalms (criticizing predestination at Psalm 108) and scholia on gospel texts.

174. Asterius the Sophist (d. c341). *Asterii Sophistae commentariorum in Psalmos quae supersunt, accedunt aliquot homiliae anonymae.* Ed. Marcel Richard. Symbolae Osloenses Fasc. Supplet. 16. Oslo: A.W. Broegger, 1956. xxxiii+273p.

Arian theologian, a disciple of Lucian of Antioch. His homilies on the Psalms provide liturgical evidence for the turn of the third century.

175. Athanasius (296?-373). *Epistle to Marcellinus.* Translated by E. Ferguson. *Ekklesiastikos Pharos* 60 (1978): 373-403. Greek and Latin texts in *Patrologia Cursus Completus, Series Graeca,* ed. J.P. Migne. Vol. 27: 11-60. Paris: J.P. Migne, 1857,

Considers the character and value of the Psalms, classifies them according to certain points of view, and indicates how they may be used in the various experiences of life.

176. _____. *St. Athanasius on the Psalms. A Letter Rendered for the First Time into English by a Religious of C.S.M.V.* London: A.R. Mowbray & Co., 1949. 43p.

177. _____. *Expositiones in Psalmos. Patrologia Cursus Completus, Series Graeca,* ed. J.P. Migne. Vol. 27: 59-590. Paris: J.P. Migne, 1857. See Hesychius.

178. Augustine of Hippo (354-430). *Enarrationes in Psalmos.* Patrologia Cursus Completus, Series Latina, ed. J.P. Migne.

Vol. 36: 21-1028; Vol.37: 1033-1968. Paris: J.P. Migne, 1841. Reprint, Turnhout, Belgium: Brepols, 1991. *Sancti Aurelii Augustini Enerrationes in psalmos*, ed. Eligius Dekkers and J. Fraipont. Corpus Christianorum 38-40. Turnhout, Belgium: Brepols, 1956. Translated into English and annotated by Scholastica Hebgin and Felicitas Corrigan. 2 vols. Ancient Christian Writers 29-30. New York: Newman Press, 1960. Vol. 1, 354p; Vol. 2, 420p. Also translated into English by A. Cleveland Coxe and published as *Expositions on the Book of Psalms* in *A Select Library of Nicene and Post-Nicene Fathers of the Christian Church.* Ed. Philip Schaff and Henry Ware. First Series, Vol. 8. New York: Christian Literature Co., 1888. Reprint, Grand Rapids, MI: William B. Eerdmans Co., 1979. 700p. *Expositions on the Book of Psalms. Translated with Notes and Indices. 6 vols. Oxford: John Henry Parker; London: F. and J. Rivington, 1847.*

For Augustine, the psalter becomes the Book of Hours of the Mystical Christ. In it we are able to enter into the consciousness of Christ as he prays, works, and suffers. In this allegorical interpretation, the Psalms represent the first phase of Christ's revelation, still veiled under carnal types which point toward the future. The Christian will thus seek Christ everywhere in the psalter.

179. _____. *Nine Sermons of Saint Augustine on the Psalms.* Translated and Introduced by Edmund Hill. London and New York: Longmans & Green, 1958. New York: Kenedy, 1959. xi+176p.

180. Baethgen, Friedrich. "Der Psalmencommentar des Theodor von Mopsuestia in syrischer Bearbeitung." *Zeitschrift für die alttestamentliche Wissenschaft* 5 (1885): 53-101.

181. _____. "Siebenzehn makkabäische Psalmen nach Theodor von Mopsuestia." *Zeitschrift für die alttestamentliche Wissenschaft* 6 (1886): 261-288; 7 (1887): 1-60.

Psalms 44, 55, 56, 57, 58, 59, 60, 62, 69, 74, 79, 80, 83, 108, 109, 144.

182. Balthasar, Hans Urs von. *Über die Psalmen. Auswahl und Übertragung.* Leipzig: J.C. Hinrichs, 1935.

183. Basil of Ancyra (c329-379). *Homiliae in Psalmos. Patrologia Cursus Completus, Series Graeca,* ed. J.P. Migne. Vol. 29: 209-494. Paris: J.P. Migne, 1857.

184. _____. *Hexaemeron. Exegetic Homilies.* Translated by Agnes Clare Way. The Fathers of the Church 46. Washington, D.C.: Catholic University of America Press, (1963). xvi+378p.

185. Berrouard, Marie-François. "Saint Augustin et la prière chrétienne des psaumes." *Lumière et Vie* 40 (1991): 107-121.

186. Bonnardière, A.M. la. "Les Enarrationes in Psalmos prêchées par S. Augustin à l'occasion de fêtes des martyrs." *Recherches Augustin* 7 (1971): 73-104.

187. Brabant, Olivia. "Classes et professions 'maudites' chez S. Augustin d'après les Enarrationes in Psalmos." *Revue Études Augustins* 17 (1971): 69-81.

188. _____. *Le Christ, centre et source de la vie morale chez S. Augustin. Études sur la pastorale des Enarrationes in Psalmos.* Recherches et synthèses. Section de morale 8. Gembloux: Éditions J. Duculot, 1971. xxiv+264p.

189. Braude, William G., Trans. "Midrash to Psalms." *Judaism* 2 (1953): 75-79.

Selections from Midrash to Psalm 18.

190. ______. *The Midrash on Psalms.* 2 vols. Yale Judaica Series XIII/1-2. New Haven, CT: Yale University Press, 1959. Vol. I, xxxvi+563p; Vol. II, 630p.

Midrash Tehillim is "a succession of homilies upon various words or phrases in the Psalter and upon related passages throughout Scripture." Its origin dates to sometime before the 9th century in Palestine. The contents of the Midrash on the Psalms shows great variety; there are frequent references to Rome, its institutions and provincial administration, as well as a wealth of parables, proverbs, etc.

Reviewed by R. Mach in *JBL* 78 (1959): 367-369; reviewed also in *CBQ* 21 (1959): 396-397.

191. Brok, Martin. "Touchant la date du Commentaire sur le Psautier de Théodoret de Cyr." *Revue d'histoire ecclésiastique* 44 (1949): 552-556.

192. Brooke, G.J. *Exegesis at Qumran: 4QFlorilegium in its Jewish Context.* Journal for the Study of the Old Testament Supplement Series 29. Sheffield: JSOT Press, 1985. xii+390p.

193. Capanaga, V. "La doctrina Augustiniana de la gracia en los Salmos." In *Studia Patristica VI. Papers Presented to the Third International Conference on Patristic Studies, held ad Christ Church, Oxford, 1959. Part IV. Theologica, Augustiniana.* Texte und Untersuchungen. 315-349. Berlin: Akademie-Verlag, 1962.

194. Carmignac, J. de, E. Cothenet and H. Lignée. *Les textes de Qumran traduits et annotés: La Règle de la Congrégationa; Recueil des Bénédictions; Interprétations de prophètes et de psaumes; Document de Damas; Apocryphe de la Genèse; Fragments des grottes 1 et 4.* Autour de la Bible 2. Paris: Letouzey et Ané, 1963. 400p.

Reviewed in *CBQ* 26 (1964): 362-363.

195. Chrysostom, John (344/354-407). *Expositio in Psalmos Patrologia Cursus Completus, Series Graeca,* ed. J.P. Migne. Vol. 55: 35-528. Paris: J.P. Migne, 1859.

196. ______. *Homilia in Psalmos. Patrologia Cursus Completus, Series Latina,* ed. J.P. Migne. Vol. 55: 531-784. Paris: J.P. Migne, 1859.

197. Cyril of Alexandria (c370-444). *Explanatio in Psalmos. Patrologia Cursus Completus, Series Graeca,* ed. J.P. Migne. Vol. 69: 697-1276. Paris: J.P. Migne, 1859.

198. Devreese, Robert. *Les anciens commentateurs grecs des psaumes.* Studi e Testi 264. Vatican City: Biblioteca Apostolica Vaticana, 1970.

The Greek Psalm commentaries from the 3rd and 4th centuries. A critical edition based on the Palestinian *catenae*.

199. Didymus the Blind (c313-398). *Expositio in Psalmos. Patrologia Cursus Completus, Series Graeca,* ed. J.P. Migne. Vol. 39: 1155-1622. Paris: J.P. Migne, 1858. German translation: *Der Psalmenkommentar von Toura. Quaternio 9.* Edited, translated and explained by Aloys Kehl. Wissenschaftliche Abhandlungen des Landes Nordrhein-

Westfalen. Papyrologica Coloniensia 1. Cologne-Opladen: Westdeutscher Verlag, 1964. 223p. Also: *Psalmenkommentar (Tura-Papyrus).* Vol. I: *Kommentar zu Psalm 20-21*, ed. and translated by L. Doutreleau, A Gesché, and M. Gronewald. Vol. II: *Psalms 22-26,10*, ed. and translated by M. Gronewald. Vol. III: *Psalms 29-34*, ed. and translated by M. Gronewald and A. Gesché. Vol. IV: *Psalms 35-39*, ed. and translated by M. Gronewald. Vol. V: *Psalms 40-44,4*, ed. and translated by M. Gronewald. Papyrologische Texte und Abhandlungen 7,4,8,6,12. Bonn: Rudolf Habelt Verlag, 1968-1970.

Among his pupils was Jerome.

200. Dillon, Richard J. "The Psalms of the Suffering Just in the Accounts of Jesus' Passion." *Worship* 61 (1987): 430-440.

201. Diodore of Tarsus (d. c392). *Commentarii in Psalmos.* Ed. J.-M. Olivier. Corpus Christianorum, Series Graeca 6. Turnhout: Brepols, 1980. cxxvi+328p. French translation: *Le commentaire de Diodore de Tarse sur les Psaumes.* Translated and ed. Louis Mariès. Paris: Didot, 1924. 127p.

Follows the historical-grammatical method of exegesis in opposition to the allegorical method of Alexandria. His two most distinguished disciples are Theodore of Mopsuestia and John Chrysostom.

202. Dorival, G. "La reconstitution du Commentaire sur les Psaumes d'Eusèbe de Césarée grâce exégétiques grecques en particulier la chaîne de Nicétas." Lecture given at the 7th International Congress for Patristic Studies, Oxford, 1975; printed in *Studia Patristica* in the series *Texte und Untersuchungen zur Geschichte der altchristlichen*

Literature. Archiv für die griechisch-christlichen Schriftsteller der ersten drei Jahrhunderte. Leipzig-Berlin: Akademie-Verlag, 1978.

203. Dupont, Dom Jacques. "L'interprétation des Psaumes dans les Actes des Apôtres." In *Le Psautier. Ses Origines. Ses problèmes littéraires. Son influence*, ed. Robert de Langhe. Orientalia et Lovaniensia 4. 357-388. Louvain: Publications Universitaires, 1962.

204. Emery, P.Y. "Les Psaumes et l'unité de l'église selon saint Augustin." *Verbum Caro* 75 (1965): 1-182.

205. Eusebius of Caesarea [Eusebius Pamphili] (c.263-c.340). *Commentaria in Psalmos. Patrologia Cursus Completus, Series Graeca,* ed. J.P. Migne. Vol. 23: 9-1396. Paris: J.P. Migne, 1857. *Due Articoli Eusebiani.* ("Commentarii in Psalmos"), Edited by Carmelo Curti. Noto: Jonica, 1971. 61p. *Il codice Patmos monastero S. Giovanni 215 e i Commentaria in Psalmos di Eusebio di Cesarea.* Studi Classici in onore de Quintino Cantardella, Vol. 2. Ed. Carmelo Curti. Catania: Università di Catania, Facoltà di lettere e filosofia, 1972. 47p. *Eusebiana I: Commentarii in Psalmos.* Saggi e testi: Classici, cristiani e medievali 1. Catania: Centro di studi sull'antico cristianesimo, Università di Catania, 1987 (1988).

Influenced by Pamphilus' interest in Origen, Eusebius' commentary is important for its citations of the *Hexapla* and Origen's commentary.

206. Ferguson, E. "Athanasius' 'Epistola ad Marcellinum in interpretationem Psalmorum.'" *Studia Patristica* 16/2 (1985): 295-308.

207. Feuer, Rabbi Avrohom Chaim. *Tehillim/Psalms -- A New Translation with a Commentary Anthologized from Talmudic, Midrashic and Rabbinic Sources.* 5 vols. ArtScroll Tanach Series: A Traditional Commentary on the Books of the Bible, ed. Rabbis Nosson Scherman and Meir Zlotowitz. Brooklyn, NY: Mesorah Publications, Ltd., 1977; reprinted as 2 vols., 1985. 1756p.

"An anthology of traditional Jewish texts and commentaries which convey the inspirational message of Tehillim. The historical background of the psalms is provided in order to show how the words flowed from the personal life of David and, in turn, the life of Israel through the ages."

208. Fischer, Balthasar. *Das Psalmen Verständnis der alten Kirche bis zu Origenes. Ps 1-20.* Katholisches Habilitations Schrift, Bonn, 1944. Portions of this unpublished dissertation (Psalms 3, 8, 16[15], 17[16], and 19[18]) are published in *Die Psalmen als Stimme der Kirche. Gesammelte Studien zur christlichen Psalmenfrömmigkeit.* Ed. Andreas Heinz on the occasion of the 70th birthday of Prof. Dr. Balthasar Fischer on September 3, 1982. 153-223. Trier: Paulinus-Verlag, 1982.

A complete history of interpretation for Psalms 1-20 from the apostolic church up to and including Origen.

209. ______. *Die Psalmenfrömmigkeit der Martyrerkirche.* Freiburg im Breisgau., 1949. Reprint, *Theologische Jahrbuch* (1960): 335-351. Revised and expanded as "Le Christ dans les psaumes." *Le Maison-Dieu* 27 (1951): 86-113. English summary in *Theological Digest* 1 (1953): 53-57; Spanish summary by A. Miller, "La visión cristiana de los salmos," *Kyrios* 1 (1958): 5-13.

This is based on Fischer's *Habilitationsschrift*, "Das Psalmenverständnis der alten Kirche bis zu Origenes," and summarizes the main conclusions.

210. _____. "Die Psalmenfrömmigkeit der Regula S. Benedicti." *Liturgie und Mönchtum* 4, (1949): 22-35; 5 (1950): 64-79. Reprinted in *Die Psalmen als Stimme der Kirche. Gesammelte Studien zur christlichen Psalmenfrömmigkeit.* Ed. Andreas Heinz on the occasion of the 70th birthday of Prof. Dr. Balthasar Fischer on September 3, 1982. 37-71. Trier: Paulinus-Verlag, 1982.

211. _____. "Conculcabis leonem et draconem. Eine deutungsgeschichtliche Studie zur Verwendung von Ps 90 in der Quadragesima." *Zeitschrift für Katholische Theologie* 89 (1958): 421-429. Reprinted in *Die Psalmen als Stimme der Kirche. Gesammelte Studien zur christlichen Psalmenfrömmigkeit.* Ed. Andreas Heinz on the occasion of the 70th birthday of Prof. Dr. Balthasar Fischer on September 3, 1982. 73-83. Trier: Paulinus-Verlag, 1982.

212. _____. "Christliches Psalmenverständnis im 2. Jahrhundert." *Bibel und Leben* 3 (1962): 111-119. French version: "Les psaumes, prière, chrétienne. Témoignage du 2ᵉ siècle." In *La prière des heures*, ed. M. Cassien and B. Botte. Lex Orandi 35. 85-99. Paris: Éditions du Cerf, 1963. German original reprinted in *Die Psalmen als Stimme der Kirche. Gesammelte Studien zur christlichen Psalmenfrömmigkeit.* Ed. Andreas Heinz on the occasion of the 70th birthday of Prof. Dr. Balthasar Fischer on September 3, 1982. 85-95. Trier: Paulinus-Verlag, 1982.

The two decisive principles for adding a Christ-dimension to the Psalms found in later Psalm interpretation, the principle *psalmus vox Christi* and the principle *psalmus vox ad Christum*, are already expressed as principles in the 2nd century. The most outstanding characteristic for both is the tendency to find the cross as the focus of the Psalms.

213. _____. "Das Taufmotiv an der Schwelle des Psalters. Die frühchristliche Deutung von Ps 1,3a und ihr Schicksal bei den lateinischen Kirchenväter." *Liturgie und Mönchtum* 33/34 (1963): 26-35. Reprinted in *Die Psalmen als Stimme der Kirche. Gesammelte Studien zur christlichen Psalmenfrömmigkeit.* Ed. Andreas Heinz on the occasion of the 70th birthday of Prof. Dr. Balthasar Fischer on September 3, 1982. 103-112. Trier: Paulinus-Verlag, 1982.

214. _____. "Psalmus est libertatis laetitia. Zum Psalmenlob des Ambrosius." In *Liturgie: Gestalt und Vollzug (Festschrift F.J. Pascher)*, ed. Walter Dürig. 98-103. Munich: M. Hueber, 1963. Reprinted in *Die Psalmen als Stimme der Kirche. Gesammelte Studien zur christlichen Psalmenfrömmigkeit.* Ed. Andreas Heinz on the occasion of the 70th birthday of Prof. Dr. Balthasar Fischer on September 3, 1982. 97-102. Trier: Paulinus-Verlag, 1982.

215. _____. "Psalmus vox Christi patientis. Selon l'épître à Marcellinus de S. Athanase." In *Politique et Théologie chez Athanase d'Alexandrie. Actes du colloque de Chantilly, 23-25 septembre 1973*, ed. Charles Kannengiesser. Théologie Historique 27. 305-311. Paris: Beauchesne, 1974. Reprinted as "Das Motiv vom Psalm als Stimme des leidenden Christus im Brief des heiligen Athanasius an Marcellinus" in *Die Psalmen als Stimme der Kirche. Gesammelte Studien zur christlichen Psalmenfrömmigkeit.* Ed. Andreas Heinz on the occasion of the 70th birthday of Prof. Dr. Balthasar Fischer on September 3, 1982. 113-119. Trier: Paulinus-Verlag, 1982.

216. _____. *Die Psalmen als Stimme der Kirche. Gesammelte Studien zur christlichen Psalmenfrömmigkeit.* Ed. Andreas Heinz on the occasion of the 70th birthday of Prof. Dr. Balthasar Fischer on September 3, 1982. Trier: Paulinus-Verlag, 1982. 247p.

217. Gastaldi, Néster J. *Hilario de Poitiers. Exegeta del Salterio. Un Estudio de su exégesis en los commentarios sobre los salmos.* (Église nouvelle, Église ancienne. Institut catholique de Paris. Thèses et traveaux de la faculté de théologie, série patristique I). Paris-Rosario: Beauchesne, 1969. 300p.

218. George, A. "Jésus et les psaumes." In *A la recontre de Dieu, Mémorial A. Gelin.* Ed. A. Barucq and Others. 297-308. Le Puy: Xavier Mappus, 1961.

219. Gesché, A. "Un document nouveau sur la christologie du IVe siècle: le commentaire sur les psaumes découvert à Toura." *Studia Patristica* III, Papers presented to the Third International Conference on Patristic Studies held at Christ Church, Oxford 1959. Part I. Introductio, Editiones, Critica, Philologica, ed. F.L.Cross. *Texte und Untersuchungen zur Geschichte der altchristlichen Literatur. Archiv für die griechisch-christlichen Schriftsteller der ersten drei Jahrhunderte* 78. Leipzig-Berlin: Akademie-Verlag, 1961-1962.

220. Goffinet, Emile. "Recherches sur quelques fragments du commentaire d'Origène sur le psaume I." *Muséon* 76 (1963): 145-196.

221. _____. *L'utilisation d"Origène dans le commentaire des psaumes de Saint Hilaire de Poitiers.* Studia Hellenistica 14. Louvain: Publications universitaires, 1965. xxi+174p.

222. ______. "Die christologische und heilstheologische Grundlage der Bibelexegese des Origenes." *Theologische Quartalschrift* 136 (1956): 1-13.

223. Golega, Joseph. *Der Homerische Psalter. Studien über dem Apolinarious von Laodikeia zugeschriebene Psalmenparaphrase.* Studia Patristica et Byzantina 6. Ettal: Buch-Kunstverlag, 1960. 200p.

224. Gourgues, Michel. *Les Psaumes et Jésus. Jésus et les Psaumes.* Cahiers Evangile 25. Service Biblique Evangile et Vie; Paris: Cerf, 1978.

225. Gregg, Robert C *The Life of Anthony and the Letter to Marcellinus.* Translation and Introduction by Robert C. Craig. Preface by William A. Clebsch. The Classics of Western Spirituality. New York: Paulist Press, 1980. xxi+166p.

226. Gregory of Nyssa (330-c.395). *In Psalmorum Inscriptiones. Patrologia Cursus Completus, Series Graeca,* ed. J.P. Migne. Vol. 44: 431-616. Paris: J.P. Migne, 1858.

227. Haendler, Gert. "Zur Auslegung der Psalmen in der Alten Kirche." *Theologische Literaturzeitung* 103 (1978): 625-632.

I. Recent research. II. Ambrose's understanding of the Psalms with examples. III. A comparison of Ambrose's and Origen's understandings. IV. Summary review of recent research.

228. Harrisville, Roy. "Paul and the Psalms." *Word and World* 5 (1985): 168-179.

229. Hesychius of Jerusalem (5th cent.). *De Titulis Psalmorum.* [Pseudo-Athanasius]. *Patrologia Cursus Completus, Series Graeca,* ed. J.P. Migne. Vol. 27: 649-1344. Paris: J.P. Migne, 1857.

Alexandrian style of exegesis.

230. ______. *Fragmenta in Psalmos. Patrologia Cursus Completus, Series Graeca,* ed. J.P. Migne. Vol. 93: 1179-1340. Paris: J.P. Migne, 1860.

231. Hilary of Poitiers (c.315-368). *Tractatus super Psalmos. Patrologia Cursus Completus, Series Latina,* ed. J.P. Migne. Vol. 9: 231-908. Paris: J.P. Migne, 1844. Reprint, Turnhout, Belgium: Brepols, 1989. Corpus Scriptorum Ecclesiasticorum Latinorum 22. Ed. Antonius Zingerle. Leipzig: G. Freytag, 1891. xxii+888p. Selections translated into English by W. Sanday and published as *Homilies on the Psalms (I, LIII[LIV], CXXX[CXXXI])* in Nicene and Post-Nicene Fathers, 2nd series, Vol. 9: 235-248.. New York: Christian Literature Co., 1895; Reprint, Grand Rapids, MI: William B. Eerdmans, 1979.

Psalms 1,2,9,13,14,51-69,91,118-150. Strongly allegorical and drawn from Origen and Eusebius.

232. Hill, Edmund. *Nine Sermons of St. Augustine on the Psalms.* London: Longmans, Green & Co., 1958. xi+177p.

Sermons on Psalms 18(19), 21(22), 25(26), 29(30), Sermons I, II and III on Psalms 30(31), and the sermon on Psalm 31(32). Reviewed in *CBQ* 21 (1959): 396.

233. Hippolytus of Rome, Antipope (c175-c.236). *In Psalmos. Patrologia Cursus Completus, Series Graeca,* ed. J.P. Migne. Vol. 10: 607-616, 711-726 (Dubius). Paris: J.P. Migne, 1857. Also in *Werke,* ed. H. Achelis, *Die griechischen christlichen Schriftsteller der ersten drei Jahrhunderte.* Vol. 1/2. 127-153. Leipzig: J.C. Hinrichs, 1897.

234. Höpfl, Hildebrand (1872-1934) *Introductionis in sacros utriusque testamenti libros compendium.* 3 vols. Rome: Libreria Spithoever, 1921. 5th ed., 1946: 311-314. 6th ed., 1958-63.

235. Jerome (Eusebius Hieronymus) (c.345-c.410). *Tractatus sive Homiliae in Psalmos.* Ed. G. Morin. Corpus Christianum, Series Latina 78. Turnhout, Belgium: Brepols, 1958. *Homilies on the Psalms.* Translated by Marie Liguori Ewald. The Fathers of the Church 48,57. New York, 1964, 1967. Also, ed. G. Morin, Anecdota Maredsolana III/1-3, 1895 to 1903.

236. Julian of Eclanum (380-c.455). *Expositionis in Psalmos.* Ed. G.J. Ascoli, Archivio glottologico italiano 5 (1878/1879): 8-610.

237. Kannengiesser, C. "Hilaire de Poitiers." In *Enchiridion Symbolorum. Definitionem et declarationum de rebus fidei et morum.* Founded by Henricus Denzinger. 34th ed. by Adolf Denzinger. 466-499. Freiburg im Breisgau and Barcelona: Herder, 1968.

An introduction to Hilary's *Tractatus super psalmos.*

238. Kistemaker, S. *The Psalm Quotations in Hebrews.* Amsterdam: Van Soest, 1961.

239. Klem, Joseph. *Hieronymi graeca in Psalmos fragmenta. Untersucht und auf ihre Herkunft geprüft.* Alttestamentliche Abhandlungen I/3. Munster i. W.: Aschendorff, 1908. 80p.

240. Knauer, Georg Nicolaus. *Psalmenzitate in Augustins Konfessionen.* Göttingen: Vandenhoeck & Ruprecht, 1955. 215p.

241. Kugel, James. "Two Introductions to Midrash." *Prooftexts: A Journal of Jewish Literary History* 3 (1983): 131-155.

A survey of the origins and development of midrash compared with other approaches to the Bible. Includes a discussion of Psalms 81 and 145.

242. Leeb, Helmut. *Die Psalmodie bei Ambrosius.* Wiener Beiträge zur Theologie 18. Vienna: Herder, 1967. 115p.

243. Lépissier, J. *Les commentaires des psaumes de Théodoret. Version slave, T.I.* Étude linguistique et philologique. Paris, 1968.

244. Linton, O. "Interpretation of the Psalms in the Early Church." In *Studia Patristica IV. Texte und Untersuchungen zur Geschichte der altchristlichen Literatur 79.* 143-156. Berlin: Akademie-Verlag, 1961.

245. Loewe, R. "Herbert of Bosham's Commentary on Jerome's Hebrew Psalter." *Biblica* 34 (1953): 44-77, 159-192, 275-298.

246. Mackay, Thomas W., and C. Wilfred Griggs. "The Recently Rediscovered Papyrus Leaves of Didymus the Blind." *Bulletin of the American Society of Papyrologists* 20 (1983): 59-60.

Commentary on the Psalms.

247. Mariès, Louis. *Etudes préliminaires à l'édition de Diodore de Tarse "Sur les Psaumes." Deux manuscrits nouveaux. Le caractère Diodorien du commentaire.* Collection d'études anciennes. Paris: Société d'édition "Les Belles Lettres," 1933. 184p.

248. Maur, H.J. auf der. *Die Psalmenverständnis des Ambrosius von Mailand. Ein Beitrag zum Deutungshintergrund der Psalmenverwendung im Gottesdienst der Alten Kirche.* Leiden: E.J. Brill, 1977. xxi+645p.

249. Meiss, Honel. *Echos des Psaumes dans le Talmud.* Nice: Soeiété Générale d'Imprimerie, 1926. 275p.

250. Mercati, G. "D'un palimpsesto Ambrosiano contenente i Salmi esapli e di un' antica versione latina del commentario perduto di Teodore di Mopsuestia al Salterio." In *Opere minori. Raccolte in occasione del settantesimo mataligioi sotto gli auspicii de S.S. Pio XI. Volume I (1891-1897).* Studii e Testi 76. 318-338. Vatican City: Vatican Library, 1937.

251. _____. *Osservazioni a proemi del Salterio di Origene, Ippolito, Eusebio, Cirilli, Allessandrino e altri con Frammenti inediti.* Studi e Testi 142. Vatican City: Vatican Library, 1948.

252. Merkelbach, R. "Konjekturen und Erläuterung zum Psalmenkommentar des Didymus." *Vigiliae christianae* 20 (1966): 214-226.

253. Methodius of Olympus (d.311). *Oration on the Psalms.* Translated into English by A. Cleveland Coxe. *The Ante-Nicene Fathers: Translations of the Writings of the Fathers Down to A.D. 325,* ed. Alexander Roberts and James Donaldson. Vol. 6: 394-398. New York: Christian Literature Co., 1861. Reprint, Grand Rapids, MI: William B. Eerdmans Co., 1978.

254. Mühlenberg, Ekkehard. *Psalmenkommentare aus der Katenenüberlieferung.* 3 vols. Patristiche Texte und Studien 15, 16, 19. Berlin: Walter de Gruyter, 1975, 1977, 1978. Vol. 1, xxxiii+375p; Vol. 2, xxxiv+398p; Vol. 3, xii+293p.

Vol. 1. Introduction to the manuscript traditions and texts -- Apollinaris of Laodicea (ca. 310-390) and Didymus the Blind (d. 398). Vol. 2. The rest of the text of Didymus, plus indices to both volumes. Vol. 3. Detailed analytical studies.

255. Müller, Paul-Gerhard. "Die Funktion der Psalmzitate im Hebräerbrief." In *Freude an der Weisung des Herrn. Beiträge zur Theologie der Psalmen. Festgabe zum 70. Geburtstag von Heinrich Gross,* ed. Ernst Haag and Frank-Lothar Hossfeld. 223-242. Stuttgart: Katholisches Bibelwerk, 1986.

256. Mussner, Franz. "Die Psalmen im Gedankengang des Paulus in Röm 9-11." In *Freude an der Weisung des Herrn. Beiträge zur Theologie der Psalmen. Festgabe zum 70. Geburtstag von Heinrich Gross,* ed. Ernst Haag and Frank-Lothar Hossfeld. 243-263. Stuttgart: Katholisches Bibelwerk, 1986.

257. Nautin, P. "L'homélie d'Hippolyte sur le psautier et les oeuvres de Josipe." *Revue de l'Histoire des Religions* 179 (1971): 137-179.

258. Nohe, A. *Der Mailänder Psalter. Seine Grundlage und Entwicklung.* Freiburger Theologische Studien XLV. Freiburg: Herder, 1936.

259. Origen (185?-254?). *Exegetica in Psalmos. Patrologia Cursus Completus, Series Graeca,* ed. J.P. Migne. Vol. 12: 1053-1686. Vol. 17: 105-150. Paris: J.P. Migne, 1857. See also C. and C.V. de la. *Patrologia Graeca* 12 (1862): 1053-1686.

260. Petrus Chrysologus (5th cent.). *Collectio Sermonum.* Corpus Christianorum, Series Latina 24. Turnhout: Brepols, 1975.

Includes *De psalmo uicesimo octauo, De psalmo quadragesimo, De psalmo primo, De Psalmo sexto, De psalmo nonagesimo quarto.*

261. Pitra, J.B. "Origenis in psalmos." *Analecta Sacra. Spicilegio Solesmensi* 2 (1884): 395-483; 3 (1884): 1-522.

262. Pizzolato, Luigi F. "Sulla genesi della ‚Explanatio Psalmorum XII' di Ambrogio: Ambrosius." In *Rivista Liturgico-Pastorale. Studi de Storia e liturgia ambrosiana* 40, Supplemento al no. 4. 1-25. Milan: Bibliotheca Ambrosiana, 1964.

263. ______. *La "Explanatio Psalmorum XII". Studio letterario sulla Esegesi di Sant' Ambrogio.* Archivio Ambrosiano XVII. Milan: Bibliotheca Ambrosiana, 1965.

Reviewed in *CBQ* 28 (1966): 255-256.

264. _____. *Commento a dodici salmi/ Sant'Ambrogio. Introduzione, Traduzione, note e indici.* 2 vol. Opere esegetiche 7. Milan: Bibliotheca Ambrosiana, 1980; Rome: Città Nouva, 1980.

265. _____. *Commento al Salmo CXVIII /Sant'Ambrogio. Introduzione, Traduzione, Note e indici.* 2 vols. Opere esegetiche 8. Milan: Biblioteca Ambrosiana, 1987; Rome: Città Nuova, 1987.

266. Popescu, G. "Les psaumes dans la prédication du bienheureux Augustin." *Studii teologice Bucuresti* 15 (1963): 155-172.

267. Prosper of Aquitaine (c.390-c.463). *Expositio Psalmorum a Centesimo Usque ad CL. Patrologia Cursus Completus, Series Latina,* ed. J.P. Migne. Vol. 51: 277-426. Paris: J.P. Migne, 1846. Reprint, Turnhout, Belgium: Brepols, 1981. Also in Corpus Christianorum, Series Latina, 68A. Turhout: Belgium: Brepols, 1972.

Psalms 100-150.

268. Puech, Henri Charles. "Origène et l'exégèse trinitaire du psaume 50,12-14." In *Aux sources de la tradition chrétienne. Mélanges offert à M. Goguel.* Bibliothèque théologique. 180-194. Neuchâtel-Paris: Delachaux & Niestlé, 1950.

269. Richard, M. "Quelques manus crits peu connu des Chaînes exégétiques et des commentaires grecs sur le psautier." *Bulletin d'information de l'Institut de recherche et d'histoire des textes* 3/1954 (Paris, 1955): 87-106.

270. _____. "Les premières Chaînes sur le psautier." *Bulletin d'information de l'Institut de recherche et d'histoire des textes* 5/1956 (Paris, 1957): 86-98.

271. Rondeau, M.-J. "Le commentaire sur les psaumes d'Évagre le Pontique." *Orientalia Christiana Periodica* 26 (1960): 307-318.

272. _____. "À propos d'une édition de Didyme l'aveugle." *Revue des Études Grecques*, Tome 81, Nos. 386-388 (Paris, 1968): 385-400.

273. _____. "Une nouvelle preuve d l'influence littéraire d'Eusèbe de Césarée sur Athanase: l'interprétation des psaumes." *Recherches de science religieuse* 56 (1968): 385-434.

274. _____. "L'Épître à Marcellinus sur les psalmes." *Vigiliae christianae* 22 (1968): 176-197.

275. _____. "Le 'Commentaire des Psaumes' de Diodore de Tarse et l'exégèse antique du Psaume 109/110." *Revue de l'histoire des religions* 176 (1969): 153-188.

276. _____. "Exégèse du Psautier et anabase spirituelle chez Gregoire de Nysse." In *Epektasis. Mélanges patristiques offert au Card. Jean Daniélou.* 517-531. Paris: Beauchesne, 1972.

277. _____. *Les Commentaires patristiques du Psautier.* 2 vols. Rome: Pontificum Istititum Studiorum Orientalium, 1982, 1985.

278. _____. "L'elucidation des interlocuteurs des Psaumes et le développement dogmatizue (IIIe-Ve siècle)." In *Liturgie und*

Dichtung, ed. H. Becker and R. Kacznysk. Vol. II: 509-577. St. Ottilien: EOS Verlag, 1983.

279. Rondet, Henri. "Notes d'exégèse augustinienne. Psalterium et Cithara." *Recherches de science religieuse* 46 (1958): 407-415.

280. _____. "Essais sur la chronologie des Enarrationes in Psalmos de saint Augustin." *Bulletin de littérature ecclésiastique* 61 (1960): 111-127, 258-286; 64 (1964): 110-136; 68 (1967): 180-202; 71 (1970): 174-200.

281. Rose, André. "L'influence des Psaumes sur les annonces et les récits de la Passion et de la Résurrection dans les Evangiles." In *Le Psautier. Ses origines. Ses problèmes littéraires. Son influence*, ed. Robert de Langhe. Orientalia et Biblica Lovaniensia 4. 297-356. Louvain: Publications Universitaires, 1962.

282. Rossi, M.A. "Recovering the Psalms Commentary of Cyril of Alexandria from Patristic Catenae." In *Annali di Storia dell' Esegesi* 1(1984), ed. P.C. Bori and M. Pesce. Bologna: Edizioni Dehoniane, 1984.

283. Sieben, Hermann-Josef. "Studien zur Psalterbenutzung des Athanasius von Alexandrien im Rahmen seiner Schriftauffassung und Schriftauslegung." Diss. Institut Catholique. Paris, 1968. Typewritten.

284. _____. "Athanasius über den Psalter, Analyse seines Briefes an Marcellinus." *Zeitschrift für Theologie und Philosophie* 48 (1973): 157-173.

285. ______. "Der Psalter und die Bekehrung der *voces* und *affectus.*" *Theologie und Philosophie* 52 (1977): 481-497.

The recitation and singing of psalms played an important role in Augustine's conversion. (See *Confessions* IX, 4, 7-11).

286. Stead, George C. "St. Anthanasius on the Psalms." *Vigiliac Christianae: A Review of Early Christian Life and Language* 39 (1985): 65-78.

Expositiones in psalmos; Epistula ad Marcellinum.

287. Stegemann, H. "Der Pešer Psalm 37 aus Höhle 4 von Qumran." *Revue de Qumrân* 14 (1963): 235-270.

288. Sunden, Hjalmer. "Saint Augustine and the Psalter in the Light of Role-Psychology." *Journal for the Scientific Study of Religion* 26 (1987): 375-382.

289. Theodore of Mopsuestia (c.350-428). *Expositio in Psalmos. Patrologia Cursus Completus, Series Graeca,* ed. J.P. Migne. Vol. 66: 647-696. Paris: J.P. Migne, 1859.

290. ______. *Commentarii in Psalmos,* ed. R. Devreesse. *Le Commentaire de Théodore de Mopsueste sur les Psaumes (I-LXXX).* Studie e Testi 93. Vatican City: Bibliothèque Apostolique, 1939. xxxii+572p.

Compares the Hebrew and Greek. Forms the much-needed beginnings of grammatical and historical exposition.

291. ______. *Theodori Mopsuesteni Expositionis in Psalmos Iuliano Aeclanensis interprete in latinum versae quae supersunt.* Ed. Lucas de Coninck with the help of Maria Josepha d'Hont.

Corpus Christianorum, Series Latina 88A. Turnhout: Brepols, 1977. xlv+410p.

Apart from some fragments preserved in the Greek *catenae*, Julian of Eclanum (380-c455) is our only source for Theodore's commentary on the Psalms. This commentary is only partially preserved. Psalms 1-16:11 is complete; the remainder offers only an epitome; for 17-40 there are only fragments.

292. ______. *Fragments syriaques du Commentaire des Psaumes. Psaume 118 et Psaumes 138-148.* 2 vols. Ed. and translated by Lucas van Rompay. Corpus scriptorum Christianorum Orientalium 435-436; Scriptores Syri 189-190. Louvan: E. Peeters, 1982.

293. Theodoret of Cyrrhus (c.393-c.458). *Patrologia Cursus Completus, Series Graeca,* ed. J.P. Migne. Vol. 80. Paris: J.P. Migne, 1859.

Of the Anthiochene school.

294. ______. *Les Commentaires des Psaumes de Théodoret (Version Slave).* Textes publiés par l'Institut d'études slaves 7. Paris: Impr. nationale, 1968.

295. Vaccari, Alberto. "Testo dei salmi nel commento di Teodoro Mopsuesteno." *Biblica* 23 (1942): 1-17.

296. ______. "I salteri de S. Girolamo e di S. Agostino." In *Scritti di erudizione e di filologia.* 207-255. Rome: Edixioni di storia e letteratura, 1952.

297. Vénard, L. "L'utilisation des Psaumes dans l'Epître aux Hebreux." In *Melanges E. Podechard. Études de sciences*

religieuses offertes pour son éméritat au doyen honoraire de la Faculté de théologie de Lyon. 253-264. Lyon: Faculté Catholiques, 1945.

298. Vesco, J.-L. "La lecture du psautier selon l'Épître de Barnabé." *Revue Biblique* 93 (1986): 5-37.

299. Vian, G.M. "Recovering the Psalms Commentary of Athanasius from Patristic Catenae." In *Annali di Storia dell' Esegesi* 1(1984), ed. P.C. Bori and M. Pesce. Bologna: Edizioni Dehoniane, 1984.

300. Vosté, J.M. "Théodore de Mopsueste sur les Psaumes." *Angelicum* 19 (1942): 179-198.

301. _____. "Mar Išoʿdad de Merw sur les Psaumes." *Biblica* 25 (1944): 261-296.

302. Weber, H. "Die Fluchpsalmen in augustinischer Sicht." *Theologie und Glaube* 48 (1958): 443-450.

See also: 51, 1056, 2486, 2592, 2657, 2658, 2781, 2912, 2925, 3246, 3268, 3293, 3294, 3296, 3304, 3308, 3339, 3349, 3360, 3362, 3550, 3601, 3610, 3677, 3713, 3773, 3775, 3776, 3909, 4001, 4036, 4177, 4208, 4409, 4431, 4448, 4450, 4453, 4455, 4464, 4475, 4543, 4589, 4601, 4602, 4604, 4607, 4628, 4777

B. 501-1800 A.D.

303. Albertus Magnus (1193-1280). *Opera omnia ad fidem codicum manuscriptorum edenda, apparatu critico, notis, prolegomenis, indicibus instruenda,* ed. Institutum Alberti

Magni Coloniense, Bernhardo Geyer praeside. Monasterii Westfalorum: In aedibus Aschendorff, 1951-.

304. Alcuin of York (735-804). *Enchiridion seu Expositio pia ac brevis in Psalmos poenitentiales, in Psalmum CXVIII et graduales. Patrologia Cursus Completus, Series Latina,* ed. J.P. Migne. Vol. 100: 569-640. Paris: J.P. Migne, 1851. Reprint, Turnhout, Belgium: Brepols, 1992.

Penitential and gradual psalms as well as Ps 118(119).

305. Alonso Schökel, Luis. "Interpretación de los Salmos desde Casiodoro hasta Gunkel. Sintesis histórica." *Estudios Biblicos* 47 (1989): 145-164.

306. Aquinus, Thomas of (1224-1274). *Expositio in Psalmos Davidis.* Ps 1-50, in Opera Omnia, Rome, 1570; Antwerp, 1612. Band 13. *Exposition in psalmos.* Psalms 1-54 in *S. Thomae Aquinatis Opera Omnia 6.* Ed. Roberto Busa. 48-130. Stuttgart: Friedrich Fromman Verlag Günter Holzboog, 1980.

307. Arnaldus, Abby of Bonneval (d. c1156). *Commentarius in Psalmum CXXXII: "Ecce quam bonum et quam jecundum habitare fratres in unum ..." Patrologia Cursus Completus, Series Latina,* ed. J.P. Migne. Vol. 189: 1569-1590. Paris: J.P. Migne, 1854.

A close friend of St. Bernard; the commentary consists of five homilies.

308. Bailey, Richard N. "Bede's Text of Cassiodorus' Commentary on the Psalms." *Journal of Theological Studies,* N.S., 34 (1983): 189-193.

309. ______, and R. Handley. "Early English Manuscripts of Cassiodorus' Expositio Psalmorum." *Classical Philology* 78 (1983): 51-55.

310. Beintker, Horst. "Gottverlassenheit und Transitus durch den Glauben (Anfechtungen des Menschen Jesus nach Luther's Auslegungen der Pss 8 und 22)." *Evangelische Theologie* 45 (1985): 108-123.

311. ______. "Christologische Gedanken Luthers zum Sterben Jesu: bei Auslegnung von Ps 8 und Ps 22 im Kommentar von 1519 bis 1521." *Archiv für Reformationsgeschichte* 77 (1986): 5-30.

312. Bellarmine, Robert (1542-1621). *Explanatio in Psalmos.* Rome, 1611. *Explanatio in Psalmos.* Editio novissima à multis mendis & omissionibus expurgata. Venice: Franciscum Zane, 1726. 602p. *Psalterium Davidis. Cum brevi et succincta paraphrasi ex Bellarmini commentario deprompta.* 2 vols. 5th ed. Augustae Taurinorum: Ex typis Hyacinthi Marietti, 1889. Edition by R. Galdos, 2vols. Rome: Vatican, 1931/1932.

Personal theologian to the pope. His commentary is noted for its literal sense and ascetic character.

313. Blemmydes, Nicephorus (c.1197-1272). *Expositio in Psalmos. Patrologia Cursus Completus, Series Graeca,* ed. J.P. Migne. Vol. 142: 1321-1622. Paris: J.P. Migne, 1885.

314. Boese, H. *Die alte "Glosa Psalmorum ex traditione Seniorum": Untersuchungen, Materialen, Texte.* Vetus Latina: Aus der Geschichte der lateinischen Bibel 9. Freiburg: Verlag Herder, 1982. 286p.

A study and partial edition of a seventh-century commentary on the Psalms which probably comes from early Benedictine circles.

315. Bossuet, Jacques Benigne (1627-1704). *Notae in Psalmos cum diddertatione in librum Psalmorum.* In *Oeuvres complètes.* Paris: J.P. Migne, 1867.

316. Boyle, Marjorie O'Rourke. "For Peasants, Psalms: Erasmus' *editio princeps* of Haymo (1533)." *Mediaeval Studies* 44 (1982): 444-469.

317. Bruno the Carthusian (c.1030-1101). *Commentarium in Psalmos. Patrologia Cursus Completus, Series Latina,* ed. J.P. Migne. Vol. 152: 637-1420. Paris: J.P. Migne, 1879.

318. Bruno of Segni (d. 1125). *Expositio in Psalmos. Patrologia Cursus Completus, Series Latina,* ed. J.P. Migne. Vol. 164" 695-1228. Paris: J.P. Migne, 1884.

319. Bruno of Würzburg (d. 1045). *Expositio in Psalmos. Patrologia Cursus Completus, Series Latina,* ed. J.P. Migne. Vol. 142: 49-530. Paris: J.P. Migne, 1880.

320. Calvin, John (1509-1564). *In Librum Psalmorum Commentarius. (Commentary on the Book of Psalms).* Original Latin version: Geneva, 1557. *Ioannis Calvini in librum Psalmorum commentarius,* ed. A. Tholuck. Berlin: Gustav Eichler, 1836. 2 vols. French version: 1563. First English translation by Arthur Golding, London, 1571. Translated from the original Latin, and collated with the author's French version by James Anderson. Edinburgh, 1845-1849. Reprint: Grand Rapids, MI: William B. Eerdmans Publishing Company, 1949. 5 vols. Vol. 1,

xlix+596p; Vol. 2, 478p; Vol. 3, 506p; Vol. 4, 494p; Vol. 5, viii+513p.

The Psalter is "An Anatomy of All Parts of the Soul" because "there is not an emotion of which any one can be conscious that is not here represented as in a mirror."

Each of the psalms is summarized and commented upon with regard to issues related to authorship and setting. A new translation is presented in sections, followed by comments on the meaning of each section. This frequently includes a critical examination of the original text and philological remarks. Concerns for the church, typological pre-figurements of Christ in the text, and the Christian life dominate. New is the combination of sound exegesis with practical application.

321. Caponetto, Salvatore. "Lutero e Savonarola." *Bollettino della Società di Studi Valdesi* 155 (1984): 41-44.

Luther's 1523 publication of Savonarola's commentaries on Psalms 30 and 50. English summary.

322. Casamassa, Antonio. "Appunti per lo studio dei 'Tractatus super Psalmos' di S. Ilario." In *Miscellanea Biblica et Orientalia R.P. Athanasio Miller, Secretario Pontificiae Commissionis Biblicae, completis LXX annis oblata cura Adalberti Metzinger, O.S.B.* Studia Anselmiana, Philosophica, Theologica 27-28. 231-238. Rome: Herder, 1951.

323. Cassiodorus, Flavius Magnus Aurelius (c.477-c.570). *Magni Aurelii Cassiodori Expositio Psalmorum. Patrologia Cursus Completus, Series Latina,* ed. J.P. Migne. Vol. 70. Paris: J.P. Migne, 1865. Also in *Corpus Christianorum, Series Latina,* Vols. 97-98. Turnhout: Brepols, 1958. *Cassiodorus.*

Explanation of the Psalms. Translated and Annotated by P.G. Walsh. 3 vols. Ancient Christian Writers 51-53. New York: Paulist Press, 1990-1991.

Cassiodorus uses the *Psalterium Romanum* as his text and draws upon the writings of Augustine, Chrysostom, Cyril of Alexandria, Hilary, Ambrose, Jerome, Leo the Great, plus several secular writers.

324. Clark, John P.H. "Walter Hilton and the Psalms Commentary *Qui Habitat.*" *The Downside Review* 100 (1982): 235-262.

Walter Hilton, an English mystic, died in 1396.

325. Colish, M.L. "Psalterium Scholasticorum: Peter Lombard and the Emergence of Scholastic Psalms Exegesis." *Speculum: A Journal of Medieval Studies* 67 (1992): 531-548.

326. Dempsey, G.T. "Aldhelm of Malmesbury and the Paris Psalter: A Note on the Survival of Antiochene Exegesis." *Journal of Theological Studies,* N.S., 38 (1987): 368-386.

Aldhelm of Malmesbury lived from *ca.* 640-709.

327. Dickson, David (1583-1662). *A Commentary on the Psalms (1653).* 3 vols. printed as 2 vols. Glasgow: John Dow, 1834. Vol. 1, 488p; Vol. 2, 535p. Reprinted as part of Geneva Commentaries Series. London, England, and Peabody, MA: Banner of Truth Trust, 1959, 1064p.

328. Dorival, Gilles. "Le Commentaire sur les Psaumes de Nicétas David (début du 10e siècle)." *Revue des Études Byzantinès* 39 (1981): 251-300.

Greek text and translation.

329. Ebeling, Gerhard. "Luthers Psalterdruck vom Jahre 1513." *Zeitschrift für Theologie und Kirche* 50 (1953): 43-99.

330. Euthymius Zigabenus (11th/12th cent.). ΕΞΗΓΗΣΙΣ ΕΙΣ ΤΟ ΨΑΛΤΗΡΙΟΝ / *Commentarius in Psalterium. Patrologia Cursus Completus, Series Graeca,* ed. J.P. Migne. Vol. 128: 41-1326. Paris: J.P. Migne, 1864.

Depends upon patristic sources, especially Chrysostom. Emphasizes the literal meaning of the text.

331. Eynde, D. van den. "Literary Notes on the Earliest Scholastic Commentarii in Psalmos." *Franciscan Studies* 14 (1954): 121-154.

332. Faber, Jacobus (Faber Stapulensis/Jacques Lefèvre d'Etaples) (c.1455-1536). *Psaterium Quincuplex.* Paris, 1509. Travaux d'humanisme et Renaissance 170. Geneva: Droz, 1979. 588p.

333. Fithian, Rosemary. "'Words of My Mouth, Meditations of My Heart': Edward Taylor's *Preparatory Meditations* and the Book of Psalms." *Early American Literature* 20 (2, 1985): 89-119.

334. Gerhoh of Reichersberg (1093-1169). *Commentarius aureus in Psalmos. Patrologia Cursus Completus, Series Latina,* ed. J.P. Migne. Vol. 193: 619-1814; Vol. 194: 9-998. Paris: J.P. Migne, 1854-1855. Vol. 194 reprinted, Turnhout, Belgium: Brepols, 1992. Psalms 31-37 and 78-117 taken from Honorius Augustodunensis.

335. Gill, John (1697-1771). *An Exposition of the Old Testament; in which the sense of the sacred text is taken; doctrinal and practical truths are set in a plain and easy light; difficult passages explained; seeming contradictions reconciled; and whatever is material in the various readings and several oriental versions is observed; the whole illustrated with notes, taken from the most ancient Jewish writings.* 6 vols., 1748-1763. Printed as 4 vols. London: William Hill Collingbridge, 1853; reprint Atlanta, GA: Turner Lassetter, 1954; also as part of *The Baptist Commentary Series,* Paris, AK: Baptist Standard Bearer, 1989.

336. Gregory I (the Great) (540-604). [Heribert de Reggio]. *In Septem Psalmos Poenitentiales. Patrologia Cursus Completus, Series Latina,* ed. J.P. Migne. Vol. 79: 549-658. Paris: J.P. Migne, 1903.

337. _____. *Pars Prima - Sup. Psalmos.* Ed. S. Paterio. *Patrologia Cursus Completus, Series Latina,* ed. J.P. Migne. Vol. 79: 819-896. Paris: J.P. Migne, 1903.

Gathered from diverse writings of Gregory the Great.

338. Gross, Julius. "Die Erbsündenlehre Manegolds von Lautenbach nach seinem Psalmen-Kommentar." *Zeitschrift für Kirchengeschichte* 71 (1960): 252-261.

Manegold of Lautenbach was a Roman Catholic scholar who lived c.1030-c.1103.

339. Hahner, Ursula. *Cassiodors Psalmenkommentar. Sprachliche Untersuchungen.* Münchener Beiträge zur Mediävistik und Renaissance-Forschung 13. Munich: Arbeo-Gesellschaft, 1973. 346p.

340. Haino of Halberstadt (d. 853). *Explanatio in Omnes Psalmos. Patrologia Cursus Completus, Series Latina*, ed. J.P. Migne. Vol. 116: 194-696. Paris: J.P. Migne, 1879.

341. Halporn, James W. "The Manuscripts of Cassiodorus' 'Expositio Psalmorum.'" *Traditio* 37 (1981): 388-396.

342. Hammer, G., and M. Biersack, eds. *D. Martin Luther. Operationes in Psalmos 1519-1521.* Teil II: *Psalm 1 bis 10 (Vulgata).* Archiv zur Weimarer Ausgabe der Werke Martin Luthers 2. Cologne: Böhlau Verlag, 1981. xcii+648p.

A critical edition of Luther's Latin text based on the earliest Wittenberg edition, all its successors described and collated.

343. Hasler, R.A. "The Influence of David and the Psalms upon John Calvin's Life and Thought." *Hartford Quarterly* 5 (1965): 7-18.

344. Hendrix, Scott H. *Ecclesia in via. Ecclesiological Developments in the Medieval Psalms Exegesis and the Dictata super Psalterium (1513-1515) of Martin Luther.* Studies in Medieval and Reformation Thought 8. Leiden: E.J. Brill, 1974. x+297p.

345. Henry, Matthew (1662-1714). *Commentary on the Whole Bible.* Edited by Leslie F. Church. Grand Rapids, MI: Zondervan Publishing House, 1961.

Henry gives a historical setting where possible for each Psalm, provides an outline, indicating the structure, and comments on the meaning of the Psalm.

346. Hobbs, R. Gerald. "How Firm a Foundation: Martin Bucer's Historical Exegesis of the Psalms." *Church History* 53 (1984): 477-491.

347. Holfelder, Hans Herman. *Tentatio et Consolatio. Studien zu Bugenhagens "Interpretation in Librum Psalmorum."* Arbeiten zur Kirchengeschichte 45. Berlin: Walter de Gruyter, 1974. 233p.

348. Honorius Augustodunensis (c.1090-c.1156). *Expositio Psalmorum selectorum. Patrologia Cursus Completus, Series Latina,* ed. J.P. Migne. Vol. 172: 269-311 (Ps 1, 50, 51, 100, 101, 150). Vol. 193: 1315-1372 (Ps 31-37). Vol. 194: 485-730 (Ps 78-117). Paris: J.P. Migne, 1895

349. Joachim of Fiore (c.1135-1202). *Psalterium decem chordarum [Psalterium of Ten Strings]. Venice, 1527. "Psalterium decem chordarum, fonte della "Concordia" con la "Novitas" francescana di Gioacchino da Fiore.* Ed. Eligio Russo. Chiaravalle: Edizione FRAMA SUD, 1983.

350. Judah ben Solomon Hakohen ibn Matqah of Toledo (fl. 1250). "The Commentary of Judah ben Solomon Hakohen ibn Matqah to Genesis, Psalms and Proverbs." Ed. David Goldstein. *Hebrew Union College Annual* 52 (1981): 203-252..

351. Kimhi, David, of Narbonne (*ca.* 1160-1235 C.E.). *The First Book of Psalms with the Longer Commentary of R. David Qimchi.* Edited by S. Schiller-Szinessy. Cambridge: Cambridge University Press, 1883.

352. ______. *The Commentary of David Kimhi on the Fifth Book of the Psalms.* Edited by J. Bosniak. New York, 1954.

Kimhi's exegesis is remarkable for its clearness and sobriety, and its adherence to the plain and literal sense of the Scriptural text. He was a well-trained philologist and an exact grammarian.

353. ______. *The Commentary of Rabbi David Kimhi on Psalms CXX-CL.* Introduction, Critical Edition, Translation and Glossary by Ernest W. Nicholson and Joshua Baker. University of Cambridge Oriental Publications No. 22. Cambridge: At the University Press, 1973. xxxii+190p.

354. ______. *The Complete Commentary on the Book of Psalms,* ed. A. Darom. Jerusalem: Mosad ha-Rav, 1967. (Hebrew). 320p.

355. Kleinhans, Arduin. "Nicolaus Trivet OP psalmorum interpres." *Angelicum* 20 (1943): 219-236.

356. ______. "Heinrich von Cossey O.F.M., ein Psalmen-Erklärer des 14. Jahrhunderts." *Studia Anselmiana* 27/28 (1951): 239-253.

357. Kraus, Hans-Joachim. "Vom Leben und Tod in den Psalmen. Eine Studie zu Calvins Psalmen Kommentar." In *Leben angesichts des Todes. Festschrift für Helmut Thielicke.* 27-46. Tübingen: J.C.B. Mohr (Paul Siebeck), 1968. Reprinted in *Biblisch-theologische Aufsätze.* 258-277. Neukirchen-Vluyn: Neukirchener Verlag, 1972.

358. Landgraf, Arthur M. "Die Zuweisung eines Psalmenkommentars an Anselm von Laon." *Biblica* 23 (1942): 170-174.

Anselm of Laon (d. 1117) was known as "Dr. Scholasticus."

359. ______. "Der *Paulinenkommentar* und der *Psalmenkommentar* des Petrus Cantor und die *Glossa magna* des Petrus Lombardus." *Biblica* 31 (1950): 379-389.

360. Lietbertus of Insulis (= Pseudo-Rufinus) (12th cent.). *In Commentarium in Psalmos LXXV. Patrologia Cursus Completus, Series Latina,* ed. J.P. Migne. Vol. 21: 633-960. Paris: J.P. Migne, 1878.

Psalms 1-75.

361. Loewe, Raphael. "Herbert of Bosham's Commentary on Jerome's Hebrew Psalter." *Biblica* 34 (1953): 44-77, 159-192, 275-298.

362. ______. "The Mediaeval Christian Hebraists of England: *The superscriptio lincolniensis.*" *Hebrew Union College Annual* 28 (1957): 205-252.

363. Ludolph of Saxony (c.1300-1378). *Le Psautier glosé et exposé de Ludolphe le Chartreux, Psaume 119. Extrait d'une traduction médiévale, manuscrit no 14 de la Bibliothèque municipale de Nancy.* Ed. Pierre Demarolle. Travaux du C.R.A.L. 4. Nancy: Presses universitaires de Nancy, (1986). 127p.

364. Luther, Martin (1483-1546). *Unbekannt Fragmente aus Luthers zweiter Psalmenvorlesung, 1518.* Ed. Erich Vogelsang. Arbeiten zur Kirchengeschichte. Berlin: Walter de Gruyter, 1940. 97p.

365. ______. *Auslegung der ersten 25 Psalmen,* 1530. *Psalmen Auslegung.* Ed. Erwin Muelhaupt. Göttingen: Vandenhoeck & Ruprecht, 1959.

366. _____. *Psalmen-Auslegung.* Ed. Erwin Mülhaupt. 3 vols. Göttingen: Vandenhoeck & Ruprecht, 1959-1965.

367. _____. "Preface to the Psalter." In *Luther's Works,* vol. 35. 253-257. Philadelphia: Fortress Press, 1960.

368. _____. *Luther's Works:* Vols. 10-11. *First Lectures on the Psalms.* Ed. Hinton C. Oswald. St. Louis, MO: Concordia Publishing House, 1974, 1976. Vol. 10: 484p; vol. 11: 579p.

369. _____. *Luther's Works:* Vols. 12-14: *Selected Psalms.* Ed. Jaroslav Pelikan. St. Louis, MO: Concordia Publishing House, 1955, 1956, 1958

Vol. 12: Psalms 2, 8, 19, 23, 26, 45, 51. Vol. 13: Psalms 68, 82, 90, 101, 110, 111, 112. Vol. 14: Psalms 117, 118, 147, The Seven Penitential Psalms (6, 32, 38, 51, 102, 130, 143), The Four Psalms of Comfort (37, 62, 94, 109), and Psalms 1 and 2.

370. _____. *Das schöne Confitemini; der 118. Psalm.* Biblische Studien 18. Neukirchen: Verlag der Buchhandlung des Erziehungsvereins, 1957. 77p.

371. Marwick, L. "A First Fragment from David b. Abraham al-Fasi's Commentary on Psalms." *Studies in Bibliography and Booklore* 6-7 (1962/1965): 53-72.

372. Melanchthon, Philip (1497-1560). *Commentarii in Psalmos.* In *Corpus R*eformatorum, ed. C.G. Bretschneider. Vol. 13: 1016-1472. Halle in Saxony: C.A. Schwetschke et Filium, 1856.

Psalms 1-118.

373. Meyer, P. Wendelin. *Psalterium Glossatum: Geschichte und Literarkritische Untersuchung eines handschriftlichen Psalmenkommentars des 14 Jahrhunderts.* Kevelaer, Rheinland: Verlag Butzon & Bercker, 1957. xiii+49p.

The glosses on this Latin Psalter were written by Frater Johannes, who was born between 1275-1280 and died between 1348-1361. He shows the influence of Peter Lombard.

Reviewed in *CBQ* 21 (1959): 93-95.

374. Neale, J.M., and R.F. Littledale. *A Commentary on the Psalms: From Primitive and Mediaeval Writers and from the Various Office-books and Hymns of the Roman, Mozarabic, Ambrosian, Gallican, Greek, Coptic, Armenian, and Syriac Rites.* 4 vols. London: John Masters; New York: Pott and Amery, 1860, 1868, 1871, 1874. 2nd ed. of vols. I and II: 1869, 1873. Vol. I (2nd ed.), 601p; Vol. II (2nd ed.), 612p; Vol. III, 527p; Vol. IV, 511p. Reprint, New York: AMS Press, 1976.

For each of the Psalms, the authors present the argument (general comments from the commentators, many of which see Christ in the psalm), list various uses of the Psalm in the church, antiphons used with the Psalm, comments of the primitive and medieval writers on the individual verses, and collects used with the Psalm.

375. Odo of Aste (d. 1120). *Expositio in Psalmos. Patrologia Cursus Completus, Series Latina,* ed. J.P. Migne. Vol. 165: 1141-1298. Paris: J.P. Migne, 1904.

376. Ortenberg, David. *Tehilah le-David. Hidushim be-divre ha-Shulhan ᶜarukh.* 3 vols. Berdichev: Y. Sheftil, 1888-1902. Reprint, Brooklyn, NY: Mesorah Publications, (1975).

Joseph ben Ephraim Karo/Shulhan ᶜarukh (1488-1575).

377. Paracelsus (Pseudonym of Philippus Aureolus Theophrastus Bombastus von Hohenheim) (1493-1541). *Auslegung des Psalters Davids.* In *Sämtliche Werke. Zweite Abteilung. Theologische und religionsphilosophischen Schriften. Theophrast von Hoheneim genannt Paracelsus.* Ed. Kurt Goldammer. Bands IV-VII. Wiesbaden: F. Steiner, 1955-1959.

IV (Psalms 75[76]-102[103]): liii+ 347p; V (Psalms 103[104]-117[118]): 260p; VI (Psalms 118[119]-137[138]): xxiii+240p; VII (Psalms 138[139]-150): 1-115p.

378. Parker, T.H.L. *Calvin's Old Testament Commentaries.* Edinburgh: T & T Clark, 1986. 239p.

379. Perez, M. "Structural Remarks in R. Moshe Ibn Gikatill's Commentary on Psalms." In *Proceedings of the Tenth World Congress of Jewish Studies; Division A: The Bible and Its World.* 87-94. Jerusalem: World Union of Jewish Studies, 1990. (Hebrew)

380. Peter Lombard (1100-1160). *Commentaria in Psalmos. Patrologia Cursus Completus, Series Latina,* ed. J.P. Migne. Vol. 191: 55-1296. Paris: J.P. Migne, 1880.

The "Master of the Sentences" completed his commentary on the Psalms by 1141.

381. Pisan, Christine de (c1363-c1431). *Les sept psaumes allégorisés [1409]. A Critical Edition from the Brussels and Paris Manuscripts.* Ed. Ruth Ringland Rains. Washington, D.C.: Catholic University of American Press, 1965. ix+181p.

382. Poole, Matthew (1624-1679). *A Commentary on the Holy Bible. 3 vols. III: 1-213. First edition,* 1685. Reprint, London: Banner of Truth Trust, 1962.

383. Potter, George R. "Zwingli and the Book of Psalms." *Sixteenth Century Journal* 10 (1979): 42-50.

384. Prijs, L. "Abraham Ibn Ezra's Commentary on Psalm 1." *Tarbiz* 28 (1959): 181-189. (Hebrew)

385. Quacquarelli, Antonio. "L'epembasi in Cassiodoro (Exp. in Ps.)." *Vetera Christianorum* 1 (1964): 27-33; reprinted in *Saggi Patristici*, Rhetorica ed esegesi biblica, 225-241; Bari, Adriatica, 1971.

Stylistic and rhetorical questions in the Psalms Commentary of Cassiodorus.

386. Raeder, Siegfried. *Das Hebräische bei Luther untersucht bis zum Ende der ersten Psalmenvorlesung.* Beiträge zur historischen Theologie 31. Tübingen: J.C.B. Mohr, 1961. vii+406p.

Reviewed by E.S. Gerstenberger in *JBL* 81 (1962): 206-207.

387. Remigius of Auxerre (c.841-908). *Enarrationes in Psalmos. Patrologia Cursus Completus, Series Latina,* ed. J.P. Migne. Vol. 131: 133-844. Paris: J.P. Migne, 1884.

Perhaps this work should be attributed to Manegold of Lautenbach (c.1030-c.1103), a contemporary of Urban II.

388. Richard of St.-Victor (c.1173). *Mysticae Adnotationes in Psalmos.* In *Patrologia Cursus Completus, Series Latina,* ed. J.P. Migne. Vol. 196: 265-402. Paris: J.P. Migne, 1880.

389. Ringgren, Helmer. "Luthers psaltarutläggning." *Svensk Exegetisk Årsbok* 50 (1985): 49-59.

390. Roehrs, Walter Robert. *Bar Salibi on the Psalms.* Chicago, IL: Private edition, distributed by the University of Chicago Libraries, 1937. 7p.

Dionysius bar Salībī (d. 1171).

391. Rolle, Richard (c1290-1349). *Richard Rolle's Version of the Penitential Psalms with His Commentary, Based on that of S. Augustine.* Rendered and edited by Geraldine Hodgson. London: Faith Press, Ltd., 1928. xix+52p.

392. Russell, S.H. "Calvin and the Messianic Interpretation of the Psalms." *Scottish Journal of Theology* 21 (1968): 37-47.

393. Saadja Al-fjjûmi. *Saadja Al-fjjûmi's arabische Psalmen Übersetzung und Commentar (Psalm 107-124).* Ed. Jacob Zallel Lauterbach. Berlin: H. Itzkowski, 1903. xxv+67p. *Saadja Al-fajjumi's arabische Psalmenübersetzung und Commentar (Psalm 125-150).* Ed. Bernhard Schreier. Berlin: H. Itzkowski, 1904. xxiii+51p.

394. Saadiah Gaon. *Tehilim. ᶜim tirgum u-ferush ha-gaᵓon Saᶜadyah ben Yosef Fayumi ve-ḫeleq ha-diq le-Maharats/Tirgem leᶜIvrit, beiᵓer ve-hekhin Yosef ben David Qafaḫ.* Jerusalem: Qeren ha-rav Yehudah Leb ve-ishto Menuḫah ḫanah Epshtayn she-ᶜal yad ha-Aqdemyah ha-Ameriqanit le-madaᶜe ha-Yahadut, 1966. 356p.

The Book of Psalms: Tafsir and Arabic Commentary, ed. and translated into Hebrew by J. Qafih.

395. Salmon ben Yeruhim (born c910). *The Arabic Commentary of Salmon ben Yeruhim the Karaite on Psalms 42-72.* Ed. from the manuscript in the State Public Library in Leningrad by Lawrence Marwick. Philadelphia: Dropsie College for Hebrew and Cognate Learning, 1956. 121p.

396. Savonarola, Girolamo Maria Francesco Matteo (1452-1498). *Prediche sopra i salmi.* Ed. Vincenzo Romano. 2 vols. Rome: Belardetti, 1969-1974.

397. Schild, Maurice E. "Approaches to Bugenhagen's Psalms Commentary (1524)." *Lutheran Theological Journal* 26 (1992): 63-71.

398. Schlieben, Reinhard. *Cassiodors Psalmenexegese. Eine Analyse ihrer Methoden als Beitrag zur Untersuchungen der Geschichte der Bibelauslegung der Kirchenväter und der Verbindung christlicher Theologie mit antiker Schulwissenschaft.* Göppinger Akademische Beiträge 110. Göppingen: Kümmerle Verlag, 1979. 292p.

399. Shunary, J. "Salmon ben Yeruham's Commentary on the Book of Psalms." *Jewish Quarterly Review* 73 (1982): 155-175.

400. Simon, Uriel. *Arba gishoth le-sepher tehillim (Four Approaches to the Book of Psalms: From Saadya Gaon to Abraham Ibn-Ezra.* Bar-Ilan University Institute for the History of Jewish Bible Research, Sources and Studies 2. Ramat-Gan, Israel: Bar-Ilan University Press, 1982. iv(English)+288(Hebrew)p. Translated into English by Lenn J. Schramm and published as *Four Approaches to the Book*

of Psalms: From Saadiah Gaon to Abraham Ibn Ezra. State University of New York Series in Judaica: Hermeneutics, Mysticism, and Religion, ed. Michael Fishbane, Robert Goldenberg, and Arthur Green. Albany, NY: SUNY Press, 1991. 400p.

401. Solomon ben Isaac (Rashi) of Troyes (1040-1105). *Tehilim. Le-hodot la-Shem.* Livorno: Yiśraᵓel Qushta va-Haverav, (1865). Reprint, Livorno: Mi-yad Shelomoh Bilforti va-Havero, (1926). 436p.

Rich in correct explanation of words, with traditions from the Midrash and Talmud scattered through it.

402. Spijker, W. van 't. "Bucers Commentaar op de Psalmen: Hebraica Veritas cum Christi Philosophia Coniungenda." *Theologia Reformata* 30 (1987): 264-280.

403. Süss, T. "Über Luthers sieben Busspsalmen." In *Vierhundertfünfzig Jahre lutherische Reformation. Festschrift für Franz Lau.* 367-383. Göttingen: Vandenhoeck & Ruprecht, 1967.

404. Talmage, Frank Ephraim. *David Kimhi: The Man and the Commentaries.* Harvard Judaic Monographs 1. Cambridge, MA: Harvard University Press, 1975. viii+236.

Reviewed in *CBQ* 39 (1977): 299-300.

405. Volz, Hans. "Luthers Arbeit am lateinischen Psalter." *Archiv für Reformationsgeschichte* 48 (1957): 11-56.

406. Vööbus, Arthur. "Die Entdeckung des Psalmenkommentars des Dawid bar ᶜAbd al-Karim." *Zeitschrift für die alttestamentliche Wissenschaft* 87 (1975): 224-226.

Announces the discovery of a complete Psalter, including Psalm 151, with a complete commentary, both in Syriac, dating from A.D. 1460/1461, the work of the Syrian monk David bar ᶜAbd al-Karim.

407. Walafrid Strabo (c.808-849). *Expositio in Viginti Primos Psalmos. Patrologia Cursus Completus, Series Latina,* ed. J.P. Migne. Vol. 114: 751-794. Paris: J.P. Migne, 1879.

Psalms 1-20.

408. Werbeck, Wilfrid. *Jacobus Perez von Valencia. Untersuchungen zu seinem Psalmenkommentar.* Beiträge zur Historischen Theologie 28. Tübingen: J.C.B. Mohr (Paul Siebeck), 1959.

15th century. Compares the exegesis of Perez on Psalms 18, 26, 39, 89, 129 (Vulgate) with the tradition of the church.

409. Wesley, John (1703-1791). *Explanatory Notes on the Old Testament.* 3 vols. Salem, OH: Schmul, 1975.

Relied on Matthew Henry and Matthew Poole.

410. Wiedermann, Gotthelf. "Alexander Alesius' Lectures on the Psalms at Cambridge, 1536." *Journal of Ecclesiastical History* 37 (1986): 15-41.

411. Zucker, M. "Notes on Saadya's Introduction into the Psalms." *Lešonenu* 33 (1968-1969): 223-230. (Hebrew)

412. Zwingli, Ulrich (Huldrych) (1484-1531). *Übersetzungen der Psalmen und Erläuterung zu einzelnen Stellen. 1525 und 1532.* Ed. Oskar Farner and Edwin Künzli. In *Huldreich Zwinglis Sämtliche Werke,* ed. Emil Egli and Georg Finsler. XIII: 467-827. Zürich: Verlag Berichthaus, 1963.

See also: 845, 1838, 1868, 2303, 2373, 2374, 2394, 2761, 2823, 2893, 3007, 3419, 3432, 3479, 3572, 3607, 3948, 4012, 4156, 4612, 4634, 4713, 4715, 4733.

C. 1801-1900

413. Alexander, Joseph Addison (1809-1860). *The Psalms, Translated and Explained.* 3 vols. Philadelphia: Presbyterian Board of Publication, (1850); New York: Baker and Scribner, 1850; Edinburgh: Andrew Elliott, 1851. Vol. I, xvi+436p; Vol. II, 349p; Vol. III, 316p. Reprint of the Edinburgh edition of 1873: Grand Rapids, MI: Baker Book House, 1975.

     Hengstenberg's Commentary forms the basis of this work.

414. Baethgen, Friedrich (1849-1905). *Die Psalmen.* Handkommentar zum Alten Testament II/2, ed. W. Nowack. Göttingen: Vandenhoeck und Ruprecht, 1904. 2nd ed., 1897. 3rd ed., 1904. l+438p.

415. Barnes, Albert (1798-1870). *Notes critical, explanatory and practical on the Book of Psalms.* 3 vols. New York, 1869/1871. Reprint, Grand Rapids, MI: Baker Book House, 1950. Vol. 1, xlviii+432p.; Vol. 2, 448p; Vol. 3, 408p.

416. Bullinger, E.W. "Introduction to the Psalms." In *Companion Bible.* 4 vols. 1893; reprint Grand Rapids, MI: Zondervan Bible Publishers, 1974.

417. Burgess, W.R. *Notes, Chiefly Critical and Philological on the Hebrew Psalms.* 2 vols. London: Williams and Norgate, 1879-1882. Vol. 1, 436p; Vol. 2, 381p.

418. Butler, James Glentworth. *The Biblework. The Old Testament. The Revised Text; with comments selected from the choicest, most illuminating and helpful thought of the Christian centuries, taken from eight hundred devout scholars.* Vols. IV-V. New York: Butler Bible-Work Co., 1892. Vol. IV (Psalms 1-72), 486p; Vol. V (Psalms 73-150), 509p.

419. Cheyne, Thomas Kelly (1841-1915). *The Book of Psalms.* London: Kegan Paul, Trench & Co., 1888. Reprint, 1904.

420. _____. *The Origin and Religious Contents of the Psalter in the Light of Old Testament Criticism and the History of Religions with an Introduction and Appendices. Eight Lectures. Preached before the University of Oxford in the Year 1889 on the Foundation of the late Rev. John Bampton, M.A., Canon of Salisbury.* London: Bampton, 1891; London: Kegan Paul, Trench, Trübner, & Co., Ltd., 1891. 517p.

The whole Psalter, with the possible exception of parts of Psalm 18, is post-exilic, belongs to the later Persian and Greek period, and contains a considerable number of Maccabean Psalms.

421. Clarke, Adam (c1762-1832). *The Holy Bible Containing the Old and New Testaments: The text carefully printed from the most correct copies of the present authorized translation, including the marginal readings and parallel texts with* A Commentary and Critical Notes *designed as a help to a better understanding of the sacred writings.* 8 vols. London: J. Butterworth & Sons, 1810-1825. A new edition, with the author's final corrections. 6 vols. 1827-1832. Reprint in 3 vols., New York: Abingdon, 1977.

The psalm titles and other information make possible a chronological arrangement of the psalms.

422. Cowles, Henry. *The Psalms with notes critical, explanatory and practical designed for both pastors and people.* New York: D. Appleton and Co., 1872. Reprint, 1891. 554p.

423. Delitzsch, Franz Julius (1813-1890). *Commentar über den Psalter.* 2 vols. Leipzig: Dörffling und Franke, 1859-1860. 5th edition by Friedrich Delitzsch, 1894. Translated from the 2nd German edition of 1867 by Francis Bolton and published as *Biblical Commentary on the Psalms.* 3 vols. Edinburgh: T.& T. Clark, 1871. Translated from the 4th German edition of 1883 by David Eaton. London: Hodder & Stoughton, 1887. Reprint, Grand Rapids, MI: William B. Eerdmans, 1959.

The time of Moses was the time of birth for Israel's national lyric. In David it attained its full maturity. 73 psalms are attributed directly to David. Other collections such as Asaph, Sons of Korah,and Ezrahite also belong to the time of David. Many psalms in the psalter come from the time of the Exile.

424. DeWette, Wilhelm Martin Leberecht (1780-1847). *Commentar über die Psalmen.* Commentar über die Schriften des alten Testaments III/2. Heidelberg: Mohr and Zimmer, 1811. 532p. 2nd ed., 1823 (586p). 3rd ed., 1829 (574p). 4th ed., 1836 (656p). 5th ed. by Gustav Baur, Heidelberg: J.C.B. Mohr, 1856. 642p.

The main classes of psalms are (1) hymns in praise of God, (2) national psalms concerned with the history of Israel as the people of God, (3) Zion and temple psalms, (4) royal psalms, (5) laments (six sub-types), and (6) general religious and moral psalms, including those expressing trust. It is not all that easy to determine the original historical setting of a psalm. One must look for the inner value of each psalm, for what is original and what is only a copy. Each breathes the inner spirit of the age in which it was composed. Historical hypotheses must give way if they do not agree with a psalm's character.

425. DeWitte, John. *The Psalms. A New Translation with Introductory Essay and Notes.* New York: Anson D.F. Randolph and Co., 1891. xxxvi+325p.

426. Duhm, Bernhard (1847-1928). *Die Psalmen.* Kurzer Handkommentar zum Alten Testament, ed. Karl Marti and Others. Abteilung XIV. Freiburg i. B., Leipzig, and Tübingen: J.C.B. Mohr (Paul Siebeck), 1899. 2nd ed., 1922. xxxii+312p. (1st ed.)

An unprejudiced critic cannot regard any Psalm as preexilic. It is even an open question whether any Psalms are as old as the Persian period; in fact, the majority of them belong to the century beginning with the Maccabean troubles and ending with the death of Alexander Jannaeus, B.C. 170-178.

The completion and final publication of the Psalter took place about 70 B.C.

427. Ewald, G. Heinrich A. von (1803-1875). *Die Psalmen und die Klagelieder.* Die Dichter des Altes Bundes, I/2. Göttingen: Vandenhoeck & Ruprecht, 1836. 3rd ed., 1866. Translated into English from the 3rd German edition by E. Johnson and published as *Commentary on the Psalms.* 2 vols. London: Williams and Norgate, 1880,1881. Vol. I, 346p; Vol. II, 353p.

The main object of the Psalter is its use in the Levitical Temple-service. Even though the Psalms themselves do not provide much information on the historical background of the individual Psalms, such information can be obtained through careful study of the Psalms. The Psalms are commented on in chronological order.

428. Fausset, Andrew Robert (1821-1910). *Studies in the CL Psalms, Their Undesigned Coincidences with the Independent Scripture Histories, Confirming and Illustrating Both..* London: Christian Book Society, 1876. xxxi+288p.

429. Forbes, John. Studies on the Book of Psalms, the Structural Connection of the Book of Psalms, Both in Single Psalms and in the Psalter as an Organic Whole. Ed. James Forrest. Edinburgh: T.& T. Clark, 1888. x+276p.

430. Gerok, Karl (1815-1890). *Die Psalmen. In Bibelstunden.* Edited by Gustav Gerok. 3 vols. Stuttgart: Carl Krabbe, 1891. Vol. 1, 459p; Vol. 2, 477p; Vol. 3, 541p.

431. Graetz, Heinrich (1817-1891). *Kritischer Commentar zu den Psalmen nebst Text und Übersetzung.* 2 vols. Breslau: Schottlaender, 1882-1883. xv+701p.

432. Grant, F.W. *The Numerical Bible: The Psalms.* Neptune, NJ: Loizeaux Brothers, 1897.

433. Hengstenberg, Ernst Wilhelm (1802-1869). *Commentar über die Psalmen.* 4 vols. Berlin: Ludwig Oehmigke, 1842-1847. Vol. 1, 475p; Vol. 2, 480p; Vol. 3, 550p; Vol. 4/1 334p; Vol. 4/2, 326p. 2nd ed., 1849-1852; Vol. 1, 480p; Vol. 2, 482p; Vol. 3, 549p; Vol. 4, 665p. Translated into English from the first German edition by Patrick Fairbairn (vols. 1-3) and John Thomson (Vols. 2-3) and published as *Commentary on the Psalms.* 3 vols. Clark's Foreign Theological Library. Edinburgh: T & T Clark, 1846-1848. Vol. 1, 539p; Vol. 2, 479p; Vol. 3, 556+xcip; 2nd edition, carefully revised, 1857; 4th cdition, carefully revised, 1869, 1870, 1863, 1896.

Hengstenberg's introductory comments appear in an appendix at the end of the last volume.

Popular lyric poetry belongs to the early history of Israel. There is no evidence, however, for a collection of Psalms prior to David. David himself is responsible for 80 Psalms, his companions 14 (Asaph, 5; the sons of Korah, 7; Solomon, 2). Of the remaining 55 (Moses had composed one), three were composed in the time of Jehoshaphat (Psalms 47, 48, 83), four in the time of the Assyrian catastrophe (Psalms 46, 75, 76, 87), one at the carrying away of the ten tribes (Psalm 81), one unknown (Psalm 85). All the rest (46 Psalms) were composed in the time immediately before, during, and after the Babylonian captivity (five Psalms of Asaph and the sons of

Korah, Psalms 77, 74, 79, 88, 89; plus Psalms 91-150, with the exception of 19 belonging to David and Solomon). Psalmodic poetry ceases after the last great occasion for singing a new song to the Lord -- the completion of the city walls under Nehemiah. The age of the superscriptions is shown by the fact that the LXX no longer understood most of them.

Collections of the Psalms of David and his singers were made at an early period. On analogy with the Pentateuch, the collector formed the Psalter into five books.

The commentary on the individual Psalms provides general comments on the meaning, structure (pointing out the importance of numbers, the number of things and their position in the psalm), and the occasion of the Psalm. Verse-by-verse comments focus on grammar, translation, and meaning.

434. Hitzig, Ferdinand (1807-1875). *Die Psalmen.* 2 vols. Leipzig and Heidelberg: C.F. Winter, 1863-1865. Vol. 1, xxx+312p; Vol. 2, xxiv+463p.

435. Hupfeld, Hermann (1796-1866). *Die Psalmen.* 4 vols. bound as 2 vols. Gotha: Friedrich Andreas Perthes, 1855, 1858, 1862. Vol. 1, xxiii+440p; Vol. 2, vi+425p; Vol. 3, 484p; Vol. 4, 478p. 2nd ed. by Riehm, 1867-1871. 3rd ed. by Nowack, 1888. 3rd ed. 1888. Vol. 3, 1860; Vol. 4, 1862.

The Psalms show us the religion of the Old Testament from inside as life is lived in the heart and as the songbook of the Jewish and Christian church received a symbolic character. Thus it is necessary to provide a *theological* interpretation. By "theological" is meant an explanation of the religious concepts and views as they are present in their particular historical form, locale, and stage of development, or such practical applications that lie within the range of the passage in question. It is also important to attend to the *grammatical* questions, in order to arrive at a more exact understanding of the linguistic and grammatical points of the most prevalent biblical concepts, style, and manner of speech.

The commentary on the individual psalms provides a new translation, a discussion of the mood and structure, and setting, plus a detailed linguistic, grammatical, and stylistic analysis of words and phrases in the psalm.

An appendix at the end of the commentary treats various introductory kinds of issues.

436. Jennings, A.C., and W.H. Lowe. *The Psalms with Introductions and Critical Notes.* 2 vols. London: Macmillan and Co., 1884-1887. Vol. 1, lxi+349; Vol. 2, 376p.

437. Kautzsch, Emil Friedrich (1841-1910). *Das Buch der Psalmen.* Die heilige Schrift des Alten Testaments. Vols. I-II. Tübingen: J.C. Mohr (Paul Siebeck), 1893. 3rd ed., 1910. 4th ed., 1922-1923.

438. Kay, William (1820-1886). *The Psalms. Translated from the Hebrew with Notes Chiefly Exegetical.* Oxford: T. and G. Shrimpton, 1864. 2nd ed., 1871. 3rd ed., London: Rivingtons, 1877. 469p.

439. Kessler, Hans. *Die Psalmen.* Strack und Zoeckler Kommentar. Kurzgefasster Kommentar zu den Heiligen Schriften Alten und Neuen Testaments sowie zu dan Apokryphen. A, Altes Testament 6/1. 2nd ed. Munich: C.H. Beck, 1899. xx+302p.

440. Kirkpatrick, Alexander Francis (1849-1940). *The Book of Psalms.* The Cambridge Bible for Schools and Colleges.

Cambridge: At the University Press, 1891-1901; reprinted 1921. cxii + 852p. Reprinted as part of Thornapple Commentaries; Grand Rapids, MI: Baker Book House, 1982. xcii+852p.

A Psalm gains in understanding if we can give it a historical or personal background, but suffers less than other parts of the Old Testament from this uncertainty because of the human and universal appeal of the Psalms. It is wrong to assign most of the Psalter to the post-exilic or even Maccabean period. Religious poetry existed before the Exile and there is no *a priori* improbability that the Psalter should contain pre-exilic Psalms. It is entirely possible that those which bear the name of David were in fact written by him. With David a new era of religious poetry commenced. The personal element entered into it. It is doubtful whether any Psalms date from the Maccabean period. The object of the Psalter was "by no means simply liturgical, but partly to unite and preserve existing collections of religious poetry, partly to provide a book of religious devotion, public and private."

The commentary proper summarizes the mood and theme of each Psalm, suggests an occasion for the writing of the Psalm, outlines the structure, and presents detailed notes based on the text of the *Cambridge Paragraph Bible*.

441. Lesêtre, Henri (1848-1914). *Le Livre des Psaumes.* La Sainte Bible, ed. Lethielleux, 1883. Paris: Lethielleux, 1886. Several reprints without change.

442. Maclaren, Alexander (1826-1910). *The Psalms.* 3 vols. The Expositor's Bible. Edited by W. Robertson Nicoll. Cincinnati, OH: Jennings & Graham, (1892); New York: Eaton & Mains, (1892). Vol. 1, 385p; vol. 2, 503p; Vol. 3, 461p.

The emphasis is on providing the exegetical, historical and theological information necessary for understanding the message of each psalm. Question of date and authorship are "all but excluded."

443. Moll, Carl Bernhard (1806-1878). *Der Psalter.* Homiletisches Bibelwerk, ed. John Peter Lange. Bielefeld and Leipzig: Velhagen und Klassing, 1869-1870. English version: *The Psalms.* Translated from the German, with additions, by Rev. Charles A. Briggs, Rev. John Forsyth, D.D., Rev. James B. Hammond, Rev. J. Fred McCurdy; Together with A New Version of the Psalms and Philological Notes by Rev. Thomas J. Conant. A Critical, Doctrinal, and Homiletical Commentary on the Holy Scriptures, IX, ed. Philip Schaff. New York: Charles Scribner's Sons, 1872; reprint, 1900. 816p.

The commentary on each Psalm presents the text in poetic form, offers (1) exegetical and critical comments on the Psalm in general and on the verses in detail, (2) doctrinal and ethical observations based on the Psalm, and (3) homiletical and practical applications of the Psalm.

444. Murphy, James G. *A Critical and Exegetical Commentary on The Book of Psalms with a New Translation.* Andover, MA: Warren Draper, 1875. Reprint, Minneapolis, MN: James Family Publishing, 1977. 694p.

Murphy's commentary "aims chiefly at bringing out the meaning and elucidating the principle of the Psalm."

For each Psalm there is a revision of the Authorized version "arranged in lines, and so printed as to indicate to the eye the divisions of thought." There is also a discussion of the occasion, subject, and arrangement of the Psalm, followed by some critical notes and general comments.

445. Olshausen, Justus (1800-1882). *Die Psalmen.* Kurzgefasstes exegetisches Handbuch zum Alten Testament 14. Leipzig: S. Hirzel, 1853. viii+505p.

This commentary is not the work of a theologian. It simply contributes, where possible, to securing a more correct philological foundation for understanding the Psalms. A recurring problem is the corruption of the text. The most natural period for the composition of the psalms seems to be the Syrian-Maccabean time.

The commentary on each of the Psalms summarizes the contents, points out the strophes, noting difficulties where they exist, indicates the historical connection, and discusses the text and meaning of the individual verses.

446. Ortenberg, Emil Fr. Jul. von. *Zur Textkritik der Psalmen.* Gottha: Perthes, 1861.

447. Patrizi, P. Fr. X., S.J. *Cento Salmi tradotti litteralmente dal testo ebraico e commentati.* Translated from Italian into French by P. Nicol. Paris: Bouchot, 1890.

448. Perowne, J.J. Stewart (1823-1879). *The Book of Psalms: A New Translation with Introductions and Notes Explanatory and Critical.* 2 vols. 1864. 3rd edition: 2 vols.; Andover, MA: Warren F. Draper, 1885. 4th edition: 2 vols.; London: George Bell and Sons, 1878. 8th edition: London: George Bell and Sons, 1892-1893; Cambridge: Deighton, Bell, and Co., 1892-1893; reprinted from the 4th edition, 2 vols.; Grand Rapids, MI: Zondervan Publishing House, 1966. Vol. I, 576p; Vol. II, 523p.; Grand Rapids,

MI: Zondervan Publishing House, 1976 (One-volume edition).

David was the greatest of the Hebrew lyric poets and in the Psalms we see much of his inner life revealed. The First Book was most likely collected by Solomon, Book Two and Three during the time of Hezekiah, and the Fourth and Fifth Book during the time of Ezra and Nehemiah. In the course of time changes were introduced into many of the Psalms.

The commentary offers a fresh translation of each Psalm, endeavors by means of introductions and explanatory notes to convey a true idea of the scope and meaning of each, employing the best commentaries available, both ancient and modern, appends a series of notes which discuss the criticism of the text, the various readings, the grammatical difficulties, and other matters of interest rather to the scholar than to the general reader.

449. Phillips, George (1804-1872). *The Psalms in Hebrew; with a Critical, Exegetical, and Philological Commentary.* 2 vols. London: John W. Parker, West Strand, 1846. Vol. I, lxxii+432p.; Vol. II, 591p.

Explains in detail the terms and construction of the Hebrew text, and thus elicits the theology which that text contains.

The commentary gives an outline of what appears to be the argument pursued by the Psalmist, states in a few words the character of the poem, as well as its age, author and subject, as far as they can be ascertained, plus criticisms on the different verses and paraphrases and explanations to which the criticisms lead.

450. Plumer, William Swan (1802-1880). Psalms. A Critical and Expository Commentary with Doctrinal and Practical Remarks on the Entire Psalter. Philadelphia, 1867. Reprinted as A Geneva Series Commentary, Edinburgh and Peabody, MA: The Banner of Truth Trust, 1975. 1211p.

451. Pridham, Arthur. *Notes and Reflections on the Psalms.* London: John Nesbit, 1869.

452. Reinke, Laurentius. *Die messianischen Psalmen. Einleitung, Grundtext und Uebersetzung nebst einem philologisch-kritischen und historischen Commentar.* Giessen: Universitätsbuchhandlung (Emil Roth), 1857-1858. Vol. 1, 450p; Vol. 2, 252+314p

453. Reischl, William Karl (1818-1873). *Das Buch der Psalmen.* 2 vols. Regensburg: Pustet, 1895.

454. Reuss, Éduard (1804-1891). *Le Psautier, ou le Livre de Cantiques de la Synagogue. La Bible. Traduction Nouvelle avec Introductions et Commentaires. L'Ancien Testament.* V: 25-417. Paris: Sandoz et Fischbacher, 1875. 2nd ed., 1879.

455. Rohling, August (1839-1931). *Die Psalmen.* Mainz: Franz Kircheim, 1871.

456. Rosenmüller, Ernst Friedrich Karl (1768-1835). *Scholia in Psalmos in compendium redacta.* Scholia in Vetus Testamentum III. Leipzig: J.A. Barth, 1831. 711p.

Marks a transition to the modern period. Mainly a compilation from older works; it is valuable for its copious citation of Jewish authorities and for its comments on the renderings of the LXX and other Versions. Draws together insights from the writings of the rabbis, Church Fathers, and medieval and Reformation scholars.

457. ______. *Annotations on Some of the Messianic Psalms. From the Commentary of Rosenmüller. With the Latin Version and Notes of Dathe.* Translated by Robert Johnson. To which is prefixed an Introduction and Preface. Edinburgh: Thomas Clark, 1841. cxxiii+320p.

Hengstenberg's Introduction to the Psalms, plus one by the translator. Psalms 2, 16, 45, 72, 110.

458. Spurgeon, Charles Haddon (1834-1892). *The Treasury of David: Containing an Original Exposition of the Book of Psalms; a Collection of Illustrative Extracts from the Whole Range of Literature; a Series of Homiletical Hints upon almost Every Verse; and Lists of Writers upon Each Psalm.* 7 vols. London: Passmore and Alabaster, 1869-1885; reprinted as 2 vols., Nashville, TN: Thomas Nelson, Inc., Publishers, 1984.

Detailed expository and homiletical comments on each of the Psalms. (There is no introduction.) I. Discussion of the title and/or subject of the Psalm and then suggests a division or outline for the Psalm. II. Exposition, containing Spurgeon's own thoughts and comments. III. Explanatory Notes and Quaint Sayings, including quotations, occasionally lengthy, from other writers, mostly from the 17th-19th centuries (especially from the Puritan divines), but with some earlier. These authors are indexed at the front of each volume. "Hints to the Village Preacher" is intended as simple suggestions on the Psalm for lay preachers.

459. Thalhofer, Valentin (1825-1891). *Erklärung der Psalmen und der im römischen Brevier vorkommenden biblischen Cantica, mit besonderer Rücksicht auf deren liturgischen Gebrauch.* 6th ed. by Peter Schmalzl. Regensburg: Nationale Verlagsanstalt Buch und Kunstdruckerei, 1895. 9th ed. by Franz Wutz, 1923.

460. Tholuck, Friedrich Augustus Gottreu (1799-1877). *Übersetzung und Auslegung der Psalmen für geistliche und Laien der christlichen Kirche.* Halle: Eduard Anton, 1843. lxxx+574p. Translated from the German edition of 1843 with a careful comparison of the Psalm-text with the original tongues by J. Isidor Mombert and published as *A Translation and Commentary of the Book of Psalms for the use of the ministry and laity of the Christian Church.* Philadelphia: William S. & Alfred Martien, 1858. 497p. Later German edition, Gotha. 1873.

The object in this commentary is "to interpret the Book of Psalms in the spirit of Calvin; and basing it on the helps derived from the newly-gained views of modern times, to adapt the volume to the wants of the people, and also to professional people, who, besides strictly grammatical Commentaries, look for a guide to the spiritual understanding of this portion of Holy Writ." There is great appreciation for Hengstenberg's Commentary on the Psalms.

The commentary on each Psalm includes a discussion of general issues related to an analysis of the psalm: classification, mood, historical setting or connection (where one can be made), psalm title (where one exists, the authenticity of its information is verified), and basic thought. Then follows the Psalm text. Commentary on the verses follows the text.

461. Vilmar, August Friedrich Christian (1800-1868). *Der Psalter.* Collegium Biblicum. Gütersloh: Bertelsman, 1882.

462. Walsh, William Pakenham (1820-1902). *The Voices of the Psalms.* London: Thomas Whittaker, 1890. xii+332p.

463. Wellhausen, Julius (1844-1918). The Book of Psalms. Critical Edition of the Hebrew Text Printed in Colors with Notes. *The Book of Psalms.* Sacred Books of the Old Testament 14, ed. Paul Haupt. English translation of notes by J.D. Prince. Leipzig: J.C. Hinrichs, 1895; The Johns Hopkins Press, 1895. 96p.

464. Wordsworth, Christopher (1807-1885). *The Book of Psalms.* Commentary on the Holy Bible. London: Rivingtons, 1867.

Full of citations from the fathers; finds in the Psalms "a prophetic Creed," "the great doctrine of Christian faith gradually revealed with greater clearness and fullness."

D. After 1900

465. Abramowski, Rudolf. *Das Buch des betenden Volkes: Die Psalmen.* 2 vols. Die Botschaft des Alten Testaments. Stuttgart: Calwer Verlag, 1938-1939. Vol. 1, 243p; Vol. 2, 263p.

466. Addis, W.E. "Psalms." In *Commentary on the Bible*, ed. Arthur S. Peake, with the assistance for the New Testament of A.J. Grieve. 366-396. New York: Thomas Nelson, 1922.

467. Aglen, Archdeacon. "The Book of Psalms." In *The Layman's Handy Commentary on the Bible*, ed. Charles John Ellicott. Grand Rapids, MI: Zondervan, 1960.

468. Alden, Robert. *Psalms.* 3 vols. Everyman's Bible Commentary Series. Chicago, IL: Moody Press, 1990.

469. Allen, Leslie C. *Psalms 101-150.* Word Biblical Commentary 21. Waco, TX: Word Books, Publisher, 1983. xx+342p.

The commentary summarizes the positions of other Old Testament scholars such as Anderson, Dahood, Gunkel, Kraus, and Weiser on the form, structure and setting of each psalm. Then comes his own explanation of its use and meaning. Here the attempt is made to trace the impact of the various psalms upon Christian thought and devotions, focusing on the New Testament uses of the Psalter; this carries with it a messianic and christological interest.

470. Anderson, Arnold. Albert. *The Book of Psalms.* 2 vols. The New Century Bible, edited by Ronald E. Clements and Matthew Black. London: Oliphants, 1972; reprinted London: Marshall, Morgan & Scott Publishing, Ltd., 1981; Grand Rapids, MI: William B. Eerdmans Publishing Co., 1981. 966p.

The large majority of the Psalms were cultic in origin and in their usage during the OT period. The three great annual festivals -- Passover and the Feast of Unleavened Bread, Harvest Festival, and Feast of Tabernacles -- provided the background for most of the Psalms. The most important of these festivals was the autumnal Feast of Tabernacles, which possessed the character of a New Year Festival.

471. Anderson, G.W. "The Psalms." In *Peake's Commentary on the Bible*, ed. Matthew Black and H.H. Rowley. 409-443. New York: Thomas Nelson and Sons, Ltd., 1962.

472. Appleton, George. *Understanding the Psalms.* Harrisburg, PA: Morehouse Publishing, 1987. 180p.

A meditative commentary on all the Psalms, plus chapters on Jesus and the Psalms, and some early Christian psalms. Index of themes included.

473. Arconada, R. *Los Salmos, versión y comentario. Reajústan S. Bartína y F.X. Rodríguez Molero.* Biblioteca de Autores Cristianos 293. Madrid: La Editorial Catolica, 1969.

See *CBQ* 32 (1970): 463.

474. Ash, Anthony L., and Clyde M. Miller. *Psalms.* The Living Word Commentary on the Old Testament 10. Austin, TX: Sweet Publishing Company, 1980. 445p.

A commentary intended primarily for lay people.

475. Baigent, John W., and Leslie C. Allen. "The Psalms." In *The International Bible Commentary with the New International Version*, ed. F.F. Bruce. 552-655. Revised edition. Grand Rapids, MI: Zondervan, 1986.

While the viewpoint of this commentary is conservative, it desires "to place in the hands of Christians of all types and denominations a volume that takes its stand upon the historical and orthodox belief in the authority of Holy Scripture." Baigent writes the commentary on Psalms 1-72, Allen on Psalms 73-150.

476. Barclay, William. *The Lord is My Shepherd: Expositions of Selected Psalms.* With an Introduction by Allan Galloway. Philadelphia: Westminster Press, 1980. 153p.

Psalms 1, 2, 8, 19, 104.

477. Barnes, W. Emery. *The Psalms, with Introduction and Notes.* 2 vols. Westminster Commentaries, ed. Walter Lock and D.C. Simpson. London: Methuen & Co., Ltd., 1931. lxxxii+698p.

The primary object of the Westminster Commentaries is to be exegetical, to interpret the meaning of each book of the Bible in the light of modern knowledge to English readers. Taking the English text in the Revised Version as their basis, the editors aim at combining a hearty acceptance of critical principles with loyalty to the Catholic Faith.

478. Beaucamp, É. *Le Psautier.* 2 vols. Sources bibliques 7. Paris: J. Gabalda, 1976, 1979. vol. 1, 331p. vol. 2, 340p.

The reader is invited to share in the prayer of Israel. The commentary aims at giving the reader what is necessary for gaining the most profit from reading the text. Comments concerning text and literary issues are made for each psalm.

479. Bellett, J.G. *Short Meditations on the Psalms.* London: G. Morrish, 1910.

480. Bentzen, Aage. *Fortolkning til de gammeltestamentlige Samler.* Copenhagen: G.E.C. Gad, 1940. xi+690p.

481. Berry, George Ricker. *The Book of Psalms.* An American Commentary. Philadelphia: The American Baptist Publication Society, 1934.

482. Bertholet, Alfred (1868-1951). *Das Buch der Psalmen.* Die heilige Schrift des Alten Testaments II. 4th ed. Tübingen, J.C. Mohr (Paul Siebeck), 1922-1923.

483. *The Bethany Parallel Commentary on the Old Testament. From the Condensed Editions of Matthew Henry; Jamison, Fausset, and Brown; and Adam Clarke. Three Classic Commentaries in One Volume.* 964-1197. Minneapolis, MN: Bethany Press, 1985.

484. Bird, T.E. *A Commentary on the Psalms.* 2 vols. London: Burns Oates & Washbourne, Ltd., 1927. Vol. 1, xiv+469p; Vol. 2, 427p.

485. ______. "The Psalms." In *A Catholic Commentary on Holy Scripture,* ed. Bernard Orchard and Others. 442-473. New York: Thomas Nelson and Sons, 1953.

486. Böhl, Franz Marius Theodor DeLiagre, and Berend Gemser. *De Psalmen: Tekst en Uitleg,* praktische bijbelverklaring door Prof. Dr. F.M.Th. Böhl en Prof. Dr. A. van Veldhuizen. 3 vols. (Vols. I & II by Böhl, Vol. III by Gemser). Groningen-Batavia: J.B. Wolters, 1946, 1947, 1949. Vol. I, 183p; Vol. II, 178p; Vol. III, 256p.

487. Bonkamp, Bernhard. *Die Psalmen nach dem hebräischen Grundtext.* Mit einem Vorwort von A. Allgeier. Freiburg im Breisgau: Verlag Wilhelm Visarius, 1949. 634p.

This is a text-critical work which applies the philological principles gained from a modern insight into the nature of language and tradition toward establishing a firm footing for understanding the often inaccessible psalms. We can only understand the Psalms when we know the circumstances out of which they arose. Tradition attributes almost half of the Psalter to David. The superscriptions, however, must be critically evaluated for their accuracy.

The texts in the psalter have been brought together from different sources. The number twelve plays a large role in this process. The Elohistic songs in Book II, Psalms 42(41)-83(82), are actually only 41 in number, Psalms 42+43 being only one psalm; they thus represent a clear contrast to the 41 Yahwistic songs of the first book. The deliberateness of the editor's work is shown by the psalms and parts of collections that appear in each book. Book IV doubles Book III (17+17). The various collections found in the five books are made up of earlier and smaller collections and go back to earlier poets, who are the actual authors of the songs.

The commentary on the psalms offers the Latin title, a German translation, and comments on the meaning, occasion and position of the Psalm.

488. Brandenburg, Hans. *Der Psalter. Das Gebetbuch des Volkes Gottes.* Die Lehrbücher des Altes Bundes. 2 vols. Giessen and Basel: Brunnen Verlag, 1967-1968. Vol. 1, 262p.; Vol. 2, 307p.

489. Brethes, C. *Mon âme, bénis le Seigneur! Commentaire et traduction en vers des Psaumes.* Paris: Apostolat des Editions, 1965. 551p.

490. Briggs, Charles Augustus, and Emile Grace Briggs. *A Critical and Exegetical Commentary on the Book of Psalms.* 2 vols.

International Critical Commentary. Edinburgh: T & T Clark, 1906-1907. Vol. 1, cx+422p; Vol. 2, 572p.

The emphasis of the commentary is on discussing the Hebrew poetry -- rhythm, meter and stophe, and parallelism, with suggestions on correcting the Hebrew text.

491. Brinke, G.R. *Skizzen über die Psalmen.* 2 vols. Bern: Ährenleseverlag, 1970-1971. Vol. 1, 276p.; Vol. 2, 285p.

492. Brug, John F. *Psalms.* 2 vols. The People's Bible, ed. Roland Cap Ehlke, John C. Jeske, and G. Jerome Albrecht. Milwaukee, WI: Northwestern Publishing House, 1989.

Brug has two goals. One is to introduce the reader to the special features and problems of Hebrew poetry. The other is to help the Bible student read through the whole book of Psalms as a connected, well-organized collection of hymns.

493. Budde, Karl F.R. *Die schönsten Psalmen, übersetzt und erklärt.* Leipzig: C.F. Amelang, 1915.

494. Buhl, Frants. *Psalmerne oversatte og fortolkrede.* Copenhagen: Gyldendalske Boghandels Forlag, 1900. lvi+889p. 2nd ed., 1918.

495. Bullough, Sebastian. "The Psalms." In *A New Catholic Commentary on Holy Scripture,* ed. R.G. Fuller. Sections 381-410. London: Thomas Nelson, 1969.

496. Buttenwieser, Moses. *The Psalms -- Chronologically Treated with a New Translation.* Chicago: University of Chicago Press, 1938. Reprinted with Prolegomenon by Nahum M.

Sarna; The Library of Biblical Studies, ed. Harry M. Orlinsky; New York: KTAV Publishing House, 1969.

497. Calès, Jean. *Le livre des Psaumes.* 2 vols. 5th ed. Paris: G. Beauchesne et ses fils, 1936. Vol. 1, 699p; Vol. 2, 687p.

The desire is to make the Psalms as intelligible as possible, in order to interest curious laity in this book, but above all in order to aid the priests and seminarians in their reciting of the Psalms in the Breviary.

498. Callan, Charles Jerome. *The Psalms. Translated from the Latin Psalter in the Light of the Hebrew, of the Septuagint and Peshitta Versions, and of the Psalterium iuxta Hebraeos of St. Jerome with Introductions, Critical Notes and Spiritual Reflections.* New York: Joseph F. Wagner, Inc., 1944. 695p.

Reviewed by J.E. Coleran in *CBQ* 8 (1946): 247-248.

499. Castellino, D. Giorgio. *Libro dei Salmi.* La Sacra Bibbia. Rome: Marietti, 1955. xi+912p.

Offers the texts of the Roman Psalter and the Vulgate, an Italian translation, and historico-literary comments on the text, as well as a religious and devotional reading of the text. The psalms are arranged according to form and content.

Reviewed in *CBQ* 19 (1957): 146-147.

500. Chouraqui, André. *Les Psaumes. Traduits et présentés.* Paris: Presses Universitaires de France, 1956.

501. Church, J.R. *Hidden Prophecies in the Psalms.* Editorial and research work by Jack Jewell and Patricia Berry. Oklahoma City, OK: Prophecy Publications, 1986. 400p.

Historical facts show how the Psalms present the ebb and flow of each year in the 20th century.

502. Clarke, Arthur G. *Analytical Studies in the Psalms.* Kilmarnock, Scotland: John Ritchie, 1949. 3rd ed., 1976. Reprint from the 3rd edition: Grand Rapids, MI: Kregel Publications, 1979. 376p.

For a true understanding of the psalms, it is necessary to study them from three distinct viewpoints: (a) the Primary Association, or Historical Aspect; (b) the Prophetic Anticipation, or Typical Aspect; and (c) the Personal Application, or Devotional Aspect.

503. Clifford, Richard J. *Psalms.* 2 vols. The Collegeville Bible Commentary, ed. Dianne Bergant and Robert J. Karris, Vols. 22-23. Collegeville, MN: The Liturgical Press, 1989.

504. Cohen, Abraham. *The Psalms: Hebrew Text, English Translation and Commentary.* The Soncino Books of the Bible. Hindhead, Surrey: Soncinco Press, 1945. xiv+488p.

The Soncino Books of the Bible series has several features. 1) Each volume contains the Hebrew text and English translation together with the commentary. 2) The exposition is designed primarily for the ordinary reader of the Bible rather than for the student. 3) The commentary is based on the received Hebrew text. 4) It offers a Jewish commentary. Without neglecting the work of Christian expositors, it takes into account the exegesis of the Talmudical Rabbis as well as of the leading Jewish commentators.

For each Psalm, the Hebrew text with the translation of the Jewish Publication Society of America is given. There are also general comments on the meaning, setting, and mood of each Psalm, plus specific comments on the individual verses.

505. Craigie, Peter C. *Psalms 1-50.* Word Biblical Commentary 19. Waco, TX: Word Books, 1983. 378p.

The Psalms contain "popular theology," which is to say that they emerge out of the broad spectrum of a life lived in relationship with God. There are different layers of theological meaning in the individual psalms. There is the original meaning of the psalm and then there is the function and significance of the psalm as it changed over the passage of time. This has two important consequences. a) If the psalm is to be fully understood, it is best to begin with its original meaning. This will help in understanding its later meaning and function. b) The reinterpretation of individual psalms provides a starting point as we attempt to reinterpret the psalm for our own contemporary use. The Ugaritic material is important for an understanding of the Hebrew psalms, yet we need to be more cautious in applying Ugaritic material to the Hebrew psalms than is Dahood. More valuable is the vocalization of the Massoretic tradition. There is the difficulty of judgment with respect to possibilities and probabilities. Firm controls (chronology, geography, literary forms, and the nature of the textual evidence) should be employed which provide the context necessary for interpreting the comparative data.

506. Creager, Harold L., and Herbert C. Alleman. *The Psalms.* Old Testament Commentary. Philadelphia: The Muhlenberg Press, 1948.

507. Dahood, Mitchell. *Psalms.* 3 vols. The Anchor Bible 16,17,17A. Garden City, NY: Doubleday & Co., 1966, 1968, 1970. Vol. 1, xiii+329; Vol. 2, xxx+399; Vol. 3, liv+491p.

This is not so much a commentary on the Psalms as a fresh translation and philological commentary that makes heavy use of the linguistic information offered by the Ras Shamra-Ugarit texts.

Vol. 1 reviewed by D.A. Robertson in *JBL* 85 (1966): 484-486; Vol. 2 reviewed by F.I. Andersen in *JBL* 88 (1969): 208-210; Vol. 3 reviewed by T.H.Gaster in *JBL* 93 (1974): 296-300. Other evaluations of Dahood's approach: John L. McKenzie, *Catholic Biblical Quarterly* 33 (1971): 421-422; A. Barucq, *Biblica* 52 (1971): 256-262; L.F. Hartman, *Catholic Biblical Quarterly* 26 (1964): 104-106; A.A. di Lella, *Catholic Biblical Quarterly* 32 (1970): 432-435; J.J. De Vault, *Theological Studies* 33 (1972): 374.

508. Davies, T. Witton. *The Psalms: LXXIII-CL.* Vol. II. The New Century Bible. Edinburgh: T.C. & E.C. Jack, 1906. 380p.

For each of the Psalms, comments are provided on the theme, (title), contents, authorship and date, followed by brief exegetical comments on selected words and phrases.

509. Davison, W.T. *The Psalms: I-LXXII.* Vol. I. The Century Bible. Edinburgh: T.C. & E.C. Jack, 1906. 365p.

The introductions to each Psalm attempt to answer questions such as Who wrote it? When? Where? For what end? and the like. The notes appended to each Psalm are brief. Attention is concentrated upon exegesis pure and simple with special emphasis upon the renderings of the Revised Version.

510. Deissler, Alphons. *Die Psalmen.* 3 vols. Die Welt der Bibel, Klein Kommentare zur Heiligen Schrift. Düsseldorf: Patmos-Verlag, 1963-1964. 3rd ed. of Vol. I, 1966; 2nd ed. of Vol. II, 1967; 2nd ed. of Vol. III, 1969. French translation from the 1st German edition of 1963-1964 by J. Décla: *Le livre des Psaumes.* Verbum Salutis, Ancient Testament, 1. Paris: Beauchesne, 1966.

In the psalms, we perceive the pulsations of the life of the people of God during the time of the Old Testament. But it is not simply Israel who speaks here; all humankind discovers in these songs and prayers those words which describe its existence before God. Hopefully this commentary will help both priests and laity as they seek to understand the meaning of these psalms.

Comments on each psalm include (a) textual issues, (b) literary genre, date and life setting, (c) interpretation of the psalm within the framework of the Old Testament, and (d) meaning of the psalm in the light of the New Testament. These comments emphasize "anthological composition" (the re-use of biblical phrases in later biblical compositions) and "re-lecture" (the re-interpretation of earlier songs through later insertions).

French version reviewed by R.E. Murphy in *JBL* 88 (1969): 371; also in *CBQ* 29 (1967): 251 (Vol. 1) and *CBQ* 31 (1969): 599-600 (Vol. 2).

511. Desnoyers, Louis. *Les Psaumes. Traduction rhthmée d'après l'hébreu.* Paris: Desclée de Brouwer, 1935. 469p.

512. Drummelow, J.R., ed. *A Commentary on the Holy Bible by Various Writers.* 321-378: "The Psalms." New York: Macmillan, 1908. 32nd printing, 1971.

513. Durham, John I. "Commentary on Psalms." In *The Broadman Bible Commentary 4: Esther Psalms,* ed. Clifton J. Allen. 153-464. Nashville, TN: Broadman Press, 1971.

514. Eaton, J.H. *Psalms: Introduction and Commentary.* Torch Bible Commentaries. London: SCM Press, 1967.

515. Eerdmans, Bernardus Dirks. *The Hebrew Book of Psalms.* Oudtestamentische Studiën 4. Leiden: E.J. Brill, 1947. viii+614p.

This commentary rejects 1) the idea that the Psalter is a Hymnbook of the Second Temple, 2) Gunkel's *Gattungsforschung,* 3) metric studies as a reliable foundation for text-emendations, 4) the compilation of the present Psalter happening over a period of time (scribes under Nehemiah's direction copied indiscriminately and pell-mell what psalms they could find or were told to them; Rabbinical scholars many centuries later, taking their cue from the doxologies, divided the Psalter into five books), 5) the literary dependence of Israelite writers on foreign literature, 6) *le* David as a reliable guide to authorship (most psalms come from the period of the monarchy, a few are post-exilic), 7) the idea of Psalms being sung to a tune or melody, 8) *lamm^{e}nasseah* as referring to a choirmaster (it refers to an overseer of laborers who keeps them working in rhythm), and 9) *selah* as a musical term (it was inserted into the Psalm long after it was written and is best understood as meaning "bow down"). The Revised Version serves as the basis of the translation, but it is modified in numerous passages. Comments are offered on the meaning, setting and date of each psalm.

516. Ehrlich, Arnold B. *Die Psalmen neu übersetzt und erklärt.* Berlin: M. Poppelauer, 1905. 438p.

517. Emmanuel (*pseud.*). *Commentaire juif des Psaumes.* Paris, Payot, 1963. 368p.

518. Farmer, Kathleen A. "Psalms." In *The Women's Bible Commentary*, ed. Carol A. Newsom and Sharon H. Ringe. 137-144. Louisville, KY: Westminster/John Knox Press, 1992.

519. Fischer, James A. *The Psalms.* Canfield, OH: Alba, 1974.

A thematic, theological, and liturgical commentary on the Psalms.

520. Freehof, Solomon B. *The Book of Psalms: A Commentary.* The Jewish Commentary for Bible Readers. Cincinnati, OH: Union of American Hebrew Congregations, 1938. 414p.

521. Gaebelein, Arno Clemens (1861-1945). *The Book of Psalms: A Devotional and Prophetic Commentary.* Neptune, NJ: Our Hope Press, 1939; reprint Neptune, NJ: Loizeaux Brothers, Inc., 1965.

522. Garcia Cordero, Maximiliano. *Libros de los Salmos I.* Biblioteca de autores cristianos. Madrid: Editorial Católica, 1963.

523. Gerstenberger, Erhard S. *Psalms, Part 1; with an Introduction to Cultic Poetry.* The Forms of the Old Testament Literature, ed. Rolf Knierim and Gene M. Tucker, vol. XIV. Grand Rapids, MI: William B. Eerdmans Publishing Company, 1988. 260p.

The structure of each Psalm is presented in outline form. The typical form is then distinguished from the individual or unique elements; this provides a basis for the determination of genre, its setting and its intention. Tradition-historical factors are discussed where relevant. A bibliography is given for each Psalm.

524. Girard, Marc. *Les Psaumes. Analyse Structurelle et Interpretation 1-50.* Recherches Nouvelle Serie-2. Montreal: Bellarmin, 1984; Paris: Cerf, 1984. 412p.

"Analyse structurelle" is the study of surface literary structure in the tradition of such scholars as Alonso-Schökel and Vanhoye. It is distinguished from "analyse structurale," which is the modern "structuralist" study of deep structures. It involves three levels: 1) syntagmatic, 2) syntactic, 3) and the unity of well-developed structures. There are four categories of psalms: those structured by 1) repetition, 2) repetition and other verbal devices, 3) relations of both words and ideas, and 4) chiefly by ideas. This intra-textual analysis of relations within the text reveals which ideas are primary and which secondary.

525. Goldingay, John. *Songs from a Strange Land. Psalms 42-51.* The Bible Speaks Today. Downers Grove, IL: InterVarsity Press, 1978. 172p.

526. González, Angel. *El Libro de los Salmos. Introducción, versión y comentariio.* Barcelona: Editorial Herder, 1966. 729p.

Special attention is given to identifying the literary forms and probable usage of the psalms.

527. Gouders, Klaus. *Herr, öffne meine Lippe. Aus dem Buch der Psalmen.* Stuttgarter Kleiner Kommentar, Altes Testament 22/1. Stuttgart: Katholisches Bibelwerk, 1974. 76p.

528. Groot, Johannes de. *De Psalmen.* Baarn: Bosch & Kreuning, 1942. 238p.

529. Gross, Heinrich, and Heinz Reinelt. *Das Buch der Psalmen.* 2 vols. Geistliche Schriftlesung, Erläuterungen zum Alten Testament für die Geistliche Lesung 9. Düsseldorf: Patmos, 1978-1980. Vol. 1, 403p; Vol. 2, 452p.

This is a devotional commentary, intended to present the text and commentary in a form suitable for prayerful study and meditation. The introduction considers historical and form-critical issues, often reflecting the views of Kraus. The psalms are divided between the two authors, who provide their own translations and commentary.

530. Guichou, Pierre. *Les Psaumes commentés par la Bible.* 3 vols. L'esprit liturgique 11-13. Paris: Les éditions du Cerf, 1958-1959.

A liturgical and devotional study of the Psalms, borrowing from many sources.

Vol. 1 reviewed in *CBQ* 20 (1958): 397-398.

531. Gunkel, Hermann (1862-1932). *Einleitung in die Psalmen: Die Gattungen der religösen Lyrik Israels.* Completed by Joachim Begrich. Göttingen Handkommentar, Ergänzungsband zur II Abteilung. Göttingen: Vandenhoeck & Ruprecht, 1933. Reprinted 1966. 464p.

§ 1. The Genres of the Psalms.

§ 2. The Hymns. I. Their Literary Forms. II. The Nature of Their Presentation. III. Their Religion. IV. Their Connections with Other Genres. V. Their Inner History.

§ 3. Songs of Yahweh's Enthronement. I. Their Forms and Contents. II. Their Cultic Situation and Their History. It is improbable that ancient Israel knew the New Year's festival. The prophetic spirit and the prophetic poets introduced the eschatological element into the enthronement songs. Deutero-Isaiah was the first to do this. This represents a completely different approach than that of Mowinckel, who wants to find the origin of eschatology in worship associated with the New Year's festival, and who makes the prophets dependent upon the psalms.

§ 4. Community Laments.

§ 5. Royal Psalms.

§ 6. Laments of the Individual.

§ 7. Thanksgiving Songs of the Individual.

§ 8. Smaller Genres. I. Blessings and Curses. II. Pilgrim Song. III. Victory Song. IV. Thanksgiving Song of Israel. V. Legend. VI. Torah.

§ 9. The Prophetic in the Psalms. I. The Eschatological Property of the Psalms. II. The Form of the Eschatological Content. III. The Penetration of the Eschatological into the Psalms. IV. The Eschatology of the Psalms in Its Relationship to the Eschatology of the Prophetical Books. The psalms are not the place of origin for eschatology (so Mowinckel); rather they presuppose the prophets. Over against them, the psalms represent a second stage and are imitations of what is original in the prophets. V. Other Prophetic Genres in the Psalms. VI. The Situation of the Prophetic Psalms. The proof for a cultic prophetic office, with which Mowinckel's thesis rises and falls, is hardly convincing. VII. Pure Intellectual Influence of the Psalms By the Prophets. VIII. The Time of the Prophetic Psalms.

§ 10. Wisdom Poetry in the Psalms.

§ 11. Mixed Types, Antiphonal Poems, and Liturgies. I. Mixed Types. These arose through the mixing of genres and the decomposition and loosening of genres. The main cause for this is the loosening of the genre from its original concrete situation, in other words, the change from cult-bound to cult-free, spiritual poetry. II. Antiphonal Poems. III. Liturgies.

§ 12. The History of Psalm Composition.

§ 13. The Collection of Psalms.

§ 14. The Superscriptions of the Psalms.

532. ______. *Die Psalmen.* 4th ed. Göttinger Handkommentar zum Alten Testament. Göttingen: Vandenhoeck & Ruprecht, 1929. 5th ed. 1968. 6th ed. 1986. xvi+639p.

533. Guthrie, Donald. *The New Bible Commentary.* Grand Rapids, MI: William B. Eerdmans Publishing Company, 1987. 1325p.

534. Hammershaimb, E. *Femten gammeltestamentlige Salmer med indledning, oversættelse og kommentar.* Bibel og historie 5. Copenhagen: Gad, 1984. 168p.

The purpose of this commentary is to help students of theology in their study of the Old Testament Psalms. The introduction includes a discussion of Hebrew poetry, the history of research with emphasis on Gunkel, Mowinckel, and the Uppsala-school. This is followed by comments on fifteen important psalms of different genres: Psalms 2, 8, 15, 23, 24, 47, 51, 60, 73, 84, 96, 101, 110, 118, and 132.

535. Hanson, Richard S. *The Psalms in Modern Speech.* 3 vols. Philadelphia: Fortress Press, 1968. Vol. 1, xlii+80p; Vol. 2, 103p; Vol. 3, 124p.

Reviewed by P.L. Garber in *JBL* 88 (1969): 368-369.

536. Harris, Arthur Emerson. *The Psalms Outlined.* Philadelphia: Judson Press, 1925.

537. Hastings, James, founder and editor, and Edward Hastings, editor. *Psalms.* 4 vols. *The Speaker's Bible.* Aberdeen, Scotland: 1923-32; reprint Grand Rapids, MI: Baker Book House, 1961-62.

The Speaker's Bible aims to preserve all that is worth preserving of the modern interpretation of the Bible. It seeks to enrich present-day preaching. It therefore offers "an exposition of every text on the Bible on which sermons are preached, with its application to modern life, all in clear order, terse language, and with pointed illustration."

538. Herkenne, Heinrich. *Das Buch der Psalmen.* Die Heilige Schrift des Alten Testaments V/2. Bonn: Peter Hanstein Verlagsbuchhandlung, 1936. xiv+466p.

In this commentary the most immediate concern is establishing the Psalm text, in order to have as firm a foundation as is possible for the exegesis. An original translation appears at the top of the page. Below this are placed deviations from the received text. Where these require a lengthy discussion, this appears in the commentary in excurses printed in smaller type. Where the reason for a change in the text is not given, those interested may refer to Gunkel's commentary. A special section discusses linguistic and literary-critical remarks which are necessary for a solid exegesis. In the interest of clarity, the comments are placed in paragraphs based on the sense of the Psalm. The leading thought of each section is printed in larger type. Many new suggestions are made for the corrections in the text.

539. Hirsch, Samson Raphael. *Die Psalmen übersetzt und erläutert.* 3rd ed. Frankfurt am Main, 1914. Another edition, 1924. Translated into English by Gertrude Hirschler and published as *The Psalms.* 2 vols. New York: Philipp Feldheim, Inc., for the Samson Raphael Hirsch Publications Society, 1960-1966.

540. Hulley, Lincoln (1865-1934). *Studies in the Book of Psalms.* New York and London: Fleming H. Revell, 1907. 178p.

541. Hylander, Ivar. *Gamla testamentets psalmbok.* Religionsvetenskapliga Skrifter 17. Uppsala: Sveriges kristliga studentrörelses bokförlag, 1937. 108p.

Hylander reflects the work of Ewald, Birkeland, and H. Schmidt, approaching the Psalms from an historical, literary, and religious point of view. He argues that the Book of Psalms grew out of religious-pedagogical concerns.

542. Ironside, Henry ("Harry") Allen (1876-1951). *Studies on Book One of the Psalms.* Neptune, NJ: Loizeaux Brothers, 1952; reprint, 1963.

The five books of the Psalms correspond in theme with the five books of the Pentateuch. The commentary is expository and homiletical, emphasizing prophetic and messianic elements; it covers Psalms 1-41.

543. Jacquet, Louis. *Les Psaumes et le couer de l'homme. Étude textuelle, littéraire et doctrinale.* 3 vols. Gembloux: Duculot, 1975, 1977, 1979. Vol. 1, 832p.; Vol. 2, 855p; Vol. 3, v+815p.

This commentary is intended not so much for the biblical scholar as for the Christian theologian and educated layperson whose concern is primarily with the teaching of the Psalms. To this end, a wide range of works and viewpoints are brought together, including major works of western and eastern religious traditions, beginning with patristic and midrashic commentators and extending down to the present, philosophical and religious comments from classical Greece, ancient Near Eastern and Far Eastern religion, and contemporary literature.

Vol. 1 reviewed by H.C. White in *JBL* 96 (1977): 432-433; also in *CBQ* 38 (1976): 394-395. Vol. 2 in *JBL* 100 (1981): 112-113; also in *CBQ* 41 (1979): 467-468. Vol. 3 in *JBL* 100 (1981): 112-113

544. Jamieson, Robert, A.R. Fausset, and David Brown. "The Book of Psalms." In *Commentary Practical and Explanatory on the Whole Bible.* 405-458. Regency Reference Library. Grand Rapids, MI: Zondervan Publishing House, 1961.

545. Johnston, Leonard. *The Psalms.* Scripture Discussion Commentary, Vol. 6. Chicago: ACTA Foundation, 1972.

546. Kalt, Edmund. *Die Psalmen übersetzt und erklärt.* Herders Bibelkommentar. Die Heilige Schrift für das Leben erklärt, Vol. VI. Freiburg im Breisgau: Verlagsbuchhandlung Herder, 1935; 2nd ed., 1937; xvi+524p; translated into English by Bernard Fritz and published as *Herder's Commentary on the Psalms*, Westminster, MD: The Newman Press, 1961. 559p.

Herder's Commentary intends to explain the biblical books with the view of aiding the formation of a practical Christian life. It looks particularly at the literal sense and emphasizes and shows the supernatural and divine in these writings. It seeks to discover what they tell us in this generation of the 20th century.

For each psalm, there is the Latin title, a sentence summarizing the Psalm, a translation of the Psalm, and comments that give some attention to historical matters but much attention to the spiritual meaning of the psalm, often highlighting the Christ dimension.

547. Kidner, Derek. *Psalms.* 2 vols. Tyndale Old Testament Commentaries, ed. D.J. Wiseman, vols. 14a and 14b. Leicester: InterVarsity Press, 1973, 1975. 492p.

The commentary focuses on the meaning and universal relevance of each psalm. An appropriate setting or situation is suggested for each psalm.

Vol. 1 reviewed in *CBQ* 37 (1975): 117-118.

548. King, Philip J., and Robert North. *The Book of Psalms.* 4 Parts. Paulist Bible Series. New York: Paulist Press, 1962-1963.

549. Kissane, Edward J. *The Book of Psalms: Translated from a Critically Revised Hebrew Text With a Commentary.* 2 vols. Dublin: Browne & Nolan, 1953-1954; Westminster, MD: The Newman Press, 1953-1954. Vol. I, xlv+319p; Vol. II, 336p; printed as one volume, Dublin: Browne and Nolan, 1964; 656p.

The chief aim in this commentary is twofold: to get back to the Hebrew text as it left the hand of the original writer, and to interpret this in the light of the religious background of Israel as revealed in the Psalter and in the Old Testament as a whole.

The commentary on the psalms discusses subject and structure, offers a translation with critical notes, suggests corrections in the Hebrew text, and comments on the meaning of the psalm. Many times a date or occasion is suggested for the psalm. When appropriate, the messianic character and/or unity of the psalm is addressed.

550. Kittel, Rudolf (1853-1929). *Die Psalmen übersetzt und erklärt.* Kommentar zum Alten Testament, ed. Ernst Sellin. Band 13. Leipzig: A. Deichert-Werner Scholl, 1914. 3rd and 4th ed., 1922. 5th and 6th ed., 1929. lvii+462p.

For each of the Psalms, the commentary provides a translation, with the meter indicated for each line. The comments begin with a general discussion of such issues as form, date, setting, and structure. The verse-by-verse comments focus on the meaning of the passages. Psalms 27 and 127 are treated as two psalms each. Psalms 42-43 are treated as one psalm. Scattered throughout the commentary are excurses on several topics: the alphabetical (acrostic) songs, protestations of innocence, Luther and Psalm 46, the eschatological Psalms (a discussion of eschatology in the

Psalms, concluding that Psalm 46 refers not to the present, but to the endtime when Yahweh will be enthroned as king over all peoples), the pious and the godless, poetic treatments of historical memories, the festival hymn (relating either to passover or the feast of tabernacles), the directions of the poor and the misfortunate, the *Ma*^{ca}*lot* or pilgrimage songs, and the participation of the community in the liturgical songs). At the end of the commentary there are two appendices, one of the idea of reward in the Psalter, the other on Babylonian and Egyptian parallels to the Psalter.

551. Knabenhauer, Josephus., S.J. *Commentarius in Psalmos.* Cursus Scripturae Sacrae. Paris: Lethielleux, 1912. 2nd ed., 1930. 492p.

552. Knight, George A.F. *Psalms.* 2 vols. The Daily Study Bible. Edited by John C.L. Gibson. Philadelphia: Westminster, 1982, 1983. Vol. 1, 337p; Vol. II, 369p.

The psalms are to be read in a number of ways all at once. 1) The psalms have come out of a particular historical period, and are conditioned by the way that period expressed itself. 2) The psalms were written by people who had already discovered the wonders of the goodness of God in making a covenant with them, a covenant of love and loyalty. 3) The psalms, being part of the word of God, are more than mere dead print. They are alive with the Spirit of God that leads us into all truth. They are alive both forwards and backwards in time. There are two patterns in the psalter. One follows the pattern of the five books of the Torah. The other is based on the whole story of God's dealings with Israel. Psalms 1-72 thus seems to concentrate on the earliest period of the formation of the nation and the great days of David and

Solomon, whereas Psalms 73-150 seem to reflect the later period of Israel's experience of God's steadfast love.

Reviewed in *CBQ* 47 (1985): 136-138; 48 (1986): 293-295.

553. König, Eduard. *Die Psalmen eingeleitet, übersetzt und erklärt.* Gütersloh: Bertelsman, 1927.

554. Kraus, Hans-Joachim. *Psalmen.* 2 vols. Biblischer Kommentar: Altes Testament 15. Neukirchen-Vluyn: Neukirchener Verlag, 1960. 2nd ed., 1962. 4th ed., 1972. 5th, completely reworked edition, 1978. vii+1171p. Translated from the 5th German edition of 1978 by Hinton C. Oswald and published as *Psalms: A Commentary.* 2 vols. Continental Commentary Series. Minneapolis, MN: Augsburg, 1988, 1989. Vol. 1, 543p; Vol. 2, 571p.

In this, 5th, completely reworked edition, it is time to depart from the approach of Gunkel and to find a new way for determining the categories of the psalms, categories that are not foreign to the Hebrew Psalter. We suggest "theme-oriented form groups." 1) "Songs of Praise" (תהלה). In form, this includes the imperative hymn, the participial hymn, and the hymn of the individual. In theme, this includes praise of the creator, harvest songs, historical songs, and entrance songs. 2) "Songs of Prayer" (תפלה). In form, this includes the prayer song of the individual, community prayer, thanksgiving song of the individual. In theme, this includes prayer songs of the sick, of the persecuted and accused, of the sinner, plus the summons to give thanks and the prayer literature (acrostic). 3) "Royal Psalms" (מעשי למלך). In form, the festival of enthronement, festival of the king and sanctuary, wedding, serious times of distress. All have reference to the king and date from the time when the monarchy existed in Jerusalem. 4) "Songs of Zion" (ציון

שיר). These are psalms that glorify Zion. They were sung as the pilgrims entered the holy place. The theme is the choosing of Zion. They are mostly pre-exilic. 5) "Didactic Poetry" (Appropriate name would be either "wisdom" [חכמות] or "understanding" [תבונות].) This is not a particular type; the psalms are related only by common language and motif. Three themes are present: a) the transitoriness of life in time; b) housebuilding, protection of the city, and the toils of labor; and c) the common life of brothers and sisters. 6) "Festival Psalms and Liturgies." Restraint must be exercised here since we know too little about the festivals of Israel and their celebration. We must not begin with great cultic rituals; rather we must attempt to work out possible cultic backgrounds case by case.

For each psalm the commmentary offers a bibliography, a translation with textual notes, and comments on the form, setting, individual verses, and purpose and thrust.

First German edition reviewed by J.J. Stamm in *Evangelische Theologie* 21 (1961): 576-581; R. Martin-Achard in *Verbum Caro* 59 (1961): 320-330.

555. Kroll, Woodrow Michael. *Psalms. The Poetry of Palestine.* New York: University Press of America, 1987. 453p.

556. Kselman, J.S., and M.L. Barré. "Psalms." In *The New Jerome Biblical Commentary*, ed. Raymond E. Brown, Joseph A. Fitzmyer, and Roland E. Murphy. 523-552. Englewood Cliffs, NJ: Prentice Hall, 1990. lxviii+1484p.

557. Lamparter, Helmut. *Das Buch der Psalmen übersetzt und ausgelegt.* Die Botschaft des Alten Testaments, 14-15. Stuttgart: Calwer Verlag, 1958-1959. Vol. I, 348p; Vol. II, 400p. 3rd ed., 1977-1978.

There are three concerns for the interpretation of the Psalms. 1) We must primarily ask about the witness to revelation in the Psalms and cannot be content with an aesthetic evaluation. 2) We must consider the function of the Psalms in the worship service and the liturgical character of their style; we should not understand them with psychological measures. 3) We must show the lines of connection between the Psalter and the entire witness of the Old Testament word of revelation as it is proclaimed through the law and the prophets; we may not consider the individual Psalms in isolation. An important part of the interpretation of the Psalms is contained in the translation. For this reason, a great amount of effort is invested in attempting to reproduce the sound and rhythm of the original. The concern in the interpretation of the Psalms is this: By an attentive overhearing of the text to work out the proclamation of the individual Psalm, as far as possible to shed light on the obscure passages, to enter into the construction of the Psalm, its structure and train of thought, and thereby to allow its particular message to come through.

558. Lancellotti, A. *I Salmi. Versione, Introduzione, Note.* Parole di Dio: Nuovissima Versione della Bibbia dai testi originali 18c. Rome: Edizioni Paoline, 1984. 999p.

Suitable for an educated but not technical readership.

559. Landersdorfer, Simon. *Die Psalmen lateinisch und deutsch für gebildete Beter bearbeitet.* Regensburg: Pustet, 1922.

560. Lattey, Cuthbert. *The Old Testament. The First Book of Psalms (Psalms i-xii).* The Westminster Version of the Sacred Scriptures. London and New York: Longmans & Green, 1939. 147p.

561. Leslie, Elmer Archibald. *The Psalms: Translated and Interpreted in the Light of Hebrew Life and Worship.* New York: Abingdon-Cokesbury, 1949. 448p.

Appreciation must be given for the work of Gunkel, Mowinckel and H. Schmidt. The origin of the individual psalms is to be found in organized public worship, the cult. For each psalm we must ask, What is its real origin and purpose? What is its setting in life? The commentary answers this for each of the psalms by organizing itself according to the major psalm types.

Reviewed by J.P. Hyatt in *JBL* 69 (1950): 184-186.

562. ______, and W.A. Shelton. "Psalms." In *The Abingdon Bible Commentary*, ed. Frederick Carl Eiselen, Edwin Lewis, and David G. Downey. 509-601. New York: The Abingdon Press, 1929.

Leslie authors the introduction and the commentary on Psalms 1-72, Shelton the commentary on Psalms 73-150.

563. Leupold, Herbert C. *Exposition of the Psalms.* Columbus, OH: The Wartburg Press, 1959. 1010p.

This is a conservative commentary on the Psalms that sifts the results of recent scholarly studies and one that intelligent laypeople can use as well as the pastor, for the Psalter still is the Prayer Book of the people of God.

564. Livingston, George Herbert, and W. Ralph Thompson. "Psalms." In *The Wesleyan Bible Commentary*, Vol. II: *Job--Song of Solomon*, ed. Charles W. Carter and Others. 177-461. Grand Rapids, MI: William B. Eerdmans Publishing Co., 1968.

The Wesleyan Bible Commentary is intended "to maintain both the spiritual insight and sound biblical scholarship of John Wesley and Adam Clarke, but to express these characteristics in the context of contemporary thought and life." It is evangelical, expositional, practical, homiletical and devotional. The American Standard Version is the basic Bible text used by the contributors. Livingston is responsible for the introduction to the Psalms as well as the commentary on Psalms 73-150. Thompson provides the commentary on Psalms 1-72. For each of the Psalms, Livingston and Thompson state the theme (including general comments on the Psalm) and offer an outline with comments on each section of the Psalm.

565. Lockyer, Herbert, Sr. *Psalms: A Devotional Commentary.* Grand Rapids, MI: Kregel Publications, 1993. 792p.

Devotional insights and notes on each of the Psalms, applying their truths to modern living. A "notebook" of a life-long study of the Psalms.

566. Lund, Emil. *The Psalms: Translated and Commented Upon.* Rock Island, IL: Augustana Book Concern (1908). 692p.

The desire is to offer a brief interpretation of the Psalter in a scientific, though popular form.

567. Luteijn, C.M. *De Psalmen.* De Bijbel en zijn boodschap. 2 vols. Leeuwarden: Johgbloed, 1961-1962.

568. M'Caw, Leslie S. "The Psalms." In *The New Bible Commentary*, ed. F. Davidson. 412-514. Grand Rapids, MI: Wm. B. Eerdmans Publishing Co., 1953. 2nd ed., 1954.

569. McCullough, W. Stewart, and William R. Taylor. "Introduction and Exegesis of the Book of Psalms." In *The Interpreter's Bible*. Edited by George Arthur Buttrick. Vol. 4: 1-763. New York: Abingdon, 1955.

Reviewed by A. Weiser in *JBL* 74 (1955): 278-279.

570. McEachern, A.H. *Psalms.* Layman's Bible Book Commentary 8. Nashville, TN: Broadman Press, 1981. 167p.

A non-technical commentary from a conservative viewpoint; it points out several of the spiritual lessons found in the Psalms.

571. Maillot, A., and A. Lelièvre. *Les Psaumes: Traduction nouvelle et commentaire.* 2 vols. Geneva: Éditions Labor et Fides, 1961, 1966. 2nd ed., 1972.

572. Mannati, M., and E. de Solms. *Les Psaumes.* Cahiers de la Pierre-Qui-Vire. Paris: Desclée de Brouwer, 1966, 1967, 1967, 1968. Vol. I., 295p; Vol. 2, 308p; Vol. 3, 302p; Vol. 4, 306p.

573. Marti, Kurt. *Annäherungen an die Psalmen.* 2 vols. Stuttgart: Radius-Verlag, 1991-1992.

574. Miller, Athanasius. *Die Psalmen übersetzt und kurz erklärt.* 2 vols. Ecclesia orans IV-V. 3rd and 4th ed. Freiburg im Breisgau: Herder, 1920.

575. Mobberley, David G. *The Psalms.* Cokesbury Basic Bible Commentary 10. Nashville, TN: Graded Press, 1988. 159p.

576. Morgan, George Campbell (1863-1945). *Notes on the Psalms.* New York: Fleming H. Revell Company, 1947. 287p.

577. Murphy, Roland E. "Psalms." In *The Jerome Biblical Commentary.* 2 vols. bound as one. Edited by Raymond E. Brown, Joseph A. Fitzmyer, and Roland E. Murphy. 570-574. Englewood Cliffs, NJ: Prentice-Hall, 1968.

578. ______. *The Psalms, Job.* Proclamation Commentaries: The Old Testament Witnesses for Preaching. Philadelphia: Fortress Press, 1977. 96p.

579. Myhre, Klare, Jens Olav Maeland, Karsten Valen, and Einar Bryn (Vol. 2). *Fortolkning til Salmenes bok.* 2 vols. Oslo: Luther Forlag and Lunde Forlag, 1985. Vol. 1, 336p.; Vol. 2, 374p.

Vol. I: Myhre: Introduction and Psalms 11-16,41-50; Maeland: Psalms 17-14; Valen: Psalms 1-10,51-72. Vol. II: Myhre: Psalms 73-87; Bryn: Psalms 88-106; Maeland: Psalms 107-132; Valen: Psalms 133-150 and Theology of the Psalms.

580. Nichol, Francis David, ed. *The Seventh Day Adventist Bible Commentary. Vol. 3: 615-944. Washington, D.C.: Review and Herald Publishing Association, 1954.*

581. Nielsen, S.A. *Salmernes bog fortolket.* Copenhagen: Det danske Bibelselskab, 1983. 285p.

The Danish Bible Society provides a popular, but scientifically-based tool to aid the understanding of the Danish translation of the Bible. Each psalm is given a title, form-critical questions are discussed, and the religious purpose of the psalm is explained.

582. Noordtzij, Arie. *Het boek der Psalmen. 2 vols.* Korte verklaring der Heilige Schrift. 2nd ed. Kampen: Kok, 1934-1935.

583. Nötscher, Friedrich. *Die Psalmen.* Die Heilige Schrift in deutscher Übersetzung, Die Echter-Bibel. Würzburg, Echter Verlag, 1947. viii+292p. Revised edition, 1953. 5th ed., 1959.

584. Oesterley, William Oscar Emil. *The Psalms, Book III, Book IV.* London: Society for Promoting Christian Knowledge, 1933.

585. ______. *The Psalms Translated with Text-Critical and Exegetical Notes.* 2 vols. London: Society for Promoting Christian Knowledge, 1939. New York: Macmillan, 1939; reprinted as one vol., 1959. xi+599p.

The following procedure is employed in dealing with the individual psalms in the commentary. First, an introductory section gives a short account of the nature and contents of the psalm; then comes the translation, as close as possible to the Hebrew and reproducing the metrical structure of the original. Text-critical and exegetical notes follow. Finally, there is a short section on the religious teaching of the psalm.

Theodore Robinson provides the commentary on twenty-two of the Psalms (55-60, 68, 73-84, 86, 88, 90) as well as four chapters in the Introduction (Chaps. I, II, IV, V).

586. Palmer, R.F. *Psalms Then and Now.* Foreword by F.H. Cosgrave. Bracebridge, Ontario: Society of Saint John the Evangelist, 1965.

A popular commentary on the entire psalter largely based on the best known works of recent years.

587. Pannier, E. *Les Psaumes.* La Sainte Bible 5. Ed. L. Pirot and A. Clamer. Paris: Letouzey et Ané, 1937.

588. _____, and H. Renard. *Les Psaumes. La Sainte Bible, texte latin et traduction française d'après les textes orignaux avec un commentaire exégétique et théologique.* Ed. Albert Clamer. Tome V: *Les Psaumes.* Paris: Letouzey et Ané, 1950. 776p.

589. Peters, Norbert. *Das Buch der Psalmen übersetzt und kurz erklärt.* Paderborn: Bonifacius-Druckerei, 1930. xii+384p.

590. Ploeg, Jan van der. *De Psalmen uit de grondtekst vertaald en van korte inleidingen en aantekeningen voorzien.* Roermond-Maaseik: J.J. Romen en Zonen, 1963.

591. _____. *Psalmen uit de grondtekst vertaald en uitgelegd.* De Boeken van het Oude Testament 7b. Roermond: J.J. Romen en Zonen. Fascicle 1 (Psalms Introduction and Psalms 1-44), 1971. p1-272. Fascicle 2 (Psalms 45-68), 1972. p273-400. Fascicle 4 (Psalms 102-121), 1975. p177-352.

The biblical poets did not feel bound to stylistic conventions; instead, they exercised considerable freedom in their choice of expressions and motifs. The psalms are either lyrical (hymns and prayers) or non-lyrical (didactic and narrative poems). A new translation, bibliography, general comments and a verse-by-verse commentary is offered for each psalm.

Reviewed in *CBQ* 34 (1972): 430-431; *CBQ* 36 (1974): 135; 37 (1975): 430-431.

592. Podechard, Emanuel. *Le Psautier. Traduction littérale et explication historique. I. Psaumes 1-75.* 2 vols. Bibliothèque de la Faculté Catholique de Théologie de Lyon 3-4. Lyon: Facultés Catholiques, 1949. I, Vol. 1, 330p; II, Vol. 2, 306p. *Le Psautier. Traduction littérale, explication historique et notes critiques. II. Psaumes 76-100 et 110.* Bibliothèque de la Faculté Catholique de Théologie de Lyon 6. Lyon: Facultés Catholiques, 1954. II, 183p.

593. Purkiser, W.T. "The Book of Psalms." In *Beacon Bible Commentary*, Vol. III: *The Poetical and Wisdom Literature*, ed. A.F. Harper and Others. 125-452. Kansas City, MO: Beacon Hill Press, 1967.

The *Beacon Bible Commentary* is offered by the Church of the Nazarene to all who love and desire better to know "the word of God, which liveth and abideth for ever." Although it is written from the viewpoint of Wesleyan-Arminian theology, the editors hope that it will have value to all who seek to know the truth as it is in Jesus.

594. Ravasi, G. *Il libro dei Salmi. Commento e attualizzazione.* 3 vols. Lettura pastorale della Bibbia 12, 14, 15. Bologna: Edizioni Dehoniane, 1981, 1983, 1984. Vol. I, 917p; Vol. II, 1065p; Vol. III.

595. ______. *I Salmi.* Bologna: Biblioteca Universale Rizzoli, 1986. 429p.

596. Rhodes, Arnold B. *The Book of Psalms.* The Layman's Bible Commentary 9. Richmond, VA: John Knox, 1960; 6th printing, 1971. 192p.

597. Ridderbos, J. *De Psalmen.* 2 vols. Commentaar op het Oude Testament, ed. G.Ch. Aalders, W.H. Gispen, and J. Ridderbos. Kampen: J.H. Kok, 1955-1958.

598. Ringgren, Helmer. *Psaltaren 1-41.* Kommentar till Gamla Testamentet. Uppsala: EFS-förlaget, 1987. 248p.

Each psalm is presented according to a four-part format: translation, notes, analysis, and exegesis. Ancient Near Eastern iconography provides helpful illustrations.

599. Rinkel, Andreas. *Psalter. Beschouwingen over de psalmen.* 2 vols. Zuthpen: G.J.A. Ruys, 1937. Vol. 1, 394p; Vol. 2, 415p.

600. Rodd, Cyril S. *Psalms.* 2 vols. Epworth Preacher's Commentaries. London: The Epworth Press, 1963-1964. Vol. 1, 136p; Vol. 2, 134p.

601. Rogerson, John William, and John William McKay. *Psalms.* 3 vols. Cambridge Bible Commentary on the New English Bible. Cambridge: Cambridge University Press, 1977. Vol. 1, 243p; Vol. 2, 193p; Vol. 3, 193p.

The aim of the Cambridge Bible Commentary series is to provide the text of the New English Bible closely linked to a commentary in which the results of modern scholarship are made available to the general reader.

Reviewed in *CBQ* 40 (1978): 615-616.

602. Rotherham, Joseph Bryant (1828-1910). *Studies in the Psalms.* 2 vols. ca. 1909. Reprint, Joplin, MO: College Press, 1970-1971. Bible Study Textbook Series. Vol. 1, 468p; Vol. 2, 439p.

For each of the Psalms, there is a descriptive title, an analysis or outline, a translation, and an exposition. The translation reproduces a revision of the Psalms text prepared for an earlier work, *The Emphasized Bible.*

603. Sabourin, Leopold. *The Psalms: Their Origin and Meaning.* 2 vols. Staten Island, NY: Alba House (Society of St. Paul), 1969. Vol. 1, xix+253p; Vol. 2, xix+373p. New, enlarged, updated edition printed as one volume, 1974. xx+450p.

The main purpose is "to present in readable form the best material now available on the biblical psalms."

Reviewed by B.S. Childs in *JBL* 89 (1970): 233-234; R. Tournay, *Revue Biblique* 78 (1971): 114-115; R.E. Murphy, *Biblica* 52 (1971): 145-146; *CBQ* 32 (1970): 631-633.

604. Schlögl, Nivard. *Die Psalmen hebraisch und deutsch mit einem kurzen wissenschaftlichen Kommentar... mit oberhirtlicher druckgenehmigung.* Graz and Vienna: Verlagsbuchhandlung "Styria," 1911. xxvii+235p.

605. ______. *Die heiligen Schriften des Alten Bundes,* III/1: *Die Psalmen.* Vienna and Leipzig: Verlagsbuchhandlung "Styria," 1915.

606. Schmidt, Hans. *Die Psalmen.* Handbuch zum Alten Testament, I,15. Edited by Otto Eissfeldt. Tübingen: J.C.B.

Mohr (Paul Siebeck), 1934; reprint Göttingen: Vandenhoeck & Ruprecht, 1950. xii+258p.

Close in point of view to Gunkel, but more reserved on textual criticism.

607. Schmidt, Ludwig. *Die Psalmen.* I Halbband. Schriftauslegung für Predigt, Bibelarbeit, Unterricht. Stuttgart: E. Klotz, 1967.

608. Schungel, Paul. *Schule des Betens. Die Klage- und Dankpsalmen.* Stuttgarter Kleiner Kommentar, AT 22/2. Stuttgart: Katholisches Bibelwerk, 1974. 76p. (See the companion volume by K. Gouders listed above.)

609. Sclater, J.R.P., Edwin McNeill Poteat, and Frank H. Ballard. "Exposition of the Book of Psalms." In *The Interpreter's Bible.* Edited by George Arthur Buttrick. Vol. 4: 17-763. New York: Abingdon, 1955.

An exposition of the Psalms based on the exegetical work of McCullough and Taylor.

610. Scroggie, W. Graham. *The Psalms: Psalms I to CL.* 4 vols. Revised edition. London: Pickering & Inglis, 1948, 1949, 1950, 1951. Reprinted as 1 vol., Old Tappan, NJ: Fleming H. Revell Company, 1965. Vol. I, 288p.; Vol. II, 301p.; Vol. III, 302p.; Vol IV, 327p.

For each Psalm, the arrangement of the text indicates the principle of parallelism, paragraphing to show the main divisions of each Psalm. There is a Title for each Psalm and at the end a Thought which is designed to fix in the mind the main lesson of the Psalm. To each is also added a note which relates the Psalm to some incident in Christian story. The Exposition aims, as far as is possible within its limits, at giving interpretive, homiletical, and devotional help.

611. Sekine, M. *Sekine Masao Chosaku-shū Dai 10, 11, 12 Kan: Kan Shihen Cyūkai* (M. Sekine Works, vols. 10, 11, and 12: A Commentary on the Psalms). Tokyo: Shinchi-shobō, 1980-1981. Vol. 10 (Psalms 1-41), 340p. Vol. 11 (Psalms 42-100), 457p. Vol. 12 (Psalms 101-150), 374p. (Japanese)

612. Simons, Joshua. *The Book of Psalms. The Hebrew Text and the English Authorized Version with a New Hebrew Commentary Beur Joshua.* New York: The Simons Family, 1953. 97p.

613. Snijdelar, E.A.A. *De Psalmen bewerkt uit de grondtekst.* Roermond: J.J. Romen en Zonen, 1949.

614. Soubigou, Louis. *Dans la beauté rayonnante des Psaumes.* Paris: P. Lethielleux, 1932.

An anthology of the psalms with translation and literary and doctrinal commentary.

615. Stadelmann, Luís I.J. *Os Salmos: Estrutura, Conteúdo e Mesagem.* Petrópolis, Brazil: Ed. Vozes, 1983. 559p.

A commentary on the Book of Psalms, including a new translation of the MT without the use of versions, variants or textual changes. The translation is supported by philology, grammar and Hebrew style. For each psalm the literary genre, strophic structure, and contents are examined and explained.

Alongside the scientific-exegetical investigation, the spiritual and Christian interests are lifted up for guidance in daily life.

616. Staerk, W. *Lyrik: Psalmen, Hoheslied und Verwandtes.* Die Schriften des Alten Testaments in Auswahl, neu übersetzt und für die Gegenwart erklärt, by H. Gressmann, H. Gunkel, M. Haller, H. Schmidt, W. Staerk and P. Volz, III/1. Göttingen: Vandenhoeck & Ruprecht, 1911. 2nd ed., 1920.

617. Stuhlmueller, Carroll. *The Psalms.* 2 vols. Old Testament Message: A Biblical-Theological Commentary 21,22. Wilmington, DE: Michael Glazier, Inc., 1983. Vol. 1, 322p; Vol. 2, 226p.

618. ______. "Psalms." In *Harper's Bible Commentary*, ed. James L. Mays and Others. 433-494. San Francisco: Harper and Row, Publishers, 1988.

619. Tate, Marvin E. *Psalms 51-100.* Word Biblical Commentary 20. Waco, TX: Word Books, 1990. xxviii+579p.

The treatment of the individual psalms gives a bibliography preceding each psalm, presents a translation with the meter of the each line being indicated in the margin, provides notes on problems of text and translation (Briggs and Gunkel are most helpful); a section on form/structure/setting (identification of genre, speaker and date, *Sitz im Leben*, outline and divisions of the psalms) discusses the current state of modern scholarship (Kraus, Weiser, and Anderson are most appreciated, with Dahood being a challenge and a stimulus); the "comments" (exegesis of the psalm by its divisions) and "explanation" (concerns and relevance for the modern believer) discuss the psalm's meaning and its relevance to the ongoing biblical revelation. Included is an excursus devoted to the problem of the identification of the "enemies" cited in so many psalms of different genres.

620. Thompson, David L. "The Psalms." in *Asbury Bible Commentary,* ed. Eugene C. Carpenter and Wayne McCown. 504-563. Grand Rapids, MI: Zondervan Publishing House, 1992.

621. Toombs, Lawrence E. "The Psalms." In *The Interpreter's One-Volume Commentary on the Bible*, ed. Charles M. Laymon. 253-303. New York: Abingdon Press, 1971; revised and concise edition, *Interpreter's Concise Commentary,* Vol. III, *Wisdom Literature and Poetry,* ed. Charles M. Layman; 42-199; Nashville, TN: Abingdon Press, 1983.

622. Tricerri, M., O.P. *I Canti divini. Introduzione -- Traduzione -- Commento estetico.* 2 vols. Turin: Marietti, 1925, 1926.

623. Ubach, Bonaventura. *El Psalteri.* 2 vols. La Biblia 10, ed. Monks of Montserrat. Monastery of Montserrat, 1932.

624. Uchelen, N.A. van. *Psalmen, Deel I (1-40)* and *Deel II (41-80).* De Prediking van het Oude Testament. Nijkerk: Callenbach, 1971 and 1977. Deel I, 275p; Deel II, 313p.

A psalm speaks for itself and of itself as a unified, self-contained whole. It does not require a setting in order to be understood. He discusses each psalm under four headings: 1) translation (original and, where possible, shows relationships among like-sounding Hebrew words), 2) introduction (important verbal and structural devices of the psalm), 3) elaboration (the verbal and structural meanings and relationships verse by verse), and 4) notes (dialogues with other scholars); a bibliography is included.

Reviewed by R.B. Coote in *JBL* 98 (1979): 126-127.

625. Vaccari, Alberto. *Il libro Giobbe e i Salmi.* 2nd ed. Rome: Pontifical Biblical Institute, 1927.

626. _____. *Il Salterio. Nuova Traduzione e Commento.* Milan: Edizioni Viola, 1951. 236p.

The purpose is to give to the Italian speaking public a translation of the Psalms which will preserve their essential nature of prayer.

Reviewed in *CBQ* 14 (1952): 291.

627. _____. *I Salmi tradotti dall'ebraico con a fronte la nuova versione latina approvata da Pio XII.* Second, completely revised ed. Turin: Marietti, 1953.

628. Valeton, J.J.P., Jr. *De Psalmen.* 2nd ed. by H.Th. Obbink. 2 vols. Nijmegen: Janssen, 1912-1913.

629. VanGemeren, Willem A. "Psalms." *The Expositor's Bible Commentary with the New International Version, Vol. 5: Psalms -- Song of Songs,* ed. Frank E. Gæbelein. 1-882. Grand Rapids, MI: Zondervan Publishing House, 1991.

The Text and Exposition on the individual psalms offers the New International Version with notes, an outline of the structure, plus discussion on historical setting, mood, genre, and meaning.

630. Vischer, Wilhelm. *Psalmen, ausgelegt für die Gemeinde.* Basel: Verlag Friedrich Reinhardt, (1944). 201p.

631. Weiser, Artur. *Die Psalmen ausgewählt, übersetzt und erklärt.* Neues Göttinger Bibelwerk, Ergänzungsband. Göttingen: Vandenhoeck & Ruprecht, 1935. 252p. 2nd ed., 1939. Revised and enlarged to include comments on all the psalms and published as *Die Psalmen übersetzt und erklärt.* 269p. 3rd ed, *Die Psalmen.* 2 vols. Das Alte Testament Deutsch. Vols. 14 and 15. 3rd. ed. Göttingen: Vandenhoeck & Ruprecht, 1950. 564p. 4th ed., 1955. 5th ed., 1959. 7th ed., 1966. Translated into English from the 5th edition by Herbert Hartwell and published as *The Psalms: A Commentary.* Old Testament Library. Philadelphia: Westminster, 1962. 841p. Paperback reprint: London: SCM Press, 1979.

The cult of the covenant renewal festival of Yahweh celebrated at New Year in the autumn is the *Sitz im Leben* for the vast majority of the psalms.

Reviewed by J.A. Sanders in *JBL* 82 (1963): 127.

632. White, R.E.O. *A Christian Handbook to the Psalms.* Exeter: The Paternoster Press, 1984; Grand Rapids, MI: William B. Eerdmans Publishing Company, 1984. 220p.

633. ______. "The Psalms." In *Evangelical Commentary on the Bible.* Ed. Walter Elwell. 367-398. Grand Rapids, MI: Baker Book House, 1989.

634. Williams, Donald M. *Psalms.* 2 vols. The Communicator's Commentary, ed. Lloyd J. Ogilvie, vols. 13 and 14. Waco, TX: Word Books, 1986, 1989. Vol. 1, 493p; Vol. 2, 543p.

The Communicator's Commentary series is offered "as a penetrating search of the Scriptures of the Old and New Testament to enable vital personal and practical communication of the abundant life."

635. Wutz, Franz. *Die Psalmen textkritisch untersucht.* Munich: Kösel & Pustet, 1925. lxi+472p.

636. Yates, Kyle M., Jr. "The Psalms." In *The Wycliffe Bible Commentary,* ed. Charles Pfeiffer and Everett F. Harrison. 491-552. Chicago, IL: Moody Press, 1962; reprint, 1990. 1525p.

637. Zolli, Eugenio. *Il Salterio. Nuova Traduzione e Commento.* Milan: Edizione Viola, 1951.236p.

Reviewed in *CBQ* 14 (1952): 291.

3. Texts and Translations

A. General Studies

639. Ackroyd, Peter R. "Some Notes on the Psalms." *Journal of Theological Studies* 17 (1966): 392-399.

Notes on Psalms 74:4; 93:1; Psalm 118 at Qumran.

640. ______, and M.A. Knibb. "Translating the Psalms." *The Bible Translator* 17 (1966): 148-162.

641. Airoldi, Noberto. "Note Critiche ai Salmi." *Augustinianum* 10 (1970): 174-180.

Psalms 38:5, 102:8, and 130:1.

642. ______. "Note ai Salmi." *Augustinianum* 13 (1973): 345-350.

Psalms 13:6c, 30:6, 31:5, 51:18.

643. Auvray, Paul. "Le Psaume I. Notes de grammaire d'exégèse." *Revue Biblique* 53 (1946): 365-371.

644. Bardtke, Hans. "Die hebräische Präposition *naegaed* in den Psalmen." In *Forschung zur Bibel. Wort, Lied und Gottespruch. Beiträge zur Septuaginta. Festschrift für Joseph Ziegler*, ed. Rudolph Schnackenburg and Josef Schreiner. 2 vols. Vol. 2, 17-27. Würzburg: Echter Verlag, 1972.

645. Barth, Christoph. "Concatenatio im ersten Buch des Psalters." *Wort und Wirklichkeit. Studien zur Afrikanistik und Orientalistik. Eugen Ludwig Rapp zum 70. Geburtstag*, ed, Brigitta Benzing, Otto Böcher, and Günter Mayer. 2 vols., Vol. 1: 30-40. Meisenheim am Glan: Hain, 1976.

646. Beaucamp, Evode. "Le texte psalmique dans le développement de la vie liturgique d'Israël." *Église et Théologie* 3 (1972): 155-191.

647. Bratcher, R.G., and W.D. Reyburn. *A Translator's Handbook on the Book of Psalms.* Helps for Translators. New York: United Bible Societies, 1991. xi+1219p.

648. Brates, L. "Algunas correcciones conjeturales en los Salmos." *Estudios Eclesiásticos* 34 (1960): 621-631.

Conjectures on the texts of Psalms 55:23-24; 75:7; 119:91,128; 126:4; 12:7.

649. Brekelmans, C. "Pronominal Suffixes in the Hebrew Book of Psalms." *Jaarbericht van het Vooraziatisch-Egyptisch Gezelschap (Genootschap) 'Ex Oriente Lux'* 17 (1964): 202-206.

650. ______. "Some Considerations on the Translation of the Psalms by M. Dahood." *Ugarit-Forschungen* 1 (1969): 5-14.

651. Dahood, Mitchell. "The root GMR in the Psalms." *Theological Studies* 14 (1953): 595-597.

652. ______. "Philological Notes on the Psalms." *Theological Studies* 14 (1953): 85-88.

653. ______. "The Divine Name ᶜELI in the Psalms." *Theological Studies* 14 (1953): 452-457.

654. ______. "Vocative *lamedh* in the Psalter." *Vetus Testamentum* 16 (1966): 299-311.

655. Driver, G.R. "Notes on the Psalms I. 1-72." *Journal of Theological Studies* 43 (1942): 149-160.

656. ______. "Notes on the Psalms. II. 73-150." *Journal of Theological Studies* 44 (1943): 12-23.

657. Eaton, J. H. "Some Questions of Philology and Exegesis in the Psalms." *Journal of Theological Studies*, N.S., 19 (1968): 603-609.

Psalms 18:45, 19:10, 41:2, 81:16, and 93:4.

658. Emerton, J.A. "Notes on Three Passages in Psalms Book III." *Journal of Theological Studies* 14 (1963): 374-381.

Psalm 74:5, 11b; 78:41.

659. Eybers, I.H. "The Stems S-P-T in the Psalms." In *Studies on the Psalms: Papers Read at the 6th Meeting of Die O.T. Werkgemeenskap in Siud-Afrika.* 58-63. Potchefstroom: Pro Rege, 1963.

660. Field, F. *Origenis Hexaplorum quae supersunt.* Tomus 2. *Jobus-Malachias.* Oxford: At the Clarendon Press, 1875.

661. Futato, Mark D. "The Preposition 'Beth' in the Hebrew Psalter." *Westminster Theological Journal* 41 (1978): 68-83.

662. Gaster, Theodor H. "Short Notes." *Vetus Testamentum* 4 (1954): 73-79.

Includes comments on Psalms 24:6; 35:11; 41:9; 68:12; 76:11; 85:14.

663. Grill, S. "Textkritische Notizen." *Biblische Notizen*, N.F., 3 (1959): 102.

Notes on Psalms 104:26a and 77:11.

664. Guillaume, Alfred. "Notes on the Psalms II (Ps 73-150)." *Journal of Theological Studies* 45 (1944): 14-15.

A reply to Driver's article in *JTS* 44 (1943): 12-23.

665. ______. "A Reply to Professor Driver." *Journal of Theological Studies* 49 (1948): 55-56.

666. Gyllenberg, Rafael. "Die Bedeutung des Wortes Sela." *Zeitschrift für die alttestamentliche Wissenschaft* 58 (1940-1941): 153-156.

667. Hammerdinger, Bertrand. "Selah." *Journal of Theological Studies*, N.S., 22 (1971): 152-153.

Selah comes from the Persian *salā* ("song") = Greek ψάλμα ("tune played on a stringed instrument"). The Alexandrian translator did not understand the word.

668. Herrmann, J. *Hebräische Wörterbuch zu den Psalmen.* Berlin: Alfred Töpelmann, 1937.

669. Hurvitz, A. "When Was the Hebrew Phrase *šlwm ^{c}l yśr* Coined?" *Lešonénu* 27-28 (1964): 297-302. (Hebrew)

The expression appears only in Psalms 125:5 and 128:6, plus 1 Chronicles 22:9. It is a late Hebrew expression, appearing only after the 6th century.

670. Irwin, William Andrew. "Critical Notes on Five Psalms." *American Journal of Semitic Languages and Literatures* 49 (1932/1933): 9-20.

671. Junker, Hubert. "Einige Rätsel im Urtext der Psalmen." *Biblica* 30 (1949): 197-212.

Psalms 87(86); 141:5-7; 139:20,24; 17:13-14.

672. Labuschagne, C.J. "Some remarks on the Translation and Meaning of $^{\supset}$*āmartī* in the Psalms." *Die Ou Testamentiese Werkgemeenskap in Suid-Africa* 5 (1962): 27-33.

673. Leveen J. "Textual Problems in the Psalms." *Vetus Testamentum* 21 (1971): 48-58.

Psalms 8:3,4,6; 9:7-8; 11:4b-5; 12:6,9; 13:5; 16:2-4,11b; 22:10,26,31,32; 27:7-9; 32:7,12,16; 36:1-2; 38:17; 40:5,8-9; 42:9,11; 46:3-5,9; 49:6.

674. Loretz, Oswald. "*^{c}d m$^{\supset}$d,* 'Everlasting Grand One' in den Psalmen." *Biblische Zeitschrift,* N.F., 16 (1972): 245-248.

675. Madros, Peter. "A Proposed Auxiliary Role of Arabic for the Understanding of Biblical Hebrew (Notes on Ps 49; 55-58)." *Studium Biblicum Franciscanum, Liber Annuus* 34 (1984): 43-52.

676. Mayer, Aloys. *Liber Psalmorum.* Stuttgart: Katholisches Bibelwerk, 1954. iii+280p.

The new Latin translation and the MT appear in parallel columns.

Reviewed in *CBQ* 17 (1955): 547.

677. _____, and Wilhelm T. Auer. *Psalmorum Liber Primus (1-41).* Editio interlinearis polyglotta quattuor linguarum. 2nd ed. Stuttgart: Katholisches Bibelwerk, 1960. 510p.

The MT, LXX, four Latin versions (New Vatican Psalter, Vulgate edition by Gramatica, and the versions of Rembold and Zorell), plus three German editions (Buber and Rosenzweig, Loch and Reischl, and Schenk).

Reviewed in *CBQ* 23 (1961): 77-78.

678. Mercati, Giovanni C. *Osservazioni a proemi del Salterio, di Origene, Ippolito, Eusebio, Cirillo Alessandrino e altri, con frammenti inediti.* Studi e Testi 142. Vatican City: Biblioteca Apostolica Vaticana, 1948. 167p.

679. _____. *Alla ricerca dei nomi degli "altri" traduttori nelle omilie sui Salmi di S. Giovanni Crisostomo e variazioni su alcune catene del Salterio.* Studi e Testi 158. Vatican City: Biblioteca Apostolica Vaticana, 1952. viii+248p.

680. _____, ed., *Psalterii hexapli reliquiae. Cura et studio.* Vatican City: Vatican Library, 1958.

681. ______. *Psalterii hexapli religuiae: Pars prima "Osservationi," Commento critico al testo dei frammenti esaplari.* Vatican City: Vatican Library, 1965.

682. Michel, Diethelm. *Tempora und Satzstellung in den Psalmen.* Abhandlungen zur Evangelischen Theologie 1. Bonn: H. Bouvier und Co. Verlag, 1960.

683. Mowinckel, Sigmund. "Zur Sprache der biblischen Psalmen." *Theologische Literaturzeitung* 81 (1956): 199-202.

684. ______. "Notes on the Psalms." *Studia Theologica* 13 (1959): 134-165.

685. ______. "Drive and/or Ride in O.T." *Vetus Testamentum* 12 (1962): 278-299.

686. Mozley, F.W. *The Psalter of the Church. The Septuagint Psalms Compared with the Hebrew, with Various Notes.* Cambridge: Cambridge University Press, 1903. xxx+204p.

687. Nestle, Eberhard. *Psalterium Tetraglottum. Graece, Syriace, Chaldaice, Latine, quadrigentesimo post primam hebraici Psalterii editionem anno (1477-1877).* Tübingen: Fr. Fues, 1879. xvi+161p.

The Peshitta text is that of the West Syrian or Jacobite church. It is a copy of the Cod. Ambrosianus B 21 inf. as found in the Milan edition of A. Ceriani.

688. Peacock, H.F. *A Translator's Guide to Selected Psalms.* Helps for Translators. New York: United Bible Societies, 1981. viii+154p.

689. Prévost, Jean-Pierre. *Petit dictionnaire des Psaumes.* Cahiers Evangile 71. Paris: Editions du Cerf, 1990. 71p.

A study of the root and usage of 40 key words of the Psalter.

690. Ringgren, Helmer. "Some Observations on the Text of the Psalms." In *Sopher Mahir: Northwest Semitic Studies Presented to Stanislav Segert*, ed. Edward M. Cook. 307-309. Winona Lake, IN: Eisenbrauns, 1990.

Critical remarks concerning the translation of Psalms 1:7; 8:2,3; 10:10; 30:6 and 31:12.

691. Schulz, Alphons. *Kritisches zum Psalter.* Alttestamentliche Abhandlungen XII, 1. Münster im Westfalen: Aschendorff, 1932. 66p.

692. ______. *Psalmen-Fragen.* Alttestamentliche Abhandlungen XIV, 1. Münster im Westfalen: Aschendorff, 1940.

693. Snaith, Norman H. "Selah." *Vetus Testamentum* 2 (1952): 43-56.

694. Thierry, G.J. "Remarks on Various Passages of the Psalms." *Oudtestamentische Studiën* 13 (1963): 77-97.

Psalms 7:15; 21:10; 22:10; 23:3,4.

695. Thomas, D. Winton. "Translating the Psalms." *St. Catharine's Society Magazine* (Cambridge, 1963): 69-73.

696. Tournay, Raymond. "Notes sur les psaumes." *Vivre et Penser* 3 (1945): 214-237.

697. _____. "En marge d'une traduction des Psaumes." *Revue Biblique* 63 (1956): 161-181, 496-512.

698. _____. "Notes sur les Psaumes: Ps 42:9; 75:7-9; 105:5; et 76:2ss." *Revue Biblique* 79 (1972): 39-58.

699. Tur-Sinai, N.H. "In the Tracts of the Language and the Scriptures: XIII. Obscure Passages in the Psalms (Concluded)." *Lešonénu* 26 (1962): 184-204. (Hebrew)

700. _____. "On Some Obscure Passages in the Book of Psalms." In *Festschrift A.H. Silver*. 1-35. New York: KTAV, 1963.

701. Uchelen, N.A. "*ʾnšy dmnm* in the Psalms." *Oudtestamentische Studiën* 15 (1969): 205-212.

702. Urbina, Pedro Antonio. "Los Salmos de David en la 'Subida del Monte Carmelo.'" *Scripta Theologica* 23 (1991): 939-959.

703. Wagner, N.E. "Rinnah in the Psalter." *Vetus Testamentum* 10 (1960): 435-441.

Rinnah is a cultic cry, a creedal statement, a confession of faith in God, who acts in the events of history.

704. Woude, A.S. van der. "Zwei alte Cruces im Psalter." *Oudtestamentische Studiën* 13 (1963): 131-136.

705. Wutz, Franz. *Systematische Wege von der Septuaginta zum hebräischen Urtext I.* Eichstätter Studien. 963-1019, 1025-126. Stuttgart: W. Kohlhammer, 1937.

706. Zenner, J. K. and H. Weismann. *Die Psalmen nach dem Urtext.* 2 vols. Freiburg im Breisgau: Herder, 1906, 1907.

707. Zuber, Beat. *Die Psalmen. Eine Studienübersetzung unter besonderer Berücksichtigung des hebräischen Tempus.* Dielheimer Blätter zum Alten Testament und seiner Rezeption in der Alten Kirche 7. Heidelberg: B.J. Diebner and C. Nauerth, 1986. 216p.

A translation of the psalms based on Zuber's rejection of the aspectual theory of the Hebrew verb system, as outlined in his *Das Tempussystem des biblischen Hebräisch* (Beihefte zur Zeitschrift für die alttestamentliche Wissenschaft 164; Berlin: Walter de Gruyter, 1986).

B. Hebrew Text

708. Baillet, Maurice. "Psaumes, hymnes, cantiques et prières dans les manuscripts de Qumrân." In *Le Psautier. Ses origines. Ses problèmes littéraires. Son Influence*, ed. Robert de Langhe. Orientalia et Biblica 4. 389-405. Louvain: Publications Universitaires, 1962.

709. Barns, J.W.B., and G.D. Kilpatrick. "A New Psalms Fragment." *Proceedings of the British Academy* 43 (1957): 229ff.

710. Bardtke, H. "Liber Psalmorum." *Biblia Hebraica Stuttgartensia*, ed. Karl Elliger et Wilhelm Rudolph. Stuttgart: Würtembergische Bibelanstalt, 1969.

Reviewed in *CBQ* 32 (1970): 254-255.

711. Bauchet, J.M. Paul. "Transcription and Translation of a Psalm from Sukenik's Dead Sea Scroll." *Catholic Biblical Quarterly* 12 (1950): 331-335.

712. Beaucamp, Évode. "Le texte psalmique dans le développement de la vie liturgique d'Israël." *Église et Théologie* 3 (1972): 155-191.

713. Diez Macho, Alejandro (with the collaboration of Angeles Navarro Peiro). *Biblia Babilónica: Fragments de Salmos, Job y Proverbios (Ms. 508 A del Seminario Teológico Judío de Neuva York).* Textos y Estudíos "Cardenal Cisneros" de la Biblia Políglota Matritense 42. Madrid: Instituto de Filología, C.S.I.C., Departamento de Filología Bíblica y de Oriente Angituo, 1987. lxxiv+106p.

This volume is part of the *Biblia Babilónica* series. The manuscript is of Yemenite origin and is the ms. referred to by P. Kahle as Enelow Memorial Collection 38.

714. Ehrlich, Arnold B. *Randglossen zur hebräischen Bibel: Textkritisches, Sprachliches und Sachliches.* Band VI: *Psalmen, Sprüche und Hiob.* 1-7. Leipzig: J.C. Hinrichs, 1913. Reprint, Hildesheim: Georg Olms Verlagsbuchhandlung, 1968. 344p.

715. Farrell, Shannon Elizabeth. "Le rouleau 11QPs[a] et le psautier biblique." *Laval théologique et philosophique* 46 (1990): 353-368.

The comparison of a psalms scroll from Cave 11 at Qumran with the biblical book of Psalms reveals several differences between the two texts. The importance of these differences is explored.

716. Ginsberg, H. "Some Emendations in Psalms." *Hebrew Union College Annual* 23 (1950-51): 97-104.

717. Goshen-Gottstein, M. "The Psalms Scroll (11QPs[a]). A Problem of Canon and Text." *Textus* 5 (1960): 22-33.

718. Hempel, Johannes. *Der hebräische Text zweier Wolfenbütteler Fragmente des Alten Testaments. Mit einem Nachtrag zu "Nachrichten" 1959.* Nachrichten der Akademie der Wissenschaften in Göttingen. I. Philologisch-Historische Klasse. Jahrg. 1962, Nr. 6. Göttingen: Vandenhoeck & Ruprecht, 1962.

719. Milik, J.T. "Fragments d'une source du Psautier." *Revue Biblique* 73 (1966): 94-104.

Discusses 4QPs89.

720. Murtonen, A. *Materials for a Non-masoretic Hebrew Grammar I: Liturgical Texts and Psalm Fragments Provided with the So-Called Palestinian Punctuation.* Helsinki: Akateeminen Kirjakauppa, 1958.

721. Ouellette, J. "Variantes qumrâniennes du livre des Psaumes." *Revue de Qumran* 7 (1969): 105-123.

722. Ploeg, J. van der. "Le Psaume xci dans une recension de Qumrân." *Revue Biblique* 72 (1965): 210-217.

723. _____. "Fragments d'un manuscript de Psaumes de Qumran (11 QPs[b])." *Revue Biblique* 74 (1967): 408-412.

724. Puech, Émile. "11QPsAp[a]: un rituel d'exorcismes. Essai de reconstruction." *Revue de Qumran* 14 (1990): 377-408.

Psalm 91 in a Qumran recension, followed by three apocryphal psalms, typical of the anthological style of the late period. The use of the tetragrammaton, far from arguing against Essene origin, points to a magical use of this material.

725. Rowley, Harold H. "The Internal Dating of the Dead Sea Scrolls." *Ephemerides theologicae lovanienses* 28 (1952): 257-276.

1QpHab and Psalm 74.

726. Sanders, James A. "The Scroll of Psalms from Cave 11 (11QPss): A Preliminary Report." *Bulletin of the American Schools of Oriental Research* 165 (1962): 11-15.

Discusses 11QPs[a].

727. _____. "Pre-Masoretic Psalter Texts." *Catholic Biblical Quarterly* 27 (1965): 114-123.

Revised in *The Dead Sea Psalms Scroll.* 9-14.

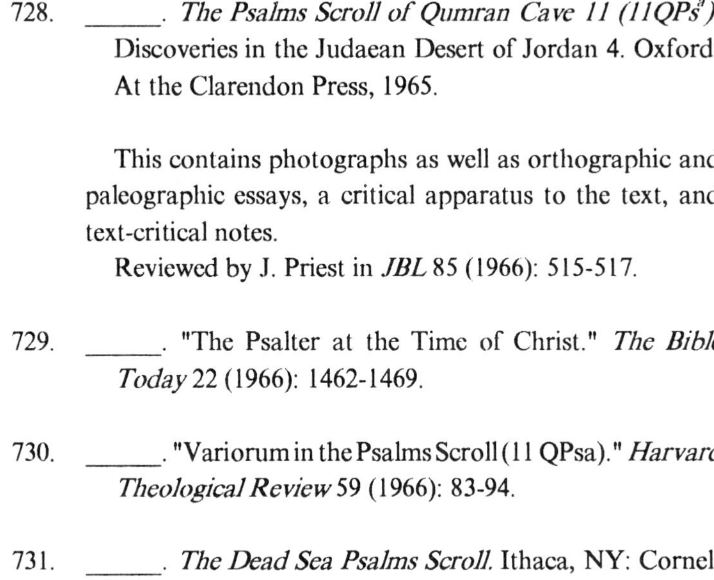

728. ______. *The Psalms Scroll of Qumran Cave 11 (*$11QPs^a$*).* Discoveries in the Judaean Desert of Jordan 4. Oxford: At the Clarendon Press, 1965.

This contains photographs as well as orthographic and paleographic essays, a critical apparatus to the text, and text-critical notes.
Reviewed by J. Priest in *JBL* 85 (1966): 515-517.

729. ______. "The Psalter at the Time of Christ." *The Bible Today* 22 (1966): 1462-1469.

730. ______. "Variorum in the Psalms Scroll (11 QPsa)." *Harvard Theological Review* 59 (1966): 83-94.

731. ______. *The Dead Sea Psalms Scroll.* Ithaca, NY: Cornell University Press, 1967.

Text and comments on the Psalms Scroll from Qumran Cave 11, which represents a radical departure from any other known recension of the Psalter.

732. ______. "Cave 11 Surprises and the Question of Canon." In *New Directions in Biblical Archaeology*, ed. David Noel Freedman and Jonas C. Greenfield. 113-130. Garden City, NY: Anchor Book (Doubleday), 1971.

A reassessment of the entire inventory of psalm discoveries, including those from Cave 4. The evidence points to a considerable flexibility among the psalms of Books 4 and 5 -- to such an extent that the Psalter of Qumran was still open-ended in the first Christian century. Translations of non-Massoretic psalms and of canonical psalms with serious variants are offered.

733. Skehan, Patrick W. "A Psalm Manuscript from Qumran (4Q Ps[b])." *Catholic Biblical Quarterly* 26 (1964): 313-322.

Discusses 4QPs[b].

734. ______. "Gleanings from Psalm Texts from Qumran." In *Mélanges bibliques et orientaux en l'honneur de M. Henri Cazelles,* ed. A. Caquot and M. Delcor. Alter Orient und Altes Testament 212. 439-452. Kevalaer: Butzon & Bercker, 1981; Neukirchen-Vluyn: Neukirchener Verlag, 1981.

735. Talmon, S. "Pisqah Be'emsa' Pasuq and 11QPs[a]." *Textus* 5 (1966): 11-21.

A longer version of this article appeared in Hebrew in *Tarbiz* (March, 1966): 214-234.

736. Wilson, Gerald H. "The Qumran Psalms Manuscripts and the Consecutive Arrangement of Psalms in the Hebrew Psalter." *Catholic Biblical Quarterly* 45 (1983): 377-388.

737. ______. "The Qumran Psalms Scroll Reconsidered: Analysis of the Debate." *Catholic Biblical Quarterly* 47 (1985): 624-642.

738. Yadin, Y. "A Fragment of the Book of Psalms." *Israel Exploration Journal* 11 (1961): 40, plus plate 20.

Discusses Nahal Hever fragment of Psalm 15:1-5 and Psalm 16:1.

739. _____. "The Excavation of Masada -- 1963/64: Preliminary Report." *Israel Exploration Journal* 15 (1965): 79-82, 103-104.

Discusses M1039-160: Psalms 81:3-85:10.

740. _____. "Another Fragment (E) of the Psalms Scroll from Qumran Cave 11 (11 QPs[a])." *Textus* 5 (1966): 1-10.

Discusses 11QPs[a] fragment E.

C. Greek Translations

741. Arconada, Ricardus. *Ecclesiae psalmi paenitentiales. Graeco-Latino textu retractato in exemplum textualis praestantiae naevorumque ecclesiastici psalterii, i.e., septuagintaviralis, quo ab apostolis graeca, gallicani, quo ab Hieronymo latina utitur ecclesia.* Rome: Pontifical Biblical Institute, 1936. 143p.

742. Barthélemy, J.D. "Le Psautier grec et le papyrus Bodmer XXIV." *Revue de Theologie et de Philosophie* III, 19 (1969): 106-110.

743. Bieler, L., ed. *Psalterium Graeco-Latinum: Codex Basiliensis A. VII.3.* Umbrae codicum occidentalium 5. Amsterdam: North Holland Publishing Co., 1960. xxii+99p.

744. Brooks, G.J. "On the Relationship between 11QPs[a] and the Septuagint on the Basis of the Computerized Data Base (CAQP)." In *Septuagint, Scrolls and Cognate Writings*, ed. George T. Brook and Barnabas Lindars. Septuagint and Cognate Studies. Atlanta, GA: Scholars Press, 1991.

745. Busto Saiz, J.R. *La Traducción de Simaco en el Libro de los Salmos.* Textos y Estudios "Cardenal Cisneros" 22. Madrid: Instituto "Arias Montano," Consejo Superior de Investigaciones Científicas, 1985. xxvi+756p.

Reviewed by A. Pietersma in *JBL* 100 (1981): 262. Reviewed also in *CBQ* 45 (1983): 98-100.

746. Caloz, Masséo. *Étude sur la LXX origénienne du Psautier. Les relations entre les leçons des Psaumes du Manuscrit Coislin 44, les Fragments des Hexaples et le texte du Psautier Gallican.* Orbis biblicus et orientalis 19. Fribourg, Switzerland: Universitaires, 1978; Göttingen: Vandenhoeck & Ruprecht, 1978. 480p.

Reviewed by A. Pietersma in *JBL* 98 (1979): 589-590; reviewed also in *CBQ* 41 (1979): 126-127.

747. Cox, Claude. "Εἰσακούω and Ἐπακούω in the Greek Psalter." *Biblica* 62 (1981): 251-258.

An attempt to clarify the reasons why Rahlfs' edition of the Greek Psalter vacillates between εἰσακούω and ἐπακούω in rendering Hebrew *'ānâ.*

748. Cutler, Anthony, and Annemarie Weyl Carr. "The Psalter Benaki 34:3: An Unpublished Illuminated Manuscript from the Family 2400." *Revue des Études Byzantines* 34 (1976): 281-323.

749. Dell'Acqua, Anna Passoni. "L'elemento intermedio nella versione greca di alcuni testi sapientizli e del libro dei Salmi." *Rivista Biblica* 30 (1982): 79-90.

Examines how various intermediate figures in creation (in Proverbs 8, Job 28, Job 38, Gen 6:1-4, some Psalms) are treated in the transition from MT into LXX.

750. Gribomont, J., and A. Thibaut. "Méthode et esprit des transductions du Psautier grec." In *Richesses et déficiences des anciens Psautiers latins,* ed. D.R. Weber. Collectanea Biblica Latina 13. 51-105. Rome: Abbaye Saint Jérôme, 1959.

751. Jellicoe, Sidney. "The Psalter-Text of St. Clement of Rome." In *Forschung zur Bibel. Wort, Lied und Gottesspruch. Beiträge zur Septuaginta. Festschrift für Joseph Ziegler,* ed. Rudolf Schnackenburg and Josef Schreiner. 2 vols. Vol. 1, 59-66. Würzburg: Echter Verlag, 1972.

Clement quotes the psalms more than any other Old Testament book, citing them 35 times in his first letter; 10 of these follow the standard LXX; yet Clement's text differs in some significant respects.

752. Kasser, Rudolphe, and Michel Testuz. *Papyrus Bodmer XXIV: Psaumes XVII-CXVIII.* Cologne and Geneva: Bibliotèque Bodmer, 1967. 235p.

753. Kooij, Arie van der. "On the Place of Origin of the Old Greek of Psalms." *Vetus Testamentum* 33 (1983): 67-74.

754. Lowden, J. "Observations on Illustrated Byzantine Psalters." *The Art Bulletin* 70 (1988): 242-260.

755. Munnich, Olivier. "Indices d'une Septante originelle dans le Psautier Grec." *Biblica* 63 (1982): 406-416.

Paul Kahle argued that there is an original version (an "*Ur-Septuaginta*") underlying the present Greek text. This thesis cannot be sustained in the Psalter.

756. ______. "La Septante des Psaumes et le group *kaigé*." *Vetus Testamentum* 33 (1983): 75-89.

An examination of the contributions of Barthélemy and Venetz regarding the relationship and possible influence of the LXX version of the Psalms and the Greek Psalms known as the *Kaigé*-group.

757. Olofsson, Staffan. *God is My Rock: A Study of Translation Technique and Theological Exegesis in the Septuagint.* Coniectanea biblica, Old Testament 31. Stockholm: Almqvist & Wiksell International, 1990. ix+208p.

An examination of the influence of theological exegesis in the LXX, particularly the Psalter, as reflected in its translation of certain Hebrew metaphorical names or epithets for God. A difference is observed between the treatment of metaphors used of God and those used in their literal or ordinary metaphorical meaning.

758. Petraglio, Renzo. "Le interpolazioni cristiane del Salterio greco." *Augustinianum* 28 (1988): 89-109.

An analysis of Christian interpolations in a series of Greek psalters, all pre-Origen.

759. Pietersma, Albert. "The Greek Psalter. A Question of Methodology and Syntax." *Vetus Testamentum* 26 (1976): 60-69.

The LXX can justifiably lay claim to front-rank position in biblical textual criticism; this is illustrated by the LXX's remarkable consistency in translating Hebrew plural verbs as plural when they are governed by a neuter plural substantive.

760. _____. *Two Manuscripts of the Greek Psalter in the Chester Beatty Library Dublin, Edited with Textual-critical Analysis and with Full Facsimile.* Analecta Biblica, 77. Rome: Biblical Institute Press, 1978. vii+79p.

Reviewed in *CBQ* 42 (1980): 548-549.

761. _____. "Articulation in the Greek Psalms: The Evidence of Papyrus Bodmer XXIV." In *Tradition of the Text: Studies Offered to Dominique Barthélemy in Celebration of His 70th Birthday*, ed. Gerard J. Norton and Stephen Pisano. Orbis Biblicus et Orientalis 109. 184-202. Freiburg, Switzerland: Universitätsverlag, 1991; Göttingen: Vandenhoeck & Ruprecht, 1991.

The Old Greek text of Psalms in its use of the definite article reflects the Hebrew more closely than appears from the text of Rahlfs.

762. _____. "Ra 2110 (P. Bodmer XXIV) and the Text of the Greek Psalter." In *Studien zur Septuaginta: Robert Hanhart zu Ehren; aus Anlass seines 65. Geburtstages*, ed. Detlef Fraenkel and Others. Abhandlungen der Akademie der Wissenschaften in Göttingen, Philologisch-historische Klass, dritte Folge 190; Mitteilungungen des Septuaginta-Unternehmens 20. 262-286. Göttingen: Vandenhoeck & Ruprecht, 1990.

763. Rahlfs, Alfred. *Septuaginta-Studien 2. Der Text des Septuaginta Psalters Nebst einen Anhang: Griechische Psalterfragmente aus Oberägypten nach Abschriften von W.C. Crum.* Göttingen: Vandenhoeck & Ruprecht, 1907. 256p.

764. ______. *Psalmi cum Odis. Septuaginta. Vetus Testamentum Graecum Auctoritate Academiae Litterarum Gottingensis editum.* Vol. 10. Göttingen: Vandenhoeck & Ruprecht, 1931. 366p.

765. Sailhammer, John H. *The Translational Technique of the Greek Septuagint for the Hebrew Verbs and Participles in Psalms 3-41.* Studies in Biblical Greek 2. New York, Bern, and Frankfurt am Main: Lang, 1991. xi+225p.

An extensive study of the equivalencies between verbal forms in the LXX and MT of Psalms 3-41. There are some differences, including an eschatological exegesis underlying the LXX handling of verbal forms in some Psalms, particularly Psalm 37. The precative perfect is apparently lost in the LXX.

766. Schenker, Adrian. *Hexaplarische Psalmenbruchstücke. Die hexaplarischen Psalmenfragmente des Handschriften Vaticanus graecus 752 and Canonicianus graecus 62.* Orbis biblicus et orientalis, 8. Freiburg: Switzerland: Universitätsverlag, 1975; Göttingen: Vandenhoeck & Ruprecht, 1975. xxvii+231p.

Reviewed by A. Pietersma in *JBL* 96 (1977): 433-436; reviewed also in *CBQ* 38 (1976): 591-592.

767. Schildenberger, Johannes. "Einige beachtliche Septuaginta-Lesarten in den Psalmen." In *Forschung zur Bibel. Wort, Lied und Gottesspruch. Beiträge zur Septuaginta. Festschrift für Joseph Ziegler*, ed. Rudolf Schnackenburg and Josef Schreiner. 2 vols. Vol. 1, 145-159. Würzburg: Echter Verlag, 1972.

Uses five examples (Psalms 4:2a, 4:3, 30:11, 45:12b, and 45:14) to illustrate how the LXX has at times preserved the original psalm reading as against the MT.

768. Soffer, Arthur. "The Treatment of Anthropomorphisms and Anthropopathisms in the LXX of Psalms." *Hebrew Union College Annual* 28 (1957): 85-107.

769. Testuz, Michel. *Papyrus Bodmer VII-IX. VII: L'epîpte de Jude; VIII: Les deux epîtres de Pierre; IX: Les psaumes 33 et 34.* Cologne and Geneva: Bibliotèque Bodmer, (c1959). 81p.

770. Venetz, Hermann-Josef. *Die Quinta des Psalteriums. Ein Beitrage zur Septuaginta und Hexaplaforschung.* Collection Massorah: Série I, Études classique et textes 2. Hildesheim: Gerstenberg, 1974. xxi+195p.

771. Wikgren, Allen. "Two Ostraca Fragments of the Septuagint Psalter." *Journal of Near Eastern Studies* 5 (1946): 181-184..

See also: 1180, 3400, 4128, 4132, 4451, 4840, 4841.

D. Other Ancient Versions

772. Allgeier, Arthur. "Das Psalterium Casineuse und die abendländische Psalmenüberlieferung." *Römische Quartalschrift für christliche Altertumskunde und Kirchengeschichte* 34 (1926): 28-45.

Codex 557 of the Benedictine Closter of Monte Cassino, a unique text of the Latin Psalter, has been influenced by the *Psalterium iuxta Hebraeos* of Jerome. It preserves in great measure the linguistic connections with its African original; it also contains many noteworthy changes according to a Hebrew text that deviate from the MT; this was done by someone who was not all that familiar with the Hebrew language.

773. _____. *Die altlateinischen Psalterien.* Prolegomena zu einer textgeschichte der hieronymianischen Psalmübersetzungen. Freiburg: Herder and Co., 1928.

774. _____. "Die erste Psalmenübersetzung des Heiligen Hieronymus und das Psalterium Romanum." *Biblica* 12 (1931): 447-482.

De Bruyne is wrong in viewing the *Psalterium Romanum* as having nothing to do with Jerome's first revision of the Old Latin.

775. _____. *Die Überlieferung der alten lateinischen Psalmenübersetzungen und ihre kulturgeschichtliche Bedeutung.* Freiburger Wissenschaftliche Gesellschaft Heft 20. Freiburg im Breisgau: Speyer und Kaerner, 1931. 27p.

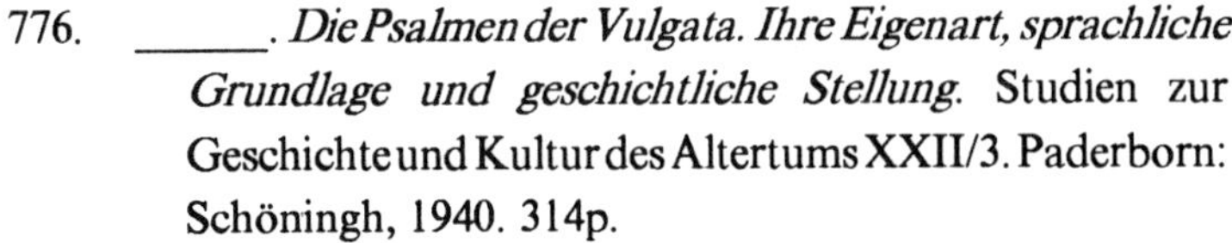

776. _____. *Die Psalmen der Vulgata. Ihre Eigenart, sprachliche Grundlage und geschichtliche Stellung.* Studien zur Geschichte und Kultur des Altertums XXII/3. Paderborn: Schöningh, 1940. 314p.

777. _____. "Methodische Folgerungen aus der neuen römischen Psalmenübersetzung." *Theologische Literaturzeitung* 73 (1948): 203-208.

778. Ammassari, Antonio. "L'anonima versione latina dei salmi secondo il Codice Cassinese 557: un'antica testimonianze Giudeo-Cristiana." *Bibbia et Oriente* 19 (1977): 242-257; 20 (1978): 27-42.

Cassinese was an early attempt at a Latin version from Hebrew. It is related to the *Romanum* as the *iuxta Hebraeos* is to the *Vulgata (Gallicanum).* There are many indications of a Judeo-Christian origin of this version.

779. _____. "Il Salterio Latino di Pietro." *Bibbia e Oriente* 32 (1990): 141-146.

The Latin text of the psalms of the Cassino Psalter (Codex Cassinese Lat. 557), translated from Hebrew by a certain Peter, offers many midrashic readings. Several psalms show readings very close to the Targum, but impossible to trace back to the LXX. The translator may have been a Judeo-Christian, not completely familiar with Latin.

780. Ayuso, Marazuela Teófilo. "El Salterio de Gregorio de Elvira y la Vetus Latina Hispana." *Biblica* 40 (1959): 135-159.

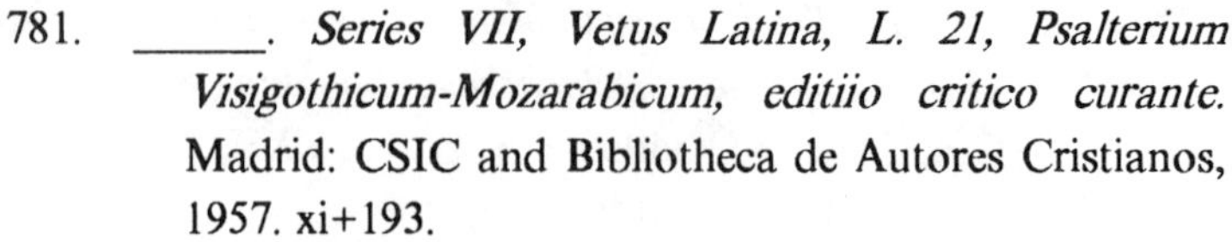

781. _____. *Series VII, Vetus Latina, L. 21, Psalterium Visigothicum-Mozarabicum, editiio critico curante.* Madrid: CSIC and Bibliotheca de Autores Cristianos, 1957. xi+193.

Reviewed in *CBQ* 24 (1962): 189-191.

782. _____. *Series VIII, Vulgata Hispana, L. 21, Psalterium S. Hieronymi de Hebraica Veritate Interpretatum, editio critica curante.* Madrid: CSIC and Bibliotheca de Autores Cristianos, 1960. xv+298.

Reviewed in *CBQ* 24 (1962): 189-191.

783. _____. *La Vetus Latina Hispana, V: El Salterio.* 3 vols. Madrid: CSIC and Bibliotheca de Autores Cristianos, 1962.

784. _____, and Others. *Biblia Polyglotta Matritensia, cura et studio. Prooemium.* Madrid: CSIC and Bibliotheca de Autores Cristianos, 1957. xii+14.

Reviewed in *CBQ* 24 (1962): 189-191.

785. Baars, W., ed. *Apocryphal Psalms. The Old Testament in Syriac According to the Peshitta Version,* ed. on behalf of the International Organization for the Study of the Old Testament by The Peshitta Institute. Vol. IV/6c. Leiden: E.J. Brill, 1973. x+10p.

The basic MS for this edition of five psalms is a 12th century Baghdad MS.

Reviewed by John W. Wevers in *JBL* 94 (1975): 455.

786. Barnes, W.E. *The Peshitta Psalter According to the West Syrian Text.* Cambridge: Cambridge University Press, 1904. Reprinted by United Bible Societies in *The New Testament and Psalms in Syriac,* ed. G.H. Gwilliam and W. Barnes. New York, 1985. 488p.

A text revised from MSS and furnished with an *Apparatus Criticus.*

787. Bea, Augustine. *Le nouveau Psautier Latin: éclaircissements sur l'origene et l'esprit de la traduction.* Paris: Desclée de Brouwer, 1947. 207p. German version: *Die neue lateinische Psalmenübersetzung. Ihr Werden und ihr Geist.* Freiburg im Breisgau: Herder-Druckerei, 1949. viii+171p.

Reviewed by David Winton Thomas in *Erasmus II* (Amsterdam, 1949): cols. 451-454.

788. *Biblia Sacra iuxta latinam Vulgatam Versionem ad codicum fidem iussu Pii PP.XII, cura et studio Monachorum Abbatiae Pontificiae Sancti Hieronymi in Urbe Ordinis Sancti Benedicti edita,* Vol. 10: *Liber Psalmorum, ex recensione Sancti Hieronymi cum praefationibus et epistula ad Sunniam et Fretelam.* Rome: Pontifical Biblical Institute, 1953. xvi+299.

The first revision by Jerome of the Old Latin Psalter is known as the Roman (384); the second (387-390) is designated as the Gallican; a third edition was the Hebrew Psalter. The text of this edition is that of the Gallican, although there are references to the Roman Psalter and the Old Latin manuscripts in the *apparatus criticus.*

Reviewed by H.S. Gehman in *JBL* 74 (1955): 134-135.

789. Bieler, L. "Notes on the Durham Copies of the Psalterium juxta Hebraeos." *Scriptorum* 12 (1958): 282-283.

790. Bloemendaal, W. *The Headings of the Psalms in the East Syriac Church.* Leiden: E.J. Brill, 1960. 94p.

The Psalms as they occur in the manuscripts and printed editions of the Peshitta are either without titles or have titles which differ completely from those in the Hebrew and Greek texts. They give a shorter or longer interpretation dependent on, for example, the circumstances under which the poet wrote the Psalm or the purpose for which it was composed. The best explanation seems to be that the translators of the Peshitta omitted them from the beginning. The primary influence on this was Theodore of Mopsuestia.

791. Boese, Helmut. *Anonymi Glosa Psalmorum ex Traditione Seniorum. Teil I: Praefatio und Psalmen 1-100.* Aus der Geschichte der Lateinischen Bibel 22. Freiburg: Verlag Herder, 1992. 471p.

792. Boylan, Patrick A. *The Psalms. A Study of the Vulgate Psalter in the Light of the Hebrew Text.* 2 vols. Dublin: M.H. Gill and Son, Ltd., 1920-1924. Vol. 1, lxix+299p; Vol. 2, 404p. 2nd ed. 1926-31.

793. Capelle, Paul. *Le text du psautier latin en Afrique.* Rome: F. Pustet, 1913. xi+267p.

794. Cardine, E. "Psautiers anciens et chant grégorien." In *Richesses et déficiences des anciens Psautiers latins,* ed. D.R. Weber. Collectanea Biblica Latina 13. 249-258. Rome: Abbaye Saint Jérôme, 1959.

795. Cooper, Charles M. "Jerome's 'Hebrew Psalter' and the New Latin Version." *Journal of Biblical Literature* 69 (1950): 233-244.

796. Díez Marino, Luis. "Haggadic Elements in the Targum on Psalms." In *Proceedings of the Eighth World Congress of Jewish Studies, Jerusalem, August 16-21, 1981. Division A: The Period of the Bible.* Jerusalem: Magnes Press (World Union of Jewish Studies), 1982.

797. ______. *Targum de Salmos: Edición Príncipe del Ms. Villa-Amil n. 5 de Alfonso de Zamora.* Bibliotheca Hispana Biblica 6. Madrid: Consejo Superior de Investigaciones Científicas, 1982. 476p.

Reviewed in *CBQ* 50 (1988): 111-113.

798. Dirksen, P.B. "Lee's Editions of the Syriac Old Testament and the Psalms, 1822-1826." *Oudtestamentische Studiën* 26 (1990): 63-71.

799. Estin, C. *Les Psautiers de Jérome à lumière des traductions juives antérieures.* Collectanea Biblica Latina 15. Rome: San Girolamo, 1984. Distributed by Turnhout: Brepols. 238p.

A study of Jerome's use of the antecedent Greek versions as presented in Origen's *Hexapla.*

800. Gaertner, Johannes A. "Latin Verse Translations of the Psalms 1500-1620." *Harvard Theological Review* 49 (1956): 271-306.

801. Gledner, Ferdinand. "Um das Psalterium Benedictinum von 1459." *Gutenberg-Jahrbuch* (1954): 71-83.

802. Gooding, D.W. "The Text of Psalms in Two Durham Bibles." *Scriptorum* 12 (1958): 94-96.

803. Grill, Severin. "Die Psalmen nach dem syrischen Text." *Bibel und Liturgie* 24 (1957): 237-241.

An introduction to the Peschitta Psalter, plus a translation of Psalms 1-4.

804. ______. "Die Psalmen nach dem syrischen Text." *Bibel und Liturgie* 24 (1957): 269-272.

Psalms 5-9.

805. Harden, J.M. *Psalterium iuxta Hebraeos. Edited with an Introduction and Apparatus Criticus.* London: S.P.C.K., 1922. xxi+195p.

806. Hiebert, Robert J.V. *The "Syrohexaplaric" Psalter.* Society of Biblical Literature Septuagint and Cognate Studies 27. Atlanta, GA: Scholars Press, 1989. xvi+352p.

807. Kubo, S. "The Influence of the Vulgate on the English Translations of Certain Psalms." *Andrews University Seminary Studies* 3 (1965): 34-41.

Psalms 8:5; 95:8; 104:4.

808. *Liber Psalmorum cum Canticis Breviarii Romani, nova e textibus primigeniis interpretatio latina cum notis criticis*

et exegeticis cura Professorum Pontificii Instituti Biblici edita. Rome: Pontifical Biblical Institute, 1945.

809. Marazuela, T. Ayuso. "Un Salterio 'juxta Hebraeos' y un Salterio Romano en un Códice tardio del Escorial." *Estudios Biblicos* 17 (1958): 5-46.

810. Marboeck, Johann. *Das Eindringen der Versio Gallicana des Psalteriums in die Psalterien der Benediktinerklöster Oberösterreichs.* Vienna: Verlag Notring, 1970. xvi+117p.

811. Marks, John H. *Der textkritische Wert des Psalterium Hieronymi juxta Hebraeos.* Winterthur: Verlag P.G. Keller, 1956. 155p.

Reviewed by A. Jeffery in *JBL* 77 (1958): 81-82.

812. Merlo, Francesca. *Il salterio di Rufino. Edizione critica e cura di Francesca Merlo. Commento da Jean Gribomont.* Collectanea Biblica Latina 14. Rome: Abbazia San Girolamo, 1972; Vatican City, Vatican Library, 1972. xi+207p.

813. Ongaro, Giovanni. "Saltero veronese e revisione Agostiniana." *Biblica* 35 (1954): 443-474.

814. Penna, Angelo. "I titoli del salterio Siriaco e S. Gerolamo." *Biblica* 40 (1959): 177-187.

815. Preuss, Horst Dietrich. "Die Psalmenüberschriften in Targum und Midrasch." *Zeitschrift für die alttestamentliche Wissenschaft* 71 (1959): 44-54.

816. Rowlands, Elwyn Richard. "Inner-Syriac Corruptions in the Book of Psalms." *Journal of Theological Studies* 42 (1941): 65-67.

817. Sainte-Marie, D. Henri de. *Sancti Hieronymi Psalterium Iuxta Hebraeos. Edition critique.* Collectanea Biblica Latina 11. Rome: Abbaye Saint-Jérôme, 1954. lxx+262p.

Reviewed by H.S. Gehman in *JBL* 76 (1957): 166-167.

818. Salmon, Petrus. "Das Problem der Psalmen. Text und Interpretation der Psalmen zur Zeit des hl. Hieronymous und hl. Augustinus." *Benediktinische Monatschrift* 30 (1954): 393-416.

I. The text of the Psalms: The Revisions of the Latin Psalters. Roman, Gallican, and Psalterium juxta Hebraeos. II. The Interpretation of the Psalms: Jerome and Augustine.

819. _____. *Les Tituli psalmorum des manuscrits latins.* Collectanea Biblica Latina 12. Rome: San Girolamo, 1959. 190p.

Six series of Latin Psalm titles.

820. Saydon, Peter P. "The Origin of the 'Polyglot' Arabic Psalms." *Biblica* 31 (1950): 226-236.

821. Sperber, Alexander, ed. *The Bible in Aramaic,* Vol. IVA: *The Hagiographa. Transition from Translation to Midrash.* Leiden: E.J. Brill, 1968. viii+206p.

822. Speyer, Wolfgang. "Der bisher älteste lateinische Psalmus abecedarius. Zur Editio princeps von R. Roca-Puig."

Jahrbuch für Antike und Christentum 10 (1967): 211-216. Reprinted in *Frühes Christentum im antiken Strahlungsfeld: Ausgewählte Aufsätze.* Wissenschaftliche Untersuchungen zum Neuen Testament 50. 64-69. Tübingen: J.C.B. Mohr (Paul Siebeck), 1989.

823. Sprenger, N. *Konkordanz zum Syrischen Psalter.* Göttinger Orientforschungen 1, Reihe Syriaca 10/8. Wiesbaden: Otto Harrassowitz, 1976. xi+331p.

824. Steiert, Barnabas. "Einführung in die neue römische Psalmenversion." *Analecta Sacri Ordinis Cisterciensis* 7 (Rome, 1951): 91-166; 11 (Rome, 1955): 199-324. Offprint, Rome: Analecta Sacra Ordinis Cisterciensis, 1951. 166p.

825. Verbraken, Patrick. "Pour une lecture chrétienne du psautier." *Bible et Vie chrétienne* 40 (1961): 71-76.

Translates and evaluates the fifth series of Latin Psalm titles.

826. Vogel, Adalbert. "Studien zum Pešitta-Psalter, besonders im Hinblick auf sein Verhältnis zu Septuaginta." *Biblica* 32 (1951): 32-56, 198-231, 336-363, 481-502.

827. Vosté, Jacques M. "Sur les titres des psaumes dans la Pesitta surtout d'après la recension orientale." *Biblica* 25 (1944): 210-235.

828. Walsh, L.G. "The Christian Prayer of the Psalms according to the 'Tituli psalmorum' of the Latin Manuscripts." *Studies in Pastoral Liturgy* 3 (Dublin, 1967): 29-73.

829. Walter, D.M., in collaboration with A. Vogel and R.Y. Ebied. *The Book of Psalms. The Old Testament in Syriac According to the Peshitta Version, Part II, Fasc. 3*, edited on behalf of the International Organization for the Study of the Old Testament by the Peshitta Institute for the University of Leiden. Leiden: E.J. Brill, 1980. xxx+173p.

830. Weber, D. Robert. "La traduction primitive de βάρις dans les psautiers latins." *Vigiliae Christianae: a Review of Early Christian Life and Language* 4 (1950): 20-32.

831. ______. *Problèmes d'édition des anciens psautiers latins.* Rome: Vatican Library, 1951.

832. ______, ed. *Le Psautier Romain et les Autres Anciens Psautiers Latins. Collectana biblica latina 10. Rome: Libreria Vaticana, 1953. xxiii+411p.*

A critical edition of the Roman Psalter and other Old Latin psalters. The text of the Roman Psalter is printed in one column, variants of the other Old Latin psalters in the other column. The Roman Psalter is considered the basic text.

Reviewed by H.S. Gehman in *JBL* 74 (1955): 135-136.

833. ______. *Liber Psalmorum ex recensione Sancti Hieronymi.* Biblia Sacra iuxta Latinam vulgatam versionem. Rome: Vatican Library, 1953.

834. ______, ed. *Richesses et déficiences des anciens Psautiers latins.* Collectanea Biblica Latina 13. Rome: Abbaye Saint Jérôme, 1959. 267p.

835. ______. *Psalterii secundum Vulgatam Bibliorum versionem nova recensio iuxta votum Synodi Generalis Abbatum Ordinis S. Benedicti.* Clervaux, 1961.

836. Weitzman, M.P. "The Peshitta Psalter and its Hebrew *Vorlage.*" *Vetus Testamentum* 35 (1985): 341-354.

The Peshitta translator consulted the LXX when in difficulties. The scribe of the *Vorlage* and the translator show themselves torn between Hebrew tradition and the contemporary Greek-speaking world.

837. Zanetti, Ugo. "La distribution des psaumes dans l'horologion copte." *Orientalia Christiana Periodica* 56 (1990): 323-369.

838. Ziegler, Joseph. "Das neu lateinische Psalterium." *Zeitschrift für die alttestamentliche Wissenschaft* 63 (1951): 1-15.

Gallican Psalter and others.

839. ______. *Antike und moderne lateinische Psalmen-übersetzungen.* Bayerische Akademie der Wissehschaften. Philosopisch-Historische Klasse. Sitzungsberichte Jahrg. 1960, Heft 3. Munich: Verag der Bayerischen Akademie der Wissenschaften in Kommision bei Beck, 1960. 68p.

840. Zimmerman, Frank. "The Text of Psalms in the Peshitta." *Journal of Theological Studies* 41 (1940): 44-46.

841. Zorell, Franz. *Psalterium ex hebraeo latinum.* 2nd ed. Rome: Pontifical Biblical Institute, 1939. xxxii+434p.

Reviewed by D.W. Thomas in *Journal of Theological Studies* 41 (1940): 289-292.

See also: 405, 4960, 4684, 4961, 4963, 4971,

E. Other Translations

842. Ahmed, Ehsan. "Clément Marot's Parallel Conversions: A Reading of the 1543 *Psaumes*." *Journal of Medieval and Renaissance Studies* 20 (1990): 137-152.

843. Althoff, E. *Myles Coverdales 'Goostly Psalmes and Spirituall Songes' and das deutsche Kirchenlied. Ein Beitrag zum Einfluss der deutschen Literatur auf die englische im 16. Jahrhundert.* Bochum-Langendreer: H. Pöppinghaus, 1935. 144p.

844. Baker, Peter S. "A Little-known Variant Text of the Old English Metrical Psalms." *Speculum: A Journal of Medieval Studies* 59 (1984): 263-281.

Trinity College MS R,17,1. Paris Psalter. Psalms 90:16-95:2.

845. Boyd, Dorothy. "Calvin's Preface to the French Metrical Psalms." *The Evangelical Quarterly* 22 (1950): 249-254.

846. Brennan, M.G. "The Date of the Countess of Pembroke's Translations of the Psalms." *Review of English Studies*, N.S., 33 (1982): 434-436.

847. ______. "Licensing the Sidney Psalms for the Press in the 1640s." *Notes and Queries* 31 (1984): 304-305.

848. Brooke, William T. *Old English Psalmody.* London: William Reeves, 1916.

849. Butterworth, Chester C. & Allen G. Chester. *George Joye 1495?-1553. A Chapter in the History of the English Bible and the English Reformation.* Philadelphia: University of Pennsylvania Press, 1962. 293p.

850. Chedozeau, Bernard. "La publication du livre des Psaumes par Port-Royal (17e siècle)." *Revue des sciences philosophiques et théologiques* 68 (1984): 355-380.

851. David, T.M., and V.L. Davis. "Edward Taylor's Metrical Paraphrases of the Psalms." *American Literature* 48 (1977): 455-470.

852. Davidsson, Carin. *Der alttschechische Wittenberger Psalter und sein Verhältnis zu den mittelalterlichen deutschen Psalterübersetzungen.* Publications de l'Institut slave d'Upsal 5. Uppsala: Almqvist & Wiksells, 1952. 111p.

853. Doelman, J. "A Seventeenth-Century Publication of Three of Sir Philip Sidney's Psalms." *Notes and Queries* 38 (1991): 162-163.

854. Duffield, G.E. "First Psalter Printed in English." *Churchman: Journal of Anglican Theology* 85 (1971): 291-293.

Bucer-Joye Psalter.

855. Eames, Wilberforce (1855-1937). *A List of Editions of the Bay Psalm Book or New England Version of the Psalms. A New Edition with a facsimile reprint of the 1st ed. of*

the Bay Psalm book, printed by S. Daye at Cambridge in New England in 1640. New York, 1885. Reprint, New York: Burt Franklin, 1973. 297p.

856. Ebeling, G. "Luthers Psalterdruck vom Jahre 1513." *Zeitschrift für Theologie und Kirche* 50 (1953): 43-99.

857. Engelbregt, J.A.H. *Het Utrechts Psalterium. Een eeuw wetenschappelijke bestudering 1860-1960.* Utrecht: Haentjens Dekker & Gumbert, 1965. 176p.

The Utrecht Psalter. A Century of Investigation, 1860-1960.

858. Fisher, J. *This treatyse concernynge the fruytfull saynges of Davyd the kynge & prophete in the seven penytencyall psalmes.* London, 1509. Facsimile edition, Amsterdam and Norwood, NJ, 1979.

859. Fisken, B.W. "'The Art of Sacred Parody' in Mary Sidney's Psalmes." *Tulsa Studies in Women's Literature* 8 (1989): 223-239.

860. Greene, R. "Sir Philip Sidney's Psalms, the Sixteenth-Century Psalter, and the Nature of Lyric." *Studies in English Literature 1500-1900* 30 (1990): 19-40.

861. Guillo, Laurent. "Le Psautier de Paris et le Psautier de Lyon: à propos de deux corpus contemporains du Psautier de Genève (1549-1561)." *Bulletin de la Société de l'Histoire du Protestantisme français* 136 (1990): 363-419.

862. Halasz, A. "Wyatt's David." *Texas Studies in Literature and Language* 30 (1988): 320-344.

863. Hannay, Margaret P. "'Psalms done into metre': The Common Psalms of John Milton and of the Bay Colony." *Christianity and Literature* 32 (3, 1983): 19-29.

Includes a chart, depicting the history of the English Psalter, 1524-1653.

864. _____. "'Wisdome the Wordes': Psalm Translation and Elizabethan Women's Spirituality." *Religion and Literature* 23 (1991): 65-82.

865. Haraszti, Zoltán. *The Enigma of the Bay Psalm Book.* Chicago, IL: University of Chicago Press, 1956. xiii+143p.

866. Hardman, C.B. "Marvell's Bermudas and Sandys's Psalms." *Review of English Studies,* N.S., 32 (1981): 64-67.

867. Heymans, J.G., ed. *Het Psalter van Leningrad.* Verzameling van middelnederlandse bijbelteksten, Kleine reeks. Afdeling V, Psalters 1. Leiden: E.J. Brill, 1973. xvi+151p.

868. _____. *Psalters der Moderne Devotie.* Corpus Sacrae Scripturae Neerlandicae Medii Aevi, Series Minor, Tom V: Psalteria, Vol. II. Leiden: E.J. Brill, 1978. xvii+354.

MSS 133 D 26 of the Royal Library, The Hague, dated 1427, and MSS BPL 46 B of the University Library, Leiden, dated at the beginning of the 15th century, are printed on opposite pages. In addition, a collation of MS 133 D 26 with MS 133 G 29, dated 1481 (Royal Library, The Hague) is included.

869. Hutchinson, E. "Attitudes toward Nature in Medieval England: The Alphanso and Bird Psalters." *Isis* 65 (1974): 5-37.

870. Jeanneret, M. *Poésie et tradition biblique au XVIe siècle: Recherches stylistiques sur les paraphrases des psaumes de Marot à Malherbe.* Paris: J. Corti, 1969. 573p.

871. Kastan, D.S. "An Early English Metrical Psalm: Elizabeth's or John Bale's?" *Notes & Queries*, N.S., 21 (1974): 404-405.

872. Keefer, S.L. "The ex libris of the Regius Psalter." *ANQ*, N.S., 3 (1990): 155-159.

873. Koropeckyj, R. "T. Ševčenko's Davydovi psalmy: A Romantic Psalter." *Slavic and East European Journal* 27 (1983): 228-244.

874. Kuhn, M. "On the Originality of the Vespasian Psalter Gloss." *English Studies* 66 (1985): 1-6. Discussion in 70 (1989): 477-483.

875. Leblanc, Paulette. *Les paraphrases français des psaumes à la fin de la période baroque, 1610-1660.* Publications de la Faculté des lettres et sciences humaines de l'université de Clermont II/9. Paris: Presses Universitaires de France, 1960. 316p.

876. Lenselink, Samuel Jan. *De Nederlandse psalmberijmingen in de 16e eeuw, van de Souterliedekens tot Datheen, met hun voorgangers in Duitsland en Frankrijk.* Assen: Van Gorcum, 1959. xii+600p.

877. _____. *Le Psautier huguenot.* Vol. 3. Assen: Van Gorcum & Comp., 1969.

878. Luther, Martin. *Das Neue Testament und die Psalmen nach der deutschen Übersetzung Martin Luthers.* Revidierter Text 1956. Stuttgart: Privilegierte Württembergische Bibelanstalt, 1956. 878p.

879. MacRobert, C.M. "What Is a Faithful Translation? Changing Norms in the Church Slavonic Version of the Psalter." *The Slavonic and East European Review* 69 (1991): 401-417.

880. Malpezzi, F.M. "Christian Poetics in Donne's Upon the Translation of the Psalmes." *Renascence* 32 (1980): 221-228.

881. Marot, Clément (c1495-1544). *Les psaumes de Clément Marot. Édition critique de plus ancien texte. (Ms. Paris B.N. Fr. 2337). Avec toutes les variantes de manuscrits et des plus anciennes éditions jusqu'à 1543, accompagnée du texte définitif de 1562 et précédée d'une étude par Samuel Jan Lenselink.* Assen: Van Gorcum & Comp., 1969. 247p.

882. O'Neill, P.P. "Old English Introductions to the Prose Psalms of the Paris Psalter: Sources, Structure, and Composition." *Studies in Philology* 78 (1981): 20-38.

883. _____. "The Lost Tabernacle of Selom: A Proposed Emendation in the Paris Psalter 77:60." *Notes and Queries* 31 (1984): 296-297.

884. _____. "A Lost Old-English Charter Rubric: The Evidence from the Regius Psalter." *Notes and Queries* 33 (1986): 292-294.

885. _____. "Another Fragment of the Metrical Psalms in the Eadwine Psalter." *Notes and Queries* 35 (1988): 434-436.

886. Prescott, A.L. "The Reputation of Clément Marot in Renaissance England." *Studies in the Renaissance* 18 (1971): 173-202.

887. Pulsiano, Phillip. "Defining the A-type (Vespasian) and D-type (Regius) Psalter-gloss Traditions." *English Studies* 72 (1991): 308-327.

888. _____. "Old English Glossed Psalters: Editions versus Manuscripts." *Manuscripta* 35 (1991): 75-95.

889. Quak, Arend. *Studien zu den altmittel- und altniederfränkischen Psalmen und Glossen.* Amsterdam Publikationen zur Sprache und Literatur 12. Amsterdam: Rodopi, 1973. 196p.

890. Raeder, Siegfried. *Das Hebräische bei Luther untersucht bis zum Ende der ersten Psalmenvorlesung.* Beiträge zur historischen Theologie 31. Tübingen: J.C.B. Mohr, 1961. vii+406p.

Reviewed by E.S. Gerstenberger in *JBL* 81 (1962): 206-207.

891. _____. *Die Benutzung des masoretischen Textes bei Luther in der Zeit zwischen der ersten und zweiten*

Psalmenvorlesung (1515-1518). Beiträge zur historischen Theologie 38. Tübingen: J.C.B. Mohr, 1967.

892. Rathmell, J.C.A., ed. *The Psalms of Sir Philip Sidney and the Countess of Pembroke*. The Stuart Editions. New York: New York University Press, 1963. 362p.

Sir Philip Sidney (1554-1586) is responsible for Psalms 1-43, the Countess of Pembroke (Lady Mary Sidney; 1561-1621)for Psalms 44-150.

893. Riese, Teut. von. *Die englische Psalmdictung im sechzehnten Jahrhundert*. Universitas-Archivanglistische Abteilung 4. Münster i. W: H. Buschmann, Abt. Helios-Verlag, 1937.

894. Rohr-Sauer, Philipp von. *English Metrical Psalms from 1600 to 1660. A Study in the Religious and Aesthetic Tendencies of the Period*. Freiburg im Breisgau: Poppen & Ortmann, 1938. 127p.

895. Rudick, M. "Two Notes on Surrey's Psalms." *Notes & Queries*, N.S., 22 (1975): 291-294.

896. Schöndorf, Kurt Erich. *Die Tradition der deutschen Psalmenübersetzung. Untersuchungen zur Verwandtschaft und Übersetzungstradition der Psalmenverdeutschung zwischen Notker und Luther*. Mitteldeutsche Forschungen 46. Cologne: Böhlau, 1967. xl+278p.

897. Sims, Phillip, and Scotty Gray. "Psalters of the Maurice Frost Collection at Southwestern Baptist Theological Seminary." *The Hymn* 30 (1979): 89-92.

898. Smith, Hallett. "English Metrical Psalms in the Sixteenth Century and their Literary Significance." *Huntington Library Quarterly* 9 (1946): 249-271.

899. Southall, R. "The Date of Wyatt's Psalms." *English Studies* 71 (1990): 497-500.

900. Stracke, J.R. "Eight Lambeth Psalter-Glosses." *Philological Quarterly* 53 (1974): 121-128.

901. Studley, M. "Milton and his Paraphrases of the Psalms." *Philological Quarterly* 4 (1925): 364-372.

902. Teudeloff, Friedrich. *Beiträge zur Uebersetzungstechnik der ersten gedruckten deutschen Bibel auf Grund der Psalmen.* Germanische Studien 21. Berlin: E. Ebering, 1922. Nedeln, Liechtenstein: Kraus Reprint, 1967. 188p.

903. Todd, R. "'So Well Attyr'd Abroad': A Background to the Sidney-Pembroke Psalter and Its Implications for the Seventeenth-Century Religious Lyric." *Texas Studies in Literature and Language* 29 (1987): 74-93.

904. ______. "Humanist Prosodic Theory, Dutch Synods, and the Poetics of the Sidney-Pembroke Psalter." *The Huntington Library Quarterly* 52 (1989): 273-293.

905. Twombly, R.G. "Thomas Wyatt's Paraphrase of the Penitential Psalms of David." *Texas Studies in Literature and Language* 12 (1970): 345-380.

906. Waller, G.F. "'This Matching of contraries': Calvinism and Courtly Philosophy in the Sidney Psalms." *English Studies* 55 (1974): 22-31.

907. Walter, J.M. "Jubilate Agno as Psalm." *Studies in English Literature 1500-1900* 20 (1980): 449-459.

908. Wyatt, Thomas (1503-1542). *Collected Poems of Sir Thomas Wyatt*, ed. K. Muir and P. Thompson. Liverpool English Texts and Studies. Liverpool: Liverpool University Press, 1969. xxvii+481p.

909. Zim, Rivkah. *English Metrical Psalms. Poetry as Praise and Prayer, 1535-1601.* Cambridge: Cambridge University Press, 1987. xvi+329p.

The 16th century was a time in which the best English lyric poets and writers began to imitate a wider range of psalm themes, tones and applications than had been the case previously. This resulted in numerous and varied metrical paraphrases of the psalms.

See also: 3583, 4515. 4516, 4288, 4354

F. Modern Translations

910. Aengenvoort, Johannes. "Die Psalmodie im 'Gotteslob.'" *Theologie und Glaube* 66 (1976): 120-132.

911. Arackal, Joseph. *The Psalms in Inclusive Language.* Collegeville, MN: The Liturgical Press, 1993. 216p.

912. Bailly, G. *Psautier Romain-Français.* Paris: Lethielleux, 1951. 619p.

Reviewed in *CBQ* 14 (1952): 208-209.

913. Beck, E., ed. *Die Psalmen. Der Ökumenische Text mit einer Einleitung und Erläuterung.* Düsseldorf: Patmos Verlag, 1979; Stuttgart: Deutsche Bibelstiftung, 1979. 150p. 2nd ed., 1977.

Critical review by Clemens Locher. "Der Psalter der 'Einheitsübersetzung' und die Textkritik." *Biblica* 58 (1977): 313-341; 59 (1978): 49-79.

914. *The Book of Psalms: A New Translation According to the Traditional Hebrew Text.* Philadelphia: The Jewish Publication Society of America, 1972.

915. Brandt, Leslie F. *God Is Here. Psalms/Now.* Art work by Corita Kent. St. Louis MO: Concordia Publishing House, 1973. 222p.

916. Buber, Martin. *Das Buch der Preisungen.* 8th ed. Heidelberg: Verlag Lambert Schneider, 1975.

917. Chamberlain, Gary. *The Psalms: A New Translation for Prayer and Worship.* Nashville, TN: The Upper Room, 1984. 186p.

918. Gerstenberger, Erhard, Konrad Jutzler and Hans Joachim Boecker. *Psalmen in der Sprache unserer Zeit.* Zürich: Benziger, 1972.

919. *Grail Breviary Psalter. The Daily Psalms, Canticles and Antiphons in Modern English.* London: The Grail, 1966.

920. Hadas, Gershon. *The Book of Psalms for the Modern Reader.* New York: Jonathan David Publishers, 1964. xii+266p.

921. Hanson, Richard S. *The Psalms in Modern Speech.* 3 vols. Philadelphia: Fortress Press, 1968. Vol. 1, xlii+80p; Vol. 2, 103p; Vol. 3, 124p.

This translation seeks to find language that communicates in contemporary idiom. It is also designed for choral recitation, as it attempts to bring out the ancient mode of recitation of each psalm. It depends heavily on the work of M. Dahood.

Reviewed by M. Dahood in *Biblica* 50 (1969): 425-426; P.L. Garber in *JBL* 88 (1969): 368-369.

922. *Holy Bible: 21st Century King James Version. Volume One: New Testament, Psalms, Proverbs, Ecclesiastes.* Gary, SD: Deuel Enterprises, Inc., 1991. xiii+248+474p.

923. *Inclusive-Language Psalms: Readings for Years A, B, & C* from *An Inclusive-Language Lectionary.* New York: The Pilgrim Press, 1987. 152p.

924. Jones, Owen. *The Psalms of David. The Great Illuminated Psalter Dedicated to Queen Victoria.* New York: Gallery Books, 1989. 108p.

925. Kleist, James A., and Thomas J. Lynam. *The Psalms in Rhythmic Prose. Translation based on the authorized Latin version rendered from the original texts by members of the Pontifical Biblical Institute.* Milwaukee: Bruce Publishing Co., (1954). xii+236p.

Reviewed in *CBQ* 18 (1956): 102-104.

926. Knox, Ronald. *The Psalms. A New Translation.* New York: Sheed & Ward, 1947. 239p.

927. Lamparter, Helmut. *Antworte Gott! Ausgewählte Psalmen.* Stuttgart: Calwer Verlag, 1982. 47p.

Twenty-two psalms in rhythmic and versified form.

928. Lattey, Cuthbert. *The Psalter in the Westminster Version of the Sacred Scriptures.* London: Sands, 1945. xvi+281p.

Seeks to reconstruct the original meter.
Reviewed by J.L. McKenzie in *CBQ* 8 (1946): 249-251.

929. Levi, Peter. *The Psalms.* Introduction by Rabbi Nicholas de Lange. New York: Penguin Books, 1976.

Attempts to present the basic Hebrew text simply and clearly. Reviewed by Robert Murray, "Presenting the Psalter Today," *The Heythrop Journal* 19 (1978): 173-174.

930. *Livre des Psaumes, Le. Texte hébreu avec traduction française d'après la Bible du Rabbinat.* New edition. Paris: Librairie Durlacher, 1957. 113p.

931. MacCauley, Sister Rose Agnes. *Vision 20/20. Twenty Psalms for the Twentieth Century.* Notre Dame, IN: Fides Publishers, 1971.

932. Mowinckel, Sigmund. "Bemerkninger til salmene i den norske bibeloversette." *Norsk Teologisk Tidsskrift* 63 (1962): 129-270.

933. Oosterhuis, Huub, Michel van der Plas, Pius Drijvers, Han Renckens, Frans Jozef van Beeck, David Smith, and Forrest Ingram. *Fifty Psalms: An Attempt at a New Translation.* New York: Herder and Herder, 1969. 156p.

934. Peterson, Eugene H. "Listen, Yahweh." *Christianity Today* 35 (January 14, 1991): 23-35.

Colloquial alternatives to Elizabethan rhythms in translations of the Psalms. Examples include Psalms 3, 5, 11, 14, 29.

935. Piatti, T. *Il Libro dei Salmi. Versione omòfona dall'originale ebraico criticamente e metricamente riconstrutto, con introduzione critica sulla poesia e la metrica ebraica.* Rome, 1954.

936. ______, and M. Imelda Bianchedi. *Nell'armonia dei Salmi. Versione poetica del Salterio su traduzione omofona del P. Piatti da M. Imelda Bianchedi.* Isola del Liri: M. Pisani, 1963. 245p.

937. *Prayer Book Psalter Revised, The.* New York: Church Hymnal Corporation, 1973.

A revision of the Prayer Book Psalter for Anglicans.

938. *The Psalms: An Inclusive Language Version Based on the Grail Translation from the Hebrew.* Chicago, IL: G.I.A. Publications, 1983, 1986. 216p.

939. *The Psalms: A New Translation: Translated from the Hebrew and Arranged for Singing to the Psalmody of Joseph Gelineau.* London: Colliers Fontana Books, 1963; Philadelphia: The Westminster Press, 1963. 255p. Paramus, NJ: Paulist Press, 1966. 258p.

940. *The Psalms. A New Translation for Worship.* London: Collins Liturgical Publications, 1977.

941. *The Psalms: Fides Translation.* Notre Dame, IN: Fides Press, 1963.

942. *Psalms for All Seasons.* Washington, DC: The Pastoral Press (National Association of Pastoral Musicians), 1987. Minister's edition, 164p; People's edition, 64p.

From the ICEL Liturgical Psalter Project. A collection of 23 of the most commonly used psalms, with notes on application in the liturgy. Inclusive language.

943. *The Psalter: A New Version for Public Worship and Private Devotion.* Introduction by Charles M. Guilbert. New York: Crossroad Books (Seabury Press), 1978.

944. *Psaumes, Les.* Paris: Desclée de Brouwer, 1973.

Translated from the MT by the monks of Saint-Lambert-les-Bois.

945. *Psautier chrétien.* 4 vols. Paris: Téqui, 1973-1976.

Volume 1 contains a translation of the Psalter from the Revised or Neo-Vulgate, done under the direction of Jean Gribomont; the Vulgate is chosen because it represents an enrichment of the Massoretic Text. Each psalm is given a Christian setting of some kind. Volumes 2 and 3, *La Tradition médite le Psautier Chrétien* (1973 and 1974), edited by Claude Jean-Nesmy, contains patristic interpretations of each psalm and of individual verses. Volume 4, *Parole et Esprit du Psautier Chrétien* (1976), by Jean-Nesmy, is a commentary on the psalms. He rejects all attempts to discover the original *Sitz im Leben* of the Hebrew psalms; the Christological interpretation is the only one recognized, and hostility is shown towards those who approach the psalms in a scientific manner.

946. *Psautier français: Une proposition oecuménique. Version nouvelle pour la prière, la lecture publique et le chant.* Paris: Cerf-Desclée, 1973.

947. *Le Psautier: Version oecumenique; texte liturgique.* Traduction approuvée par les Conférences épiscopales de Belgique, du Canada, de France, du Luxembourg, de Suisse et d'Afrique du Nord. Paris: Cerf, 1977. 381p.

A refinement of *Psautier français.*

Jean-Luc Vesco, "Traductions liturgiques du psautier." *La Maison-Dieu* 118 (1974): 76-86, reviews *Psautier Chrétien* (largely unsatisfactory for Christian liturgy), and *Psautier français,* a preliminary Psalter which has now become *Le Psautier: Version oecumenique; texte liturgique* (one of the best liturgical Psalters at the present time).

948. *Revised Psalms of the New American Bible, The.* Authorized by the Board of Trustees of the Confraternity of Christian Doctrine and approved by the Administrative Committee/Board of the National Conference of Catholic Bishops and the United States Catholic Conference. New York: Catholic Book, 1992.

949. Rosenberg, David. *Blues of the Sky. Interpreted from the Original Hebrew Book of Psalms.* New York: Harper and Row, 1976.

Twenty psalms are here put into poetic form by a poet, who attempts to translate not the precise words but "the original atmosphere."

950. Schoenbechler, Roger. *Book of Psalms. An Interpretative Version in Measured Rhythm.* Large Print Edition for Easy Reading. Collegeville, MN: The Liturgical Press, 1978.

Based on the 1945 Latin Psalter and on the revised Latin text as given in the new *Liturgia Horarum* (1972-1974). The "measured rhythm" does not coincide with the parallel poetic lines of the Hebrew.

951. Schonfeld, S. *A New-Old Rendering of the Psalms.* London: The Uniby Press, 1980. xvi+288p.

952. Schreck, Nancy, and Maureen Leach. *Psalms Anew: In Inclusive Language.* Winona, MN: St. Mary's Press, 1984. 200p.

953. Schuller, Eileen. "Inclusive-Language Psalters." *The Bible Today* 26 (1988): 173-179.

954. Shepherd, Massey H., Jr. *A Liturgical Psalter for the Christian Year.* Minneapolis, MN: Augsburg Publishing House, 1976.

955. Sullivan, Francis Patrick. *Lyric Psalms: Half a Psalter.* Washington, DC: The Pastoral Press, 1983. 191p.

956. _____. *Tragic Psalms.* Washington, DC: The Pastoral Press, 1987. 225p.

957. Thomas, D. Winton. *The Text of the Revised Psalter.* London: SPCK, 1963.

958. _____. "The Revised Psalter." *Theology* 66 (1963): 504-507.

959. Tournay, Raymond-Jacques. "A propos du 'Psautier de Jérusalem." *Lumière et Vie* 40 (1991): 41-53.

960. Untermeyer, Louis, ed. *Songs of Joy from the Books of Psalms.* Illustrated by Joan Berg Victor. Cleveland, OH: The William Collins + World Publishing Co., 1967.

A selection of Psalms written in the King James Version, illustrated with pencil drawings.

961. Waltke, Bruce K. "The *New International Version* and Its Textual Principles in the Book of Psalms." *Journal of the Evangelical Theological Society* 32 (1989): 17-26.

962. Willesen, Folker. "Bemerkninger til proeveoversaettelsen af Psalmenes Borg." *Dansk Teologisk Tiddskrift* 42 (1979): 153-184.

A review essay of the Book of Psalms published in 1977 by the Danish Bible Society.

963. Wright, W. Aldis, ed. *The Hexaplar Psalter.* Cambridge: Cambridge University Press, 1911. Anglistica & Americana 55. Reprint, Hildesheim and New York: G. Olms, 1969. vi+389p.

Contains six versions arranged in parallel columns: Coverdale (1535); Coverdale *revised,* i.e. the Great Bible (1539); Geneva (1560); Bishops' (1568); "Authorised" (1611); "Revised" (1885). These versions are reproduced in the original spelling. In the Great Bible (= Prayer Book) words and phrases found in the Vulgate, but absent from the Hebrew, are printed within the brackets assigned them in

1539 (These brackets have disappeared from modern editions of the Prayer Book).

964. Zerr, Bonaventure. *The Mount Angel Psalter: The Psalms Translated from the Hebrew.* Mount Angel Abbey, OR: Mount Angel Abbey. Revised edition: *The Psalms*, by the Monks of Mount Angel Abbey. St. Benedict. Mount Angel Abbey, OR: Mount Angel Abbey, 1975. Reprinted as *Psalms: A New Translation.* New York, NY, and Ramsey, NJ: Paulist Press, 1979. xii+331p.

A modern lyrical translation that attempts to make use of new information about the thought world and cultural milieu of ancient Israel, relying heavily on the work of Dahood.

965. Zink, J. *Er wird meine Stimme hören. Psalmen des Alten und Neuen Testaments.* Stuttgart: Kreuz Verlag, 1967. Reprinted as Gütersloher Taschenbüchern/Siebenstern 361, Gütersloh: Gerd Mohn, 1980. 126p.

A fresh translation of the Psalms, arranged according to themes, for the purpose of prayer.

4. Poetry

966. Airoldi, Norberto. "L'antico mondo poetico dei Salmisti [The Ancient Poetic World of the Psalmists]." *Bibbia e Oriente* 14 (1972): 97-105.

967. Alden, Robert L. "Chiastic Psalms: A Study in the Mechanics of Semitic Poetry in Psalms 1-50, 51-100, 101-150." *Journal of the Evangelical Theological Society* 17 (1974): 11-28; 19 (1976): 191-200; 21 (1978): 199-210.

968. Alonso Schökel, Luis. *Treinta Salmos: Poesía y oración. Institución San Jerónimo para la investigación bíblica.* Estudios de Antiguo Testamento 2. Valencia: Institución San Jerónimo, 1981; Madrid: Ediciones Cristiandad, 1981. 470p.

Psalms 3, 4, 8, 11, 19, 23, 29, 30, 37, 42/42, 45, 46, 50 and 51 (treated as a redactional unit), 58, 65, 73, 76, 82, 90, 98, 121-125, 136, 148, 149.
Reviewed in *CBQ* 45 (1983): 446-448.

969. ______. "The Imaginative Language of the Psalms." (Spanish). 1982. Reprinted in *Hermeneutica de la Palabra. II. Interpretación Literaria de Textos Bíblicos.* Academia Christiana 38. 271-284. Madrid: Ediciones Cristiandad, 1987. 542p.

970. ______. *A Manual of Hebrew Poetics.* Translated from the Spanish by Adrian Graffy. Subsidia Biblica 11. Rome: Pontifical Biblical Institute, 1988. x+228p.

971. Alter, Robert. "From Line to Story in Biblical Verse." *Poetics Today* 4 (1983): 615-637.

An examination of the striking avoidance of narrative in biblical Hebrew poetry.

972. ______. *The Art of Biblical Poetry.* New York: Basic Books, 1985.

973. ______. "The Psalms -- Beauty Heightened Through Poetic Structure." *Bible Review* 2 (3,1986): 28-41.

974. ______. "The Characteristics of Ancient Hebrew Poetry." Chap. in *The Literary Guide to the Bible,* ed. Robert Alter and Frank Kermode. 611-624. Cambridge, MA: The Belknap Press of Harvard University Press, 1987. 678p.

The two most common structures of biblical poetry are (1) a movement of intensification of images, concepts, themes through a sequence of lines, and (2) a narrative movement -- which most often pertains to the development of metaphorical acts but can also refer to literal events.

975. Andersen, Francis I. "Orthography in Repetitive Parallelism." *Journal of Biblical Literature* 89 (1970): 343-344.

976. Avishur, Yitzhak. *Stylistic Studies of Word-Pairs in Biblical and Ancient Semitic Literatures.* Alter Orient und Altes

Testament 210. Neukirchen-Vluyn: Neukirchener Verlag, 1984; Kevelaer: Butzon & Bercker, 1984. xii+804p.

977. Balocco, A. "'Ritornelli' e 'Selah' nella scansione stróﬁca dei Salmi." *Revista Biblica (Italiana)* 19 (1971): 187-201.

978. Barré, Lloyd M. "*Halělû yāh*: A Broken Inclusion." *Catholic Biblical Quarterly* 45 (1983): 195-200.

979. Barré. Michael L. "The Formulaic Pair טוב (ו) חסד in the Psalter." *Zeitschrift für die alttestamentliche Wissenschaft* 98 (1986): 100-105.

980. Bazak, Jacob/Yaaqov. *Structures and Contents in the Psalms: Geometric Structural Patterns in the Seven Alphabetic Psalms.* Tel Aviv: Dvir, 1984. (Hebrew)

981. _____. "הערות לבקורתו של מיכאל שׁשר." *Beth Mikra* 32 (1986/1987): 95-98.

Responds to Shashar's article, citing references to the visual arrangement of poetry in ancient Greek poetry.

982. _____. "Numerical Devices in Biblical Poetry." *Vetus Testamentum* 38 (1988): 332-337.

Psalms 23:4; 92:9; 81:9; and 34:7,8 are constructed through numerical techniques.

983. _____. "Unrecognized Literary Embellishment in Biblical Poetry -- Arithmetic Decoration." *Beth Mikra* 34 (1988/1989): 39-40. (Hebrew)

Arithmetic principles, which were first applied to the Bible in the sixteenth century, have been found to underlie the structure of literary works by Edmund Spenser, John Dryden, and John Milton. The main concept of several Psalms (e.g., Psalms 1, 23, 92, 9, 33, 25, 95, 34, 107, 81, and 104) is located at their arithmetic center.

984. Beaucamp, E. "Structure Strophique des Psaumes." *Recherches de Science Religieuse* 56 (1968): 199-224.

985. Bee, R.E. "The Mode of Composition and Statistical Scansion." *Journal for the Study of the Old Testament* 6 (1978): 58-68.

986. ______. "The Use of Syllable Counts in Textual Analysis." *Journal for the Study of the Old Testament* 10 (1978): 68-70.

987. Bélanger, J. "Traduction du Psautier; la strophique des psaumes." *Meta* 15 (1970): 18-25.

988. Berlin, Adele. "Grammatical Aspects of Biblical Parallelism." *Hebrew Union College Annual* 50 (1979): 17-43. Reprinted in *Beyond Form Criticism: Essays in Old Testament Literary Criticism,* ed. Paul R. House. Sources for Biblical and Theological Studies 2. 311-348. Winona Lake, IN: Eisenbrauns, 1992.

Grammatical parallelism is "the alteration of grammatical structure in parallel stichs, or, better, the pairing of two different grammatical structures in parallel stichs." Psalm 92 serves as an example.

989. ______. *The Dynamics of Biblical Parallelism.* Bloomington, IN: Indiana University Press, 1985. xii+179p.

Roman Jakobson takes a broad approach to parallelism, defining it as the "phenomenon of combining elements which are in some way linguistically equivalent." Thus parallelism is not confined to the level of the couplet but includes the entire poem. Four aspects of parallelism are examined: grammatical, lexical, semantic, and phonological. Reviewed in *CBQ* 50 (1988): 107-108.

990. ______. "Lexical Cohesion and Biblical Interpretation." *Hebrew Studies* 30 (1989): 29-40.

"If word X is used in connection with idea A and then with idea B, the two ideas are in some way equated, or drawn together in a unified field of vision." The examples include Psalms 25:2-3, 111:9-10, 125:1-2, and 147:4-5.

991. ______. *Biblical Poetry through Medieval Jewish Eyes.* Indiana Studies in Biblical Literature. Bloomington and Indianapolis, IN: Indiana University, 1991. xvii+205p.

A survey of the views on biblical poetry current among representative medieval and Renaissance Jewish scholars, followed by a more detailed study of 17 authors from the 9th-17th centuries.

992. Bickell, Gustav. *Metrices biblicae regulae exemplis illustratae.* Innsbruck: Wagner, 1879.

Hebrew poetry follows the method of Syriac poetry, where the measure of the verse is marked by regular alternation of accented and unaccented syllables. As a rule, the accent is on the penult. The constant alternation of rise and fall only allows for iambic and trochaic feet. Frequent altering of vowel pronunciation and numerous alterations of the consonantal text undergird this theory.

993. ______. *Carmina Veteris Testamenti metrice.* Innsbruck: Wagner, 1882.

994. ______. *Dichtungen der Hebräer.* Innsbruck: Wagner, 1882-1883.

995. ______. "Die hebräische Metrik." *Zeitschrift der Deutschen Morgenländischen Gesellschaft* 34 (1880): 557-563; 35 (1881): 415-422,

996. Birkeland, H. *Akzent und Vokalismus im althebräischen.* Skrifter utgitt av Det Norske Videnskaps-Akademi i Oslo, II Hist.-Filos. Klasse II/3. Oslo: Jacob Dybwad, 1940. 130p.

997. Bliese, Loren F. "Structurally Marked Peak in Psalms 1-24." *OPTAT: Occasional Papers in Translation and Text Linguistics* 4 (1990): 265-321.

In Psalms 1-24, there are 28 metrical chiasms and 12 metrically homogeneous line sequences. The former are used to mark a central peak, the latter to indicate a final peak.

998. Boling, Robert G. "'Synonymous' Parallelism in the Psalms." *Journal of Semitic Studies* 5 (1960): 221-255.

999. Bratcher, Robert G. "Dividing the Psalms into Strophes." *The Bible Translator* 29 (1978): 425-427.

1000. Breck, John. "Biblical Chiasmus: Exploring Structure for Meaning." *Biblical Theology Bulletin* 17 (1987): 70-74.

1001. Brongers, Hendrik Antonie. "Merismus, Synekdoche und Hendiadys in der Bibel-Hebräischen Sprache." *Oudtestamentische Studiën* 14 (1965): 100-114.

1002. _____. "Alternative Interpretationen des sogenannten Waw copulativum." *Zeitschrift für die alttestamentliche Wissenschaft* 90 (1978): 273-277.

1003. Bronznick, Norman M. "'Metathetic Parallelism' -- An Unrecognized Subtype of Synonymous Parallelism." *Hebrew Annual Review* 3 (1979): 25-39.

1004. Bruno, D. Arvid. *Der Rhythmus der alttestamentlichen Dichtung -- Eine Untersuchung über die Psalmen I-LXII.* Leipzig: A. Deichertsche Verlagsbuchhandlung D. Werner Scholl, 1930. iv+349p.

1005. _____. *Die Psalmen. Eine rhythmische und textkritische Untersuchung.* Stockholm: Almqvist & Wiksell, 1954. 282p.

1) The rhythmical element is the accented word; (2) the rhythmical unit is the strophe; (3) a poem is a series of rhythmically equal strophes (except for certain isolated strophes); (4) an extended portion of the Old Testament writings lend themselves to this measurement.

Reviewed by B.M. Waggoner in *JBL* 75 (1956): 156-157.

1006. Budde, K. "Das hebräische Klagelied." *Zeitschrift für die alttestamentliche Wissenschaft* 2 (1882): 1-52.

"A" verses in laments have a tendency to be somewhat longer than corresponding "B"'s, "A" having generally three stresses and "B" usually having two; this is the *qinah* or lament meter.

1007. Byington, Steven T. "A Mathematical Approach to Hebrew Metres." *Journal of Biblical Literature* 66 (1947): 63-77.

1008. Ceresko, Anthony R. "The Chiastic Word Pattern in Hebrew." *Catholic Biblical Quarterly* 38 (1976): 303-311.

1009. ______. "Function of Chiasmus in Hebrew Poetry." *Catholic Biblical Quarterly* 40 (1978): 1-10.

1010. ______. "Recent Study of Hebrew Poetry: Implications for Theology and Worship." *Toronto Journal of Theology* 1 (1985): 98-112.

1011. Cloete, W.T.W. "The Concept of Metre in Old Testament Studies." *Journal of Semitics* 1 (1989): 39-53.

1012. Collins, Terence. "Line-forms in Hebrew Poetry." *Journal of Semitic Studies* 23 (1978): 228-244.

Both a parallelism of meaning (semantic) and a metrical (phonetic) approach are unsatisfactory. Better is a new (syntactical) method for the analysis of Hebrew poetry: "an analysis of lines based on grammatical structure."

1013. Condamin, Albert. *Poèmes de la Bible: Avec une introduction sur lat strophique hébraique.* Paris: Beauchesne, 1933. vii+285p.

Instead of the alternating strophe of Zenner, there is a mediating strophe between the choral responses.

1014. Craigie, Peter C. "The Comparison of Hebrew Poetry." *Semitics* 4 (1974): 10-21.

1015. Cross, Frank Moore, Jr, and David Noel Freedman. *Studies in Ancient Yahwistic Poetry.* Ph.D. dissertation, Harvard University, 1950. Reprinted as Society of Biblical Literature Dissertation Series 21; Missoula, MT: 1975. vii+191p.

Reviewed by M. Dahood in *JBL* 96 (1977): 581-582.

1016. Crumpacker, Mary M. "Formal Analysis and the Psalms." *Journal of the Evangelical Theological Society* 24 (1981): 11-21.

Formal analysis is a technique for approaching poems as artistic wholes to discover a system of inner relationships in which form and content are inseparable. This is applied to Psalms 1 and 51.

1017. Culley, Robert C. *Oral Formulaic Language in the Biblical Psalms.* Near and Middle East Series 4. Toronto: University of Toronto Press, 1967. 137p.

Psalms with high formulaic content are more likely to be oral formulaic compositions or to come from a period when this form of composition was being practiced. The major device in Hebrew oral composition was the formula.

Reviewed in *CBQ* 30 (1968): 438-439.

1018. Dahood, Mitchell. "A New Metrical Pattern in Biblical Poetry." *Catholic Biblical Quarterly* 29 (1967): 574-582.

1019. ______. "Additional Pairs of Parallel Words in the Psalter and in Ugaritic. In *Forschung zur Bibel. Wort, Lied und Gottespruch. Beiträge zur Septuaginta. Festschrift für Joseph Ziegler*, ed. Rudolph Schnackenburg and Josef Schreiner. 2 vols. Vol. 2, 35-40. Würzburg: Echter Verlag, 1972.

1020. Fecht, Gerhard. *Metrik des Hebräischen und Phönischen.* Ägypten und Altes Testament: Studien zu Geschichte, Kultur und Religion Ägyptens und des Alten Testaments 19. Wiesbaden: Harrassowitz, 1990. viii+211p.

A study of metrics according to quantity, accent and syllable-counting, largely following J. Ley and E. Sievers. Prose and poetic passages scanned include Psalms 124 and 139. Phoenician inscriptions are also scanned.

1021. Fensham, F.C. "The Use of the Suffix Conjugation and the Prefix Conjugation in a Few Old Hebrew Poems." *Journal of Northwest Semitic Languages* 6 (1978): 9-18.

1022. Freedman, David Noel. "Acrostics and Metrics in Hebrew Poetry." *Harvard Theological Review* 65 (1972): 367-392. Reprinted in *Pottery, Poetry, and Prophecy: Studies in Early Hebrew Poetry.* 51-76. Winona Lake, IN: Eisenbrauns, 1980. xiii+376.

1023. ______. "Acrostic Poems in the Hebrew Bible: Alphabetic and Otherwise." *Catholic Biblical Quarterly* 48 (1986): 408-431.

A study of the metrical structure of alphabetic acrostic poems in the Hebrew Bible, with special attention to Lamentations 5 and Psalms 33 and 94. All three poems are actually non-alphabetic acrostics of 22 or 23 lines.

1024. Garr, W. Randall. "The Qinah: A Study of Poetic Meter, Syntax and Style." *Zeitschrift für die alttestamentliche Wissenschaft* 95 (1983): 54-75.

1025. Geller, Stephen A. *Parallelism in Early Biblical Poetry.* Harvard Semitic Monographs 20. Missoula, MT: Scholars Press, 1979. 389p.

Reviewed by D.K. Stuart in *JBL* 100 (1981): 272-273.

1026. Gevirtz, Stanley. *Patterns in the Early Poetry of Israel.* Studies in Ancient Oriental Civilization 32. Chicago: University of Chicago Press, 1963.

Reviewed by D.N. Freedman in *JBL* 83 (1964): 201-203.

1027. Goldingay, John. "Repetition and Variation in the Psalms." *Jewish Quarterly Review* 68 (1978): 146-151.

Delitzsch observed that refrain-like thoughts in the psalms are not repeated exactly. Many refrains do occur exactly, but others with variations have several possible explanations.

1028. Gray, George Buchanan. *The Forms of Hebrew Poetry considered with Special Reference to the Criticism and Interpretation of the Old Testament.* London: Hodder and Stroughton, 1915. Reprinted, with a Prolegomenon by David Noel Freedman (vii-lvi), New York: KTAV

Publishing House, 1972. 303p. "Prolegomenon" by Freedman reprinted in *Pottery, Poetry, and Prophecy: Studies in Early Hebrew Poetry.* 23-50. Winona Lake, IN: Eisenbrauns, 1980.

1029. Grimme, Hubert. "Abriss der biblisch-hebräischen Metrik." *Zeitschrift der Deutschen Morgenländische Gesellschaft* 50 (1896): 529-584; 51 (1897): 683-712.

1030. _____. *Grundzüge der hebräischen Accent- und Vocallehre.* Collectanea Friburgensia 5. Freiburg in Switzerland: Kommissionsverlag der Universitäts-buchhandlung (B. Veith), 1896.

Vowel-signs actually receive a very different value from that assigned to them by others. Each syllable and each syllable beat is given a definite quantity, a definite number of *morae.* Every final principal-tone syllable of an act of speech counts as a rise; whether other syllables are to be reckoned rises or not is determined by counting, according to fixed rules, the value of the *morae* of the syllables which fall within the same sphere. The number of rises determines the species of verse. There are verses (*i.e.*, lines) with 2, 3, 4, 5 rises, but the verse with 2 rises occurs only as an accompanying meter to that with 4 and 5 rises. Very few changes in the text are needed.

1031. _____. *Psalmenprobleme. Untersuchungen über Metrik, Strophik und Paseq des Psalmenbuches.* Collectanea Friburgensia, N.F., 3. Freiburg in Switzerland: Kommissionsverlag der Universitätsbuchhandlung (B. Veith), 1902. 204p.

1. Meter in the Psalms. Overview of the Rules of Hebrew Meter. Emendations with Particular Attention to Metrical Form. 2. Psalms with Changing Meter. 3. On Strophes in the Psalms. 4. *Paseq-L^{e}garmeh* in the Psalms.

1032. Grol, H.W.M. van. "Paired Tricola in the Psalms, Isaiah and Jeremiah." *Journal for the Study of the Old Testament* 25 (1983): 55-73.

A large number of all pairs of tricolon-bicolon (and vice versa) occurring in the Bible have to be described as paired tricola.

1033. ______. "De exegeet als restaurateur en interpreet. Een verhandeling over de bijbelse poëtica met Ps. 121 als exempel." *Bijdragen: Tijdschrift voor Filosofie en Theologie* 44 (1983): 234-261, 350-365.

1034. Grossberg, Daniel. "The Disparate Elements of the Inclusio in Psalms." *Hebrew Annual Review* 6 (1982): 97-104.

A study of inclusion that brackets an entire psalm and whose morphology, phonetics, semantics or syntax are altered in the closing element (Psalms 26, 29, 47, 82 and 97). The variations were prompted by an artistic desire to guard against mechanical composition or monotony. The result is an element of surprise into an overall impression of symmetry and unity.

1035. ______. *Centripetal and Centrifugal Structures in Biblical Poetry.* Society of Biblical Literature Monograph Series 39. Atlanta, GA: Scholars Press, 1989. 111p.

"Centripetal" features highlight the unity of the whole; "centrifugal" emphasize the parts. Concentration is focused on the Songs of Ascent (Psalms 120-134), the Song of Songs, and Lamentations. Centrifugal and centripetal features are balanced in the Songs of Ascent; Song of Songs is near the centrifugal extreme; Lamentations is the most centripetal of the three.

1036. Grossman, William. *Euphony in the Book of Psalms* (תפארת הלשון בספר תהלים). (Hebrew) Brooklyn, NY: "Ezra" Linotyping and Printing, 1952. 61p.

Stylistic rules that govern the diction of the Bible in general and of the Psalter in particular.

Reviewed by M. Tsevat in *JBL* 75 (1956): 160.

1037. ______. *Poetic Devices in the Book of Psalms* (דרכי המלישה בספר תהלים). (Hebrew) New York: Bloch, 1954. 32p.

Reviewed by M. Tsevat in *JBL* 75 (1956): 160.

1038. Gunkel, Hermann. "The Poetry of the Psalms: Its Literary History and Its Application to the Dating of the Psalms." In *Old Testament Essays.* Edited by D.C. Simpson. 118-142. London: Griffin, 1927.

1039. Herder, J.G. *The Spirit of Hebrew Poetry.* 1782-83. Translated by James Marsh. Burlington, VT: E. Smith, 1833. Reprint, Naperville, IL: Aleph Press, 1971.

Parallelism is the force underlying the development of meter.

1040. Houk, Cornelius B. "Syllables and Psalms: A Statistical Linguistic Analysis." *Journal for the Study of the Old Testament* 14 (1979): 55-62.

A syllable-word structure analysis of Psalms 42-43, 66, 102, 130, and 146.

1041. Hugger, Pirmin. "Die Alliteration im Psalter." In *Forschung zur Bibel. Wort, Lied und Gottespruch. Beiträge zur Septuaginta. Festschrift für Joseph Ziegler*, ed. Rudolph Schnackenburg and Josef Schreiner. 2 vols. Vol. 2, 81-90. Würzburg: Echter Verlag, 1972.

A study of the history of alliteration, its use in Semitic and Germanic languages, and an almost complete listing of alliteration possibilities for the Psalter.

1042. Hunter, J.H. "The Irony of Meaning: Intertextuality in Hebrew Poetical Texts." *Journal of Semitics* 1 (1989): 229-243.

The two sides of intertextuality (borrowing vs. originality) should both be recognized in order to do justice to the creative abilities of individual authors in texts. This is illustrated by Psalms 114 and 115.

1043. Kirkconnell, W. "Translating the Psalter; the Problem of Metre." *Meta* 15 (1970): 10-17.

1044. Kleist, J.A. "Toward a More Rhythmical Rendering of the Psalms." *Catholic Biblical Quarterly* 11 (1949): 66-75.

1045. Kodell, Jerome. "The Poetry of the Psalms." *The Bible Today* 65 (1973): 1107-1113.

1046. Korpel, Marjo C.A., and Johannes C. de Moor. "Fundamentals of Ugaritic and Hebrew Poetry." *Ugarit-Forschungen* 18 (1986): 173-212. Reprinted in *The Structural Analysis of Biblical and Canaanite Poetry*, ed. Willem van der Meer and Johannes C. de Moor. Journal for the Study of the Old Testament Supplement 74; 1-61; Sheffield: JSOT Press, 1988.

1047. Krašovec, Jože. *Der Merismus im biblischen-hebräischen und nordwest-semitischen.* 1977. Biblica Orientalia 33. Rome: Pontifical Biblical Institute, 1977. xvi+184p.

Reviewed in *CBQ* 40 (1978): 246-248.

1048. ______. "Merism-Polar Expression in Biblical Hebrew." *Biblica* 64 (1983): 231-239.

1049. ______. *Antithetic Structure in Biblical Hebrew Poetry.* Supplements to Vetus Testamentum 35. Leiden: E.J. Brill, 1984. xiv+143p.

1050. Kugel, James L. *The Idea of Biblical Poetry. Parallelism and its History.* New Haven, CT: Yale University Press, 1981. xii+339p.

Parallelism is, indeed, of the essence of biblical poetry, but its effect is not to produce a simple equation (such terms as "synthetic" and "antithetic" parallelism are meaningless): parallelism always implies a "plus" or a "what's more." It is found almost as much in "prose" as it is in "poetry." What constitutes biblical poetry? What is called biblical "poetry" is "a complex of heightening effects used in combinations and intensities that vary widely from composition to composition." Poetry and prose are to be distinguished only in degree. Meter is not a distinguishing factor.

A critical review by Alan Cooper, "On Reading Biblical Poetry." *Maarov* 4 (1987): 221-241. Reviewed by Francis Landy, "Poetics and Parallelism: Some Comments on James Kugel's *The Idea of Biblical Poetry.*" *Journal for the Study of the Old Testament* 28 (1984): 61-87; Patrick D. Miller, Jr. "Meter, Parallelism and Tropes: The Search for Poetic Style." *Journal for the Study of the Old Testament* 28 (1984): 99-106; Wilfred G.E.Watson. "A Review of Kugel's *The Idea of Biblical Poetry.*" *Journal for the Study of the Old Testament* 28 (1984): 89-98.

1051. ______. "Some Thoughts on Future Research into Biblical Style: Addenda to *The Idea of Biblical Poetry.*" *Journal for the Study of the Old Testament* 28 (1984): 107-117.

1052. Kunz, Lucas. "Zur symmetrischen Struktur der Psalmen." In *Misc. H. Anglés I.* 453-464. Barcelona: Consejo Superior de Investigaciones Cientificas, 1961.

1053. ______. "Untersuchungen zur Textstruktur solistischer Psalmen." *Kirchenmusikalisches Jahrbuch (Köln)* 45 (1961): 1-37.

Attempts to find the same number of words for each strophe.

1054. Ley, Julius. *Die metrischen Formen der hebräischen Poesie. Des Vers- und Strophenbaues in der hebräischen Poesie. Nebst Analyse einer Auswahl von Psalmen und anderen strophischen Dichtungen der verschiedenen Vers- und Strophenarten mit vorangehendem Abriss der Metrik der hebräischen Poesie.* Halle: Buchhandlung des Waisenhauses, 1875. ix+266p.

1055. ______. *Leitfaden der Metrik der hebräischen Poesie nebst dem ersten Buch der Psalmen. Nach rhythmischer Vers- und Strophenabteilung mit metrischer Analyse.* Halle: Buchhandlung des Waisenhauses, 1887. vi+60p.

Meter depends upon accents, and relies upon alliteration, assonance and rhyme as subordinate features. Every word that conveys an idea has a tone-syllable, certain words may have more than one. Every tone-syllable forms, along with the preceding unaccented syllables and the following syllable of the falling tone, one meter. The number of unaccented syllables makes no difference, so that a significant word of a single syllable may have the same metrical value as a whole series of syllables. The kind of verse is determined by the number of such meters. The unit ('verse') is the verse formed by parallel lines; the caesuras serve to divide the individual lines from one another. In this way it becomes possible to unite lines of very different lengths in the same verse. For the most part, we may accept the traditional vocalization and accentuation. Stress is the sole significant element in Hebrew poetry.

1056. ______. "Origenes über hebräische Metrik." *Zeitschrift für die alttestamentliche Wissenschaft* 12 (1892): 212-217.

1057. Loretz, Oswald. *Die Psalmen. Teil II. Beitrag der Ugarit-Texte zum Verständnis von Kolometrie und Textologie der Psalmen, Ps. 90-150.* Alter Orient und Altes Testament, 207/2. Kevelaer: Butzon & Bercker, 1979; Neukirchen-Vluyn: Neukirchener Verlag, 1979. viii+522p.

A transliterated consonantal text of Psalms 90-150 set out in cola.

Reviewed in *CBQ* 43 (1981): 279-280.

1058. _____, and Ingo Kottsieper. *Colometry in Ugaritic and Biblical Poetry. Introduction, Illustrations and Topical Bibliography.* Akademische Bibliotek: Ugaritisch-Biblische Literatur 5. Altenberge and Soest: CIS Verlag, 1987. 166p.

1059. Lowth, Richard. *De sacra poesi Hebraeorum praelectiones academicae Oxonii habitae.* Lectures delivered at Oxford. 1753. Translated from the Latin by G. Gregory and published as *Lectures on the Sacred Poetry of the Hebrews.* 2 vols. London: J. Johnson, 1787. Reprinted, Andover, MA: Codman, 1829. Reprinted, New York: Garland Publishing, Inc., 1971. Vol. I, 387p; Vol. II, 449p.

1060. Lugt, P. van der. *Strofische Structuren in de Bijbels-Hebreeuwse Poëzie. De geschiedenis van het onderzoek en een bijdrage tot de theorievorming omtrent de strofenbouw van de Psalmen.* Dissertationes Neerlandicae. Series Theologica. Kampen: Kok, 1980. xiv+614p.

A review of the history of strophic analysis of the psalms, a study of the nature of the poetic forms and a detailed analysis of more than fifty psalms, looking both at indications of regularity and diversity, and commenting on details of word echoes and marker words.

Reviewed in *CBQ* 44 (1982): 655-657.

1061. Magne, Jean. "Répétitions de mots et exégèse dans quelques Psaumes et le Pater." *Biblica* 39 (1958): 177-197.

Psalms 1, 29, 51, 91, 137, Matthew 6:9-13.

1062. Magonet, Jonathan. "Some Concentric Structures in Psalms." *The Heyworth Journal* 23 (1982): 365-376.

1063. Miller, Patrick D., Jr. "Synonymous-Sequential Parallelism in the Psalms." *Biblica* 61 (1980): 256-260.

A familiar but little recognized form of Hebrew poetry is synonymous-sequential parallelism. It occurs when "two elements of a sequential relationship are broken up by a pair of synonymous or nearly parallel elements." The examples include Psalms 18:42, 22:22, and 88:2.

1064. Monloubou, Louis. "Les psaumes -- le symbole -- le corps." *Nouvelle Revue Théologique* 102 (1980): 35-42.

1065. ______. *L'Imaginaire des Psalmistes: Psaumes et Symboles.* Lectio Divina 101. Paris: Éditions du Cerf, 1980. 136p.

The texts have power to produce something. Is there a symbolic system that helps us understand and appreciate the ancient poetry of the psalms? Helpful in this regard is G. Durand (*L'imagination symbolique*, 1968), whose theory of the organization of symbols understands symbols as primordial gestures through which the human mind constructs its symbolic world. Thus bodily gestures and symbolic presentations come together. There are three basic symbolic patterns: standing, sitting and walking. The standing person symbolizes the place of humanity in creation and its sense of power and grandeur. The sitting person symbolizes the intimate life of the home, security and peace. The walking person symbolizes humanity on the move, mastering the universe. Part I studies the imaginary in the Psalms. Part II deals with understanding the structure of the symbolism used in the Psalms.

Reviewed by J.W. Betlyon in *JBL* 101 (1982): 604-605; reviewed also in *CBQ* 44 (1982): 299-300.

1066. Moor, Johannes C. de. "The Art of Versification in Ugarit and Israel." In *Studies in Bible and the Ancient Near East. Present to Samuel E. Loewenstamm on his Seventieth Birthday,* ed. Y. Avishur and J. Blau. 136ff. Jerusalem: E. Rubinstein's Publishing House, 1978.

1067. _____. "The Art of Versification in Ugarit and Israel. II: The Formal Structure." *Ugarit-Forschungen* 10 (1978): 187-217.

1068. _____. "The Art of Versification in Ugarit and Israel. III: Further Illustrations of the Principle of Expansion." *Ugarit-Forschungen* 12 (1980): 311-315.

1069. Mowinckel, Sigmund. "Zum Problem der hebräischen Metrik." In *Festschrift Alfred Bertholet zum 80. Geburtstag,* ed. W. Baumgartner and Others. 379-394. Tübingen: J.C.B. Mohr (Paul Siebeck), 1950.

1070. _____. "Zur hebräischen Metrik II." *Studia Theologica cura ordinum Theologorum Scandinavorum edita* 7 (1953): 54-85.

1071. _____. "Metrischer Aufbau und Textkritik an Ps 8 illustriert." In *Studia Orientalia Johanno Pedersen Septuagenario ... dicata.* 250-262. Hauniae: Einar Munksgaard, 1953.

1072. _____. "Marginalien zur hebräischen Metrik." *Zeitschrift für die alttestamentlichen Wissenschaft* 67 (1956): 97-123.

1073. _____. *Real and Apparent Tricola in Hebrew Psalm Poetry.* Avhandinger utgitt av Det Norske Videnskaps - Akademi i Oslo, II. Hist. Filos Klasse, II, 1957. Kristiania: Jacob Dybwad: 1958.

1074. _____. "Notes on the Psalms." *Studia Theologica cur ordinum Theologorum Scandinavorum edita* 13 (1959): 134-165.

1075. Müller, David Heinrich (1846-1912). *Strophenbau und Responsion.* Biblischen Studien II. Vienna: A. Hölder, 1898. 2nd ed., 1904. 86p.

Strophes are based upon three fundamental principles -- the *responsio*, the *concatenatio*, and the *inclusio.* Examples include Psalms 46, 54, 64, 76, 107, 119, 150.

1076. _____. *Komposition und Strophenbau.* Biblischen Studien III. Vienna: A. Hölder, 1907.

Includes a study of Psalm 105.

1077. _____. *Strophenbau und Responsion in Ezechiel und den Psalmen. Biblische Studien* IV. Vienna: A. Hölder, 1908. 64p.

Includes studies of Psalms 46, 54, 64, 76, 107, 119, 140, 105, and 78.

1078. O'Connor, Michael Patrick. *Hebrew Verse Structure.* Winona Lake,IN: Eisenbrauns, 1980. xviii+629.

An attempt at constructing a new framework in which the whole matter of Hebrew poetry can be discussed. Part I comprises a introduction, followed by fourteen poems (Genesis 49; Exodus 15, Numbers 23-24; Deuteronomy 32 and 33; Judges 5; 2 Samuel 1; Habakkuk 3; Zephaniah 1, 2, and 3; and Psalms 78, 106, and 107, translated with notes). Part II deals with micro-structure of these poems and examines the line, repetition, "coloration" (word-pairs, construct chains), "matching" (chiasmus), "gapping" (ellipsis) and clause patterning. Part III is a statistical analysis of these micro-structural features within the poems.

1079. ______. "The Pseudosorites: A Type of Paradox in Hebrew Verse." In *Directions in Biblical Hebrew Poetry*, ed. Elaine R. Follis. Journal for the Study of the Old Testament, Supplement Series 40. 161-172. Sheffield: JSOT Press, 1987.

A pseudosorite is a form of paradox which ties two or three clauses together by repetition, anaphora, or their equivalents.

1080. Pardee, Dennis. "Ugaritic and Hebrew Metrics." *Ugarit and Retrospect: 50 Years of Ugarit and Ugaritic*, ed. Gordon D. Young. 113-130. Winona Lake, IN: Eisenbrauns, 1981.

1081. Parunak, H. van Dyke. "Oral Typesetting; Some Uses of Biblical Structure." *Biblica* 62 (1981): 153-168.

1082. Paul, Shalom M. "Polysensuous Polyvalency in Poetic Parallelism." In *"Sha'arei Talmon": Studies in the Bible, Qumran, and the Ancient Near East Presented to*

Shemaryahu Talmon, ed. Michael Fishbane and Emanuel Tov. 147-163. Winona Lake, IN: Eisenbrauns, 1992.

1083. Raabe, Paul R. *Psalm Structures. A Study of Psalms with Refrains.* Journal for the Study of the Old Testament Supplement Series 104. Sheffield: JSOT Press, 1990. 240p.

"Our goal is to describe the 'building blocks' that Hebrew lyric poets use to construct a psalm." The discussion is limited to specific psalms with refrains: 42-43, 46, 49, 56, 57, 59, with a brief treatment of 39, 67, 80, 90 in an appendix. The refrain is extrinsic to a stanza.

1084. _____. "Deliberate Ambiguity in the Psalter." *Journal of Biblical Literature* 110 (1991): 213-227.

"Sometimes, maybe more often than we think, a word, phrase, or sentence could be understood in two (or more) ways because both were intended, it is deliberately ambiguous."

1085. Rand, Herbert. "Numerological Structure in Biblical Poetry." *The Jewish Bible Quarterly* 20 (1991-1992): 50-56.

1086. Ridderbos, Nic. H. "The Psalms: Style-Figures and Structure (Certain considerations, with special reference to Pss. xxii, xxv, and xlv)." Oudtestamentische Studiën 13 (1963): 43-76. Reprinted as "De Psalmen: Stijlfiguren en structuur (enige overwegingen, speciaal met betrekking tot de Psalmen 22, 25 en 45)." In *Psalmenstudie. Prof. Nic. H. Ridderbos en het boek der Psalmen. Opstellen van prof. dr. Nic. H. Ridderbos,* ed. C. Van Ginkel and P.J. van Midden. 92-112. Kampen: Kok, 1991.

1087. Robertson, David A. *Linguistic Evidence in the Dating of Early Hebrew Poetry.* Society of Biblical Literature Dissertation Series 3. Missoula, MT: Scholars Press, 1972.

Reviewed by N.M. Sarna in *JBL* 95 (1976): 126-129.

1088. Robinson, T.H. "Anacrusis in Hebrew Poetry." In *Werden und Wesen des Alten Testaments. Festschrift für Claus Westermann zum 70. Geburtstag.* Ed. R. Albertz and Others. 37ff. Göttingen: Vandenhoeck & Ruprecht, 1980; Neukirchen-Vluyn: Neukirchener Verlag, 1980.

1089. Ryken, Leland. "Metaphor in the Psalms." *Christianity and Literature* 31 (3, 1982): 9-29.

1090. Sauer, Georg. "Erwägungen zum Alter des Psalmendichtung in Israel." *Theologische Zeitschrift (Basel)* 22 (1966): 81-95.

1091. Schedl, Claus. *Psalmen im Rhythmus des Urtextes: Eine Auswahl.* Klosterneuburg: Klosterneuburger Bibelapostolat, 1964. 95p.

Reviewed in *CBQ* 26 (1964): 515-516.

1092. Schildenberger, J. "Bemerkungen zum Strophbau der Psalmen." *Estudios Eclesiásticos* 34 (1960): 673-687.

1093. Segert, Stanislav. "Vorarbeiten zur hebräischen Metrik." *Archiv Orientalni* 21 (1953): 481-542.

1094. ______. "Versbau und Sprachbau in der althebräischen Poesie." *Mitteilungen des Instituts für Orientforschung* 15 (1969): 312-321.

1095. Shashar, Michael. "מזמורים גיאומטריים מאת יעקב בזק." *Beth Mikra* 32 (1986/1987): 92-94.

Challenges Bazak's contention that biblical psalms can be interpreted on the basis of their visual arrangement (*Shir Shel Yom Bitehillîm* [Jerusalem: 1985]).

1096. Sievers, Eduard. *Studien zur hebraeischen Metrik* I,2. II, III. 1901. Abhandlungen der Philologisch-historischen klasse der königliche sächssischen Gesellschaft der Wissenschaften 21/1-2; 23/1-2; 4; 35/1-2. Leipzig: B.G. Teubner, 1901-1919.

Contrary to what others may argue, it is not simply the accented syllables that are to be counted. The unaccented syllables are also fixed in number, with two for every accented syllable. When only one or no unaccented syllables appear between two accented syllables, the missing units of the measure are contained within the preceding or following accented syllables.

1097. Slotki, Principal Israel W. "Typographic Arrangement of Ancient Hebrew Poetry: New Light on the Solution of Metrical and Textual Difficulties." *Zeitschrift für die alttestamentliche Wissenschaft* 49 (1931): 211-222.

1098. Soden, Wolfram von. "Rhythmische Gestaltung und intendierte Aussage im Alten Testament und in babylonische Dichtungen." *Zeitschrift für Althebraistik* 3 (1990): 179-206.

Recent studies on Babylonian metrics have shown a certain regularity in the sequence of stressed and unstressed syllables. This can also be observed in Old Testament poetry.

1099. Soll, William Michael. "Babylonian and Biblical Acrostics." *Biblica* 69 (1988): 305-323.

1100. Stieb, Robert. "Die Versdoubletten des Psalters." *Zeitschrift für die alttestamentliche Wissenschaft* 57 (1939): 102-110.

1101. _____. "Noch einmal: Die Versdubletten des Psalters." *Zeitschrift für die alttestamentliche Wissenschaft* 62 (1950): 317-318.

1102. Stuart, Douglas K. *Studies in Early Hebrew Meter.* Harvard Semitic Monographs 13. Missoula, MT: Scholars Press, 1976. 245p.

Argues for the method of syllabic counting which is actually found in the original poetry.
Reviewed by E.M. Good in *JBL* 97 (1978): 273-274; reviewed also in *CBQ* 40 (1978): 255-256.

1103. Trublet, Jacques. "La poétique des psaumes." *Lumière et Vie* 40 (1991): 55-73.

Hebrew poetry consists of four features: Rhythm, rhetoric, syntax, and semantic structures.

1104. Watson, Wilfred G.E. *Classical Hebrew Poetry. A Guide to Its Techniques.* Journal for the Study of the Old Testament Supplement Series 26. Sheffield: JSOT Press, 1984. xx+457p. Reprint, 1986.

1105. Weiss, Meir. "Wege der neuen Dichtungswissenschaft in ihrer Anwendung auf die Psalmenforschung (Methodologische Bemerkungung, dargelegt am Beispiel von Psalm XLVI)." *Biblica* 42 (1961): 255-302. Reprinted with an addendum bringing the discussion up to date in *Zur Neueren Psalmenforschung*, ed. Peter H.A. Neumann, 400-451; Darmstadt: Wissenschaftliche Buchgesellschaft, 1976.

1106. Westhuizen, J.P. van der. "Assonance in Biblical and Babylonian Hymns of Praise." *Semitics* 7 (1980): 81-101.

1107. Zenner, J.K. *Die Choresänger im Buche der Psalmen*. 2 vols. Freiburg im Breisgau: Herder, 1896.

Argues for a system of strophes and counter-strophes which are divided between alternating choirs. An alternating strophe is inserted in the middle and its verses fall alternately to the two choirs. Changes in the text and the bringing together of independent songs are the means for making this system work.

1108. Zevit, Ziony. "Psalms at the Poetic Precipice." *Hebrew Annual Review* 10 (1986): 351-366.

The strong influence of linguistics, especially through the work of Roman Jakobson, on biblical Hebrew poetry, with an analysis of three "sloppy psalms" (Psalms 125, 133, and 134) illustrating how ancient Israelite poets could achieve the "appearance of parallelism" at the "outer limit of biblical poeticity."

See also: 1211, 1504.

5. Literary Criticism and Historical Issues

1109. Ackroyd, Peter R. "Criteria for the Maccabean Dating of Old Testament Literature." *Vetus Testamentum* 3 (1953): 113-132.

1110. Arens, Anton. *Die Psalmen im Gottesdienst des alten Bundes. Eine Untersuchung zur Vorgeschichte des christlichen Psalmengesangs.* Trierer theologische Studien 11. Trier: Paulinus Verlag, 1961. xix+228.

A study of the liturgical development in Israel from its beginning to late Judaism. There are parallel thought patterns in the corresponding three-year cycle readings. Genesis 1-2 and Psalms 1-2; Genesis 49-50 and Psalm 41; Exodus 1-2 and Psalms 42-43; Exodus 39-40 and Psalm 72; Leviticus 1-2 and Psalm 73; Leviticus 26-27 and Psalm 89; Numbers 1-2 and Psalm 90; Numbers 35-36 and Psalm 118; Deuteronomy 1-2 and Psalm 119; Deuteronomy 33-34 and Psalm 150.

Reviewed by E.S. Gerstenberger in *JBL* 81 (1962): 105; reviewed also in *CBQ* 24 (1962): 209-210. Reviewed by H. Schneider in *Theologische Revue* 58 (1962): 225-234.

1111. ______. "Hat der Psalter seinen 'Sitz im Leben' in der synagogalen Leseordnung des Pentateuch?" In *Le Psautier: Ses origines. Ses problèmes littérraires. Son influence*, ed. Robert de Langhe. Orientalia et Biblica Lovaniensia, IV. 107-131. Louvain: Publications Universitaires, 1962.

There is a formal correspondence of the arrangement and division of the three-year lectionary of the Pentateuch and the Psalter.

1112. Auffret, Pierre. *Le sagesse a bâti sa maison. Etudes de structures littéraires dans l'Ancien Testament et spécialement dans les psaumes.* Orbis Biblicus et Orientalis 49. Fribourg Suisse: Editions Universitaires, 1982; Göttingen: Vandenhoeck & Ruprecht, 1982.

A series of studies on the crafting of poetic construction. Genesis 2-4, 11:1-9, and 2 Samuel 13, plus 11 psalms: (1) a study of Psalm 2 and (2) a study of the balances between Psalms 15 and 24, 16 and 23, 17 and 22, 18 and 20/21, leading to Psalm 19 as the center-point with its two halves related, the first half looking forward to Psalms 20-24, the second half looking back to Psalms 15-18.

Reviewed in *CBQ* 48 (1966): 99-101.

1113. _____. "Les Psaumes 15 à 24 comme ensemble structure." In *Le sagesse a bâti sa maison. Etudes de structures littéraires dans l'Ancien Testament et spécialement dans les psaumes.* Orbis Biblicus et Orientalis 49. 407-438. Fribourg Suisse: Editions Universitaires, 1982; Göttingen: Vandenhoeck & Ruprecht, 1982.

1114. _____. "La collection des psaumes des montees comme ensemble structure." In *Le sagesse a bâti sa maison. Etudes de structures littéraires dans l'Ancien Testament et spécialement dans les psaumes.* Orbis Biblicus et Orientalis 49. 439-531. Fribourg Suisse: Editions Universitaires, 1982; Göttingen: Vandenhoeck & Ruprecht, 1982.

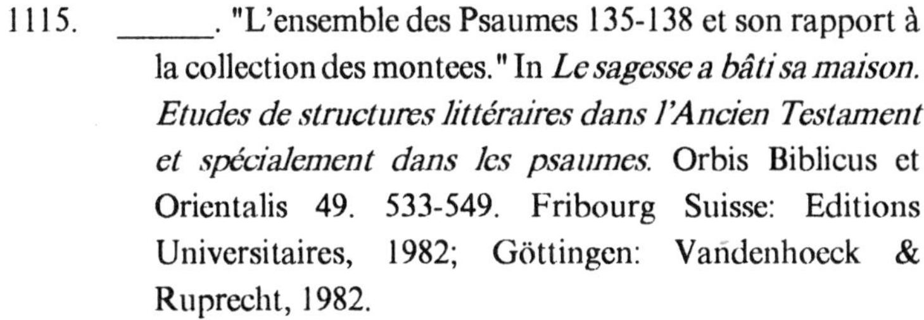

1115. _____. "L'ensemble des Psaumes 135-138 et son rapport à la collection des montees." In *Le sagesse a bâti sa maison. Etudes de structures littéraires dans l'Ancien Testament et spécialement dans les psaumes.* Orbis Biblicus et Orientalis 49. 533-549. Fribourg Suisse: Editions Universitaires, 1982; Göttingen: Vandenhoeck & Ruprecht, 1982.

1116. _____. *Voyez de vos yeux. Étude structurelle de vingt psaumes, dont le psaume 119.* Supplements to Vetus Testament 48. Leiden: E.J. Brill, 1993.

A structural analysis of Psalms 52, 54-60, 108, 62, 64-66, 78-80, 91-91, plus the lengthy Psalm 119.

1117. Baumann, Eberhard. "Struktur-Untersuchungen im Psalter." *Zeitschrift für die alttestamentliche Wissenschaft* 61 (1945-1948): 114-176.

Psalms 4, 8, 13, 18, 26, 32, 36, 39, 40:2-12, 50, 56, 57.

1118. _____. "Struktur-Untersuchungen im Psalter II." *Zeitschrift für die alttestamentliche Wissenschaft* 62 (1949-1950): 115-152.

Psalms 59, 60, 72, 73, 84, 110, 126 and 85, 135, 144:1-11, 144:12-15.

1119. Bazak, Yaakov/Jacob. "The Six Chapters of the 'Hallel' -- The Numerological Ornamentation and Formal Structure (Psalms 113-118)." *Beth Mikra* 35 (1989-1990): 182-191. (Hebrew)

There is an underlying unity to Psalms 113-118. At the center of these Psalms lies Psalm 116:8, which expresses the theme of the whole (thanksgiving) in exactly 26 words -- the numerical value of the tetragrammaton. The tetragrammaton appears elsewhere in units of 26 words or 26 words from the beginning and end of literary units.

1120. ______. "The Set of the Six Chapters of the 'Hallel,' -- Numerological Ornamentation and Formal Structure." *Beth Mikra* 36 (1990-1991): 91-93. (Hebrew)

1121. Beaucamp, Evode. "L'unité du recueil des montées, Psaumes 120-134." *Liber Annuus Biblici Franciscani* 29 (1979): 73-90.

Despite the fact that 11QPs[a] has separated Psalms 133 and 134 from the collection, both Jewish and Christian liturgy presume the unity of the "songs of ascents." They were probably composed by northern pilgrims to Jerusalem recently freed from the Assyrian yoke in the time of Josiah.

1122. Bellinger, W.H., Jr. *Psalmody and Prophecy.* Journal for the Study of the Old Testament Supplement Series 27. Sheffield: JSOT Press, 1984. 146p.

1123. Bonnard, Pierre E. *Le Psautier selon Jérémie: influence littéraire et spirituelle de Jérémie sur trente-trois psaume.* Lectio divina 26. Paris: Cerf, 1960. 281p.

It has long been recognized that a relationship exists between various sayings of Jeremiah, particularly his confessions, and certain of the psalms. Which way does the line of dependence run? Jeremiah was imitated by the authors of the final forms of some 33 psalms. The arguments are based on similar patterns and expressions and assume that Jeremiah was a creative enough writer that others would have imitated him rather than the other way around.

Reviewed by John E. Huesman, *Catholic Biblical Quarterly* 23 (1961): 337-338; J. Bright, *Journal of Biblical Literature* 80 (1961): 298-299.

1124. Bonnes, Jean Paul. *David et les Psaumes.* Paris: Éditions du Seuil, 1957. 191p.

1125. Boson, Biustino. "Una divisione logica del Salterio." *Miscellanea Biblica et Orientalia R.P. Athanasio Miller, Secretario Pontificiae Commissionis Biblicae, completis LXX annis oblata cura Adalberti Metzinger O.S.B. 195-207. Rome, Pontifical Biblical Institute, 1951.*

1126. Bourguet, Daniel. "La structure des titres des psaumes." *Revue d'histoire et de philosophie religieuses* 61 (1981): 109-124.

1127. Brueggemann, Walter. "Bounded by Obedience and Praise: The Psalms as Canon." *Journal for the Study of the Old Testament* 50 (1991): 63-92.

The placement and sequence of Psalms make a theological assertion.

1128. Buss, Martin J. "The Psalms of Asaph and Korah." *Journal of Biblical Literature* 82 (1963): 382-392.

The Psalms can be divided into three main groups, following the lines of their attribution. David Psalms comprise essentially individual laments and related types. Asaph and Korah Psalms exhibit the following genres:

collective lament; deuteronomic Levitical Psalms of judgment, law, and history (so among Asaph Psalms); songs of Zion (so among Korahite Psalms); and a few personal Psalms involving cult personnel and bring wisdom reflection. Psalms with no attribution are primarily hymns. The first group may be called Psalms of laity; the second, presentations of clergy; the third group may well be considered appropriate for both groups.

1129. Cazelles, H. "La question du *lamed auctoris.*" *Revue Biblique* 56 (1949): 93-101.

The *lamed* prefixed to proper names in the psalms' headings was probably understood at first as a *lamed of attribution* or of *classification,* not of author.

1130. Chernoff, Robert. "Tehillim -- the Psalms." *The Jewish Bible Quarterly* 19 (1990-1991): 191-194.

The psalter was intended to be the common prayer book of the Jerusalem Temple as well as of outlying synagogues during the Second Temple period.

1131. Childs, Brevard S. "Psalm Titles and Midrashic Exegesis." *Journal of Semitic Studies* 16 (1971): 137-150.

1132. Collins, Terence. "Decoding the Psalms: A Structural Approach to the Psalms." *Journal for the Study of the Old Testament* 37 (1987): 41-60.

An asynchronic approach to the Psalter. Three binary oppositions appear in the Psalms: Blessed/cursed, wicked/faithful, success/failure. An actantial model reveals the story of the psalms with relationships and the flow of a plot.

1133. Cooper, A.M. "King David's Life and Times According to the Psalms." In *The Poet and the Historian: Essays in Literary and Historical Biblical Criticism*, ed. R.E. Friedman. Harvard Semitic Studies 26. Chico, CA: Scholars Press, 1983.

1134. Delekat, L. "Probleme der Psalmenüberschriften." *Zeitschrift für die alttestamentliche Wissenschaft* 76 (1964): 280-297.

1135. Deursen, Arie van. *De Achtergrond der Psalmen*. Baarn: J. Bosch & Kreuning, 1947. 260p.

1136. Eerdmans, Bernardus Dirks. "Essays on Masoretic Psalms." *Oudtestamentische Studiën* 1 (1942): 105-300.

Includes essays on "On the Road to Monotheism," "Foreign Elements in pre-exilic Israel," "The Songs of Ascents," "Thora-Songs and Temple-Singers in the pre-exilic period," "The Chasidim," "Psalm XIV-LIII and the Elohim-psalms," and "Psalms XL, XLI, LV, LXVIII."

1137. Eissfeldt, Otto. "Die Psalmen als Geschichtsquelle." In *Near Eastern Studies in Honor of William Foxwell Albright*, ed. Hans Goedicke. 97-112. Baltimore, MD: Johns Hopkins Press, 1971.

1138. Enciso Viana, Jesús. "Indicaciones musicales en los titulos de los Salmos." In *Miscellanea Biblica B. Ubach*, ed. R. M. Díaz Carbonell. 185-200. Montserrat: (Imprenta-Escuela of Barcelona), 1953.

1139. _____. "Los titulos de los Salmos y la historia de la formación del Salterio." *Estudios Biblicos* 13 (1954): 135-165

1140. _____. "Los Salmos-prólogos." Misc. Bibl. A. Fernandez. *Estudios Eclesiasticos* 34 (1960): 621-631.

1141. _____. "Como se formó la prima parte del libro de los Salmos." *Biblica* 44 (1963): 129-158.

1142. Fabry, Heinz-Josef. "11 Q Psa und the Kanonizität des Psalters." In *Freude an der Weisung des Herrn. Beiträge zur Theologie der Psalmen. Festgabe zum 70. Geburtstag von Henrich Gross*, ed. Ernst Haag and Frank-Lothar Hossfeld. 45-79. Stuttgart: Katholisches Bibelwerk, 1986.

1143. Feinberg, Charles Lee. "The Date of the Psalms." *Bibliotheca Sacra and Theological Review* 104 (1947): 426-440.

1144. _____. "Are There Maccabean Psalms in the Psalter?" *Bibliotheca Sacra and Theological Review* 105 (1948): 44-55.

1145. _____. "The Uses of the Psalter." *Bibliotheca Sacra and Theological Review* 105 (1948): 154-169.

An insistence on a liturgical approach to the Psalter obscures the devotional purpose of the Psalms.

1146. Finkelstein, L. "The Origin of the Hallel (Pss. 113-118)." *Hebrew Union College Annual* 23 (1950/1951): 319-337.

1147. Füglister, Notker. "Die Verwendung und das Verständnis der Psalmen und des Psalters um die Zeitwende." In *Beiträge zur Psalmenforschung,* ed. Josef Schreiner. 319-384. Forschung zur Bibel 60. Würzburg: Echter Verlag, 1988.

There is no evidence for the psalter being the official hymnal of the Temple in first-century Judaism.

1148. Gese, Hartmut. "Die Entstehung der Büchereinteilung des Psalters." In *Forschung zur Bibel. Wort, Lied und Gottesspruch. Beiträge zur Septuaginta. Festschrift für Joseph Ziegler,* ed. Rudolf Schnackenburg and Josef Schreiner. 2 vols. Vol. 1, 57-64. Würzburg: Echter Verlag, 1972; reprinted in *Vom Sinai zum Zion: Alttestamentliche Beiträge zur biblischen Theologie.* Beiträge zur Evangelische Theologie 64. 159-167. Munich: Kaiser, 1974.

The books of psalms are quite different in size and the doxologies are not uniform. They could not have come from one hand, but are the result of a long process. There are actually nine collections of psalms that have been gradually assembled through the influence of the musical guilds even as late as the 2nd century B.C. Thus any five-book division is artificial. Arens' theory of an association with the three-year reading cycle of the Pentateuch and Prophets is rejected.

1149. Gevaryahu, Haim M.I. "Biblical Colophons: A Source for the 'Biography' of Authors, Texts and Books." In *Congress Volume. Edinburgh 1974.* Supplements to Vetus Testamentum 28. 42-59. Leiden: E.J. Brill, 1975.

1150. ______. "Tehilim: The Book of Psalms." *Dor Le Dor* 16 (1987/1988): 235-241.

The book of Psalms is a collection of votive prayers, originally written on wooden tablets or leather skins, which were displayed in the Temple court or on the city gates. Others may have been copied from engraved stones or walls.

1151. ______. "Tehillim: The Book of Psalms." *Dor le Dor* 17 (1988/1989): 83-90.

There is reason to assume that the current superscriptions were meant to indicate authorship. They include various kinds of information on the collection of the psalms.

1152. Glueck, J.J. "Some Remarks on the Introductory Notes of the Psalms." In *Studies on the Psalms: Papers Read at the 6th Meeting of Die O.T. Werkgemeenskap in Suid-Afrika.* 30-39. Potchefstroom: Pro Rege, 1963.

1153. Goldstain, J. *Le monde des Psaumes.* Paris: Les Editions de la Source, 1964. 413p.

1154. Goossens, E. *Die Frage nach makkabäischen Psalmen.* Münster-en-W.: Aschendorff, 1914. x+72p.

There are no Maccabean psalms, including Psalms 44, 74, 79, and 83, which have sometimes been considered Maccabean psalms that have been interpolated into the psalter.

1155. Goulder, Michael D. "The Fourth Book of the Psalter." *Journal of Theological Studies* 26 (1975): 269-289.

The Fourth Book is the shortest and the most homogeneous of the books in the Psalter. This arrangement was not merely liturgical in orientation; by the 5th century B.C. Psalms 90-106 were fitted to the morning and evening celebrations for the eight-day Tabernacles festival. The even-numbered psalms were used in the evening, the odd-numbered psalms in the morning. Some of the psalms were adapted specifically for Tabernacles; others may have been composed for the renewed fall festival. Genesis 1 was composed to match Psalm 104.

1156. _____. *The Psalms of the Sons of Korah.* Journal for the Study of the Old Testament, Supplement Series, 20. Sheffield: JSOT Press, 1983. xiv+302p.

All psalms in the psalter have been funnelled through the Jerusalem community who found them in some way useable. All of the Korah psalms are public and all are part of the Dan Tabernacles liturgy, the great autumn festival in the month of Bul. The order of the psalms, as they stand corresponds to the order of the ritual, day by day, in 8th century Dan. The Dan and Tabor psalmodies were taken south after the catastrophe of 722 and eventually accepted, along with their bearers (the Korahite and Ethanite priesthoods) into a place in the Jerusalem establishment.

1157. _____. *The Prayers of David. (Psalms 51-72): Studies in the Psalter, II.* Journal for the Study of the Old Testament, Supplement Series 102. Sheffield: JSOT Press, 1990. 266p.

These psalms were composed by a court poet during David's lifetime, probably one of David's sons, in response to situations David faced from the Uriah incident to the accession of Solomon. The order of these psalms follows the chronological order of their writing. The idea behind the historical notes in the headings is correct, though not the historical notes themselves. The present Succession Narrative is a fuller version of an earlier account seen in 2 Samuel 15:7-1 Kings 1, the "Passion of David." It has a liturgical character to it; David's movements were retraced in Jerusalem and its environs in a national ritual involving the king of Judah. The "Passion of David," along with Psalms 51-72, was recited during this ritual. Sections of the "Passion of David" were read after the *selahs* in Psalms 52-60.

Reviewed by M.L. Barré in *JBL* 111)1992): 527-528.

1158. Guilding, Aileen. "The Arrangement of the Pentateuch and Psalter." In *The Fourth Gospel and Jewish Worship. A Study of the Relation of St.John's Gospel to the Ancient Jewish Lectionary System.* 24-44. Oxford: At the Clarendon Press, 1960.

The Psalter, like the Pentateuch and Prophets, was recited over a three year period; the number of Psalms corresponds to the number of sabbaths in three lunar years; the arrangement of the Psalter seems to have been influenced by liturgical considerations.

1159. Haag, H. "Jerusalemer Profanbauten in den Psalmen." *Zeitschrift des deutschen Palästina-Vereins* 93 (1977): 87-96.

Reflections about non-sacral structures in Jerusalem which are mentioned in the Psalms: *hêkāl, 'armĕnôt, migdālîm, ḥêl, ḥômôt, šĕʻārîm.*

1160. Haran, Menahem. "11QPs[a] and the Composition of the Book of Psalms." In *"Sha'arei Talmon": Studies in the Bible, Qumran and the Ancient Near East Presented to Shemaryahu Talmon,* ed. Michael Fishbane and Emanuel Tov. 123*-128*. Winona Lake, IN: Eisenbrauns, 1992. (Hebrew)

According to Sanders, the approximately forty canonical psalms in 11QPs[a] plus the eight extra-canonical texts represent a pre-canonical stage in the composition of the Psalter. The Qumran community, however, accepted the scroll as its official psalter, and ascribed its entire contents to David.

1161. Hauret, Ch. "Un problème insoluble? La chronologie des psaumes." *Recherches de Science Religieuse* 35 (1961): 225-256.

A survey of various opinions and methods in Psalm chronology.

1162. Heredia, F. Marín. "Los cinco libros del Salterio." *Carthagiensia* 7 (1991): 3-17.

There are noteworthy correspondences between the five "books" of the Psalter and those comprising the Pentateuch. Genesis, e.g., parallels Book I of the Psalms, Exodus Book II, etc.

1163. Hockey, F. "*Cantica Graduum.* The Gradual Psalms in Patristic Tradition." *Studia Patristica* 10 (= *Texte und Untersuchungen* 107) (1970): 355-359.

1164. Howard, David M., Jr. "Editorial Activity in the Psalter: A State-of-the-Field Survey." *Word & World* 9 (1989): 274-285.

1165. Illman, Karl-Johan. *Thema und Tradition in den Asaf-Psalmen.* Meddelanden från Stiftelsens för Åbo Akademi Forskningsinstitut 13. Åbo, Finland: Stiftelsens för Åbo akademi forskningsinstitut, 1976. 81p.

There is little formal conformity in the Asaph psalms (Psalms 50, 73-83). Themes and aspects of tradition history in these psalms include topics such as creation, salvation history, Yahweh's judgment, confidence in God, but with differing emphasis and contexts. There is no evidence for a uniform process of transmission nor for an Asaph guild of singers. In sum, these psalms tell us very little about the Asaph temple-singers and their relationship to the Asaph psalms.

Reviewed by E.S. Gerstenberger in *JBL* 97 (1978): 284-285.

1166. Jenni, Ernst. "Zu den doxologischen Schlussformeln des Psalters." *Theologische Zeitschrift* 40 (1984): 114-120.

The original purpose of the doxologies of Psalms 41:14, 72:18-19, 89:53, 106:48 was something other than the late one of dividing the Psalter into five "books."

1167. Keet, Cuthbert C. *A Study of the Psalms of Ascents: A Critical and Exegetical Commentary upon Psalms CXX to CXXXIV.* London: Mitre Press, 1969. viii+192p.

Psalms 120-134 form a unity. An examination of the title reveals that these psalms are closely attached to the feast of first-fruits and to the holy pilgrimage to Jerusalem associated with it. The study includes a detailed commentary on each of the psalms and a discussion of the Psalms of Ascents in Jewish life and liturgy.

Reviewed by E. Gerstenberger in *JBL* 92 (1973): 284-285. Reviewed in *CBQ* 34 (1972): 83.

1168. Lassalle, S. "Onias III et les Psaumes macchabéens." *Bulletin de la Société Ernest-Renan* 85 (1961): 7-9.

1169. Lelièvre, André. "Qui parle dans les Psaumes?" *Foi et Vie* 87 (1988): 3-13.

1170. Liebreich, Leon J. "The Songs of Ascents and the Priestly Blessing." *Journal of Biblical Literature* 74 (1955): 33-36.

1171. Lindblom, J. "Bemerkungen zu den Psalmen I." *Zeitschrift für die alttestamentliche Wissenschaft* 59 (1942/43): 1-13.

1172. Luria, B.Z. "Psalms from Ephraim." *Beth Mikra* 23 (1978): 151-161 (Hebrew).

Psalms 76, 77, 80, and 81 come from the Northern Kingdom.

1173. McCann, J. Clinton. "The Psalms as Instruction." *Interpretation* 46 (1992): 117-128.

Although the Psalms may have originated primarily within the liturgical life of ancient Israel and Judah, they were nonetheless appropriated, preserved, and transmitted as instruction for the faithful.

1174. Maertens, Thierry. "Jérusalem, cité de Dieu." *Paroisse et Liturgie* 17 (1954): 1-25; 18 (1954): 1-14; 19 (1954): 1-19; 20 (1954): 1-15; 21 (1954): 2-9. 2nd, reworked and enlarged ed., *Jérusalem, Cite de Dieu (Pss 120-128).* Collationes Lumière et Vie 3. Bruges, Belgium: Editions de l'Abbaye de Saint-Andre, 1954. 149p.

A study of Psalms 121-128 from the point of view of the historico-topographical development and the development of the literary theme "Jerusalem." The stages of development are from geography to history, from history to story, from story to cult, from cult to moral, from moral to eschatology, from eschatology to church.

1175. May, Herbert Gordon. "^{c}AL in the Superscriptions of the Psalms." *American Journal of Semitic Languages and Literatures* 58 (1941): 70-83.

1176. Mays, James Luther. "The David of the Psalms." *Interpretation* 40 (1986): 143-155.

The Old Testament notion of the David of the Psalms is an intra-textual reality, which warns against treating the character of David only or primarily as an historical problem.

1177. Miller, Patrick D., Jr. "Psalms and Inscriptions." *Congress Volume. Vienna 1980, ed.* J.A. Emerton. Supplements to Vetus Testamentum 32. 311-332. Leiden: E.J. Brill, 1980.

1178. Nasuti, Harry P. *Tradition History and the Psalms of Asaph.* Society of Biblical Literature Dissertation Series, 88. Atlanta, GA: Scholars Press, 1988. vii+204p.

In response to K.-J. Illman's *Thema und Tradition in den Asaf-Psalmen* (1976), we need a renewed effort at identifying the tradition circle/current which expresses itself in the Asaph psalms. The language of Psalms 50, 73-83, their literary forms, and the extra-Psalter data concerning Asaph and his line point toward the long-lived "Ephraimite" tradition stream which had its start in the North but eventually relocated in the South and which had special affinities with the cult.

1179. Phillips, G.E. *The Imagery of the Pilgrim Psalms.* London: S.P.C.K., 1957. 64p.

Explains the imagery found in Psalms 120-134.

1180. Pietersma, Albert. "David in the Greek Psalms." *Vetus Testamentum* 30 (1980): 213-226.

Do the additional *ldwd superscriptions of Psalms in the LXX (over the MT) pre- or post-date the Greek translations?* "Though the translator of Psalms consistently rendered *ldwd* by τῷ δαυίδ, in the process of textual transmission the latter was frequently changed to τοῦ δαυίδ, in an apparent effort to clarify Davidic authorship." Rahlf's ready acceptance of the phrase as Old Greek is suspect.

1181. Pinto, Basil de. "The Torah and the Psalms." *Journal of Biblical Literature* 86 (1967): 154-174.

Does the Torah and the way of life it represents constitute an intrinsic element in the structure of the Book of Psalms? Is the Torah mentality a part at least of its fundamental orientation? Yes. "It seems to be a valid conclusion that a spirituality of the Torah has been inserted into the framework of the psalter as a whole, and is one of the foremost guidelines of interpretation of the book, a real key to its understanding."

1182. Press, Richard. "Die zeitgeschichtliche Hintergrund der Wallfahrtpsalmen." *Theologische Zeitschrift* 14 (1958): 401-415.

The pilgrimage psalms stem from the last period of the Babylonian exile. Their eschatological faith and their superscriptions contain prophetic presuppositions similar to the proclamation of Deutero-Isaiah.

1183. Qimron, E. "Post-exilic Language in the Book of Psalms." *Beth Mikra* 23 (1978): 139-150. (Hebrew)

According to Hurvitz, late linguistic features date Psalms 103, 104, 107, 111, 119, 124, 135, 137, 143, 145, and 146 to the post-exilic period. Psalms 123, 129, and 136 should also be ascribed to this period.

1184. Reindl, Joseph. "Weisheitliche Bearbeitung von Psalmen. Ein Beitrag zum Verständnis der Sammlung des Psalters." In *Congress Volume, Vienna 1980*, ed. J.A. Emerton. Supplements to Vetus Testamentum 32. 333-356. Leiden: E.J. Brill, 1981.

1185. Rendsburg, Gary A. *Linguistic Evidence for the Northern Origin of Selected Psalms.* Society of Biblical Literature Monograph Series 43. Atlanta, GA: Scholars Press, 1991. xi+143p.

Psalms 9-10, 16, 29, 36, 45; the Korah group, 53, 58, 74; and the Asaph group, 116, 132, 133, 140 and 141 are probably the only psalms of northern provenance. A list of grammatical and lexical criteria used in the study are offered for identifying dialect variation synchronically in the Hebrew Bible.

1186. Rost, Leonhard. "Ein Psalmproblem." *Theologische Literaturzeitung* 93 (1968): 241-246.

The treatment of the terms for the offering shows that the authors of the psalms were not priests. The psalms were not only intended for the laity; they were also an expression of their piety.

1187. Sarna, Nahum M. "The Psalm Superscriptions and the Guilds." In *Studies in Jewish Religious and Intellectual History, Presented to Alexander Altmann on the Occasion of His Seventieth Birthday,* ed. Siegfried Stein and Raphael Loewe. 281-300. London: Institute for Jewish Studies, 1979.

1188. Sawyer, J.F.A. "An Analysis of the Context and Meaning of the Psalm-Headings." *Transactions of Glasgow University Oriental Society* 22 (1967-1968): 26-38.

1189. Schneider, H. "Die Psalterteilung in Fünfziger- und Zehnergruppen." In *Universitas. Festschrift A. Stohr. I.* 36-47. Mainz: Matthias Grünewald Verlag, 1960.

1190. Schulz, Alphons (1871-1947) *Psalmenfragen. Mit einem anhang. Zur Stellung der Beifügung im hebräischen.* Alttestamentliche Abhandlungen 14/1. Münster: Aschendorff, 1940. 128p.

1191. Seidel, Hans. "Wallfahrtslieder." In *Das Lebendige Wort. Festgabe für Gottfried Voigt zum 65. Geburtstag,* ed. Hans Seidel and Karl-Heinrich Bieritz. 26-40. Berlin: Evangelische Verlagsanstalt, 1982.

Psalms 120-134 have a common genre, structure, and provenance in the Levitical preaching between 515-400 B.C. In these psalms we do not encounter the prophetic word of God but a meditative reflection upon the significance of transpired events.

1192. Selms, A. van. "Historiese en geografiese name in die boeck van die Psalmen." *Hervormde Teologiese Studies* 14 (1958): 1-12. (Afrikaans)

Historical and geographical names in the book of Psalms.

1193. Seybold, Klaus. *Die Wallfahrtspsalmen. Studien zur Entstehungsgeschichte von Psalm 120-134.* Biblisch-theologische Studien 3. Neukirchen-Vluyn: Neukirchener Verlag, 1978. 108p.

Psalms 120-134 have received several redactional additions. Their common features are narrow-minded social origins, provincial geographical origins, Aramaisms, and greetings or blessings formulas. With the exception of Psalm 132, a product of the Jerusalem liturgy, the "pilgrimage psalms" were the works of ordinary pilgrims who employed stock greetings or blessings formulas in creating these mementos, which they then left at the sanctuary as part of their thanksgiving. After their deposit at the sanctuary (cf. Psalm 40:8) these compositions were redacted (generalized, formularized, liturgically adjusted) into a small psalter for use by pilgrims to Jerusalem. The emphasis of this redaction on Zion as a focus of divine blessing accounts for the presence of Psalm 132 in the collection. Later this collection was incorporated into the Psalter.

Reviewed in *CBQ* 42 (1980): 110-111.

1194. _____. "Die Redaktion der Wallfahrtspsalmen." *Zeitschrift für die alttestamentliche Wissenschaft* 91 (1979): 247-268.

1195. _____. "Toward an Understanding of the Formation of Historical Titles in the Book of Psalms." *Zeitschrift für die alttestamentliche Wissenschaft* 91 (1979): 350-380.

1196. Skehan, Patrick W. "Borrowings from the Psalms in the Book of Wisdom." *Catholic Biblical Quarterly* 10 (1948): 384-397.

1197. _____. "A Liturgical Complex in 11QPs[a]." *Catholic Biblical Quarterly* 34 (1973): 195-205.

The canonical Psalter existed and was fixed prior to the writing and copying of the Psalms Scroll from Cave 11; furthermore, the peculiar arrangement of materials in the scroll was due first of all to a liturgical grouping and secondly to a collection of writings to honor David, the psalmist. A simplified version of this article appears in "An Old Testament Service of Praise." *The Bible Today* 67 (1973): 1236-1241.

1198. Slomovic, Elieser. "Toward an Understanding of the Formation of Historical Titles in the Book of Psalms." *Zeitschrift für die alttestamentliche Wissenschaft* 91 (1979): 350-380.

"Connective midrash," used by the rabbis in associating certain events or persons with various psalms, is illustrated to show that analogies together with a congruity of images serve as stimuli for connecting the Psalms with persons and events and that certain parts that lack a connecting element are glossed over. This explains Psalm headings in the LXX as well as those in the Masoretic text. The same midrashic process of placing certain Psalms into specific historical situations is employed by the author of 1-2 Chronicles.

1199. Solah, Arieh. "The Psalms of Ascent." *Beth Mikra* 47 (1971): 457-475. (Hebrew)

1200. Stamm, J.J. "Eine Bemerkung zum Anfang des achten Psalms." *Theologische Zeitschrift (Basel)* 13 (1957): 470-478.

Psalms 8:3; 44:17; 89:11; 140:8; Matthew 21:16.

1201. Toit, S. du. "Psalms and History." In *Studies on the Psalms: Papers Read at the 6th Meeting of Die. O.T. Werkgemeenskap in Suid-Africa.* 18-29. Potchetstroom: Pro Rege, 1963.

1202. Torrance, T.F. "The Last of the Hallel Psalms." *Evangelical Theology* 28 (1956): 101-108.

1203. Tournay, Raymond J.. "Les psaumes complexes." *Revue Biblique* 54 (1947): 521-542; 56 (1949): 37-60.

1204. ______. "Sur quelques rubriques des Psaumes." In *Mélanges bibliques rédigés en l'honneur de André Robert.* Trauvaux de l'Institut Catholique de Paris 4. 197-204. Paris: Bloud & Gay, 1959.

1205. _____. "Recherches sur la chronologie des Psaumes." *Revue Biblique* 65 (1958): 321-357.

1) Principles and Examples. 2) Psalms from the Time of Josiah. a) The Psalm of Nahum. b) The Victory Song in Exodus 15. (Cont.)

1206. _____. "Recherches sur la chronologie des Psaumes." *Revue Biblique* 66 (1959): 161-190.

c) A Liturgy of Enthronement (Psalms 20 and 21).

1207. Treves, Marco. *The Dates of the Psalms. History and Poetry in Ancient Israel.* Pisa: Giardini Stampaton, 1988. 109p.

The 150 psalms fit in the historical setting of the period 170-103 B.C. The various criteria for recognizing the second century B.C. setting of the psalms include borrowings from Greek literature and dependence on other late Old Testament literature. Isaiah 40-66, for example, is also Maccabean. They mostly come from within the Hasidean community. The "I" who speaks in the different psalms can be identified with one or another of the Maccabees from Judas to Hyrcanus.

1208. Tsevat, Matitiahu. *A Study of the Language of the Biblical Psalms.* Journal of Biblical Literature Monograph Series 9. Philadelphia: Society of Biblical Literature, 1955. viii+153p.

Reviewed by S. Mowinckel in *Theologische Literaturzeitung* 81 (1956): 199-202.

1209. Tur-Sinai, Naftali Herz. "The Literary Character of the Book of Psalms." *Oudtestamentlische Studiën* 8 (1950): 263-281. Translated into German by Fritz Grosspietsch and printed as "Zum literarischen Charakter der Psalmen," in *Zur Neueren Psalmenforschung*, ed. Peter H.A. Neumann, 217-233; Darmstadt: Wissenschaftliche Buchgesellschaft, 1976.

1210. Viviers, H. "Die opbou van die *ma*^{ca}*lōt*-bundel (Ps 120-134)." *Nederduits Gereformeerde Teologiese Tydskrif* 33 (1992): 11-22.

Auffret is wrong in seeing a logical-dramatic movement in these psalms. This lack of movement argues against the widely-held view that the collection was put together for cultic purposes. It is rather best seen as a post-exilic "book of meditation" designed to provide comfort and evoke renewed confidence in Yahweh.

1211. ______. "Klank-inhoud-chiasme in die Ma^{c}alot-Psalms (Psalms 120-134)." *Skrif en Kerk* 13 (1992): 65-79.

Sound-content chiasm is a recognized pattern in classical Hebrew poetry. In each of the "Ascent Psalms" the technique links adjacent elements and subtly emphasizes themes. It also helps to unify the individual psalms of the collection with each other.

1212. Waltke, Bruce K. "Superscripts, Postscripts, or Both." *Journal of Biblical Literature* 110 (1991): 583-596.

In the Psalter *lmnsh* + optional prepositional phrase is a frozen postscript originally appended to the preceding psalm (cf. Hab 3:19). Postscripts include terms for the psalm's performance; superscriptions contain matter about the psalm's composition. *Lmnsh* + prepositional phrases is appended only to pre-exilic psalms.

1213. Walton, John H. "Psalms: A Cantata about the Davidic Covenant." *Journal of the Evangelical Theological Society* 34 (1991): 21-31.

Is there a rationale behind the arrangement of the Psalter? If so, is it tied to content or to the authority of the editor as opposed to the original psalmist(s)? Organization by content is feasible, but the question of authority cannot be answered.

1214. Wanke, Gunter. "Prophecy and Psalms in the Persian Period." In *The Cambridge History of Judaism,* ed. W.D. Davies and L. Finkelstein. Vol. I: 162-188. Cambridge: Cambridge University Press, 1984.

1215. Weiser, Asher. "Historic Underpinnings of Psalms." *Beth Mikra* 63 (1975): 536-544. (Hebrew)

1216. Westermann, Claus. "Zur Sammlung des Psalters." *Theologica Viatorum* 8 (1972): 278-284. Reprinted in *Forschung am Alten Testament.* Theologische Bücherei 24. 336-343. Munich: Chr. Kaiser Verlag, 1964. Reprinted in *Lob und Klage in den Psalmen.* Göttingen: Vandenhoeck & Ruprecht, 1977. Translated into English by Richard N. Soulen and published as "The Formation of the Psalter," in *Praise and Lament in the Psalms,* 250-258; Atlanta, GA: John Knox Press, 1981.

Two basic distinctions seem to have been made in the collecting process -- individual or community, lament or praise.

1217. Wilson, Gerald Henry. "The Qumran Psalms Manuscripts and the Consecutive Arrangement of Psalms in the Hebrew Psalter." *Catholic Biblical Quarterly* 45 (1983): 377-388.

Thus this study supports Sander's theory of the gradual stabilization of the Psalter from beginning to end. It also "affirms a gradual conformity of psalms MSS to the canonical arrangement which reached its height about the middle of the first century A.D. and prevailed thereafter."

1218. ______. "Evidence of Editorial Divisions in the Hebrew Psalter." *Vetus Testamentum* 34 (1984): 337-352.

1219. ______. *The Editing of the Hebrew Psalter.* Society of Biblical Literature Dissertation Series 76. Chico, CA: Scholars Press, 1985. xiv+278p.

Comparative materials (Mesopotamia and Qumran) and recent scholarly studies help us understand the editorial principles underlying the present psalter.

1220. ______. "The Use of 'Untitled' Psalms in the Hebrew Psalter." *Zeitschrift für die alttestamentliche Wissenschaft* 97 (1985): 404-413.

The occurrence of untitled psalms in Books I-III is directly related to a real tradition of combination. The Psalter editor(s) was aware of alternate traditions for the combination/division of these psalms and desired to preserve both traditions. This technique is most likely active in those cases of isolated, untitled psalms in Books One to Three of the Psalter and may be extended to some examples of

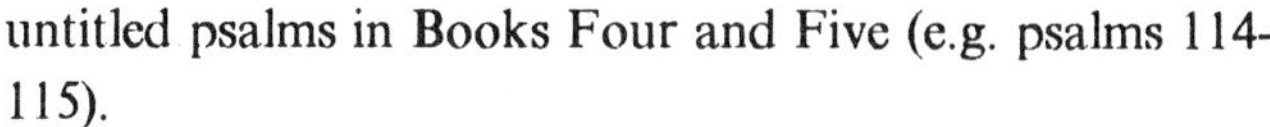

untitled psalms in Books Four and Five (e.g. psalms 114-115).

1221. _____. "The Use of Royal Psalms at the 'Seams' of the Hebrew Psalter." *Journal for the Study of the Old Testament* 35 (1986): 85-94.

1222. _____. "The Shape of the Book of Psalms." *Interpretation* 46 (1992): 129-142.

The Psalter exhibits a complex literary structure that not only determines its shape but also provides the reader with interpretive clues for reading both the whole and its parts.

1223. Yates, Kyle M. *Studies in the Psalms.* Nashville, TN: Broadman Press, 1953.

1224. Zeitlin, Solomon. "Hallel: A Historical Study of the Canonization of the Hebrew Liturgy." *Jewish Quarterly Review* 53 (1962): 22-29.

1225. Zenger, Erich. "Israel und Kirche im gemeinsamen Gottesbund: Beobachtungen zum theologischen Programm des 4. Psalmenbuchs (Ps 90-106)." In *Israel und Kirche heute. Für E.L. Ehrlich,* ed. Marcel Marcus and Others. 236-254. Freiburg im Breisgau: Herder Verlag, 1991.

1226. _____. *Ich will die Morgenröte wecken: Psalmenauslegungen.* Freiburg, Basel, and Vienna: Herder, 1991. 268p.

The title, "I will awake the dawn," comes from Psalm 57:9(8). Twenty-five psalms of various literary types are translated and explained.

1227. Zimmerli, Walter. "Zwillingspsalmen." In *Forschung zur Bibel. Wort, Lied, und Gottesspruch. Beiträge zu Psalmen und Propheten. Festschrift für Joseph Ziegler*, ed. Rudolf Schnackenburg and Josef Schreiner. 2 vols. Vol. 2, 105-113. Würzburg: Echter Verlag, 1972; reprinted in *Studien zur alttestamentlichen Theologie und Prophetie; Gesammelte Aufsätze*, Band II. 261-271. Theologische Bücherei 51. Munich: Kaiser Verlag, 1974.

A study of doublets and the juxtaposing of psalms in the Psalter, particularly the twin psalms: Psalms 111 and 112, Psalms 105 and 106. In the first pair there seems to be a contrast between the response of the one who fears the Lord (Psalm 111) and the response of the godless (Psalm 112). In the second pair there is a contrast between the faithfulness of God (Psalm 105) and the faithlessness of God's people (Psalm 106).

See also: 2, 814, 997.

6. Form-Criticism and Tradition History

1228. Aejmelaeus, A. *The Traditional Prayer in the Psalms.* Beihefte zur Zeitschrift für die alttestamentliche Wissenschaft 167. Berlin: Walter de Gruyter, 1986.

1229. Airoldi, Norberto. "La Consultazione divina nella Malattia in Israele." *Bibbie e Oriente* 15 (1973): 163-172.

1 Kings 14:1-19 and Isaiah 38 illustrate the type of background implied in the psalms of the sick. These psalms, explicitly or implicitly, look to an expected divine oracle that has been sought by consultation. This oracle is the decisive factor in the healing process.

1230. Anderson, A.A. "Psalms." In *It is Written: Scripture Citing Scripture. Essays in Honor of Barnabas Lindars, SSF*, ed. D.A. Carson and H.G.M. Williamson. 56-66. Cambridge: Cambridge University Press, 1988.

Studies the way in which the Psalms uses antecedent Scripture.

1231. Barucq, A. "La lode divina nei Salmi." *Bibbia e Oriente* 1 (1959): 66-77.

1232. Bazak, Jacob. "Songs of Prophetic Drama in the Book of Psalms." *Beth Mikra* 33 (1987/1988): 339-345. (Hebrew)

In the book of Psalms the first person most often refers to the worshipper; sometimes, however, it refers to God, whose part may have been spoken by a cultic prophet.

1233. Becker, Joachim. "Die kollektive Deutung der Königspsalmen." *Theologie und Philosophie* 52 (1977): 561-578.

The royal theology was transferred to the entire people in exilic and post-exilic times. This "democratizes" most of the messianic psalms.

1234. Begrich, Joachim. "Die Vertrauensäusserung im israelitischen Klagelied des Einzelnen und in seinem Babylonischen Gegenstück." *Zeitschrift für die alttestamentliche Wissenschaft* 46 (1928): 221-260. Reprinted in *Gesammelte Studien zum Alten Testament.* Theologische Bücherei 21. 168-216. Munich: Chr. Kaiser Verlag, 1964.

There are some rather striking differences between expressions of confidence in the Israelite lament of the individual and their Babylonian counterpart. Those in the Israelite laments are particular rather than general, colorful rather than flat, varied in form and content rather than formalized, and most importantly, expressive of a strong personal relationship to Yahweh. If Israel learned anything about the lament from Babylon, Israel managed to put a surprisingly new element of life into the lament.

1235. ______. "Das priesterliche Heilsorakel." *Zeitschrift für die alttestamentliche Wissenschaft* 52 (1934): 81-92. Also published in *Gesammelte Studien zum Alten Testament*;

Theologische Bücherei 21; 217-231; Munich: Chr. Kaiser, 1964.

1236. _____. "Die priesterliche Tora." In *Werden und Wesen des Alten Testaments,* ed. Paul Volz, Friedrich Stummer, and Johannes Hempel. Beihefte zur Zeitschrift für die alttestamentliche Wissenschaft 66. 63-88. Berlin: Alfred Töpelmann, 1936. Reprinted in *Gesammelte Studien zum Alten Testament.* Theologische Bücherei 21. 232-260. Munich: Ch. Kaiser, 1964.

1237. Bellinger, W.H., Jr. *Psalmody and Prophecy.* Journal for the Study of the Old Testament Supplement 27. Sheffield: JSOT Press, 1984. 146p.

A study of various aspects of the relationship between psalmody and prophecy, especially of prophetic elements in psalms of individual and community lament. "There are clearly significant relationships between psalmody and prophecy in terms of form, vocabulary and function."

1238. _____. "Psalms of the Falsely Accused: A Reassessment." *Society of Biblical Literature Seminar Papers* 25 (1986): 463-469.

1239. Bernini, Giuseppe. *Le preghiere penitenziali del Salterio.* Analecta Gregoriana 62. Rome: Gregorian University Press, 1953.

Psalms 19, 25, 32, 38-41, 51, 65, 69, 79, 85, 90, 103, 106, 130, and 143.

1240. Beyerlin, Walter. *Herkunft und Geschichte der ältesten Sinaitraditionen.* Tübingen: J.C.B. Mohr (Paul Siebeck),

1961. Translated into English by S. Rudman and published as *Origins and History of the Oldest Sinaitic Traditions.* Oxford: Basil Blackwell, 1965. 191p.

Noth and von Rad reach the conclusion that the Sinai tradition is distinct from that of the Exodus. Not so. The influence of the pattern of the Hittite treaties is apparent in all strands of the Covenant tradition. The calling-out of Israel and her Covenant obligations are interwoven from the beginning. Cult and history are interwoven from the beginning. References include Psalms 24, 47, 48, 78, 80, 95, 96, 97, 99, 105, and 132.

1241. ______. "Die *tôdā* der Heilsverkündigung in den Klageliedern des Einzelnen." *Zeitschrift für die alttestamentliche Wissenschaft* 79 (1967): 208-224.

The feeling of *tôdā*, a combination of praise and thanksgiving, can be expressed in a lament not because deliverance has already happened, but because the psalmist has so much faith in the divine power and in the past signs of divine benevolence of God that he is able to celebrate this in the very midst of suffering; for example, this appears in Psalms 9 and 10; 26:6-7 and 40:2-12. This type of lament psalm should be distinguished from others where no such confession-thanksgiving is present.

1242. ______. *Die Rettung der Bedrängten in den Feindpsalmen der Einzelnen.* Forschungen zur Religion und Literatur des Alten und Neuen Testament 99. Göttingen: Vandenhoeck und Ruprecht, 1970. 174p.

The cultic nature of 25 individual psalms against enemies: Psalms 3-5, 7, 9-10, 11, 12, 17, 23, 25-27, 54-57, 59, 62-64,

86, 94, 140, 142, 143. An examination of the psalms suggests that 14 psalms (Psalms 9-10, 55, 56, 62, and 94 definitely do not; Psalms 12, 25, 64, 86, 140, 142, and 143 most likely do not) do not refer to a cultic-sacral institution. There is a clear reference to a cultic institution in 11 psalms (Psalms 3, 4, 5, 7, 11, 17, 23, 26, 27, 57, 63). Schmidt and Delekat are wrong in their assessment of the role of Yahweh's protection and judgment in these 11 psalms. The motif of God's protection does not represent an integral part of those psalms which are related to a cultic institution (contrary to Delekat); this motif is subordinated to the dominant motif of judgment. The background to these psalms is not the institution of asylum which supposedly provides an oracle of salvation (contrary to Delekat), nor an investigative imprisonment (contrary to Schmidt); rather it is the institution of a cultic judgment of God at the Yahweh sanctuary to which the oppressed could turn as a last court of appeal; it is independent of the annual festival cult and does not require the presence of the community; the function of these psalms is thus to bring about the decisive act of judgment. These 11 psalms are not to be classified as psalms of lamentation; rather they are prayers of supplication.

Reviewed by G.F. Hasel in *JBL* 89 (1970): 470-472.

1243. ______. "Kontinuität beim 'berichtenden' Lobpreis des Einzelnen." In *Wort und Geschichte. Festshrift für K. Elliger*, ed. H. Gese and others. Alter Orient und Altes Testament 18. 17-24. Neukirchen-Vluyn: Neukirchener Verlag, 1973.

1244. Booij, Thijs. *Godswoorden in de Psalmen, Hun functie en achtergronden, in het bijzonder het godswoord na klachten en gebeden en de goddelijke terechtqijzing.* 2

vols. Rodopi: Academisch proefschrift, Vrije Universiteit te Amsterdam, 1978. 414p.

Others have viewed the divine oracles in the Psalms as mere literary devices, as spoken by psalmists posing as prophets, as citations of previously spoken prophetic oracles, or as actual divine oracles. There is some truth in the first three, very little in the last approach. Linguistic and structural arguments confirm these divine utterances as original. A distinction must be made between human and divine utterances. There are three categories of the divine: a previous divine speech is cited directly, a divine speech becomes part of a separate literary element, and a divine speech occurs independently at the moment of recitation or composition. Since it is only in this last category that a distinct divine "I" is actually speaking, we concentrate on its structure, genre, *Sitz im Leben*, and function. Psalms 12, 60, 85, and 132 are complaints or appeals. Psalms 81 and 95 are liturgical hymns from the pre-exilic temple. Psalm 50 is a theophany-description. Who is this divine "I?" It is not a prophet but a temple-singer carrying on in the prophetic spirit. Mowinckel's claim that there were actual prophets serving as cultic functionaries is to be rejected. Those who speak as God and for God in the Psalms do so as prophets, but only in the extended meaning of the term. An English summary appears at the end of volume one.

Reviewed by S.J. De Vries in *JBL* 99 (1980): 451-453. Reviewed in *CBQ* 42 (1980): 532-533.

1245. Bout, H. *Het zondebesef in het Bock der Psalmen. Een exegetisch-theologische Studie.* Leiden: E.J. Brill, 1952.

A study of the penitential prayers in the Psalms.

1246. Brongers, H.A. "Die Rache- und Fluchpsalmen im Alten Testament." *Oudtestamentische Studiën* 13 (1963): 21-42.

1247. Broyles, Craig C. *The Conflict of Faith and Experience in the Psalms: A Form-Critical and Theological Study.* Journal for the Study of the Old Testament, Supplement Series 52. Sheffield: JSOT Press, 1989. 272p.

The lament psalm is examined as it goes through its stages of composition: from the distress that occasions it to the interpretation of that distress to the appeal made to God concerning it. A distinction should be made within the category between psalms of plea, which affirm the praise of God, and psalms of complaint, which charge God with failing certain traditions normally expressed as praise.

1248. Brueggemann, Walter. "From Hurt to Joy, from Death to Life." *Interpretation* 28 (1974): 3-19.

The lament was built on real life experience and honest confrontation. It is a corrective to running from reality and to the euphoric celebration of life that would overlook the dark side of things.

1249. ______. "The Costly Loss of Lament." *Journal for the Study of the Old Testament* 36 (1986): 57-71.

The presence of lament arises from both the protest for justice on the social level and the need for self-affirmation by another in order to attain authenticity on the psychological level.

1250. Bückers, Hermann. "Zur Verwertung der Sinaitraditionen in den Psalmen." *Biblica* 32 (1951): 401-422.

There is no support for Weiser's theory of a covenant festival.

1251. Budde, K. "Das hebräische Klagelied." *Zeitschrift für die alttestamentliche Wissenschaft* 2 (1882): 1-52.

1252. Burger, J. "Wysheidskriteria vir die klassifikasie van psalms as wysheidspsalms." *Hervormde Teologiese Studies* 47 (1991): 213-230.

Criteria for Identifying Wisdom Psalms.

1253. Cartledge, Tony W. "Conditional Vows in the Psalms of Lament: A New Approach to an Old Problem." In *The Listening Heart. Essays in Wisdom and the Psalms in honor of Roland E. Murphy, O.Carm.*, ed. Kenneth G. Hoglund and Others. Journal for the Study of the Old Testament Supplement 58. 77-94. Sheffield: JSOT Press, 1987.

The usual form of conditional vows in the psalms of lament is entreaty, complaint, trust, vow, confidence.

1254. Ceresko, A. "The Sage in the Psalms." In *The Sage in Israel and the Ancient Near East*, ed. John G. Gammie and Leo G. Perdue. Winona Lake, IN: Eisenbrauns, 1990.

1255. Coats, George W. *Rebellion in the Wilderness. The Murmuring Motif in the Wilderness Traditions of the Old Testament.* Nashville, TN: Abingdon Press, 1968. 288p.

A study of the nature and history of the murmuring motif in the wilderness traditions and its significance for defining the relationship between positive and negative interpretations of the wilderness traditions. Includes a discussion of Psalms 78 and 106.

1256. ______. "Self-Abasement and Insult Formulas." *Journal of Biblical Literature* 89 (1970): 14-26.

Questions such as "What is man that you should remember him, or the son of man, that you should visit him?" (Psalm 8:5) do not make their point immediately clear. Questions like this basically represent one formula -- a self-abasement or insult formula according to the point of reference for the speaker. Job 7:17 parodies the concept of humankind presented in Psalm 8:6-9, but it does not parody Psalm 8:5; Psalm 144:3, on the other hand, does seem to be a conscious imitation of Psalm 8:5.

1257. Coetzee, J.H. "Die funksioniering van spanningselement in 'n aantal klaagpsalms." *Nederduits Gereformeerde Teologiese Tydskrif* 30 (1989): 6-20.

The Function of Elements of Tension in a Number of Lament Psalms. Yahweh "hides his face" in a series of laments: Psalms 9/10; 13; 22; 27; 44; 69; 88; 102 and 143. Various sorts of "tensions" are present here, including tension between the complaint and the appeal directed to Yahweh, between the psalmists and his enemies. Such "tensions" reflect the psalmist's concern to persuade Yahweh to intervene on his behalf.

1258. Coppens, J. *Het Onsterfelijkheidsgeloof in het Psalmboek.* Med. Kon. Vl. Acad. Wet. Lett. Sch. Kunsten van België XIX/3. Brussels, 1957.

1259. Crim, Keith R. *The Royal Psalms.* Richmond: John Knox Press, 1962. 127p.

Reviewed by E.S. Gerstenberger in *JBL* 81 (1962): 325-326.

1260. Crüsemann, Frank. *Studien zur Formgeschichte von Hymnus und Danklied in Israel.* Wissenschaftliche Monographien zum Alten und Neuen Testament 32. Neukirchen-Vluyn: Neukirchener Verlag, 1969. ix+348p.

A re-examination of the categories of the hymn and of the psalms of thanksgiving in Israel, including an attempt at reconstructing their pre-exilic forms. (The "call to joy" reflects the fertility cult; it is often addressed to a land or city as a feminine figure; it is not found in the Psalter.)

There are three types of hymns: (a) The imperative hymn (song of praise). The basic model is found in Exodus 15:21; in the Psalter the clearest example is Psalm 117. Other examples in the Psalter are Psalms 96, 98, 100, and 136. Here the imperative to sing "to Yahweh" is followed by *kî* and a verb of the perfect tense. Its *Sitz im Leben* is the regular cultus, its original content the experience of Yahweh's historical treatment of Israel. (b) The participial hymn. Parallels in the ancient Near East, especially Babylonia, point out the importance of this form. It is found in the prophecy of Deutero-Isaiah, in laments, requests, and in wisdom. Many are connected with the phrase "Yahweh is his name." Here the attempt is made to claim descriptions of other gods for Yahweh. Unfortunately, only fragments and mixtures of this form exist in Old Testament literature. (c) The hymn of the individual. This must be clearly distinguished from the *todah*, the thanksgiving song of the individual. Examples of this are Psalms 8 and 104. Direct address to god is originally part of "individual hymns."

Gunkel is correct in recognizing the category of the individual psalm of thanksgiving. Its structure has two parts: one directed to Yahweh in connection with (or in symbolic allusion to) the presentation of a sacrifice, the other directed to surrounding persons in a way that tells of Yahweh's deed. The psalm of thanksgiving (and the *toda*-formula) finds its original and normal place with the sacrifice of thanksgiving. Psalm 118 is the beginning point of analysis. Psalm 40 is also examined.

We must reject the existence of a category of collective psalms of thanksgiving distinct from hymns (against Gunkel). Psalms 124 and 129, 64A, 67 and 65 are examined. The "wish for praise" is common in the ancient oriental hymns as a way of praising gods and divine nature, and well as the powers of nature. In its pure form it is relatively rare in Israel. However, it was transformed and became part of one of the most important parts of the hymn in Israel -- the imperative. It is addressed to Yahweh and is analogous to a wish for blessing expressed to human addressees.

Reviewed by M.J. Buss in *JBL* 89 (1970): 466-468; reviewed also in *CBQ* 33 (1971): 250-251.

1261. _____. "Im Netz. Zur Frage nach der 'eigentlichen Not' in den Klagen der Einzelnen." In *Schöpfung und Befreiung. Für Claus Westermann,* ed. Rainer Albertz. 139-148. Stuttgart: Calwer Verlag, 1989.

In the psalms of individual lament we must not look for a single form or cause of distress; rather the individual is caught in a net of many distresses, with one form causing or attracting another.

1262. Curtis, A.H.W. "The 'subjugation of waters' motif in the Psalms: Imagery or Polemic?" *Journal of Semitic Studies* 23 (1978): 245-256.

1263. Davies, G.H. "The Ark in the Psalms." In *Promise and Fulfillment: Essays Presented to Professor S.H. Hooke*, ed. F.F. Bruce. 51-61. Edinburgh: T & T Clark, 1963.

1264. Delekat, L. *Asylie und Schutzorakel am Zionheiligtum: Eine Untersuchungen zu den Privaten Feindpsalmen mit zwei Exkursen.* Leiden: E.J. Brill, 1967. 432p.

The private complaint psalm against enemies has its *Sitz im Leben* in temple prayer inscriptions. A private individual, who has fled for safety to an asylum, records the answer to his prayer in an epigram *(miktam)*. Several small collections of these psalms exist in the Psalter: Psalms 3-7, 9/10-13, 16-17, 25-28, 31AB, 34-36, 54-55, 56-59(+60), 61-65, 69-71, 140-143. In some cases these collections have been provided with introductory and concluding psalms from other sources. These collections all come from the collection of prayer inscriptions at the Zion sanctuary. They date from different periods; generally the progression is chronological. The oldest collection is Psalms 3-7. Psalms 56-60 come from the time shortly after 800 B.C. Psalms 3-7(+8), 9/10-13(+14), 54-54 are older; Psalms 36, 61-64, 140-143 span the time until 721, which is reached in Psalm 143; Psalms (15+)16/17,22, 25-28, 31AB, and 40 originate after 721, as does Psalm 69, while Psalms 70 and 71 are probably older.

How is it determined whether God grants the individual asylum and refuge in the temple? Several means are available: incubation, sacrifice, and the priestly oracle. What form does the priest use in communicating the divine decision to the one seeking asylum? The priestly oracle of salvation. Most of those who come for asylum are poor and fearful of imprisonment or enslavement for debt. They have suffered acts of violence and are suspected of robbery. The speech of salvation serves as their letter of safe-conduct.

If the refugee is found guilty, he remains in the holy precincts; the priest cannot force him out; the priest, however, can help the guilty person to flee. Who may seek asylum in the temple precincts? Psalm 15 offers a few examples. Once asylum has been granted, it can be used as a weapon against those who have accused and threatened the refugee.

What happens to the refugees who could not leave the temple area? How can they support themselves? They can become temple-singers or precinct guards. In an act of self-dedication, the refugees take hold of the horns of the altar and say, "In the Lord I take refuge." Some could be anointed for priestly service; this was determined through questioning by the king. The ultimate goal of all who seek asylum is to be able to leave the place of asylum. This becomes possible when it is safe to leave, namely when the enemy receives an affliction (especially a sudden death) that is viewed by the public as a punishment for a false accusation. That is why many pray that God will kill the slanderer.

Two excursuses discuss the nature of the asylum outside the psalms: (1) sanctuaries of asylum for killers; the asylum and the king; (2) cities of asylum or refuge; the concept עצור. There are also an excursus on *Elohim* in the 2nd and 3rd Book of the Psalter, observations on determining the smallest literary units in the Psalms, and remarks on a few criticisms of Delekat's 1964 book *Katoche, Hierodulie und Adoptionsfreilassung.*

Reviewed in by B.S. Childs in *JBL* 88(1969): 104-105.

1265. Dell'Acqua, Anna Passoni. "Il Genere letterario dell' Inno e del Canto di Ringraziamento nell'antico e nel nuovo Testemento e negle Inni di Qumrân (IQH)." *Ephemerides Liturgicae* 90 (1976): 99-116.

A study comparing the nature of hymns and thanksgiving psalms in both the Old and New Testament and at Qumran (the Hodayot). There is some evolution in the genres as well as some contamination, especially in the Hodayot, where a sectarian heaviness is often observed. The hymn and the song of thanksgiving are two different ways of expressing joy; this joy is pure and disinterested in the hymn; it becomes more personal and living in the song of thanks.

1266. Del Páramo. S. "El género literario de los Salmos." *Estudios Biblicos* 6 (1947): 241-264, 450-451.

1267. Descamps, Albert. "Pour un classement littéraire des Psaumes." In *Mélanges bibliques rédigés en l'honneur de André Robert.* Trauvaux de l'Institut Catholique de Paris 4. 187-196. Paris: Bloud & Gay, 1959.

1268. Eaton John H. *Kingship and the Psalms.* Studies in Biblical Theology, Second Series 32. London: SCM Press, 1976. 2nd ed., London: JSOT Press, 1986. xii+247p.

The list of royal psalms is more extensive than has been admitted by others. Based on a variety of criteria, there are 31 psalms with clearly royal content (Psalms 3, 4, 7, 9-10, 17, 22, 23, 27, 28, 35, 40, 41, 57, 59, 61, 62, 63, 66, 69, 70, 71, 75, 89, 91, 92, 94, 108, 118, 138, 140, 143); 22 others are less clear cases (Psalms 5, 11, 16, 31, 36, 42-43, 51, 52, 54, 55, 56, 73, 77, 86, 102, 109, 116, 120, 121, 139, 141, 142). An examination of the royal rites outside and within Israel,

Mowinckel's autumn festival, and Gunkel's royal psalms confirms that the dramatic celebration of Yahweh's kingship in the autumn festival also entailed a dramatic presentation of the Davidic office. While the exact order of the ceremonies and texts remains uncertain, "the chief elements of the royal suffering and exaltation are strongly attested, as is also the close relation to the assertion of Yahweh's own kingship." An entirely eschatological interpretation of this ritual, however, is ruled out. The Psalter definitely has a royal aspect, being something like the king's collection of prayers. The royal psalms have not been "democratized." The second edition includes a discussion of works published in the last decade.

Reviewed in *The Expository Times* 88 (1976): 65-67; by R. Murray in *The Heythrop Journal* 19 (1978): 108-110.

1269. Eichhorn, D. *Gott als Fels, Burg und Zuflucht. Eine Untersuchungen zum Gebet des Mittlers in den Psalmen.* Bern: Herbert Lang, 1972.

1270. Frost, S.B. "Asservation by Thanksgiving." *Vetus Testamentum* 8 (1958): 380-390.

1271. Galling, Kurt. "Der Beichtspiegel: Eine gattungsgeschichtliche Studie." *Zeitschrift für die alttestamentliche Wissenschaft* 47 (1929): 125-130. Reprinted in *Zur Neueren Psalmenforschung*, ed. Peter H.A. Neumann, 168-175; Darmstadt: Wissenschaftliche Buchgesellschaft, 1976.

1272. Gelander, Shamai. "Convention and Originality: Identification of the Situation in the Psalms." *Vetus Testamentum* 42 (1992): 302-316.

It is possible to discern a personal, unique situation for the psalms even when these psalms have been identified as cultic and formulaic. Psalm 5 and the phrase "under the shadow of your wings" from Psalm 17:8 demonstrate this thesis.

1273. Gelin, A. "La question des 'relectures' bibliques à l'intérieur d'une tradition vivante." *Sacra Pagina. Miscellanea biblica Congressus Internationalis Catholici de Re Biblica.* Ed. J. Coppens, A. Descamps, and E. Massaux. Bibliotheca ephemeridum theologicarum lovaniensium 13. I: 203-215. Gembloux: J. Duculot, 1959.

Psalm 47; Psalm 22 and Isaiah 53; Zechariah 3:9; Psalm 78; Psalm 110:3 (LXX).

1274. _____. *La Prière des Psaumes.* 2nd ed. Paris: Editions de L'Epi, 1961. 107p.

1275. George, A. "Prier les Psaumes." *Foi Vivante* 15 (1965): 15-224.

1276. Gerstenberger, Erhard S. "Der klagende Mensch." In *Probleme biblischer Theologie: G. von Rad zum 70. Geburtstag,* ed. H.W. Wolff. 64-72. Munich: Chr. Kaiser Verlag, 1971.

1277. _____. "Psalms." In *Old Testament Form Criticism,* ed. J. H. Hayes. 179-223. Trinity University Monographs Series in Religion 2. San Antonio, TX: Trinity University Press, 1974.

1278. _____. *Der bittende Mensch. Bittritual und Klagelied des Einzelnen im Alten Testament.* Wissenschaftliche

Monographien zum Alten und Neuen Testament 51. Neukirchen: Neukirchener Verlag, 1980. x+195p.

The Laments of the Individual are formularies distilled from general experience, the work of ritual experts who presented them with ritual acts on behalf of the client or patient. An examination of procedures and wording of petitions to human beings in the Old Testament narratives, the combination of ritual and utterance in Babylonian exorcism, and modern social studies confirm their original purpose. The texts must be understood as only the spoken part of the ritual; such procedures occur in the primary social group rather than then state cult; the expert is more of a seer than a priest.

1279. _____. *Wesen und Herkunft des "Apodiktischen Rechts."* Wissenschaftliche Monographien zum Alten und Neuen Testament. Neukirchen-Vluyn: Neukirchener Verlag, 1965. 162p.

Contrary to the commonly accepted view that apodictic law is "genuinely Israelite," and that it finds its life-setting in the liturgy (covenant renewal), the literary genre of "apodictic" law has to be broken down; moreover, it is not typically Israelite (contrary to the opinion of many), nor bound to the liturgy, and it covers many different legal genres. The origin of the prohibitions is not to be found in an act of covenanting; rather the prohibitions are best located in the life of the tribe; they are the authoritative commands of the clan elders, which derive their binding power from the sacral order they are designed to preserve.

Reviewed by R.E. Murphy in *JBL* 85 (1966): 503-504.

1280. Gese, Hartmut. "Abraham unser Vater." In *Abraham unser Vater. Juden und Christen im Gespräch über die Bibel. Festchrift für Otto Michel zum 60. Geburtstag,* ed. Otto Betz, Martin Hengel, and Peter Schmidt. 222-234. Leiden: E.J. Brill, 1963. Reprinted in *Vom Sinai zum Zion.* Beiträge zur Evangelische Theologie 64. 147-158. Munich: Kaiser, 1974.

1281. _____. "Der Davidsbund und die Zionserwählung." *Zeitschrift für Theologie und Kirche* 61 (1964): 10-26. Reprinted in *Vom Sinai zum Zion: Alttestamentliche Beiträge zur biblischen Theologie.* Beiträge zur Evangelische Theologie 64. 113-129. Munich: Kaiser, 1974.

1282. _____. "Bemerkungen zur Sinaitradition." *Zeitschrift für die alttestamentliche Wissenschaft* 79 (1967): 137-154. Reprinted in *Vom Sinai zum Zion: Alttestamentliche Beiträge zur biblischen Theologie.* Beiträge zur Evangelische Theologie 64. 31-48. Munich: Kaiser, 1974.

1283. Gevaryahu, Haim. "Amen and Hallelujah." *Dor le Dor* 13 (1984/1985): 93-97.

The first originated in private prayer; the second was part of the temple liturgy that eventually found its way into the synagogue through the recitation of the Psalms.

1284. Ginsberg, H.L. "Psalms and Inscriptions of Petition and Acknowledgement." In *Louis Ginsberg Jubilee Volume.* 159-171. American Academy for Jewish Research. New York, 1945.

1285. _____. "A Strand in the Cord of Hebraic Hymnody." *Eretz Israel* 9 (1969): 45-50.

Psalms 29, 96, 98, 147, and Deutero-Isaiah.

1286. Gómez, Humberto Jiménez. "Los Géneros Literarios en los Salmos." *Seminario Conciliar* 6 (1961): 9-25.

1287. González, Ruiz José M. "Las teofanias en los Salmos." *Estudios Biblicos* 13 (1954): 267-287.

A distinction needs to be made between theophany psalms in the narrow sense (Psalms 18 and 50) and those in the wider sense. The latter include those which speak of God's presence as a) a cosmic appearance: Psalms 29, 33, 104; b) a human event: Psalms 66, 68, 76, 81; c) the royal majesty of Yahweh: Psalm 47, 93, 95-99. Although the assumption of an "enthronement festival" (Mowinckel) or of a "covenant festival" (Weiser) is lacking concrete proof, the cultic character of these psalms cannot be disputed.

1288. Grill, Severin. "Die Regenbitten in den Psalmen." *Bibel und Liturgie* 24 (1957): 265-269.

Psalms 4, 28(29), 41(42), 64(65), 67(68), 83(84), probably also all the Gradual Psalms (119-132 [120-133]), 133(134), 146(147:1-11).

1289. Gunkel, Hermann. *Ausgewählte Psalmen.* Göttingen: Vandenhoeck & Ruprecht, 1904. 4th ed., 1917. 270p.

Most of the Psalm interpretations found in this book of selected Psalms were printed previously (1900-1903) in a few German and North American journals. Questions about where and when a Psalm was composed have little weight beside the more important issue of what a Psalm means. Our real purpose is "to make clear to the modern reader the piety of the psalmists and to lay it to heart." Translations and interpretations are offered for Psalms 1, 2, 8, 19, 20, 22, 23, 24, 26, 29, 39, 42-43, 45, 46, 50, 51, 79, 82, 85, 90, 91, 95, 97, 103, 104, 114, 121, 122, 123, 124, 125, 126, 128, 129, 130, 131, 139, 149, 1 Samuel 2:1-10, and Jonah 2:2-10.

1290. _____. *Reden und Aufsätze von Hermann Gunkel.* Göttingen: Vandenhoeck & Ruprecht, 1913.

Articles related to the Psalms include "Die Endhoffnung der Psalmisten" (123-130). "Ägyptische Parallelen zum Alten Testament" (131-141), and "Ägyptische Danklieder" (141-149).

1291. _____. "Die Königspsalmen." *Preussische Jahrebücher* 158 (1914): 42-68.

1292. _____. "Formen der Hymnen." *Theologische Rundschau* 20 (1917): 265-304.

1293. _____. "Danklieder im Psalter." *Zeitschrift für Missionskunde und Religionswissenschaft* 34 (1919): 177-184, 211-228.

1294. _____. "Die alttestamentliche Literaturgeschichte und die Ansetzung der Psalmen." *Theologische Blätter* 7 (1928): 85ff.

1295. _____. *Was bleibt vom Alten Testament?* Göttingen: Vandenhoeck & Ruprecht, 1916. 34p. Translated into

English by A.K. Dallas and published as *What Remains of the Old Testament*. London: Allen & Unwin, 1928.

Contains English translations of five essays originally written in German, including "The Religion of the Psalms" (*Die Christliche Welt* 36 [1922]: nos. 1, 2, 5, 6, 7).

1296. Habel, Norman C. "Yahweh, Maker of Heaven and Earth: A Study in Tradition Criticism." *Journal of Biblical Literature* 91 (1972): 321-337.

The roots, function, and modulation of the title, "Yahweh, maker of heaven and earth," as a formula within the liturgical and prophetic contexts of the religion of Israel.

1297. Haglund, Erik. *Historical Motifs in the Psalms*. Coniectanea Biblica Old Testament Series 23. Malmö and Uppsala: CWK Gleerup, 1984. 144p.

These motifs have developed in two settings. 1) One is the covenant cult, in which hymns with the motifs of exodus and conquest are used in the Autumn Festival. Psalms of lament connected with the same cult use similar motifs. Royal psalms of lament refer to the David traditions. In the covenant cult the historical motifs serve as expressions of God's faithfulness. 2) The other setting is the Holy war, where the motifs of exodus and conquest appear in the form of theophanies in hymns and lament. Here the historical motifs express God's power and intervention. They are used as reasons for praise, as objects of meditation and as profession of trust; they often represent a literary stage that is older than the traditions preserved in the narrative works; however, the Deuteronomic-Deuteronomistic circles have created psalms of their own.

Reviewed in *CBQ* 48 (1986): 533-535.

1298. Harvey, Julien. "La typologie de l'Exode dans les Psaumes." *Sciences Ecclésiastiques* 15 (1963): 383-405.

1299. Hayes, John H. "The Tradition of Zion's Inviolability." *Journal of Biblical Literature* 82 (1963): 419-426.

1300. Heinen, Karl. "Das nomen *t*^{e}*fillā* als Gattungsbezeichnung." *Biblische Zeitschrift* 17 (1973): 103-105.

T^{e}*fillā* ("prayer of lament and intercession") was the earlier and better designation than *t*^{e}*hillim* ("praises") for the Psalms.

1301. Hesse, Fr. "Würzelt die prophetische Gerichtsrede im israelitischen Kult?" *Zeitschrift für die alttestamentliche Wissenschaft* 65 (1953): 45-53.

1302. Holm-Nielsen, S. *Die Geschichtsmotive in den alttestamentlichen Psalmen.* Annales academiae scientiarum fennicae 16/1. Helsinki: Suomalainen Tiedeakatemia, 1945.

1303. ______. "Die alttestamentliche Psalmentradition." *Dansk teologisk Tidsskrift* 18 (1955): 123-148, 193-215.

The late Jewish psalm poetry of Psalms of Solomon, on the one hand, and the Psalms in the Old Testament outside the psalter, on the other hand, show how the old cultic *Sitz im Leben* can be lost. The later period used the Psalms as wisdom literature, sought allusions to historical situations, and placed the Psalms in a new cult situation (synagogue).

1304. ______. "De sidste årtiers salme -- og profetforskning; nogle synspunkter." *Dansk Teologisk Tidsskrift* 35 (1972): 30-46.

1305. Horst, Friedrich (1896-1962). "Segen und Segenshandlungen in der Bibel." *Evangelische Theologie* 7 (1947-1948): 23-37. Reprinted in *Gottes Recht. Gesammelte Studien zum Recht im Alten Testament von Friedrich Horst. Aus Anlass der Vollendung seines 65. Lebensjahres*, ed. H.W. Wolff. 188-202. Munich: Ch. Kaiser, 1961.

1306. Hunter, J.H. "The Literary Composition of Theophany Passages in the Hebrew Psalms." *Journal of Northwest Semitic Languages* 15 (1989): 97-107.

The invariables in the Theophany Psalms (18, 50, 68, 97, 144) are the coming of God and the effect of this coming on nature. Each psalmist appropriated both the argumentation and the poetry of the theophanic tradition to create new meanings in a new poem.

1307. Hurvitz, Avi. "Wisdom Vocabulary in the Hebrew Psalter: A Contribution to the Study of 'Wisdom Psalms.'" *Vetus Testamentum* 38 (1988): 41-51.

1308. Hyde, Clark. "The Remembrance of the Exodus in the Psalms." *Worship* 62 (1988): 404-414.

1309. James, Fleming. *Thirty Psalmists: A Study in Personalities of the Psalter as Seen Against the Background of Gunkel's Type-Study of the Psalms.* New York: G.P. Putnam's Sons, 1938. xv+261p. 2nd ed. (Paperback), 1965.

1310. Janowski, Bernd. "Keruben und Zion. Thesen zur Entstehung der Ziontradition." In *Ernten was man sät. Festschrift für Klaus Koch zu seinem 65. Geburtstag*, ed. Dwight R. Daniels. 232-264. Neukirchen-Vluyn: Neukirchener Verlag, 1991.

Many scholars follow Alt in tracing the origins of the Zion tradition back to David's bringing the ark to Jerusalem. More likely, the decisive impetus for the development of this tradition emanates from Solomon's construction of a cherubim throne for Yahweh in the Jerusalem temple.

1311. Jansen, H.Ludin. *Die spätjudische Psalmendictung, ihr Entstehungskreis und ihr "sitz im Leben"*. Skrifter utgitt av Det Norske Videnskaps-Akademi i Oslo, II. Hist.-Filos. Klasse 3. Oslo: Jacob Dybwad, 1937. 147p.

1312. Janzen, Waldemar. "*ᵓAshrê* in the Old Testament." *Harvard Theological Review* 58 (1965): 215-226.

1313. ______. *Mourning Cry and Woe Oracle*. Beihefte zur Zeitschrift für die alttestamentliche Wissenschaft 125. Berlin: Walter de Gruyter, 1972. 91p.

A survey of the semantic range of *hôy* from its *Sitz im Leben* as a funerary expression of lament to its use in prophetic oracles of impending punishment.

Reviewed by Ludwig R. Dewitz in *JBL* 93 (1974): 301-302.

1314. Jasper, F.N. "Early Israelite Traditions and the Psalter." *Vetus Testamentum* 17 (1967): 50-59.

Only Psalms 44, 47, 60, 68, 77, 78, 80, 81, 99, 105, 106, 114, 135, and 136 "afford a recognizable link with the traditions of Israel's origins as a people." A knowledge of the Pentateuch allows the construction of a coherent narrative from these "historical psalms"; however, only in Psalms 78, 105, 106, 135, and 136 is there an attempt to give a chronological record of the events; these five are probably fairly late in their present form. The other ten psalms belong to "the early, spontaneous group"; since they were already part of the established liturgy, they remained as they were, even though the disappearance of the monarchy called for modifications.

1315. Jeremias, Jörg. *Theophanie. Die Geschichte einer alttestamentlichen Gattung.* Wissenschaftliche Monographien zum Alten und Neuen Testament 10. Neukirchen-Vluyn: Neukirchener Verlag, 1965. 182p. 2nd ed., 1977.

The theophany is an independent type which grew gradually. The original and shortest form consisted of two parts: Yahweh comes and there is a reaction in nature (Amos 1:2; Micah 1:3f; Psalm 46:7 and Isaiah 63:19b; perhaps also underlying Judges 5:4f and Psalm 68:8f). As the form developed, it was given a new content or was simply expanded with new motifs. In some instances, the two parts of the form separated from one another and became independent. A dissolution of the form takes place in texts that introduce the clouds as God's chariots or describe the various weapons of God.

A survey of the literature of Israel's neighbors reveals certain parallels in the way theophanies are described: a) Yahweh rides upon the clouds; b) Yahweh's voice is heard in the thunder; c) Yahweh sends his lightning as arrows; d)

Yahweh is in the storm; e) the earth trembles before Yahweh's voice; f) the mountains tremble before Yahweh and heaven and earth shudder; g) Yahweh's power makes the mountains tremble; h) the earth trembles before the din of the chariot of Yahweh; i) Yahweh makes the deep tremble; j) Yahweh makes fiery coals rain upon his enemies; k) Yahweh fights against his enemies with the weapons of nature. The traditions of the conquest of primeval chaos, the miracle of the deliverance at the sea, and the Day of the Lord also contributed to the development of the theophany as a literary type. The description of the Sinai theophany, on the other hand, is not the prototype of other theophany texts; it is still possible, though, that the idea of Yahweh's coming is a reflection of the Sinai event. Also considered are the ark tradition, the tradition of Yahweh as a heavenly king, Yahweh's coming in the stilling of the storm, as well as an excursus on Yahweh's place of departure.

The *Sitz im Leben* of the theophany is not the Jerusalem liturgy, as Mowinckel and Weiser have argued; rather, based on the various contexts in which theophanic texts occur (the hymn to Yahweh and the prophetic proclamations of judgment and salvation), the theophanic form is more firmly rooted in the hymn, specifically in the victory songs of the wars of Yahweh (as reflected in the song of Deborah). This explains the coming of Yahweh with the forces of nature as Yahweh's weapons. With the coming of the monarchy and the use of mercenaries, victory celebrations took on a secular character; the theophany thus was loosed from its original setting, appearing in passages such as Psalm 46, Deuteronomy 33 and the writing prophets. Throughout its history, the theophany serves as an expression of Israel's belief in Yahweh's irresistible power and Yahweh's dynamic intervention in order to destroy his enemies and to deliver his people. In the course of the study, references are made to Psalms 18, 29, 46, 48, 50, 68, 76, 77, 97, 99, 104, 114, 144.

Reviewed by R.E. Murphy in *JBL* 85 (1966): 107-108.

1316. _____. "Lade und Zion. Zur Entstehung der Ziontradition" In *Probleme biblischer Theologie. Festschrift G. von Rad zum 70. Geburtstag*, ed. H.W. Wolff. 183-198. Munich: Chr. Kaiser, 1971.

1317. Käser, W. "Beobachtungen zum alttestamentlichen Makarismus." *Zeitschrift für die alttestamentliche Wissenschaft* 82 (1970): 225-250.

1318. Kevers, P. "Wisdom Elements in the Psalms." In *Wie wijsheid zoekt, vindt het Leven. De wijsheidsliteratur van het Oude Testament*, ed. Erik Fynikel. Leuven: Vlaamse Bijbelstichting/Acco, 1991; Boxtel: Katholieke Bibjel Stichting, 1991. (Dutch)

1319. Kim, Ee Kon. *The Rapid Change of Mood in the Lament Psalms: A Matrix for the Establishment of a Psalm Theology*. Seoul, Korea: Korea Theological Study Institute, 1985. 267p.

1320. Kirchner, Dankwart. "Gruppendynamische Untersuchung zu Struktur und Geschichte der Klage im Alten Testament." *Theologische Literaturzeitung* 114 (1989): 785-796.

1321. Koch, Klaus. "Tempeleinlassliturgien und Dekalog." In *Studien zur Theologie der alttestamentlichen Überlieferungen. Festschrift Gerhard von Rad*, ed. R. Rendtorff and K. Koch. 45-60. Neukirchen-Vluyn: Neukirchener Verlag, 1961.

Psalms 15 and 24:4ff; Isaiah 33:14ff; Micah 6:6ff; Ezekiel 18:5ff.

1322. Kraus, Hans-Joachim. "Zum Thema 'Exodus.'" In *Biblisch-theologische Aufsätze.* 109-119. Neukirchen-Vluyn: Neukirchener Verlag, 1972.

1323. _____. "Tore der Gerechtigkeit." In *Ernten was man sät. Festschrift für Klaus Koch zu seinem 65. Geburtstag,* ed. Dwight R. Daniels. 265-272. Neukirchen-Vluyn: Neukirchener Verlag, 1991.

Explores the connection between righteousness and access to Yahweh in worship, as presented in Psalms 15 and 24, the prophetic adaptations in Micah 6:6-8, Isaiah 33:14-16, Ezekiel 18, as well as the Temple Sermon in Jeremiah 7.

1324. Küchler, F. "Das priesterliche Orakel in Israel und Juda." In *Abhandlungen zur semitischen Religionskunde und Sprachwissenschaft, W.W. Graften von Baudissin überreicht.* Beihefte zur Zeitschrift für die alttestamentliche Wissenschaft 33. 285-301. Giessen: Alfred Töpelmann, 1918.

A priestly oracle intervenes at the place just before the sudden change of mood. In this oracle the priest or cultic person assures the lamenter that Yahweh has heard his or her petition.

1325. Kuntz, J. Kenneth. "Theophany and the Book of Psalms." Chap. in *The Self-Revelation of God.* 169-214. Philadelphia: Westminster Press, 1967.

In the Psalms (18, 50, and 97) the theophany has a partiality for metaphor and elaborate description and moves away from the strict theophanic form.

1326. _____. "The Canonical Wisdom Psalms: Their Rhetorical, Thematic and Formal Dimensions." In *Rhetorical Criticism. Essays in Honor of James Muilenburg*, ed. Jared J. Jackson and Martin Kessler. 186-222. Pittsburgh, PA: Pickwick, 1974.

Psalms 1, 32, 34, 37, 49, 112, 127, 128, and 133 are wisdom psalms. Seven rhetorical elements (none contains all seven), 64 sapiential words, and four thematic elements appear in the wisdom psalms.

1327. _____. "The Retribution Motif in Psalmic Wisdom." *Zeitschrift für die alttestamentliche Wissenschaft* 89 (1977): 223-233.

1328. Kunz, P. Lucas. "Selah, Titel und authentische Gliederung der Psalmen." *Theologie und Glaube* 46 (1956): 363-369.

1329. _____. "Zur Liedgestalt der ersten fünf Psalmen." *Biblische Zeitschrift* 7 (1963): 261-270.

1330. Lauha, Aarre. *Die Geschichtsmotive in den alttestamentlichen Psalmen*. Annales Academiae Scientiarum Fennicae, B LVI,1. Helsinki: Druckerei A.-G. der Finnischen Literaturgesellschaft, 1945. 148p.

1331. Lindblom, J. "Bemerkungen zu den Psalmen." *Zeitschrift für die alttestamentliche Wissenschaft* 58 (1942-1944): 1-13.

1332. ______. "Theophanies in Holy Places in Hebrew Religion." *Hebrew Union College Annual* 32 (1961): 91-106.

1333. Lipiński, Edouard. "Les psaumes de supplication individuelle." *Revue Ecclésiastique de Liège* 53 (1967): 129-138.

1334. ______. "Les psaumes d'action de grâce individuelle." *Revue Ecclésiastigue de Liège* 53 (1967): 346-366.

1335. ______. "Macarismes et psaumes de congratulation." *Revue Biblique* 75 (1968): 321-367.

1336. ______. *La liturgie pénitentielle dans la Bible.* Lectio Divina 52. Paris: Les Éditions du Cerf, 1969. 117p.

The penitential liturgies represent the best attested forms of cultic life of ancient Israel; they come as a result of natural phenomena and before or after battle; if necessary, they were repeated several times. When the need arose, the Israelites observed a fast, followed by sacrifices and petitions to God in the local sanctuary. Penitential liturgies were also one aspect of Hebrew funeral rites. The elements that make up this category -- invocation, complaint (with its "Why?" addressed to God), expression of sorrow, accusation of the enemy, and plea for help -- are all compared, both within the Bible and outside the Bible; the evolution of the form is described. There are relatively few psalms of national supplication in the Psalter (Psalms 44:10-15,18-27; 60:3-7,8-14; 74; 79; 80; 83; 85:2-8; 89:39-52; and 94:1-7); originally they came about as a result of the suppliant's appeal to Yahweh for help.

Reviewed by L.T. Whitelocke in *JBL* 90 (1971): 492-494.

1337. Luke, F. "The Songs of Zion as a Literary Category of the Psalter." *Indian Journal of Theology* 14 (1965): 72-90.

1338. Luyten, J. "Het Zelfbeklag in de Psalmen." *Ephemerides Theologicae Lovanienses* 39 (1963): 501-538.

The self-lament in the Psalms.

1339. McConville, J.G. "Statement of Assurance in Psalms of Lament." *Irish Biblical Studies* 8 (1986): 64-75.

The real explanation for the change in mood in the lament psalms is the ability of these texts to effect a similar change in the mood of the user.

1340. McKay, J.W. "Psalms of Vigil." *Zeitschrift für die alttestamentliche Wissenschaft* 91 (1979): 229-247.

There are about 8 or 9 psalms that appear to be the prayers of a distressed worshipper keeping vigil at the sanctuary. He tells of suffering, of a sense of dereliction and of a spiritual conflict with grotesque enemies. His purpose is to seek God's healing presence by watching for the dawn which, as it vanquishes the powers of darkness, symbolizes for him the coming of God's salvation. These psalms were probably composed for use by individuals, but in some kind of community setting.

1341. McKenzie, J.L. "The Imprecations of the Psalter." *American Ecclesiastical Review* 111 (1944): 81-96.

1342. Maiberger, P. "Zur Problematik und Herkunft der sogenannten Fluchpsalmen." *Trierer Theologische Zeitschrift* 97 (1988): 183-216.

These psalms are not the outpouring of sheer unbridled anger, or of human wickedness. Rather their ultimate source is the holy and just God "who speaks his curse against anyone who does not turn from evil."

1343. Mand, Fritzlothar. "Die Eigenständigkeit der Danklieder des Psalters als Bekenntnislieder." *Zeitschrift für die alttestamentliche Wissenschaft* 70 (1958): 185-199.

1344. Mannati, Marina. *Pour prier avec les psaumes.* Cahiers Evangile 13. Paris: Cerf, 1966.

1345. ______. "Les psaumes graduels constituent-ils un genre littéraire distinct à l'interieur du psautier biblique?" *Semitica* 29 (1979): 85-100.

The recognition of the "gradual psalms" as a separate literary genre clarifies their meaning. The genre is determined not by the structure of the individual psalm but by the cumulative course or movement of the entire group.

1346. Martin-Achard, R. "La prière des malades dan le psautier d'Israël." *Lumiere et Vie* 86 (1968): 25-43.

1347. Mbon, Friday M. "Deliverance in the Complaint Psalms: Religious Claim or Religious Experience." *Studia Biblica et Theologica* 12 (1962): 3-15.

Psalms 6 and 32 concern deliverance from sickness. Psalms 18 and 28 provide insight into the meaning of deliverance from enemies. The psalmist's "death experience" in Psalms 30 and 116 results in deliverance from the fear and threat of death. No explanation is offered on how the deliverance takes place. None may be possible.

1348. Millàs Vallacrosa, J.M. "La tradución del Salmo penitencial en la poesia hebraica postbiblica." In *Miscellanea Biblica B. Ubach*, ed. R. Díaz. 243-278. Montserrat: Imprinta-escuela of Barcelona, 1953.

1349. Miller, Patrick D., Jr. "Trouble and Woe: Interpreting the Biblical Laments." *Interpretation* 37 (1983): 32-45.

1350. Morgenstern, J. "The Cultic Setting of the 'Enthronement Psalms.'" *Hebrew Union College Annual* 35 (1964): 1-42.

1351. Mowinckel, Sigmund. "Psalms and Wisdom." In *Wisdom in Israel and in the Ancient Near East. Presented to Professor Harold Henry Rowley by the Society for Old Testament Study in association with the Editorial Board of Vetus Testamentum, in Celebration of His Sixty-fifth Birthday, 24 March 1955*, ed. M. Noth and D. Winton Thomas. Supplements to Vetus Testamentum 3. 205-244. Leiden: E.J. Brill, 1955. Translated into German and printed as "Psalmen und Weisheit" in *Zur Neueren Psalmenforschung*, ed. Peter H.A. Neumann, 341-366; Darmstadt: Wissenschaftliche Buchgesellschaft, 1976.

There is no cultic background for the wisdom psalms; they are something less than "real" psalms.

1352. Müller, H.-P. "Die kultische Darstellung der Theophanie." *Vetus Testamentum* 14 (1964): 183-191.

1353. Murphy, Roland E. "A New Classification of Literary Forms in the Psalms." *Catholic Biblical Quarterly* 21 (1959): 64-87.

1354. _____. "An Approach to the Psalms." Chap. in *Seven Books of Wisdom.* 28-52. Milwaukee, WI: Bruce Publishing Co., 1960.

1355. _____. "A Consideration of the Classification, 'Wisdom Psalms.'" In *Congress Volume, Bonn 1962. Supplements to Vetus Testamentum* 9. 156-167. Leiden: E.J. Brill, 1962; reprinted in *Studies in Ancient Israel, selected, with a Prolegomena by James L. Crenshaw.* The Library of Biblical Studies, ed. Harry M. Orlinsky. 456-467. New York: KTAV Publishing House, 1976.

1356. _____. *Wisdom Literature and the Psalms.* Nashville, TN: Abingdon, 1983.

1357. Nicolsky, N.M. *Spuren Magischen Formeln in den Psalmen.* Authorized translation of the Russian manuscript by Georg Petzold. Beihefte zur Zeitschrift für die alttestamentliche Wissenschaft 46. Giessen: Alfred Töpelmann, 1927. 97p.

1358. _____. "Das Asylrecht in Israel." *Zeitschrift für die alttestamentliche Wissenschaft* 48 (1930): 146-175.

1359. Niemeyer, Cornelius T. *Het Problem van de Rangschikking der Psalmen.* Leiden: Luctor et emergo, 1950. 166p.

1360. Norden, Eduard (1868-1941) *Agnostos Theos. Untersuchungen zur Formgeschichte religiösen Rede.* Leipzig: B.G. Teubner, 1913. x+410p. 4th ed., Darmstadt: Wissenschaftliche Buchgesellschaft, 1956. Reprint, 1974.

1361. Norin, Stig I.L. *Er Spaltete das Meer: Die Auszugüberlieferung in Psalmen und Kult des Alten*

Israel. Coniectanea Biblica, Old Testament 9. Translated from the Swedish by Christiane Boehncke Sjöberg. Lund: Gleerup, 1977. xiii+235p.

Reviewed by D.F. Morgan in *JBL* 98 (1979): 128-129; reviewed also in *CBQ* 40 (1978): 612-613.

1362. O'Brien, Julia M. "Because God Heard My Voice: The Individual Thanksgiving Psalm and Vow-Fulfillment." In *The Listening Heart. Essays in Wisdom and the Psalms in honor of Roland E. Murphy, O.Carm.*, ed. Kenneth G. Hoglund and Others. Journal for the Study of the Old Testament Supplement 58. Sheffield: JSOT Press, 1987.

1363. Pidoux, G. "Quelques allusions au droit d'asile dans les Psaumes." In *Maqqél shâqéd. La branche d'amandier. Hommage à Wilhelm Visscher.* 181-190. Montpellier: Causse Graille Castelnau, 1960.

1364. Ploeg, J. van der. "Réflexions sur les genres littéraires des Psaumes." In *Studia biblica et semitica. Theodoro Christiano Vriezen qui munere Professoris Theologiae per XXV Annos functus est, ab Amicis, Collegis, Discipulis dedicata.* 265-277. Wageningen: H. Veenman & Zonen, 1966.

1365. Press, R. "Das Ordal im alten Israel." *Zeitschrift für die alttestamentliche Wissenschaft* 51 (1933): 121-140, 227-255.

1366. ______. "Die Gerichtspredigt der vorexilischen Propheten und der Versuch einer Steigerung der kultischen Leistung." *Zeitschrift für die alttestamentliche Wissenschaft*, N.S., 29 (1958): 181-184.

1367. Quell, G. *Das kultische Problem der Psalmen.* Beiträge zur Wissenschaft vom Alten und Neuen Testament, N.F., 11. Berlin: W. Kohlhammer, 1926.

The psalms can be divided into three main groups. (1) Cultic Group A includes 62 psalms (Psalms 1, 2, 12, 14, 15, 20/21, 24, 29, 33, 44-48, 50, 58, 60, 65, 67, 68, 72, 74, 76, 78-83, 85, 87, 90, 93, 95-100, 102, 105, 107, 110, 112-114, 117, 124-126, 128, 129, 132-136, 147-150); these are dominated by cultic ideas or reveal liturgical patterns. (2) Cultic-Religious Mixed-Group B includes 75 psalms (All those not in A or C); here cultic elements are mixed with non-cultic religious thoughts). (3) Religious Group C includes 13 psalms (Psalms 6, 19:1-7, 38, 39, 41, 88, 91, 102A, 120, 127, 131, 139, 143); only cult-free religious expressions are found in these psalms. None of these form-critical studies proves the existence of cult prophets; historical proof, not form-critical proof, is necessary to establish this. It is too easy for prophetic words to be imitated in the liturgy.

1368. Rad, Gerhard von. "Erwägungen zu den Königspsalmen." *Zeitschrift für die alttestamentliche Wissenschaft* 58 (1940/41): 216-222; reprinted in *Zur Neueren Psalmenforschung*, ed. Peter H.A. Neumann, 176-184; Darmstadt: Wissenschaftliche Buchgesellschaft, 1976.

1369. ______. "Der Lobpreis Israels." In *Antwort: Karl Barth zum siebzigsten Geburtstag am 10. Mai 1956.* Ed. E. Wolf, Ch. von Kirschbaum, and R. Frey. 676-687. Zollikon-Zürich: Evangelischer Verlag, 1956.

1370. Rao, T.J. Raja. "Agony and Anguish: the Psalmist in His Sufferings." *Jeevadhara* 18 (1988): 94-100.

1371. Reindl, Joseph. "Weisheitliche Bearbeitung von Psalmen." *Congress Volume. Vienna, 1980.* Supplement to *Vetus Testamentum* 32. 333-356. Leiden: E.J. Brill, 1981.

1372. Rendtorff, K.G. "Sejrshymnen i Exodus 15 og dens forhold til tronbestigelsessalmerne." *Dansk Teologisk Tidsskrift* 22 (1959): 65-81, 156-171.

1373. Reventlow, Henning Graf. "Kultisches Recht im Alten Testament." *Zeitschrift für Theologie und Kirche* 60 (1963): 267-304.

The origin of the prophetic message formula and lies in the giving of the law in the covenant feast. Thus the prophetic office is firmly based in the cult and mediates the law.

1374. Ridderbos, Nicolaas Hermann. "De plaats van het loven en van het bidden in het Oude Testament." 1970. Reprinted in *Psalmenstudie. Prof. Nic. H. Ridderbos en het boek der Psalmen. Opstellen van prof. dr. Nic. H. Ridderbos,* ed. C. van Ginkel and P.J. van Midden. 144-169. Kampen: Kok, 1991.

1375. ______. *Die Psalmen. Stilistische Verfahren und Aufbau mit besonderer Berucksichtigung von Ps 1-41.* Translated from the Dutch by Karl E. Mittring. Beihefte zur Zeitschrift für die alttestamentliche Wissenschaft 117. Berlin: Walter de Gruyter, 1972. xii+305p.

Reviewed in *CBQ* 35 (1973): 403-405.

1376. Robert, A. "L'exégèse des Psaumes selon les méthodes de la 'Formgeschichte' exposé et critique." *Miscellanea Biblica*

B. Ubach, ed. R. Díaz. 211-225. Montserrat: Imprinta-escuela of Barcelona, 1953.

1377. Rost, L. *Die Überlieferung von der Thronnachfolge Davids.* Beiträge zur Wissenschaft von Alten und Neuen Testament 3/6. Stuttgart: Kohlhammer, 1926.

1378. Ruppert, Lothar. "Klage oder Bitte? Zu einer neuen Sicht der individuellen Klagelieder." *Biblische Zeitschrift* 33 (1989): 252-255.

The basic component of this literary form is not as lament but as (petitionary) prayer; it is marked by the use of traditional vocabulary and motifs.

1379. Sabourin, Leopold. *Un Classement Littéraire des Psaumes.* Bruges, Belgium: Desclée de Brouwer, 1964. [= *Sciences Ecclésiastiques* 1964 23-58]. 58p.

Reviewed in *CBQ* 26 (1964): 515-516.

1380. Scharbert, Josef. *Solidarität im Segen und Fluch im Alten Testament und in seiner Umwelt I.* Bonner Biblische Beiträge 14. Bonn: P. Hanstein, 1958.

1381. ______. "Die Geschichte der *barūk*-Formel." *Biblische Zeitschrift*, N.F., 17 (1963): 1-28.

1382. Schenker, Adrian. "Gelübde im Alten Testament: unbeachtete Aspekte." *Vetus Testamentum* 39 (1989): 87-91.

In addition to the common vow of petition, there are several other kinds of vows in the Old Testament.

1383. Schilling, Othmar. "Noch einmal die Fluchpsalmen." *Theologie und Glaube* 47 (1957): 177-185.

1384. Schmidt, Hans. "Das Gebet der Angeklagten im Alten Testament." In *Old Testament Essays. Papers read before the Society for Old Testament Study at its eighteenth meeting, held at Keble College, Oxford, September 27th to 30th, 1927*, 143-155. London: Charles Griffen and Company, Limited, 1927. Reprinted in *Zur Neueren Psalmenforschung*, ed. Peter H.A. Neumann, 156-167; Darmstadt: Wissenschaftliche Buchgesellschaft, 1976. This lecture in expanded form with footnotes added was published under the same name in *Beiheft zur Zeitschrift für die alttestamentliche Wissenschaft* 49. Giessen: Alfred Töpelmann, 1928.

1385. _____. "Grüsse und Glückwünsche im Psalter." *Theologische Studien und Kritiken* 103 (1931): 141-150.

1386. Schmidt, Ludwig. *Beobachtungen zu der Plagenerzählung in Exodus VII 14-XI 10*. Studia Biblica 4. Leiden: E.J. Brill, 1990. v+119p.

There are four levels of tradition in the formation of the plague literature: Jahwist (J), Jehowist, P, and a final redactor. Psalms 78:44-51 and 105:28-38 presuppose the final form of the plague cycle.

1387. Schottroff, Willy. *Der altisraelitische Fluchspruch*. Wissenschaftliche Monographien zum Alten und Neuen Testament 30. Neukirchen-Vluyn: Neukirchener Verlag, 1969. 280p.

The curse formula has its origin not in cultic activities but in a conflict situation within a clan or family group.

Reviewed by E.S. Gerstenberger in *JBL* 90 (1971): 108-110; reviewed also in *CBQ* 34 (1972): 390-392.

1388. Seybold, Klaus. *Das Gebet des Kranken im Alten Testament: Untersuchungen zur Bestimmung und Zuordnung der Krankheits- und Heilungspsalmen.* Beiträge zur Wissenschaft vom Alten und Neuen Testament 99. Stuttgart: W. Kohlhammer, 1973.

1389. Snaith, Norman. *The Seven Penitential Psalms.* London: Epworth Press, 1964. 109p.

The Seven penitential psalms are Psalms 6, 32, 38, 51, 102, 130, and 143. They "have to do mostly with the humbled, the afflicted ones, those who for one reason or another, were conscious of indignities and of the almost unbearable disabilities from which they suffered."

1390. Sperling, Uwe. *Das theophanische Jahwe-Überlegenheitslied: Forschungsbericht und gattungskritische Untersuchung der sogennanten Zionlieder.* European University Studies 23/426. Frankfurt am Main: Lang, 1991. 472p.

The first half of the book surveys the history of form-critical scholarship on the so-called "Songs of Zion" (Psalms 46, 48, 76, 84, 87, and 122): Gunkel and Begrich, Mowinckel, Weiser, and Kraus. The second half analyses the methodological foundations underlying the form-critical criteria for the genre.

1391. Steingrimsson, Sigurdur. Örn. *Tor der Gerechtigkeit: Eine literaturwissenschaftliche Untersuchung der sogenannten Einzugsliturgien im AT: Ps 15; 24,3-5 und Jes 33,14-16.* Münchener Universitätsschriften: Arbeiten zu Text und Sprache im Alten Testament 22. St. Ottilien: Eos Verlag, 1984. xiv+188p.

Psalm 15 belongs to the Josiah period; Psalm 24:3-5 and Isaiah 33:14-16 are later adaptations.

Reviewed in *CBQ* 48 (1986): 322-323.

1392. Stolz, Fritz. *Psalmen im nachkultischen Raum.* Theologische Studien 129. Zurich: Theologischer Verlag, 1983. 78p.

A study of the "post-cultic" use and interpretation of forms which had their origin in the cult.

1393. Stummer, Friedrich. "Die Psalmengattungen im Lichte der altorientalischen Hymnenlitteratur." *Journal of the Society of Oriental Research* 8 (1924): 123ff.

In contrast to Gunkel and based on the Babylonian pattern, we divide the Psalms into only monologues or private prayer-songs and dialogues or public prayer-songs.

1394. Szörényi, Andreas. *Psalmen und Kult im Alten Testament (Zur Formgeschichte der Psalmen).* Budapest: Sankt Stefans Gesellschaft, 1961.

There was no special feast of Yahweh's enthronement.

1395. Timko, Philip. "The Psalms: An Introduction to their Historical and Literary Character." *The Bible Today* 65 (1973): 1095-1099.

1396. Towner, W. Sibley. "'Blessed be YHWH' and 'Blessed art Thou, YHWH.'" *Catholic Biblical Quarterly* 30 (1968): 386-399.

1397. Trublet, Jacques. "Le Corpus Sapientiel et le Psautier: Approche Informatique du Lexique." In *Congress Volume: Leuven, 1989*, ed. J.A. Emerton. Supplements to *Vetus Testamentum* 43. 248-263. Leiden: E.J. Brill, 1991.

1398. Vesco, Jean-Luc. "Hymne et Supplication dans la Prière du Psautier." *La Maison-Dicu* 121 (1975): 22-55.

1399. Vetter, D. *Jahwcs Mit-Sein: Ein Ausdruck des Segens.* Stuttgart: Calwer, 1971.

1400. Virgulin, Stefano. "'Che io non si svergognato!' La preghiera dei salmisti." *Parola Spirito e Vita* 20 (1989): 75-86.

1401. Wambacq, Benjamin N. "Les Origines du Psautier." *Angelicum* 52 (1974): 445-449.

Most of the psalms came to be used in the public worship of Israel; however, this does not mean that they were all composed directly for liturgical usage.

1402. Watts, John D.W. "Psalms of Trust, Thanksgiving, and Praise." *The Review and Expositor* 81 (1984): 395-406.

1403. Wehmeier, G. *Der Segen im Alten Testament.* Basel: Reinhardt, 1970.

1404. Weiser, Artur. "Zur Frage nach den Beziehungen der Psalmen zum Kult: Die Darstellung der Theophanie in Psalmen und in Festkult." In *Glaube und Geschichte in Alten Testament. Festschrift Alfred Bertholet*, ed. W. Baumgartner and Others. 303-321. Tübingen: J.C.B. Mohr (Paul Siebeck), 1950. Reprinted in *Ausgesammelte Schriften.* 303-321.

1405. Westermann, Claus. *Das Loben Gottes in den Psalmen.* Berlin: Evangelische Verlagsanstalt, 1953. 124p. Translated from the 2nd German edition of 1961 by Keith R. Crim and published as *The Praise of God in the Psalms.* Richmond, VA: John Knox, 1965. 171p. The 5th German edition appears in *Lob und Klage in den Psalmen.* Göttingen: Vandenhoeck & Ruprecht, 1977. English translation in *Praise and Lament in the Psalms.* 15-162. Atlanta, GA: John Knox Press, 1981.

The "categories" of the Psalms are not first of all literary or cultic in nature. Rather they designate the basic modes of what occurs when humans turn to God with words: plea and praise. As these two basic modes of "prayer" change and expand, the categories also change and expand.

Das Loben Gottes in den Psalmen, 2nd ed., reviewed by E.S. Gerstenberger in *JBL* 81 (1962): 207-208.

1406. _____. "Struktur und Geschichte der Klage im Alten Testament." *Zeitschrift für die alttestamentliche Wissenschaft* 66 (1954): 44-80. Reprinted in *Forschung am Alten Testament II*, ed. Rainer Albetz and Eberhard Ruprecht; Theologische Bücherei 24; 266-305; Munich:

Chr. Kaiser Verlag, 1964; reprinted in *Lob und Klage in den Psalmen*; Göttingen: Vandenhoeck & Ruprecht, 1977; translated into English by Richard N. Soulen and published as "The Structure and History of the Lament in the Old Testament," in *Praise and Lament in the Psalms*, 165-213; Atlanta, GA: John Knox Press, 1981.

The practice of calling on God in time of need in order to secure God's help existed in Israel from the earliest to the latest periods of her history. Nothing ever caused this to change. The Lament always had three components -- the one who laments, God, and the others (that circle of people among whom or against whom the lamenter raises a complaint). What did change dramatically, however, was the way in which one called upon God.

1407. ______. "Vergegenwärtigung der Geschichte in den Psalmen." In *Zwischenstation. Festschrift für Karl Kupisch zum 60. Geburtstag* (Munich: Chr. Kaiser Verlag, 1963), 253-280; reprinted in *Forschung am alten Testament*; Theologische Bücherei 24; 306-335; Munich: Chr. Kaiser Verlag, 1964; reprinted in *Lob und Klage in den Psalmen*; Göttingen: Vandenhoeck & Ruprecht, 1977; translated into English by Richard N. Soulen and published as "The Re-presentation of History in the Psalms," in *Praise and Lament in the Psalms*, 214-249; Atlanta, GA: John Knox Press, 1981.

The purpose of "re-presenting" the history of the beginning has nothing to do with creating an interest in the past; rather the purpose is future directed -- in times of crisis, to persuade God to do what God had done earlier, in times of praise to extol the Lord who is present with the community and is leading the community into the future.

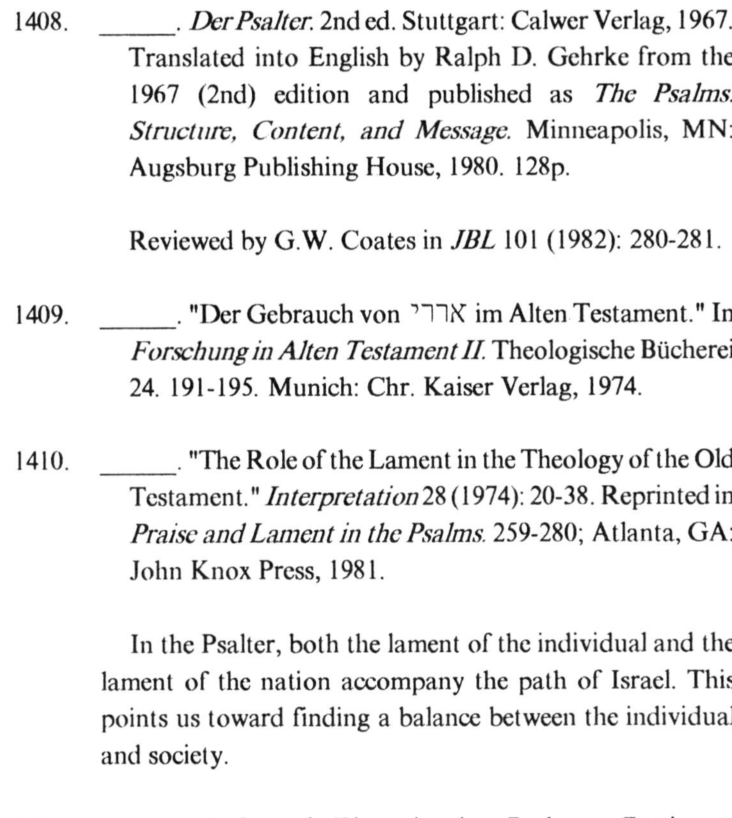

1408. _____. *Der Psalter.* 2nd ed. Stuttgart: Calwer Verlag, 1967. Translated into English by Ralph D. Gehrke from the 1967 (2nd) edition and published as *The Psalms: Structure, Content, and Message.* Minneapolis, MN: Augsburg Publishing House, 1980. 128p.

Reviewed by G.W. Coates in *JBL* 101 (1982): 280-281.

1409. _____. "Der Gebrauch von אדרי im Alten Testament." In *Forschung in Alten Testament II.* Theologische Bücherei 24. 191-195. Munich: Chr. Kaiser Verlag, 1974.

1410. _____. "The Role of the Lament in the Theology of the Old Testament." *Interpretation* 28 (1974): 20-38. Reprinted in *Praise and Lament in the Psalms.* 259-280; Atlanta, GA: John Knox Press, 1981.

In the Psalter, both the lament of the individual and the lament of the nation accompany the path of Israel. This points us toward finding a balance between the individual and society.

1411. _____. *Lob und Klage in den Psalmen.* Göttingen: Vandenhoeck und Ruprecht, 1977. Translated into English by Keith R. Crim and Richard N. Soulen and published as *Praise and Lament in the Psalms.* Atlanta, GA: John Knox Press, 1981. 301p.

Book One, "The Praise of God in the Psalms," is a reprint of *The Praise of God in the Psalms.*

Book Two, "Lament in the Psalms," includes chapters on "The Structure and History of the Lament in the Old Testament," "The 'Re-presentation' of History in the Psalms," "The Formation of the Psalter," and "The Role of the Lament in the Theology of the Old Testament," all previously published.

1412. ______. "Anthropologische und theologische Aspekte des Gebets der Psalmen." *Theologische Jahrbuch* (1979): 51-62.

1413. ______. *Ausgewählte Psalmen.* Göttingen: Vandenhoeck & Ruprecht, 1984. Translated into English by J.R. Porter and published as *The Living Psalms.* Grand Rapids, MI: William B. Eerdmans Publishing Company, 1989; Edinburgh: T&T Clark, 1989. 306p.

1414. Wevers, John W. "A Study of the Form Criticism of Individual Complaint Psalms." *Vetus Testamentum* 6 (1956): 80-96.

The existence of a pronouncement of a "salvation oracle" by a priest in response to the individual complaint has not been proved and is even unnecessary. The invocation of the divine name Yahweh accounts for the sudden shift from anxiety to confidence. Psalms 4, 12 and 16 are given particular attention.

1415. Weymann, Volker. "Loben und Klagen in den Psalmen." *Bibelarbeit in der Gemeinde* 4 (1982): 15-32.

1416. Williams, Walter G. "Liturgical Problems in Enthronement Psalms." *Journal of Bible and Religion* 25 (1957): 118-122.

1417. Wolff, Hans Walter. "Die Aufruf zur Volksklage." *Zeitschrift für die alttestamentliche Wissenschaft* 76 (1964): 48-65. Reprinted in *Gesammelte Studien*;

Theologische Bücherei 22; 2nd ed. 392-401. Munich: Chr. Kaiser Verlag, 1973.

1418. Würtwein, Ernst. "Der Ursprung der prophetischen Gerichtsrede." *Zeitschrift für Theologie und Kirche* 49 (1952): 1-16.

The prophetic *Gerichtsrede* originated in the cult. This speech form must have a distinctive setting because it is used so frequently and in a constant form. The setting is the cultic accusation and judgment from Yahweh pronounced by cultic personnel, most likely cultic prophets.

1419. ______. "Kultpolemic oder Kultbescheid? Beobachtungen zu dem Thema 'Prophetie und Kult.'" In *Tradition und Situation: Studien zur alttestamentlichen Prophetie (Artur Weiser zum 70. Geburtstag)*, ed. Ernst Würtwein and Otto Kaiser. 115-131. Göttingen: Vandenhoeck & Ruprecht, 1963.

Prophetic sayings opposing the cult have their setting in the divine reply given to prayer which was pronounced by the cult prophet. The canonical prophets take the positive reply to prayer and make it into a negative one in order to announce judgment against particular cultic acts.

1420. Zirker, H. *Die kultische Vergegenwärtigung der Vergangenheit in den Psalmen.* Bonner Biblische Beiträge 20. Bonn: P. Hanstein, 1964. xvii+158p.

The Liturgical Re-presentation of the Past as exemplified in the Psalms.

See also: 14, 1494, 1786, 1787.

7. Worship in Ancient Israel

1421. Albright, William Foxwell. "Baal Zaphon." In *Festschrift Alfred Bertholet zum 80 Geburtstag. Gedwidmet von Kollegen und Freunden,* ed. Walter Baumgartner and Others. 2-14. Tübingen: J.C.B. Mohr (Paul Siebeck), 1950.

1422. Anderson, Gary A. *A Time to Mourn, A Time to Dance: The Expression of Grief and Joy in Israelite Religion.* University Park, PA: Pennsylvania State University, 1991. xvii+139p.

1423. Anderson, George W. "'Sicut Cervus': Evidence in the Psalter of Private Devotion in Ancient Israel." *Vetus Testamentum* 30 (1980): 388-397.

There is little evidence of "inner devotional experience of individual Israelites" in the prophetic oracular words of a few psalms. It is more evident from words which ask for God's presence or God's deliverance. Psalm 73 and 139 also express an "intimate personal relationship" between the worshipper and God.

1424. Auerbach, E. "Das Fest der Lese am Abschluss des Jahres." *Vetus Testamentum* 3 (1953): 186-187.

1425. ______. "Die Feste im Alten Testament." *Vetus Testamentum* 8 (1958): 1-18.

1426. _____. "Neujahrsfest und Versöhnungsfest in den biblischen Quellen." *Vetus Testamentum* 8 (1958): 337-343.

1427. Beaucamp, Evode. "Liturgia e Salmi nelle grandi tappe della storia d'Israel." *Bibbia e Oriente* 13 (1971): 9-25.

1428. Bentzen, Aage. "The Cultic Use of the Story of the Ark of Samuel." *Journal of Biblical Literature* 67 (1948): 37-53.

1429. Bič, M. "Das erste Buch des Psalters: eine Thronbesteigungsfestliturgie." *Atti dell'VIII Congresso Internazionale di Storia delle Religioni (Roma 17-23 Aprile 1955).* 268-270. Florence: G.C. Sansoni, 1956.

1430. Boguslawski, Steven R. "The Psalms: Prophetic Polemics Against Sacrifices." *Irish Biblical Studies* 5 (1983): 14-41.

Psalms 40:6-8, 50:7-15, 51:16, and 141:2. The psalms examined echo the prophetic call to authentic worship.

1431. Buss, M.J. "The Meaning of 'Cult' and the Interpretation of the Old Testament." *Journal of Bible and Religion* 32 (1964): 317-325.

1432. Cazelles, Henri. "Nouvel An. IV. Le Nouvel An en Israël." In *Dictionnaire de la Bible, Supplément VI.* Cols. 620-645. Paris: Letouzey & Ané, 1960.

1433. Clines, David-J.A. "The Evidence for an Autumnal New Year in Pre-exilic Israel Reconsidered." *Journal of Biblical Literature* 93 (1974): 22-40.

The arguments for and against an autumn new year are inconclusive. The same is also true about a spring new year.

1434. Davis, Eli. "The Psalms in Hebrew Medical Amulets." *Vetus Testamentum* 42 (1992): 173-178.

1435. Eaton, John H. "The Psalms and Israelite Worship." In *Tradition and Interpretation. Essays by Members of the Society for Old Testament Study,* ed. G.W. Anderson. Oxford: At the Clarendon Press, 1979.

1436. ______. *Vision in Worship. The Relation of Prophecy and Liturgy in the Old Testament.* London: SPCK, 1981; New York: Seabury Press, 1981. ix+115p.

"The great occasions of Israelite worship were experienced as meetings with God, and moreover, with God active in his fundamental work of judgment and salvation." Prophecy is not a separate movement breaking in upon the liturgy; rather it grows out of it.

1437. ______. *The Psalms Come Alive: An Introduction to the Psalms through the Arts.* Mowbray's Christian Studies. Oxford: A.R. Mowbray, 1984. x+165p, including 13 illustrations.

1438. Gese, Harmut. "Zur Geschichte der Kultsänger am zweiten Temple." In *Abraham unser Vater. Juden und Christen im Gespräch über die Bibel. Festschrift für Otto Michel zum 60. Geburtstag,* ed, O. Betz, M. Hengel, and P. Schmidt. Arbeiten zur Geschichte des Spätjdentums und Urchristentums. 222-234. Leiden: E.J. Brill, 1963. Reprint in *Vom Sinai zum Zion: Alttestamentliche Beiträge zur biblischen Theologie.* Beiträge zur Evangelische Theologie 64. 147-158. Munich: Kaiser, 1974.

1439. Gross, H. "Lässt sich in den Psalmen ein 'Thronbesteigungsfest Jahwes' nachweisen?" *Trier Theologische Zeitschrift* 65 (1956): 24-40.

1440. Guillaume, Alfred. *Prophecy and Divination among the Hebrews and Other Semites.* The Bampton Lectures, 1938. London: Hodder and Stoughton, 1938. xviii+434p.

1441. _____. "Magical Terms in the Old Testament." *Journal of the Royal Asiatic Society of Great Britain and Ireland* (1942): 111ff; (1943): 251ff; (1946): 79ff.

1442. Gunkel, Hermann. "Die Frömmigkeit der Psalmen." *Die Christliche Welt* 36 (1922): nos. 1,2,5,6,7. Translated into English by A.K. Dallas and published as "The Religion of the Psalms," in *What Remains of the Old Testament and Other Essays.* Preface by James Moffatt. 69-114. London: George Allen & Unwin Ltd., 1928; New York: Macmillan, 1928.

1443. Hermisson, Hans-Jürgen. *Sprache und Ritus im altisraelitischen Kult. Zur 'Spiritualisierung' der Kultbegriffe im Alten Israel.* Wissenschaftliche Monographien zum Alten und Neuen Testament 7. Neukirchen-Vluyn: Neukirchener Verlag, 1965. 165p.

Reviewed by A.L. Merrill in *JBL* 85 (1966): 113-114.

1444. Hillers, Delbert R. "The Effective Simile in Biblical Literature." *Journal of the American Oriental Society* 103 (1983): 181-185.

"Effective" similes are those pronouncements intended to produce what is indicated by the comparison. There is a relationship between such pronouncements and analogic magic.

1445. Humbert, Paul. *Le terou'a: Analyse d'un rite Biblique.* Université de Neuchâtel. Recueil de travaux publiépar la Faculté des Lettres 23. Neuchatel: Université de Neuchâtel, 1946. 48p.

1446. Jeppesen, Knud. "The Day of Yahweh in Mowinckel's Conception Reviewed." *Scandinavian Journal of the Old Testament* 2 (2,1988): 42-55.

1447. Jeremias, Jörg. *Kultprophetie und Gerichtsverkündigung in der späten Israels.* Wissenschaftliche Monographien zum Alten und Neuen Testament 35. Neukirchen Vluyn: Neukirchener Verlag, 1970. viii+214.

(1) Cultic prophets preached against wrongdoers within Israel, not against Israel as a whole, (2) their preaching was conducted primarily within lamentation rituals associated with times of fasting and distress, (3) unlike the classical prophets, cultic prophets did not proclaim total judgment and destruction, and (4) cultic prophets were organized into guilds, served the king, and functioned in the temple.

Reviewed by J.H. Hayes in *JBL* 90 (1971): 112-114.

1448. Johnson, Aubrey R. "The Role of the King in the Jerusalem Cultus." In *The Labyrinth. Further Studies in the Relation between Myth and Ritual in the Ancient World,* ed. S.H. Hooke. 71-111. London: Oxford University Press, 1935.

1449. ______. "The Prophet in Israelite Worship." *The Expository Times* 47 (1936): 312-319.

Prayer as well as the oracular elements in psalms may come from cult prophets.

1450. ______. *The Cultic Prophet in Ancient Israel.* Cardiff: University of Wales, 1944. 2nd ed., 1962.

The early נביאים are closely associated with the formal worship of Yahweh in the sanctuary; they are cultic specialists. The status of the cult prophets was not a subordinate one but was at least as high as that of the priests. They are responsible for the prophetic elements in the Psalms.

1451. ______. *The Cultic Prophet and Israel's Psalmody.* Cardiff: University of Wales Press, 1979. xii+467p.

The role of the cultic prophet (1) in regular worship, (2) in times of crisis, and (3) in times of personal crisis.

1452. Kapelrud, Arvid S. "Tradition and Worship: The Role of the Cult in Tradition Formation and Transmission." In *Tradition and Theology in the Old Testament,* ed. Douglas A. Knight. 101-124. Philadelphia: Fortress Press, 1977.

Poetic literature often represents a conservative tendency; "the psalms show better than any other medium how the different elements were welded together and combined in a way which actually created a new set of traditions." There is a "fluid orthodoxy" in the psalms where most elements converged.

1453. Kippenberg, H.G. *Religion und Klassenbildung im antiken Judäa.* 2nd ed. Göttingen: Vandenhoeck and Ruprecht, 1982.

1454. Liebreich, L. "Aspects of the New Year Liturgy." *Hebrew Union College Annual* 34 (1963): 125-176.

1455. McCullough, W.S. "The 'Enthronement of Yahweh' Psalms." In *A Stubborn Faith. Papers on Old Testament and Related Subjects. Presented to Honor W.A. Irwin,* ed. E.C. Hobbs. 53-61. Dallas: Southern Methodist University Press, 1956.

1456. McRae, G.W. "The Meaning and Evolution of the Feast of Tabernacles." *Catholic Biblical Quarterly* 22 (1960): 251-276.

1457. Maertens, Thierry. *C'est fête en l'honneur de Jahvé.* Collection Thèmes Bibliques. Bruges: Desclée de Brouwer, 1961. 224p. Translated into English by Kathryn Sullivan and published as *A Feast in Honor of Yahweh.* Notre Dame, IN: Fides, 1965. 245p.

Reviewed by R.B.Y. Scott in *JBL* 81 (1962): 209. French edition reviewed in *CBQ* 24 (1962): 79-80; English translation reviewed in *CBQ* 27 (1965): 447-448.

1458. Maier, J. *Das altisraelitische Ladeheiligtum.* Beihefte zur Zeitschrift für die alttestamentliche Wissenschaft 93. Berlin: Alfred Töpelmann, 1965.

Reviewed by M. Haran in *JBL* 85 (1966): 248-249.

1459. Metzger, M. "Himmlische und irdische Wohnstatt Jahwes." *Ugarit-Forschungen* 2 (1970): 139-158.

1460. Michel, Diethelm. "Studien zu den sogenannten Thronbesteigungspsalmen." *Vetus Testamentum* 6 (1956): 40-68. Reprinted in *Zur Neueren Psalmenforschung*, ed. Peter H.A. Neumann, 367-399; Darmstadt: Wissenschaftliche Buchgesellschaft, 1976.

1461. Morgenstern, Julian. "Trial by Ordeal among the Semites and in Ancient Israel." *Hebrew Union College Jubilee Annual* (1925): 113-143. Reprint, New York: KTAV, 1968.

1462. Mowinckel, Sigmund. *Kongesalmerne i det Gamle Testament.* Kristiana: Jacob Dybwad, 1916.

1463. ______. "Tronstigningssalmerne og Jahves tronstigningsfest." *Norsk Teologisk Tidsskrift* 18 (1917): 13-79.

1464. ______. *Psalmenstudien 1. ʾAwen und die individuellen Klagespalmen.* Skrifter utgitt av Det Norske Videnskaps-Akademi i Oslo, II. Hist.-Filos. Klasse. Kristiana: Jacob Dybwad, 1921. Reprint, Amsterdam: Verlag P. Schippers N.V., 1966. vi+181p.

I. The Way to the Soul of the Word. 1) *ʾAun* and Doers of *ʾAun*. The Point of Departure. 2) The Doers of *ʾAun* as Murderers. 3) The Doers of *ʾAun* as Robbers and Stealers of Property. 4) *ʾAun* as a Cause of Illness. 5) *Aun* as an Art or Means of Prediction. 6) The Secretive and Malicious Activities of the Doers of *Aun*. 7) The Tongue and the Emphatic Words as a Means of the *Aun*-Man. 8) The Doers of *Aun* and the Power. 9) Sleights of Hand and Other External Means of Aun. 10) Aun = Magic. 11) Etymology.

II. Development. 1) General Meaning. The basic meaning of און is magic power, magic, sorcery. It can refer to the means of magic, the acts of magic (almost = sorcery), the results brought about by sorcery, and a religious and moral judgment. 2) און = Disaster and Destruction Caused by Magic. 3) און = Disaster, Destruction. 4) Sorcery as a Type of Hostility to God and Sin. 5) און as the Designation of an Illegitimate Cult. 6) Sorcery as "Lie" and "Deceit."

III. Results Regarding Magic in Israelite Popular Belief. 1) There is often no essential distinction between the external actions of religion and magic. However, magicians work with an evil power, while servants of the cult reach their goal through the good power. Further, magicians do not use the *rite vocati et ordinati* of the community; rather they use that of private individuals who have no power in the community. Their actions can contradict the interest of the community. Thus they practice their art mostly in secret. Their intent is almost without exception evil. The Psalms don't contain many concrete references concerning the means used by the Aun-people. The main one, however, is the "symbolic" action that creates power and the formula that creates power, the magical word. The actions are mostly formed on the principle of *similia similibus.* The words have the character of effective curses. 2) Results. a) Summary of Chapter I. b) Covenant of the Aun-People with Sheol and the Demons. c) Demons in the Psalms (Psalms 59, 22)

IV. The Enemies in the Individual Psalms of Lament. 1) The Usual Approach to the Problem. 2) Thesis. The Enemies Are the Magicians. 3) The Proof by Analogy: The Enemies in the Babylonian Psalms of Lament. 4) The Direct Proof. 5) The Enemy in the Individual Psalms of

Thanksgiving corresponds exactly to that in the psalms of lament.

V. The Individual Psalms of Lament as Cult Psalms. 1) If fear of magic played a role in the life of ancient Israel, there must have been cultic actions through which one was purified from magic and freed from the evil consequences of *aun.* 2) The Thesis. A Priori and Ex Analogia. What Gunkel did not see, and in fact denied, was that the psalms of lament now in the psalter are actual cult psalms. 3) Traces of Cultic Use in the Psalms of Lament. 4) Toward an Religious Appreciation of the Psalms of Lament.

VI. The End of the Cultic Rites for Healing an Illness. 1) Giving a New Meaning to the Individual Psalms of Lament. 2) The Causes of the New Meaning Being Given to a Psalm.

1465. ______. *Psalmenstudien 2. Das Thronbesteigungsfest Jahwäs und der Ursprung der Eschatologie.* Skrifter utgitt av Det Norske Videnskaps-Akademi i Oslo, II. Hist.-Filos. Klasse. Kristiana: Jacob Dybwad, 1922. Reprint, Amsterdam: Verlag P. Schippers N.V., 1966. xvi+347p.

First Part. The Enthronement Psalms and the Enthronement Festival of Yahweh.

I. The Enthronement Psalms and Their Meaning. 1) The Material and Its Unity. 2) The Situation of the Psalms. a) The Enthronement of the Earthly Kings. b) The Enthronement of Yahweh According to the Psalms. 3) Earlier Attempts at Interpretation. a) The Historical Interpretation. b) The Eschatological Interpretation. 4) The Cultic Interpretation. a) The Principle. The customary view of the psalms has been that they are either historical or eschatological. This was based on the failure of theologians to recognize the liturgical character of the psalms, and to represent correctly the essence and manner of a cultic religion. b) The Cult as Creative Drama. In the cult a reality is simulated and thereby brought forth. The cult is everywhere and always a drama. This drama is more than a simple drama; it has the power to bring forth a holy reality; it is a sacrament. The contents of this drama form the mythical or historical events on which the religious community builds its faith, its hope, and its life, its existence. Each time this drama is repeated in the community it creates anew the reality and power of these events. c) Traces of the Cult Drama in Israel cannot be found in the post-exilic priestly code but in the psalter. d) Yahweh's Enthronement Day as an Annual Festival Day. If the enthronement psalms are cultic songs, then the enthronement of Yahweh must have taken place not in the eschatological future nor in the wishes and fantasies of the believers, but in the cult as a religiously experienced reality. This means that the enthronement day of Yahweh must have been celebrated in the cult on a specific recurring festival day; since the cultic festival cycle was the yearly cycle, the enthronement day of Yahweh was celebrated each year on a certain time. II Samuel 6, I Kings 8, and I Chronicles 16 seem to suggest a one-time event; this, however, is only an appearance. The harvest and New Year's festival has features of just such a festival.

II. The Enthronement Festival (The Day) of Yahweh. 1) The Cult Myth of the Festival. (a) The Creation and Dragon Conflict Myth. (b) Myth About the Fight of Gods. (c) Exodus Myth. Creation is completed only with the creation and settling of Israel in the promised land. (d) Myth About the Fight of Nations. (e) Myth of Judgment. α) Judgment. The victory brings a judgment against the enemies and the other gods. β) Determining the Destiny. (f) Deliverance out of distress. 2) The Terminology of the Festival. a) The New

Year's Day. The enthronement day of Yahweh is the New Year's Day, the day of the festal shout or the day of the ram's horn. b) The Great Autumn Festival. The New Year's festival on the first of Tishri as a one-day festival is a late development. In an earlier period there were three festivals: New Year's festival on the first of Tishri, the great festival of atonement on the tenth of Tishri, and the Feast of Tabernacles on the 15th-21st of Tishri. When we speak of the enthronement festival of Yahweh, we must think not exclusively of the isolated New Year's Day but of the great autumn festival. 3) The Rites of the Festival. a) Preliminary Issues. The old autumn and New Year's festival appears to have a double character. It is a festival of the royal dominion of Yahweh and an agricultural festival. The agrarian cult and myth is older and more original than the royal elements of this festival. In late Judaism the great night festival in the temple formed the beginning of the festivities. Nothing certain can be said about the 2nd-6th day. The seventh day was the "great" day of the festival. It was marked with the ceremony of pouring out water and by going around the altar seven times. It all came to an end with the (Aaronite) blessing of the High Priest, followed by a feast. Many of these rites go back to the pre-exilic time. In the older period the royal procession of Yahweh occurred on the last day as the high point of the entire festival. b) The Individual Rites and Their Meaning. In its most original nature the autumn festival was an agricultural New Year's festival. It was a preparation for the new year, an attempt to secure blessing and fertility. c) The Entrance of Yahweh. In the ancient royal period of the cult, Yahweh comes as king and creates things from which salvation comes. The main theme of the festival is the coming of the personal God; the dramatic presentation of this is the most important rite of the festival and with it the festival reaches its high point. The accounts of the entrance of the ark into the city of David in II Samuel 6 (‖ I Chronicles 15-16) and I Kings 8 (‖ II Chronicles 5-7) are shaped according to the customs of their own time, thus reflecting an annual event. d) Traces of Other Festival Performances. Psalms 48 and 46, 33 and 76. e) The Processional Street must have led from the western part of the city to Zion, i.e, the east hill, the city of David and the mount of the temple. 4) The Mood of the Festival. The two poles of mood in Israelite religion are fear before Yahweh and joy in Yahweh. Fear is the normal attitude; joy belongs above all to the festival. And yet, people come to the festival with a whole range of religious feelings and moods, because here they experience the entirety of religion. In this festival the people see only the beginning of what Yahweh will do in the course of thc upcoming year. Expectation is thus the underlying tone of the entire year.

III. The Royal Government (Kingdom) of Yahweh. The community prays for the realization of the gifts and blessings promised to the community in the cultic experience. 1) The Gifts. A covenant that brings blessings and power, fruitfulness of the land and people and a warlike spirit and energetic activity. The king incorporates in himself the fortune of the people. 2) The Demands. The divine grace is attached to certain conditions. The "writing prophets" did not create the ethical current in the religion. 3) Universalism and Nationalism. Both universalism and nationalism were a part of the kingdom of God concept from the beginning. Universalism did not develop out of nationalism.

IV. The Age of the Festival. 1) General Considerations and Literary Attestations outside the Psalter. There can be no doubt that the ideas and religious notions present in the festival belong not to Judaism but to the pre-exilic national cult religion of the people of Israel. 2) The Age of the Different Enthronement Psalms. 3) The Probable Age of the

Festival. The Israelites took over the Canaanite autumn festival as their most important festival, thus putting the probably older and Israelite passover temporarily in the shadows. The specific Jerusalemite festival, with which we have to do here, naturally is not older than David. 4) On the History of the Festival. The festival went through a certain development in its rites and in its religious ideas. The idea that Yahweh's struggle against the enemies came after the enthronement is a later displacement; originally the sequence was creation = struggle against the enemies, then triumph and enthronement. Already by the latest pre-exilic time the ancient Israelite festival of Passover had regained its earlier importance. Originally Passover had nothing to do with the exodus; in the psalms the autumn festival is the exodus festival. The grounding of the Passover in the exodus is to be attributed to the Deuteronomist. The real golden age of the enthronement festival was in the older pre-exilic period. The dismantling of the original autumn festival into three independent festivals -- New Year's, Atonement, and Tabernacles -- took place between 586 and ca. 460. With this, the New Year's Day was loosened from the autumn festival and lost its connection with the economic and popular life. Much of the contents of the enthronement day was transferred to the Feast of Tabernacles.

Second Part. The Origin of Israelite Eschatology.

I. The Problem and the Thesis. 1) The Cultic Enthronement Day of Yahweh (Summary of the First Part). 2) The Problem -- Critique of Gressmann, Gunkel, Sellin. 3) The Thesis. The contents of eschatology stemmed from the cultic enthronement festival; in the contents and mood of the festival we have the root of the complete eschatology. This eschatology arose so that everything that was originally expected each year as the immediate results of the annual cultic enthronement of Yahweh, results that came true in the course of that year, would be deferred to an indefinite future, when Yahweh takes his throne for the last time.

II. Outline of the Argument. The Day of Yahweh. 1) End-History = Primeval History. 2) The Day of Yahweh is the Day of Enthronement. The (eschatological) day of Yahweh is the future, final enthronement day of God that outshines all others. 3) The Day of Theophany and the Terror Associated with the Revelation. The fearful, crushing side of the Yahweh revelation relates to its being a day of terror and shame and of the downfall of the enemies of Yahweh and Israel. 4) Natural Catastrophes and the Destruction of the World. The day of Yahweh is not a day of natural catastrophes; these are simply to be considered as ornaments of the theophany. 5) The Time of the Oppressions and the Deliverance from the Misery Caused by the Enemies. The presupposition of the coming of Yahweh for the enthronement is the fact that his people Israel is being oppressed by fearful enemies. This presupposition holds true for eschatology as well as the cult myth. 6) Salvation and Disaster. Yahweh's day of enthronement brings disaster upon Israel's enemies and salvation upon Israel. Deutero-Isaiah retains this double-sided quality. 7) The Day of Judgment. The transference of the disaster of the heathen to Israel can also be observed when the day of Yahweh is viewed as a day of judgment for Israel. It is possible, although it cannot be proven, that this idea existed before Amos. Deutero-Isaiah splits the judgment into two parts; Israel has already been judged and punished through the exile. 8) The Remnant. A distinction must be made in the idea of a remnant between form and content; in its content, it is later than Amos, who separated salvation and disaster and made disaster absolute, final. In form, Isaiah's characteristic expression is "become converted" ("return"); this clearly belongs to the eschatology of salvation. 9) The

New Creation. The original sense of the new creation was not the restoration of a cosmos that had been completely destroyed by some kind of world catastrophe, but that of a new revival secured by new powers in the cult. The "last," the eschatological new creation was probably also understood in this sense originally as a restoration of the original magnificent conditions, which existed at the time when God saw for the first time that everything was very good. 10) The Turning of the Destiny. In the enthronement myth the time of salvation stands out as a turning of the destiny, a thought that is a favorite in certain eschatological passages. 11) The New Covenant. The day of enthronement was a repeating of the liberation from Egypt, to which the covenant at Sinai attached itself; thus the covenant is renewed on New Year's Day. It makes sense, then, that the eschatological coming of Yahweh reaches its climax in the renewing of the covenant. The result of concluding the covenant is peace, which comes chiefly to Israel and Yahweh, not to the enemies who are destroyed or the remaining nations that become vassals. This covenant of peace extends to the wild animals and the stones of the field. 12) The Worldwide Kingdom of God. The eschatological kingdom of Yahweh is a worldwide kingdom. The main interest, however, lies with the salvation of Israel, not with the other nations who are destroyed. Deutero-Isaiah advances beyond this to a universalism of religion where the entire world is converted rather than forced. 13) The Eschatological Meal. The festival day of Yahweh ended with a festal meal. It is not surprising, then, to encounter eschatological depictions of a festal meal of Yahweh, which he prepares for the people at the end of the day; this is the coronation meal. 14) The Messiah. An eschatological king does not develop directly from the idea of an enthronement festival. A messiah beside the king Yahweh is superfluous and a kind of double of Yahweh. The messiah resulted from projecting the ideal type of the divine Davidic king into the picture of the future; the messiah is an eschatological mirroring of the divine earthly king, not the other way around. 15) Summary. All of the more important ideas of eschatology can be explained on the basis of the enthronement myth and the circle of ideas associated with the festival. Israel possessed (and created) an eschatological picture, which can be grasped simply as an enthronement festival of Yahweh which takes place in the future.

III. From Experience to Hope. Eschatology is faith and hope. Primarily, faith and hope are based only on experience. Most often, eschatology is faith whose original connection with experience has been cut off. How has experience become hope? The goal of the cult, the festival, is to create a new reality that will bring salvation for the immediate future, for the coming year. The coming of Yahweh brings certain expectations. Already, then, the enthronement festival has a tug which leads into an eschatology.

Conclusion. Is Israelite eschatology of foreign or native origin? Gressmann favors the first, Sellin the second. In general, Sellin is right. To be sure, the ideas of the cultic enthronement of a god are not Israelite, but common to the orient; nevertheless, the autumn and enthronement festival was a genuine expression of the old Israelite religion in a way unlike any other part of the cult.

1466. ______. *Psalmenstudien 3. Kultusprophetie und prophetische Psalmen.* Skrifter utgitt av Det Norske Videnskaps-Akademi i Oslo, II. Hist.-Filos. Klasse. Kristiana: Jacob Dybwad, 1923. Reprint, Amsterdam: Verlag P. Schippers N.V., 1966. 118p.

I. Introduction and Background. 1) The Problem. Gunkel has argued that almost all of the psalms as they presently exist were not original psalms of the cult. The prophetic element in the psalms is the result of a double borrowing: the prophets copied the psalmists and produced a mixed prophetic style (the prophetic was dominant); later the psalmists copied this mixed style and produced the prophetic psalms, this time, however, simply as a literary form. Gunkel is wrong. The following thesis is proposed: With little exception, biblical psalms were composed as psalms of the cult; whatever prophetic element there is in the psalms is not to be explained as a borrowing but as actually cultic. 2) Cult and Prophecy. a) General Issues. b) Seer and Priest. c) The Priest as a Mediator of Revelation. d) The Nabi as a Servant of the Cult. Since prophetic ecstasy was induced and maintained by music, the nebiim are related to the music of the cult. Thus the professional cultic prophets and the poets of the prophetic psalms are to be sought among the temple singers. Sometime during the post-exilic period the cult prophets are absorbed into the ranks of the Levitical singers. At that point they are primarily singers and only secondarily prophets. Cult prophecy as such has died out. e) Form and Technique of the Cultic Oracle. f) Cult Prophecy and Psalmistry. The composition of the poetic psalms is based on a special inspiration; the poet was a divinely inspired person who had received a supernatural gift; the nabi was a poet. Prophet and poet thus were closely related. Whoever can compose poetry is inspired, and under certain conditions can also prophesy. The close connection between prophets and temple singers and psalm-poets is confirmed by the book of Habakkuk and the book of Joel.

II. The Individual Psalms. This material must now be related to the individual biblical psalms and their cultic settings. 1) Prophecies at the Great Yearly Festival. 2)

Prophetic Oracles in the Occasional Worship Services of the Community. 3) Royal Oracles.

1467. ______. *Psalmenstudien 4. Die technischen Termini in den Psalmenüberschriften.* Skrifter utgitt av Det Norske Videnskaps-Akademi i Oslo, II. Hist.-Filos. Klasse. Kristiana: Jacob Dybwad, 1923. Reprint, Amsterdam: Verlag P. Schippers N.V., 1966. vi+52p.

Introduction. 1) The psalms in the psalter are actual cult songs, which can only be understood in connection with specific cultic actions and situations. The following explanations presuppose this. 2) There is no doubt that the use made of these psalms by the latest period of the Jewish temple and the Mishnah and synagogue in many cases does not correspond to the original sense of these psalms. The explanations offered here are based on the belief that the superscriptions to the psalms are generally related to the original sense and usage; there are some exceptions to this.

A) General and Special Designations of the Psalms and Cult Songs. B) Musical Statements. These concern mainly the instruments used in the presentation of the psalms. C) Statements Concerning the Purpose of Particular Psalms. D) Statements of Cultic Actions and Situations.

1468. ______. *Psalmenstudien 5. Segen und Fluch in Israels Kult und Psalmdichtung.* Skrifter utgitt av Det Norske Videnskaps-Akademi i Oslo, II. Hist.-Filos. Klasse. Kristiana: Dybwad, 1924. Reprint, Amsterdam: Verlag P. Schippers N.V., 1966. viii+144p.

Introduction. Among the psalms of the psalter there are psalms of blessing (e.g., 128), psalms of cursing (e.g., 109, 137), and also psalms which exhibit in a weakened form the double schema of blessing and curse (1, 112). What's the origin of this schema? Gunkel traces the blessing and cursing psalms back to cultic acts.

I. The Blessing in Cult and Psalm Poetry. 1) Blessing (see J. Pedersen). 2) The Blessing in the Cult. 3) Psalms of Blessing. The actual form of the cultic word is the rhythmic-metrical poetic form. It was spoken as a kind of recitative, i.e., sung, and was delivered by a choir of priests rather than by an individual.

II. The Curse in Cult and Psalm Poetry. 1) The Curse. 2) The Curse in the Cult. 3) Cursing Psalms.

III. The Two-Membered Blessing and Cursing Formula in Cult and Psalm Poetry. 1) The Two-Membered Blessing and Cursing Formula. 2) Poetic Imitations and Echoes of the Scheme.

Conclusion: Religious-Historical Summary. Blessings as well as curses are found in the cult; both occasional words and regularly-repeated words appear. From these, liturgies and psalms are formed. The blessing gathers unto itself all that the nation and the individuals expect of the cult and of religion. The religion develops from a belief in an impersonal power to a belief in a personal idea of God, from the automatic formula to the prayer for blessing and to praise. Cursed was all which stood in the way of fortune and self-affirmation of the people, all which worked against the righteousness of the people. Both were brought into connection with moral and religious demand, in order to keep watch over the moral consciousness of the nation and the ethical impetus of religion, and to create a pure cultic community. These words took on an important role in educating the community; the origin of the decalogue in cultic words of blessing and curse confirms this.

1469. ______. *Psalmenstudien 6. Die Psalmdichter.* Skrifter utgitt av Det Norske Videnskaps-Akademi i Oslo, II. Hist.-Filos. Klasse. Kristiana: Dybwad, 1924. Reprint, Amsterdam: Verlag P. Schippers N.V., 1966. 101p.

I. Introduction. The statements about authorship do not correspond to the actual facts, but were added later by the copyists, the collectors and scholars. Although the authors use the I-Style, they are not pure individuals; rather they depict typical experiences and moods and feelings of the members of a great circle; allusions to the individual are never clearly present. Thus, the task can only be one of ascertaining the circle out of which the psalms arose.

II. Destination of the Psalms. Private or Cultic Songs? Gunkel believed that a) the various psalm forms originated in the cult, but that the actual psalms were imitations of this form and were later spiritualized compositions by an individual, and b) the individual psalms of lament originated in private circles and were composed and sung for private devotion. If the psalms can be explained satisfactorily as cult psalms, there is simply no reason to draw upon any other explanation, let alone to give it the priority. The main mass of the psalms are not private, originally non-cultic poems, but actual, genuine cult songs. Psalms 1, 127 and perhaps 112, are the only psalms which were not composed for a cultic purpose.

III. The Actual Psalmists. The psalms originated in the circle of temple personnel, specifically among the levitical singers, who have some connection with the temple prophets.

IV. Origin of the False Assertions Concerning the Composer. In contrast to the relatively correct assertions about Asaph, Heman, Ethan, and the Korahites, the statements about Moses, David and Solomon are false and completely unhistorical. The statements about Moses and Solomon have the character of a midrash and thus belong to the latest notices added to the superscriptions. The question of authorship is a secondary one for a cult psalm; of more importance religiously are the useability of the psalm, its acceptance to God, its reflection of God and of the divine laws and cultic-liturgical conditions. The superscription *l David* actually meant "written for David and used by him and other kings." Statements in the superscriptions about the historical situations lying behind the psalms are completely worthless and are simply midrashic combinations and speculations. They presuppose Davidic authorship and thus are later additions to an older *l David.*

The six *Psalmenstudien* were reprinted as 2 volumes in 1961.

1470. _____. *Offersang og sangoffer. Salmediktningen i Bibelen.* Oslo: Aschehoug, 1951. xv+664p. Revised by Mowinckel, translated into English by D.R. Ap-Thomas and published as *The Psalms in Israel's Worship.* 2 Vols. bound as one. New York: Abingdon, 1962. Reprint, Sheffield: JSOT Press, 1992.

Norwegian edition reviewed by G.W. Anderson in *JBL* 82 (1953): 329-332. English revision and translation reviewed by E.S. Gerstenberger in *JBL* 82 (1963): 333-336.

1471. _____. *Zum israelitischen Neujahr und zur Deutung der Thronbesteigungspsalmen.* Avhanglinger utgitt av det Norske Videnskaps-Adademi i Oslo. II. Hist.-Filos. Kl. Oslo: Jacob Dybwad, 1952. 68p.

1) Aalen's thesis of the relative meaninglessness of the yearly cycle is wrong. Ancient Israel had an exact

understanding of when the year began and when it ended. 2) Snaith is wrong in considering the enthronement psalms as being originally "sabbath psalms." Contrary to Aalen, the enthronement psalms are not simply "morning prayers"; they are connected with the New Year celebration and its ideology.

1472. ______. *Religion und Kultus.* Translated by A. Schauer. Göttingen: Vandenhoeck and Ruprecht, 1953. 164p.

1473. ______. "Gottesdienst, II. Im AT." In *Die Religion in Geschichte und Gegenwart,* ed. Kurt Galling. 3rd ed. II: 1752-1756. Tübingen: J.C.B. Mohr (Paul Siebeck), 1958.

1474. Nielsen, E. "Some Reflections on the History of the Ark." In *Congress Volume. Oxford 1959.* Supplements to Vetus Testamentum 7. 61-74. Leiden: E.J. Brill, 1960.

1475. Noth, M. "Jerusalem und die israelitische Tradition." *Oudtestamentische Studien* 8 (1950): 28-46. Also published in *Gesammelte Studien.* Theologische Bücherei 6. 3rd ed. 172-187. Munich: Chr. Kaiser Verlag, 1966. Translated into English and published as "Jerusalem and the Israelite Tradition." In *The Laws in the Pentateuch and Other Essays.* Translated by D.R. Ap-Thomas. 132-144. Edinburgh: Oliver and Boyd, 1966. Philadelphia: Fortress, 1966.

1476. Oesterley, William Oscar Emil. "Early Hebrew Festival Rituals." In *Myth and Ritual. Essays on the Myth and Ritual of the Hebrews in Relation to the Cultic Pattern of the Ancient East,* ed. S.H. Hooke. 111ff. London: Oxford University Press, 1933.

1477. Patai, R. "Hebrew Installation Rites." *Hebrew Union College Annual* 20 (1947): 143-225.

1478. Perdue, Leo G. *Wisdom and Cult: A Critical Analysis of the Views of Cult in the Wisdom Literature of Israel and the Ancient Near East.* Society of Biblical Literature Dissertation Series 30. Missoula, MT: Scholars Press, 1977. xiii+390p.

Reviewed by R.E. Murphy in *JBL* 97 (1978): 583-584.

1479. Plantin, Henry. "Leviternas veckodagspsalmer i templet." *Svensk Exegetisk Årsbok* 48 (1983): 48-76.

The Hymns of Levites for the days of the week which are mentioned in the Mishna *Tamid* 7.4 and in the headings of six psalms in the LXX were originally two groups of psalms from the Assyrian period. Psalms 24, 92, 48, 93, 97 originated at the time of Hezekiah's reform and 81, 94 at the time of the Covenant Festival celebrated by Josiah. These two groups of psalms were united and become psalms for the days of the week when the temple service was restored in 165 B.C. At the same time these psalms were translated into Greek (LXX).

1480. ______. "Deuteronomium och lövhyddofestens psalmer i b Sukka 55 a." *Svensk Exegetisk Årsbok* 55 (1990): 7-38.

Deuteronomy and the Feast of Booths Psalms in b. Sukka 55 a. According to b. Sukka 55a, Psalms 50, 81, 94, 82, and 29 were sung at the feast of Tabernacles. The first four are influenced by the book of Deuteronomy which, according to Deuteronomy 31:10-11, was to be read during the same feast at the end of the seventh year. Psalm 29 is the eighth day's psalm in the LXX. Both the hymn of Deuteronomy 33 and this psalm are theophanies and have influenced each other in the LXX, indicating that they were united in the eighth day's liturgy at the time they were translated into Greek.

1481. Poulssen, N. *König und Tempel in Glaubenzeugnis des Alten Testaments.* Stuttgarter biblische Monographien 3. Stuttgart: Katholisches Bibelwerk, 1967.

1482. Ricotti, Anna Luisa. "I Salmi nel culto Giudaico." *Bibbia e Oriente* 3 (1961): 161-174.

Psalms in the daily cult, on festival days, and with other events, covering the period down to the New Testament (in the second Temple and in the synagogue).

1483. Ridderbos, Nicolaas Hermann. *Psalms en Kultus. Rede uitgesproken bij de aanvaarding van het ambt van hoogleraar in de theologie aan de Vrije Universiteit te Amsterdam op vrijdag 30 Juni 1950.* 3-29,32-40. Kampen: J.H. Kok N.V., 1950. 40p. Translated from Dutch into German by Heinz Wolters and printed as "Psalmen und Kult" in *Zur Neueren Psalmenforschung*, ed. Peter H.A. Neumann, 234-279; Darmstadt: Wissenschaftliche Buchgesellschaft, 1976. Reprinted in *Psalmenstudie. Prof. Nic. H. Ridderbos en het boek der Psalmen. Opstellen van prof. dr. Nic. H. Ridderbos*, ed. C. Van Ginkel and P.J. van Midden. 19-50. Kampen: Kok, 1991.

1484. Ringgren, Helmer. "Enthronement Festival or Covenant Renewal?" *Biblical Research* 7 (1962): 45-48.

1485. Ripoli, F. "The Psalms or Israel at Prayer." *Biblehashyam* 5 (1979): 133-138.

1486. Rowley, H.H. *Worship in Ancient Israel: Its Forms and Meaning.* 173-212: "Psalmody and Music." London: SPCK, 1967.

1487. Schmid, H. "Jahwe und die Kulttraditionen von Jerusalem." *Zeitschrift für die alttestamentliche Wissenschaft* 67 (1955): 168-197.

1488. Schmidt, Hans. "Rezension über: Sigmund Mowinckel, Psalmenstudien II: Thronbesteigungsfest Jahwäs und der Ursprung der Eschatologie." *Theologische Literaturzeitung* 49 (1924): 77-81; reprinted in *Zur Neueren Psalmenforschung*, ed. Peter H.A. Neumann, 55-61; Darmstadt: Wissenschaftliche Buchgesellschaft, 1976.

1489. ______. *Die Thronfahrt Jahwes am Fest der Jahreswende im Alten Israel.* Sammlung gemeinverständlicher Vorträge und Schriften aud dem Gebiet der Theologie und Religiongeschichte 122. Tübingen: J.C.B. Mohr, 1927.

1490. Schneider, H. "Die Psalmen in Gottesdienst des Alten Bundes." *Theologische Revue* 58 (1962): 225-234.

1491. Seybold, Klaus. "Krankheit und Heilung. Soziale Aspekt in den Psalmen." *Bibel und Kirche* 26 (1971): 107-111.

1492. Snaith, Norman H. *The Jewish New Year Festival, Its Origins and Development.* London: SPCK, 1947. vi+230p.

1493. Soleh, M.Z. "The Festive Assembly on the First of the Seventh Month in the Time of Ezra and Nehemiah." *Beth Mikra* 29 (1983/1984): 381-383. (Hebrew)

There is no evidence anywhere in the Hebrew Bible that the first day of the seventh month was a New Year celebration. Since Solomon's Temple was dedicated in the seventh month, it seems to have been an ancient Israelite tradition which was preserved by the exiled Judeans rather than an imitation of Babylonian practice.

1494. Springer, Simone. *Neuinterpretation im Alten Testament. Untersucht an den Themenkreisen des Herbstfests und der Königspsalmen.* Stuttgarter Biblische Beiträge. Stuttgart: Katholisches Bibelwerk, 1979. 208p.

A study of the process of re-interpretation (=relecture) within the Old Testament, using the fall festival and Israel's royal psalms as test cases. There is the question of bringing "what is valid in the past" into "the need of the present." Implied in this is the belief that a tradition is living rather than static.

1495. Steiner, Anton. "Psalmen im Tempelgottesdienst Israels." *Bibelarbeit in der Gemeinde* 4 (1982): 33-42.

1496. Toorn, K. van der. "Ordeal Procedures in the Psalms and the Passover Meal." *Vetus Testamentum* 38 (1988): 427-445.

There was a nocturnal ordeal procedure in which the guilty could lose his life (i.e., not wake from sleep). The ordeal itself is viewed as a drinking ordeal. The cup would be drunk as part of a sacred meal in connection with an oath ceremony. The wine, since it was sacred, would presumably "turn against" an untruthful oath-taker.

1497. Tournay, R.J. *Seeing and Hearing God in the Psalms: Prophetic Liturgy from the Second Temple in Jerusalem.* Translated by J. Edward Crowley. Journal for the Study of the Old Testament, Supplement Series, 118. Sheffield: JSOT Press, 1991. 311p.

Psalms sung by the Levitical singers of the Second Temple made up for the silence of the classical prophets. An idealized David, musician and prophet, is depicted as leader of the cultic prophets and of the entire inspired community. Theophanic descriptions and oracular material in the style of the classical prophets were developed and preserved through the psalms.

Reviewed by C. Stuhlmueller in *JBL* 112 (1993): 135-137.

1498. Uffenheimer, Binyamin. "The Psalmist's Religious Experience and the Prophetic Mind." *Immanuel* 21 (1987): 7-27.

Prophecy should be understood as an organic development out of popular Israelite religion.

1499. Volz, Paul. *Das Neujahrfest* (Laubhüttenfest). Sammlung Gemeinverständlicher Vorträge und Schriften aus dem Gebiet der Theologie und Religionsgeschichte 67. Tübingen: J.C. Mohr (Paul Siebeck), 1912.

1500. Willems, G.F. "Les psaumes dans la liturgie juive." *Bijdragen: Tijdschrift voor Filosofie en Theologie* 51 (1990): 397-417.

The use of the Psalms in the Jewish liturgy of the second Temple period and of today.

See also: 29, 1394, 1581, 1794, 1795, 1796, 1821, 1822, 1837, 1846, 1849, 1850, 1852, 1856, 1862, 1865, 1869, 1870, 1871.

8. Ancient Near Eastern Parallels/ Comparative Studies

1501. Adam, Alfred. *Die Psalmen des Thomas und das Perlenlied als Zeugnisse vorchristlicher Gnosis.* Beihefte zur Zeitschrift für die neutestamentliche Wissenschaft und die Kunde der älteren Kirche 24. Berlin: A. Töpelmann, 1959. 90p.

    Reviewed in *CBQ* 22 (1960): 109-111.

1502. Ahlers, Julia, Rosemary Broughton, and Carl Koch, eds. *Womenpsalms.* Winona, MN: St. Mary's Press (Christian Brothers Publications), 1992. 144p.

1503. Albertz, R. *Persönliche Frömmigkeit und offizielle Religion.* Stuttgart: Calwer, 1978.

1504. Albright, William Foxwell. *Yahweh and the Gods of Canaan: A Historical Analysis of Two Contrasting Faiths.* The Jordan Lectures 1965, Delivered at the School of Oriental and African Studies, University of London. Garden City, NY: Doubleday & Company, 1968. 294p.

1505. Allberry, C.R., and H. Ibscher. *A Manichaean Psalmbook.* Stuttgart: Kohlhammer, 1938.

1506. Assmann, J. *Ägyptische Hymnen und Gebete.* Zurich: Artemis, 1975.

1507. Auffret, Pierre. *Hymnes d'Egypt et d'Israël. Études de structures littéraires.* Orbis biblicus et orientalis 34. Fribourg, Switzerland: Éditions Universitaires, 1981; Göttingen: Vandenhoeck & Ruprecht, 1981. 316p.

I. An analysis of the structures of the stele of Neb-Re, Psalms 33, 34, 42-43, and 147. II. An analysis of Psalm 104 and the Hymn to Aton.

Reviewed in *CBQ* 44 (1982): 289-290.

1508. Baars, W. "Psalms of Solomon." In *Peshitta -- The Old Testament in Syriac,* Part IV. Leiden: E.J. Brill, 1972.

1509. Barucq, Andre. "Péché et innocence dans les Psaumes bibliques et les textes religieux du Nouvel Empire." In *Études de critique et d'histoire religieuse.* 111-127. Paris, 1948.

1510. ______. *L'expression de la louange divine et de la prière dans la Bible et en Égypte. Contribution aux études de comparitisme biblique.* Bibliotheque d'Étude Tom.33. Cairo: Institut Francais d'Archeologie Orientale, 1962.

1511. Blackman, Aylward M. "The Psalms in the Light of Egyptian Research." In *The Psalmists: Essays on their religious experience and teaching, their social background, and their place in the development of Hebrew Psalmody,* edited with an Introduction by D.C. Simpson. 177-197. London: Oxford University Press (Humphrey Milford), 1926. 197p; translated into German by Hermann-Josef Dirksen and printed as "Die Psalmen in Ägyptologischer Sicht," in *Zur Neueren Psalmenforschung,* ed. Peter H.A. Neumann, 134-155; Darmstadt: Wissenschaftliche Buchgesellschaft, 1976.

1512. Böcher, O. *Dämonenfurcht und Dämonenabwehr.* Beiträge zur Wissenschaft vom Alten und Neuen Testament 90. Stuttgart: Kohlhammer, 1970.

1513. Böhl, F.M. Th. de Liagre. *Mimus en drama op het Babylonische Nieuwjaarsfeest en konigsdag in Babylon en in Israël. Rede, uitgesproken bij de aanvaarding van het hoogleeraarsambt aan de Rijksuniversiteit te Leiden op 23 November 1927.* Groningen-Den Haag, 1927; reprinted in *Opera Minora. Studies en bijdragen op assyriologisch en oudtestamentisch terrein*, 261-281 and 502-504; Groningen: J.P. Wolters, 1953.

1514. Buccellati, G. "The Enthronement of the King and the Capital City in Texts from Ancient Mesopotamia and Syria." In *From the Workshop of the Chicago Assyrian Dictionary. Studies Presented to A. Leo Oppenheim, June 7, 1964.* 54-61. Chicago: University of Chicago Press, 1964.

1515. Butterworth, E.A.S. *The Tree at the Navel of the Earth.* Berlin-New York: Walter de Gruyter, 1970. xii+239p; 31pl.

1516. Caplice, R. "Participants in the Namburbi-Rituals." *Catholic Biblical Quarterly* 29 (1967): 346-352.

1517. ______. *The Akkadian Namburbi Texts.* Sources from the Ancient Near East 1/1. Los Angeles, CA: Undena Publications, 1974.

1518. Caquot, André., M. Sznycer, and A. Herdner. *Textes ougaritiques I: Mythes et Légendes.* Paris: Editions du Cerf, 1974.

1519. _____, and Jean-Michael de Tarragon. *Textes ougaritiques II: Textes religieux et rituels: Introduction, traduction, commentaire*; Jesús Cunchillos, *Correspondance: Introduction, traduction, commentaire*. LAPO 14. Paris: Editions du Cerf, 1989. 480p.

1520. Carmignac, J., and P. Guilbert. *Les Textes de Qumran traduits et annotés: La Règle de la Communauté; Le Règle de la Guerre; Les Hymnes*. Autour de la Bible. Paris: Letouzey et Ané, 1961. 284p.

Reviewed in *CBQ* 24 (1962): 101-103.

1521. Castellino, Raffaele Giorgio. *Le lamentazioni individuali e gli inni in Babilonia e in Israele, raffrontati riguardo all forma e al contenuto*. Torino: Società Editrice Internazionale, 1939. xxviii+283p.

1522. _____. "Lamentazioni individuali Accadiche ed Ebraiche." *Salesianum* 10 (1948): 145-162.

1523. Cervo, N.A. "'Of Pious Hymns and Psalms': Tennyson's Saint Simeon Stylites and the Penitential Psalms." *English Language Notes* 28 (1991): 37-41.

1524. Charlesworth, James H., ed. *The Old Testament Pseudepigrapha*, Vol. 2: *Expansions of the "Old Testament" and Legends, Wisdom and Philosophical Literature, Prayers, Psalms and Odes, Fragments of Lost Judeo-Hellenistic Works*. 607-771. Garden City, NY: Doubleday & Company, 1985.

English translations and discussions of Psalms 151-155, the Prayer of Manasseh, Psalms of Solomon, Hellenistic

Synagogal Prayers, the Prayer of Joseph, the Prayer of Jacob, and the Odes of Solomon.

1525. Clifford, Richard J. *The Cosmic Mountain in Canaan and the Old Testament.* Harvard Semitic Monographs 4. Cambridge, MA: Harvard University Press, 1972. 221p.

Reviewed by D.L. Petersen in *JBL* 92 (1973): 443-444.

1526. _____. "Cosmogonies in the Ugaritic Texts and in the Bible." *Orientalia* 53 (1984): 183-201.

1527. Cohen, Mark E. *Sumerian Hymnology: The Eršemma.* Hebrew Union College Annual Supplements 2. Cincinnati [New York: Ktav], 1981. xii+217p.

Reviewed in *CBQ* 44 (1982): 478-479.

1528. _____. *The Canonical Lamentations of Ancient Mesopotamia.* 2 vols. Bethesda, MD: Capital Decisions Limited Press, 1988. 843p.

1529. Contenau, Georges. *La magie chez les Assyriens et les Babyloniens.* Paris: Payot, 1947. 298p.

1530. Coogan, Michael David. *Stories from Ancient Canaan.* Philadelphia: Westminster, 1978. 120p.

Reviewed in *JBL* 98 (1979): 580-582.

1531. Coppens, Joseph. "Les Parallels du Psáutier avec les Textes de Ras-Shamra-Ougarit." *Bulletin d'histoire et exegése de l'Ancien Testament* 18 (1946): 113-142. Published as an extract of *Mélanges Lefort, Muséon* 59 (1946): 113-142.

1532. _____. "Trois parallèles ougaritiens du Psautier." *Ephemerides Theologicae Lovanienses* 23 (1947): 173-177.

Psalms 110:3,6b; 82:7.

1533. Cumming, Charles Gordon. *The Assyrian and the Hebrew Hymns of Praise.* Columbia University Oriental Studies 12. New York: Columbia University Press, 1934. Reprint, New York: AMS Press, Inc., 1966. 176p.

1) The Hebrew Hymns of Praise. 2) The Assyrian Hymns of Praise. 3) A Comparison of the Assyrian and the Biblical Hymns.

1534. Dahood, Mitchell. *Ugaritic-Hebrew Philology: Marginal Notes on Recent Publications.* Biblica et Orientalia 17. Rome: Pontifical Biblical Institute, 1965. Reprinted 1976. viii+89p.

1535. _____. "Eblaite and Biblical Hebrew." *Catholic Biblical Quarterly* 44 (1982): 1-24.

1536. Day, John. *God's Conflict with the Dragon and thc Sea. Echoes of a Canaanite Myth in the Old Testament.* University of Cambridge Oriental Publications, 35. Cambridge: Cambridge University, 1985. xii+233p.

The imagery is Canaanite, not Babylonian in origin, and had its *Sitz im Leben* at the Autumn festival.

Critiqued by N. Wyatt in "Killing and Cosmogony in Canaanite and Biblical Thought," *Ugarit-Forschungen* 17 (1986): 375-381.

1537. Deichgräber, Reinhard. *Gotteshymnus und Christushymnus in der frühen Christenheit: Untersuchungen zu Form, Sprache und Stil der frühchristlichen Hymnen.* Studien zur Umwelt des Neuen Testaments 5. Göttingen: Vandenhoeck & Ruprecht, 1967.

Reviewed in *CBQ* 30 (1968): 440-441.

1538. Delcor, M. "Cinq nouveaux psaumes esséniens?" *Revue de Qumran* 1 (1958): 85-102.

1539. _____. *Les Hymnes de Qumrân. Texte hébreu, introduction, traduction, commentaire.* Autour de Bible. Paris: Letouzey et Ané, 1962. 342p.

1540. Dietrich, Manfried, Oswald Loretz, and Others, eds. *Ugaritische Bibliographie 1928-1966.* 4 vols. Alter Orient und Altes Testament 20/1-4. Neukirchen-Vluyn: Neukirchener Verlag, 1973.

1541. _____ and W.C. Delsman, eds. *Ugarit-Bibliographie 1967-1971: Titel, Nachträge, Register.* Alter Orient und Altes Testament 20/5. Kevelaer: Butzon und Bercker, 1986; Neukirchen-Vluyn: Neukirchener Verlag, 1986. 814p.

1542. Dijk, J.J. A. van. *La sagesse suméro-accadienne. Recherches sur les genres littéraires des textes sapientiaux.* Commentationes orientales 1. Leiden: E.J. Brill, 1953. vii+146p.

1543. _____. *Sumerische Götterlieder II.* Abhandlungen der Heidelberger Akademie der Wissenschaften, Phil.-hist. Klasse. Heidelberg: C. Winter, 1960.

1544. Dijkstra, M. "A Ugaritic Pendant of the Biblical Expression 'Pure in Heart' (Ps 24:4; 73:1)." *Ugarit-Forschungen* 8 (1976): 440.

1545. Donner, Herbert. "Ugaritismen in der Psalmenforschung." *Zeitschrift für die alttestamentliche Wissenschaft* 79 (1967): 322-350.

Psalms 8:2, 19:2-5a, 29:2, 42:2, 73:9, 74:13-14, 92:10, 93:3.

1546. Doriani, B.M. "'Then have I ... said with David': Anne Bradstreet's Andover Manuscript Poems and the Influence of Psalm Tradition." *Early American Literature* 24 (1989): 52-69.

1547. Driver, Godfrey R. "The Psalms in the Light of Babylonian Research." In *The Psalmists: Essays on their religious experience and teaching, their social background, and their place in the development of Hebrew Psalmody,* edited with an Introduction by D.C. Simpson. 109-175. London: Oxford University Press (Humphrey Milford), 1926. 197p. Translated into German by Anne G. Preiswerk and printed as "Die Psalmen im Lichte Babylonischer Forschung," in *Zur Neueren Psalmenforschung,* ed. Peter H.A. Neumann, 62-133; Darmstadt: Wissenschaftliche Buchgesellschaft, 1976.

1548. ______. *Canaanite Myths and Legends.* Old Testament Studies 3. Edinburgh: T. & T. Clark, 1956.

1549. Drower, E.S. *The Canonical Prayerbook of the Mandaeans.* Berlin: Akademie, 1959.

1550. Dubinski, Roman. "Donne's Holy Sonnets and the Seven Penitential Psalms." *Renaissance and Reformation* 10 (1986): 202-216.

1551. Dupont, J. "'Béatitudes' égyptiennes." *Biblica* 47 (1966): 185-222.

1552. Dürr, L. "Reichsgründungsfeiern im Antiken Orient." *Theologie und Glaube* 20 (1928): 305-320.

1553. Ebeling, Erich. *Tod und Leben nach den Vorstellung der Babylonier.* Vol. I, *Texte.* Berlin-Leipzig: Walter de Gruyter, 1931.

1554. _____. "Ein Loblied auf Nabû aus neuassyrischer Zeit." *Die Welt des Orients* 1 (1947-1952): 476-479.

1555. _____. *Die akkadische Gebetsserie "Handerhebung."* Deutsche Akademie der Wissenschaften zu Berlin. Veröffentlichungen des Instituts für Orientforschung 20. Berlin: Akademie Verlag, 1953. 171p.

1556. ______. *Aus dem Tagebuch eines assyrischen Zauberpriesters.* Mitteilung der altorientalischen Gesellschaft 5/3. 2nd ed. Osnabrück: O. Zeller, 1972. 52p.

1557. Engnell, Ivan. *Studies in Divine Kingship in the Ancient Near East.* Uppsala: Almqvist and Wiksell, 1943. Reprinted with a preface by G.W. Anderson, an appreciation of the author by C.R. North, a supplementary bibliography by G.W. Anderson, and a bibliography of Engnell's writings by A. Carlson: Oxford: Basil Blackwell, 1967. xxvii+261p.

Reviewed by M. Pope in *JBL* 87 (1968): 486-487.

1558. Erichsen, Wolja. *Demotische Orakelfragen.* Copenhagen: E. Munksgaard, 1942. 19p.

1559. Falkenstein, Adam. "Gebet I. Das Gebet in der sumerischen Überlieferung." In *Reallexikon der Assyriologie*, ed. Erich Ebeling and Bruno Meissner. Vol. III/2: 156-160. Berlin and Leipzig: Walter de Gruyter, 1959.

1560. _____. "Akitu-Fest und akiti-Festhaus." In *Festschrift Johannes Friedrich zum 65. Geburtstag am 27. August 1958 gewidmet,* ed. R. von Kienle and Others. 147-182. Heidelberg: C. Winter, 1959.

1561. _____. *Sumerische Götterlieder I.* Abhandlungen der Heidelberger Akademie der Wissenschaften, Phil.-hist. Klasse. Heidelberg: C. Winter, 1959.

1562. _____ and W. von Soden. *Sumerische und akkadische Hymnen und Gebete.* Die Bibliothek der Alten Welt, Reihe Der Alte Orient, ed. K. Hoenn. Zurich: Artemis, 1953. Excerpts from the introduction printed as "Sumerische und akkadische Hymnen und Gebete" in *Zur Neueren Psalmenforschung*, ed. Peter H.A. Neumann, 280-314; Darmstadt: Wissenschaftliche Buchgesellschaft, 1976.

1563. Feinberg, Ch.L. "Parallels to the Psalms in Near Eastern Literature." *Bibliotheca Sacra and Theological Review* 104 (1947): 290-321.

1564. Fisher, Loren R, ed. *Ras Shamra Parallels: The Texts from Ugarit and the Hebrew Bible.* 2 vols. Analecta Orientalia

49-50. Rome: Pontifical Biblical Institute, 1972, 1975. Vol. I, xxiii+535p; Vol. II, xiii+508p.

1565. _____, ed. *The Claremont Ras Shamra Tablets.* Rome: Pontifical Biblical Institute, 1971.

1566. Frankfort, Henri. *Ancient Egyptian Religion. An Interpretation.* 1946. Reprint, New York: Harper Torchbooks (The Cloister Library), 1961. x+172p.

1567. _____. *Kingship and the Gods: A Study of Near Eastern Religion as the Integration of Society and Nature.* Chicago: University of Chicago, 1948; reprint Chicago: University of Chicago Press, 1978. xxiii+444p.

Reviewed by A. Haldar in *JBL* 69 (1950): 186-189.

1568. _____. *The Problem of Similarity in Ancient Eastern Religions.* The Frazer Lecture, 1951. Oxford: At the Clarendon Press, 1951. 23p.

1569. Frazer, James George. *The Golden Bough: A Study in Magic and Religion.* 12 vols. London: Macmillan and Co., 1911-1919.

1570. Furlani, Giuseppe, and H. Otten. "Gebet und Hymne in Hatti." In *Reallexikon der Assyriologie*, ed. Erich Ebeling and Bruno Meissner. III/3: 170-175. Berlin: Walter de Gruyter, 1964.

1571. Gadd, Cyril John. "Babylonian Myth and Ritual." In *Myth and Ritual. Essays on the Myth and Ritual of the Hebrews in Relation to the Culture Pattern of the*

Ancient East, ed. S.H. Hooke. 40-67. London: Oxford University Press, 1933.

1572. ______. *Ideas of Divine Rule in the Ancient Near East.* The Schweich Lectures of the British Academy for 1945. London: Oxford University Press (For the British Academy), 1948. 101p.

1573. García Martínez, Florentino. "Salmos Apócrifos in Qumran." *Estudios Bíblicos* 40 (1982): 197-220.

The "Apocryphal Psalms": Psalm 151 A+B, 11QPs[a] xxviii,3-4; Psalm 154, 11QPs[a] xviii,1-16; Psalm 155, 11QPs[a] xxiv,3-17; Sir 51:13ff, 11QPs[a] xxi,11-17, xxii,1; "Plea for Deliverance," 11QPs[a] xix,and Ps[b] frag. a,y,b; "Hymn to Zion," 11QPs[a] xxii,1-15; "Hymn to the Creator," 11QPs[a] xxvi,9-15; an eschatological hymn, 4QPs[f] ix; "Apostrophe to Judah," 4QPs[f] x,5-14; Psalms against demons, 11QPsAp[a].

1574. Gaster, Theodore. *Thespis: Ritual, Myth and Drama in the Ancient Near East.* New York: Henry Schuman, Inc., 1950; revised edition, New York: Doubleday & Co., 1961; reprinted, New York: Harper Torchbooks (Harper and Row), 1966. 512p.

Reviewed by A.M. Honeyman in *JBL* 70 (1951): 165-167.

1575. Gennep, Arnold van. *Rites de passasge. Etude systématique des rites de la porte et du seuil, de l'hospitalité, de l'adoption, de la grossesse et de l'accourchement, de la naissance, de l'enfance, de la puberté, de l'initiation, de l'ordination, du couronnement des fiançailles et dur mariage, des funérailles, des saisons, etc.* Paris: E. Nourry, 1909. ii+288p. Reprint, Paris: A. & J. Picard,

1981. Translated into English by M.B. Vizedom and G.L. Caffee and published as *The Rites of Passage.* Introduction by Solon T. Kimball. Chicago: University of Chicago Press, 1960. xxvi+198p.

1576. Gese, Harmut, Maria Höfner, and Kurt Rudolph. *Die Religionen Altsyiens, Altarabiens, und der Mandäer.* Die Religionen der Menschheit 10/2/ Stuttgart: W. Kohlhammer, 1970. viii+491.

1577. Gibson, John C.L. *Canaanite Myths and Legends.* 2nd ed. Edinburgh: T & T Clark, 1978. xx+168p.

Reviewed by R.J. Clifford in *JBL* 98 (1979): 580-582.

1578. Goldammer, Kurt. "Elemente des Schamanismus im Alten Testament." *Studies in the History of Religion* 21/2 (1972): 266-285.

1579. Gray, John. "Canaanite Mythology and Hebrew Tradition." *Glasgow University Oriental Society Transactions,* 1954.

1580. _____. *The Legacy of Canaan. The Ras Shamra texts and their relevance to the Old Testament.* Supplements to Vetus Testamentum 5. Leiden: E.J. Brill, 1957; 2nd ed., 1965. x+348p.

1581. _____. "Sacral Kingship in Ugarit." *Ugaritica* 6 (1969): 289ff.

1582. Greenfield, Jonas C. "Aspects of Aramean Religion." In *Ancient Israelite Religion: Essays in Honor of Frank Moore Cross,* ed. Patrick D. Miller,Jr., Paul D. Hanson, and S. Dean McBride. 67-78. Philadelphia: Fortress Press, 1987.

1583. _____. "Two Notes on the Apocryphal Psalms." In *"Sha'arei Talmon": Studies in the Bible, Qumran and the Ancient Near East Presented to Shemaryahu Talmon*, ed. Michael Fishbane and Emanuel Tov. 309-314. Winona Lake, IN: Eisenbrauns, 1992.

11QPs^{a} 19:14-16 and 11QPs^{a} 155:5-8.

1584. Greenwood, Theresa. *Psalms of a Black Mother.* Anderson, IN: The Warner Press, 1970.

1585. Grønbæk, Jakob H. "Jahves kamp med dragen." *Dansk Teologisk Tidsskrift* 47 (1984): 81-108.

Yahweh's Battle with a Dragon.

1586. _____. "Baal's Battle with Yam -- A Canaanite Creation Fight." *Journal for the Study of the Old Testament* 33 (1985): 27-44.

The battle of Baal and Yam was an ahistorical moment imaginatively celebrating the renewal of the cosmos through the cult of New Year festival. It was not directly related to an agrarian background.

1587. Gross, D. "Trollope's Mr. Quiverful: An Addendum to John W. Clark's The Language and Style of Anthony Trollope." *English Language Notes* 17 (1979): 122-124.

1588. Gross, Heinrich. *Die Idee des ewigen und allgemeinen Weltfriedens im Alten Orient und im Alten Testament.* Trier: Paulinus Verlag, 1956. xvii+185.

Reviewed by S.N. Kramer in *JBL* 77 (1958): 386-388.

1589. Gryglewicz, F. "Die Herkunft der Hymnen des Kindheitsevangeliums des Lucas." *New Testament Studies* 21 (1974-1975): 265-273.

1590. Gunkel, Hermann. *Schöpfung und Chaos in Urzeit und Endzeit. Eine religiongeschichtliche Untersuchung über Gen. 1 und Ap. Joh. 12.* Göttingen: Vandenhoeck und Ruprecht, 1895. 2nd ed., 1921.

1591. _____. "Ägyptische Parallelen zum Alten Testament." In *Reden und Aufsätze von Hermann Gunkel.* 131-141. Göttingen: Vandenhoeck & Ruprecht, 1913.

1592. _____. "Ägyptische Danklieder." *Reden und Aufsätze von Hermann Gunkel.* 141-149. Göttingen: Vandenhoeck & Ruprecht, 1913.

1593. _____. "Die Lieder in der Kindheitsgeschichte Jesu bein Lukas." In *Festgabe von Fachgenossen und Freunden A. von Harnack zum siebzigsten Geburtstag dargebracht.* 43-60. Tübingen: J.C.B. Mohr, 1921.

1594. Güterbock, H.G. "The Composition of Hittite Prayers to the Sun." *Journal of the American Oriental Society* 78 (1958): 237-245.

1595. Haldar, Alfred. *Associations of Cult Prophets among the Ancient Semites.* Uppsala: Almqvist & Wiksells Boktryckeri AB, 1945.

In Israel the נביא is an ecstatic cult functionary, a phenomemon no different from that found in the nations surrounding Israel. The canonical prophets are part of the cult prophet phenomenon. These cultic prophets were part of a group that with a leader (at times the king) performed their functions at local sanctuaries and the various cultic festivals, reciting oracles and rituals. Through the means of divination they had special knowledge of God and communicated this word from the Lord in the cult.

1596. ______. *The Notion of the Desert in Sumero-Accadian and West-Semitic Religions.* Uppsala Universitets Årsskrift 1950: 3. Leipzig: Otto Harrassowitz, 1950. 70p.

Reviewed by J. Muilenburg in *JBL* 70 (1951): 340-341.

1597. Hallo, William W. "Individual Prayer in Sumerian. The Continuity of a Tradition." *Journal of the American Oriental Society* 88 (1968): 71-89; this issue of the journal also was printed as *Essays in Memory of E.A. Speiser*, ed. William W. Hallo; American Oriental Series, vol. 53; New Haven, CT: American Oriental Society, 1968.

1598. ______. "Sumerian Literature -- Background to the Bible." *Bible Review* 4 (3,1988): 28-38.

Wisdom literature, literature centered on royal themes, and literature devoted to the Sumerian gods.

1599. Hann, R.R. *The Manuscript History of the Psalms of Solomon.* Septuagint and Cognate Studies 13. Chico, CA: Scholars Press, 1982.

1600. Healey, John F. "The Immortality of the King: Ugarit and the Psalms." *Orientalia* 53 (1984): 245-254.

1601. Heiler, Friedrich. *Das Gebet. Eine religiongeschichtliche und religionspsychologische Untersuchung.* Munich: E. Reinhardt, 1918. 4th ed.,1921. 5th ed., 1923. Translated into English and edited by Samuel McComb with the assistance of J. Edgar Park, and published as *Prayer. A Study in the History and Psychology of Religion.* London: Oxford University Press, 1932. Reprint, 1958. xxviii+376p.

1602. Heimpel, W. "The Nahshe Hymn." *Journal of Cuneiform Studies* 33 (1981): 65-139.

Unlike most Sumerian hymns, it expresses a concern for moral problems as seen from the viewpoint of the officials responsible for the temple cult.

1603. Hempel, Johannes. "Die israelitischen Anschauungen von Segen und Fluch im Lichte altorientalischen Parallelen." *Zeitschrift der Deutschen Morganländischen Gesellschaft* 79 (1925): 20-110.

1604. Herdner, A. *Corpus des Tablettes en Cunéiformes Alphabétiques, découvertes à Ras Shamra -- Ugarit de 1929 à 1939.* Mission de Ras Shamra X. 2 vols. Paris: Paul Geuthner, 1963.

1605. Hess, Richard S. "Hebrew Psalms and Amarna Correspondence from Jerusalem: Some Comparisons and Implications." *Zeitschrift für die alttestamentliche Wissenschaft* 101 (1989): 249-265.

1606. Hoenig, S.B. "Qumran Liturgic Psalms." *Jewish Quarterly Review* 57 (1967): 327-332.

1607. Hofius, Otfried. *Der Christushymnus Philipper 2,6-11: Untersuchungen zu Gestalt und Aussage eines urchristlichen Psalms.* Wissenschaftliche Untersuchungen zum Neuen Testament 17. Tübingen: J.C.B. Mohr, 1976. viii+118.

Reviewed in *CBQ* 40 (1978): 635.

1608. Holm-Nielsen, Svend. *Hodayot. Psalms from Qumran.* Translated with notes, introduction and analysis. Acta Theologica Danica, II. Leiden: E.J. Brill, 1960. 366p.

Reviewed in *CBQ* 23 (1961): 365-376.

1609. _____. "Die Psalmen Salomos." In *Jüdische Schriften aus hellenistisch-römische Zeit 4,* ed. W.G. Kümmel and Others. 51-112. Gütersloh: Gerd Mohn, 1977.

1610. Hooke, S.H. "The Babylonian New Festival." *Journal of the Manchester Egyptian and Oriental Society* 13 (1927): 29-38.

1611. _____, ed. *Myth and Ritual: Essays on the Myth and Ritual of the Hebrew in Relation to the Cultic Pattern of the Ancient East.* London: Oxford University Press, 1933.

Contains "The Myth and Ritual Pattern of the Ancient East" by Hooke; "Myth and Ritual in Ancient Egypt" by A.M. Blackman; "Babylonian Myth and Ritual" by Gadd; "Traces of the Myth and Ritual Patter in Canaan" by Hooke; "The Sun Cult and the Temple at Jerusalem" by Hollis; "Early Hebrew Festival Rituals" by Oesterley; "Initiatory Rituals" by James; and "Hebrew Myths" by Robinson.

1612. _____, ed. *The Labyrinth: Further Studies in the Relation between Myth and Ritual in the Ancient World.* London: Oxford University Press, 1935. xiv+288p.

1613. _____. *The Origins of Early Semitic Ritual.* Schweich Lectures of the British Academy, 1935. London: Oxford University Press, 1938.

1614. _____. "Myth, Ritual and History." *Folklore* 50 (1939): 137-147.

1615. _____, ed.. *Myth, Ritual and Kingship. Essays on the Theory and Practice of Kingship in the Ancient Near East and in Israel.* Oxford: At the Clarendon Press, 1958. xi+308p.

Lectures given at the University of Manchester in the autumn of 1955 and the spring of 1956, published with one addition.

1616. _____. *Babylonian and Assyrian Religion.* London and New York: Hutchinson's University Library, 1953. Reprint, Oxford: Basil Blackwell, 1962; Norman, OK: University of Oklahoma Press, 1963. xii+128.

Reviewed by W.W. Hallo in *JBL* 82 (1963): 338-339.

1617. Houwink, P.H.J. "Hittite Royal Prayers." *Numen* 16 (1969): 81-98.

1618. Jacobsen, Thorkild. "Religious Drama." In *Unity and Diversity*, ed. H. Goedicke and J.J.M. Roberts. 65-97. Baltimore: Johns Hopkins University Press, 1975.

1619. Jefferson, H.G. "Canaanite Literature and the Psalms." *The Personalist* 39 (1958): 356-360.

1620. Jirku, Anton. "Kanaanäische Psalmenfragmente in der vorisraelitischen Zeit Palästinas und Syriens." *Journal of Biblical Literature* 52 (1933): 108-120.

1621. Jones, D. "The Background and Character of the Lukan Psalms." *Journal of Theological Studies* 19 (1968): 19-50.

1622. Kaiser, Otto. *Die mythische Bedeutung des Meeres in Ägypten, Ugarit und Israel.* Beihefte zur Zeitschrift für die alttestamentliche Wissenschaft 78. Berlin: Alfred Töpelmann, 1959. viii+161p. 2nd ed., 1962.

Reviewed by J.C. Greenfield in *JBL* 80 (1961): 91-92.

1623. Kapelrud, Arvid Schou. "Jahves tronstigningsfest og funnene i Ras Sjamra." *Norsk Teologisk Tidsskrift* 41 (1940): 38-58.

1624. ______. "The Gates of Hell and the Guardian Angels of Paradise." *Journal of the American Oriental Society* 70 (1950): 151-156.

1625. Keel, Othmar. *Die Welt der altorientalischen Bildsymbolik und das Alte Testament: Am Beispiel der Psalmen.* Zürich: Benziger Verlag, 1972; Neukirchen-Vluyn: Neukirchener Verlag, 1972. 2nd, improved and expanded ed., 1977. 391p. Translated into English by Timothy J. Hallet with additions and corrections by the author and published as *The Symbolism of the Biblical World. Ancient Near Eastern Iconography and the Book of Psalms.* New York: Seabury, 1978. 422p.

Review of German edition by W.E. Lemke in *JBL* 94 (1975): 126-128.

1626. _____, and Christoph Uehlinger. *Göttinen, Götter und Gottessymbole: Neue Erkenntnisse zur Religionsgeschichte Kanaans und Israels aufgrund bislang unerschlossener iconographischer Quellen.* Quaestiones Disputatae 134. Freiburg: Herder, 1992. xiv+526p.

A survey of iconographical evidence from about 1800 to 450 B.C., which sheds light on ancient Near Eastern gods and goddesses and their symbols.

1627. Kees, Hermann. *Totenglauben und Jenseitsvorstellungen der alten Ägypter. Grundlagen und Entwicklung bis zum Ende des Mittleren Reiches.* Leipzig: J.C. Hinrichs. 2nd ed. Berlin: Akademie Verlag, 1956. 315p.

1628. King, L.W. *Babylonian Magic and Sorcery, being "The Prayers of the Lifting of the Hand." The Cuneiform texts of a group of Babylonian and Assyrian incantations and magical formulae, edited with transliterations, translations and full vocabulary from tablets of the*

Kuyunjik collections preserved in the British Museum. London: Luzac and Co., 1896. xxx+199p. Reprint, New York: AMS Press, 1976.

1629. Kittel, Bonnie Pedrotti. *The Hymns of Qumran: Translation and Commentary.* Society of Biblical Literature Dissertation Series 50. Chico, CA: Scholars Press for the Society of Biblical Literature, 1981. xii+222p.

Reviewed in *CBQ* 45 (1983): 660-661.

1630. Kramer, Samuel Noah. *The Sacred Marriage Rite.* Bloomington, IN: Indiana University Press, 1969.

1631. ______. *Sumerian Mythology: A Study of Spiritual and Literary Achievement in the Third Millennium B.C.* Memoirs of the American Philosophical Society 21. Philadelphia: American Philosophical Society, 1944. xiv+125p.

Reviewed by F.J. Stephens in *JBL* 64 (1945): 282-284.

1632. ______, and M. Weinfield. "Prolegomena to a Comparative Study of the Book of Psalms and Sumerian Literature." *Beth Mikra* 56 (1973): 8-24. (Hebrew)

1633. Krecher, J. *Sumerische Kultlyrik.* Wiesbaden: Otto Harrassowitz, 1966.

1634. Kutsch, Ernst. *Salbung als Rechtsakt im Alten Testament und im Alten Orient.* Beihefte zur Zeitschrift für die alttestamentliche Wissenschaft 87. Berlin: Alfred Töpelmann, 1963. 78p.

I. The Anointing with Oil and Its Meaning. II. Anointing as a Judicial Act.

1635. Laessoe, J. *Studies on the Assyrian Ritual and Series bît rimki.* Copenhagen: Munksgaard, 1955.

1636. Lambert, Wilfred G. *Babylonian Wisdom Literature.* Oxford: At the Clarendon Press, 3rd ed., 1960,. Reprint, 1975.

1637. ______. "The Great Battle of the Mesopotamian Religious Year. The Conflict in the Akītu House (A Summary)." *Iraq* 25 (1963): 189-190.

1638. Langdon, Stephen. *Sumerian and Babylonian Psalms.* Paris: Geuthner, 1909.

1639. ______. *Babylonian Penitential Psalms.* Oxford Editions of Cuneiform Texts 6. Paris: Geuthner, 1927.

1640. Langhe, Robert de. *Les Textes de Ras Shamra-Ugarit et leurs Rapports avec le Milieu Biblique de l'Ancient Testament.* 2 vols. Gembloux: J. Duculot; Paris: Desclée de Brouwer, 1945.

Reviewed by C.H. Gordon in *JBL* 66 (1947): 248.

1641. Langton, Edward. *Essentials of Demonology. A Study of Jewish and Christian Doctrine, Its Origin and Development.* London: Epworth Press, 1949. xxii+234p.

1642. Lebrun, René. *Hymnes et prières hittites.* Homo Religiosus 4. Louvain-la-Neuve, Belgium: Centre d'Histoire des Religions, 1980. 500p.

1643. Lehmann, Manfred R. "11Q Ps[a] and Ben Sira." *Revue de Qumran* 11 (1983): 239-251.

11QPs[a] was intended for liturgical use.

1644. Lewandowska, M.L. "The Words of Their Roaring: Roethke's Use of the Psalms of David." In *The David Myth in Western Literature*, ed. R.-J. Frontain and J. Wojcik. 156-167. West Lafayette, IN: Purdue University Press, 1980.

1645. Loretz, Oswald. "Psalmenstudien I." *Ugarit-Forschungen* 3 (1971): 101-115.

1646. ______. "Die Ugaritistik in der Psalmeninterpretation." *Ugarit-Forschungen* 4 (1972): 167-169.

Reflections on the work of Dahood.

1647. ______. "Psalmenstudien II." *Ugarit-Forschungen* 5 (1973): 213-218.

1648. ______. "Psalmenstudien III." *Ugarit-Forschungen* 6 (1974): 175-210.

1) Review of Kraus' 4th ed. of his Psalms' commentary. 2) *Mgn* Gift in the Psalms. 3) *ᶜām* "Strong One" in the Psalms. 4) *Hdrt qdš* (Ps 29,2) and ug. *hdrt* (CTA 14 III 155). 5) Psalm 19. 6) Psalm 23. 7) Psalm 29. 8) Psalm 47. 9) Psalm 80. 10) Psalm 95. 11) Psalm 100. 12) Stichometry of Psalm 106. 13) Psalm 107.

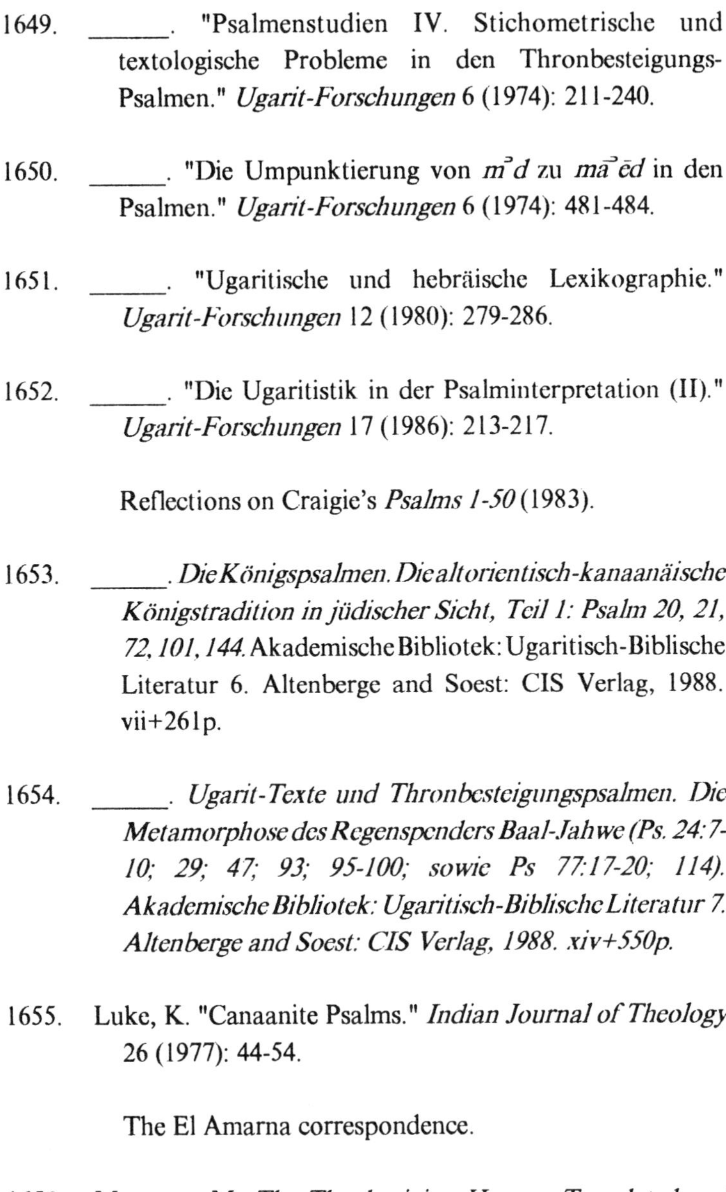

1649. _____. "Psalmenstudien IV. Stichometrische und textologische Probleme in den Thronbesteigungs-Psalmen." *Ugarit-Forschungen* 6 (1974): 211-240.

1650. _____. "Die Umpunktierung von *mʾd* zu *maʾēd* in den Psalmen." *Ugarit-Forschungen* 6 (1974): 481-484.

1651. _____. "Ugaritische und hebräische Lexikographie." *Ugarit-Forschungen* 12 (1980): 279-286.

1652. _____. "Die Ugaritistik in der Psalminterpretation (II)." *Ugarit-Forschungen* 17 (1986): 213-217.

Reflections on Craigie's *Psalms 1-50* (1983).

1653. _____. *Die Königspsalmen. Die altorientisch-kanaanäische Königstradition in jüdischer Sicht, Teil 1: Psalm 20, 21, 72, 101, 144.* Akademische Bibliotek: Ugaritisch-Biblische Literatur 6. Altenberge and Soest: CIS Verlag, 1988. vii+261p.

1654. _____. *Ugarit-Texte und Thronbesteigungspsalmen. Die Metamorphose des Regenspenders Baal-Jahwe (Ps. 24:7-10; 29; 47; 93; 95-100; sowie Ps 77:17-20; 114). Akademische Bibliotek: Ugaritisch-Biblische Literatur 7. Altenberge and Soest: CIS Verlag, 1988. xiv+550p.*

1655. Luke, K. "Canaanite Psalms." *Indian Journal of Theology* 26 (1977): 44-54.

The El Amarna correspondence.

1656. Mansoor, M. *The Thanksgiving Hymns. Translated and annotated with an introduction.* Studies on the Texts of the Desert of Judah, ed. J. van der Ploeg. Leiden: E.J. Brill, 1961. xii+227p.

1657. Margulis, B. "A Ugaritic Psalm (RŠ 24.252)." *Journal of Biblical Literature* 89 (1970): 292-304.

1658. Martinez, Ernest R. *Hebrew-Ugaritic Index to the Writings of Mitchell J. Dahood: A Bibliography with Indices of Scriptural Passages, Hebrew and Ugaritic Words, and Grammatical Observations.* Rome: Pontifical Biblical Institute, 1967. 120p.

1659. ______. *Hebrew-Ugaritic Index to the Writings of Mitchell J. Dahood: A Bibliography with Indices of Scriptural Passages, Hebrew, Ugaritic and Eblaitc Words, and Grammatical Observations, Critical Reviews, Doctoral Dissertations and Related Writings.* Subsidia Biblica 4. Rome: Pontifical Biblical Institute, 1981. 155p.

1660. Mayer, Werner R. *Untersuchungen zur Formensprache der babylonischen "Gebetsbeschwörung."* Studia Pohl Series Maior 5. Rome: Pontifical Biblical Institute, 1976.

1661. ______. "'Ich rufe dich von ferne, höre mich von nahe!' Zu einer babylonischen Gebetsformel." In *Werden und Wirken des Alten Testaments. Festschrift für Claus Westermann zum 70. Geburtstag,* ed. R. Albertz, R. Müller, H.-P. Wolff, and W. Zimmerli. 302-317. Göttingen: Vandenhoeck & Ruprecht, 1980; Neukirchen-Vluyn: Neukirchener Verlag, 1980.

An analysis of the Babylonian prayer-formula, which is helpful in understanding the Psalm prayers, especially the idea of "near" and "far."

1662. _____. "Ein neues Königsritual gegen feindliche Bedrohung." *Orientalia* 57 (1988): 145-164.

1663. Metzger, Martin. *Königsthron und Gottesthron. Thronformen und Throndarstellungen in Ägypten und im Vodereren Orient im dritten und zweiten Jahrtausend vor Christus und deren Bedeutung für das Verständnis von Aussagen über den Thron im Alten Testament.* Alter Orient und Altes Testament 15/1-2. Neukirchen-Vluyn: Neukirchener Verlag, 1985; Kevelaer: Butzon & Bercker, 1985. Vol. 1, xi+391p; Vol. 2, viii+272.

Reviewed in *CBQ* 49 (1987): 484.

1664. Millás Vallicrosa, José Ma. "La tradición del Salmo penitencial en la poesía hebraica postbíblica." In *Miscellanea biblica B. Ubach,* ed. R.M. Díaz Carbonell. 243-278. Montserrat: Imprinta-escuela of Barcelona, 1953.

A summary of post-biblical Hebrew poetry, plus examples of penitential psalms from the third century to the present.

1665. Miller, Patrick D., Jr. *The Divine Warrior in Early Israel.* Harvard Semitic Monographs 5. Cambridge, MA: Harvard University Press, 1973. 279p.

Reviewed by D.F. Morgan in *JBL* 95 (1976): 474-476.

1666. ______. "Vocative Lamed in the Psalter: A Reconsideration." *Ugarit-Forschungen* 11 (1979): 617-637.

"We are not yet able to include vocative *lamed* in the grammars of Hebrew."

1667. Monteiro, G. "Ernest Hemingway, Psalmist." *Journal of Modern Literature* 14 (1987): 83-95.

1668. Moor, Johannes C. de. *New Year with Canaanites and Israelites.* 2 parts. Kamper Cahiers 21-22. Kampen: J.H. Kok, 1972. Part 1, 31p; Part 2, 35p.

I. The Canaanite and Israelite New Year festivals. A seven-day festival began with a new moon in the fall, the time of the resurrection of Baal, corresponding to the end of the dry season. The ritual included a celebration of kingship, ritual combat, establishment of the destinies of the coming year, sacred marriage, communion with the dead, and the liberal consumption of new wine. The Israelite New Year was taken over from the Canaanites and was virtually the same during the period of the judges and the united monarchy; it, however, focused on Yahweh, eliminated the sacred marriage, and played down the role of the king and the consumption of wine. When the Babylonian practice of beginning the year in the spring was adopted in the late 7th century, the fall festival in Judah was no longer thought of as a New Year celebration. II. The Canaanite sources.

Reviewed by D.F. Morgan in *JBL* 93 (1974): 112; C.E. L'Heureux in *JBL* 98 (1979): 416-417.

1669. Morgenstern, J. "The King-God among the Western Semites and the Meaning of Epiphanes." *Vetus Testamentum* 10 (1960): 138-197.

1670. Moroder, R.J. "Ugaritic and Modern Translation of the Psalter." *Ugarit-Forschungen* 6 (1974): 249-264.

1671. Moyer, James C. "Hittite and Israelite Cultic Practices: A Selected Comparison." In *Scripture in Context II. More Essays on the Comparative Method*, ed. William W. Hallo and Others. Winona Lake, IN: Eisenbrauns, 1983.

1672. Müller, K.F. *Das assyrische Ritual I: Texte zum assyrischen Königsritual.* Mitteilungen der vorderasiatisch-ägyptischen Gesellschaft XLI, 3. Leipzig: J.C. Hinrich, 1937.

1673. Muntingh, L.M. "A few social concepts in the Psalms and their relationship to the Canaanite residential area." In *Studies on the Psalms: Papers Read at the 6th Meeting of Die O.T. Werkgemeenskap in Suid-Afrika.* 48-57. Potchefstroom: Pro Rege, 1963.

1674. Nitzan, Bilhah. "Songs of Praise from Qumran (4Q 510 and 4Q 511)." *Tarbiz* 57 (1987/1988): 603-605. (Hebrew)

4Q 510 cannot be read as Baumgarten proposed, and 4Q 511 draws on phrases from Psalm 91.

1675. Nötscher, F. *"Das Angesicht Gottes schauen" nach biblischer und babylonischer Auffassung.* 2nd ed. Darmstadt: Wissenschaftliche Buchgesellschaft, 1969.

1676. Obermann, Julian. "An Antiphonal Psalm from Ras Shamra." *Journal of Biblical Literature* 55 (1936): 21-42.

1677. O'Callaghan, Roger T. "Echoes of Canaanite Literature in the Psalms." *Vetus Testamentum* 4 (1954): 164-176.

1678. Oesterley, William Oscar Emil (1866-1950). *The Sacred Dance. A Study in Comparative Folklore.* Cambridge:

Cambridge University Press, 1923. x+234p. Reprint, Brooklyn, NY: Dance Horizons, (1968).

1679. Oldenburg, U. *The Conflict between El and Baʿal in Canaanite Religion.* Leiden: E.J. Brill, 1969. xiv+217p.

1680. Patai, Raphael. *Man and Temple in Ancient Jewish Myth and Ritual.* London, 1947. 2nd, enlarged edition with a new introduction and postscript. New York: KTAV Publishing House, 1967. xiv+247p.

1681. Patton, John Hastings. *Canaanite Parallels in the Book of Psalms.* Baltimore, MD: Johns Hopkins Press, 1944. 68p.

Ugaritic poetry provides a better key for understanding Hebrew prosody than does Babylonian and Egyptian poetry. All this "points to a direct influence of the Canaanite of Ugarit upon the composition of the Psalms."

Reviewed by J.A. Montgomery in *JBL* 63 (1944): 418-419.

1682. Peterson, R.S. *Imitation and Praise in the Poems of Ben Jonson.* New Haven, CT: Yale University Press, 1971.

1683. Pope, Marvin H. *El in the Ugarit Texts.* Supplements to Vetus Testamentum 2. Leiden: E.J. Brill, 1955. x+116p.

Reviewed by W.F. Albright in *JBL* 75 (1956): 255-257.

1684. _____. "The Status of El at Ugarit." *Ugarit-Forschungen* 19 (1987): 219-230.

1685. _____. and W. Röllig. "Die Mythologie der Ugariter und Phönizier." In *Wörterbuch der Mythologie. I. Die Alten*

Kulturvölker. Edited by H.W. Haussig. 217-312. Stuttgart: E. Klett, 1965. xii+601p.

1686. Pritchard, James B., ed. *Ancient Near Eastern Texts Relating to the Old Testament.* Princeton, NJ: Princeton University Press, 1950. 2nd ed., enlarged and corrected, 1955. xxi+544p.

1687. Proosdij, B.A. van. *L.W. King's Babylonian Magic and Sorcery.* Leiden: E.J. Brill, 1952.

1688. Reiner, E. *Šurpu: A Collection of Sumerian and Akkadian Incantations.* Archiv für Orientforschung 11. Graz: Akademie, 1958.

1689. Ringgren, Helmer. "Hieros Gamos i Egypten, Sumer och Israel." *Religion och Bibel* 18 (1959): 23-51.

1690. _____. "Ugarit und das Alte Testament: Einige methodologische Erwägungen." *Ugarit-Forschungen* 11 (1979): 719-721.

1691. Roeder, Günther. *Kulte, Orakel und Naturverehrung im alten Ägypten.* Zurich: Artemis-Verlag, 1960. 462p.

1692. Rummel, Stan (ed.). *Ras Shamra Parallels: The Texts from Ugarit and the Hebrew Bible, Vol. III.* Analecta Orientalia 51. Rome: Pontifical Biblical Institute, 1981. xiii+618p.

1693. Ruppert, Lothar. "Klagelieder in Israel und Babylonien -- verschiedene Deutungen der Gewalt." In *Gewalt und Gewaltlosigkeit im Alten Testament*, ed. Ernst Haag and

Others. Quaestiones disputatae 96. Frieburg: Herder, 1983. 256p.

Compares the understanding of violence in the individual laments of the Psalter with that in similar Babylonian literature; the Psalter demythologizes the hostile agents.

1694. Sanders, James A. "Two Non-canonical Psalms in 11Q Ps^{a}." *Zeitschrift für die alttestamentliche Wissenschaft* 76 (1964): 57-75.

1695. Sanders, J.T. *New Testament Christological Hymns: Their Historical and Religious Background.* Cambridge: Cambridge University Press, 1971.

1696. Sauer, G. "Die Ugaritistik und die Psalmenforschung." *Ugarit-Forschungen* 6 (1974): 401-406; 10 (1978): 357-386.

A basically negative analysis of Dahood's Anchor Bible commentary on the Psalms.

1697. Savignac, J. de. "Theologie Pharaonique et Messianisme d'Israel." *Vetus Testamentum* 7 (1957): 82-90.

1698. Scheele, Paul-Werner. *Opfer des Wortes. Gebete der Heiden aus fünf Jahrtausenden.* Paderborn: Schöningh, 1960. 288p.

1699. Schegget, G.H. ter. *Het lied van de Mensenzoon -- Studie over de Christus-Psalm in Fil 2:6-11.* Baarn: Wereldvenster, 1975.

1700. Schiffmann, Lawrence H., and Michael D. Swartz. *Hebrew and Aramaic Incantation Texts from the Cairo Genizah: Selected Texts from Taylor-Schechter Box K1.* Semitic Texts and Studies 1. Sheffield: JSOT, 1992. 183p.

1701. Schmid, H. H. "*Šālōm: 'Frieden' im alten Orient und im Alten Testament.* Stuttgarter Bibelstudien 51. Stuttgart: Katholisches Bibelwerk, 1971.

1702. Schmidt, Werner H. *Königtum Gottes in Ugarit und Israel.* Beihefte zur Zeitschrift für die alttestamentliche Wissenschaft 80. Berlin: Töpelmann, 1961. 90p. 2nd ed., 1966. 105p.

2nd ed. reviewed by J.A. Scoggin in *JBL* 86 (1967): 120.

1703. Schuller, Eileen M. *Non-Canonical Psalms from Qumran: A Pseudepigraphic Collection.* Harvard Semitic Studies 28. Atlanta, GA: Scholars Press, 1986. xii+297p.+ 9 pl.

Reviewed in *CBQ* 50 (1988): 335-336.

1704. Schüpphaus, Joachim. *Die Psalmen Salomos: Ein Zeugnis jerusalemer Theologie und Frömmigeit in der Mitte des vorchristlichen Jahrhunderts. Arbeiten zur Literatur und Geschichte des hellenistischen Judentums 7. Leiden: E.J. Brill, 1977.*

Reviewed in *CBQ* 41 (1979): 657-658.

1705. Seters, John van. "The Creation of Man and the Creation of the King." *Zeitschrift für die alttestamentliche Wissenschaft* 101 (1989): 333-342.

A recently published Neo-Babylonian text describes the creation of the king by the gods, alongside the creation of humanity in general, in which the king is endowed with the regalia for ruling humanity and all the divine qualities for kingship, in the likeness of various gods. Cf. Ezekiel 28:12-19, Genesis 2-3 (J), and Genesis 1:26-28 and Psalm 8.

1706. Seux, M.-J. *Hymnes and prières aux dieux de Babylonie et d'Assyrie.* Paris: Cerf, 1976.

1707. Smick, Elmer B. "Ugaritic and the Theology of the Psalms." in *New Perspectives on the Old Testament,* ed. J. Barton Payne. 104-116. Waco, TX: Word, 1970.

1708. ______. "Mythopoetic Language in the Psalms." *Westminster Theological Journal* 44 (1982): 88-98.

1709. Smith, Mark S. "The Near Eastern Background of Solar Language for Yahweh." *Journal of Biblical Literature* 109 (1990): 29-39.

1710. Smith, S. "The Practice of Kingship in Early Semitic Kingdoms." In *Myth and Ritual. Essays on the Myth and Ritual of the Hebrews in Relation to the Culture Pattern of the Ancient East,* ed. S.H. Hooke. 22-73. Oxford: Oxford University Press, 1933.

1711. Soden, W. von. "Gebet II (babylonisch und assyrisch)." In *Reallexikon der Assyriologie,* ed. E. Ebeling and B. Meissner. Vol. III: 160-170. Berlin: Walter de Gruyter, 1959-1964.

1712. Soll, Will. "Babylonian and Biblical Acrostics." *Biblica* 68 (1988): 305-323.

1713. Spronk, K. *Beatific Afterlife in Ancient Israel and the Ancient Near East.* Alter Orient und Altes Testament 219. Kevelaer: Butzon & Bercker; Neukirchen-Vluyn: Neukirchener Verlag, 1986. ix+398p.

Belief in a happy hereafter can be traced back to Canaanite (Ugaritic) tradition and persisted beyond the Old Testament period.

Reviewed by Mark S. Smith and Elizabeth M. Block-Smith, in "Death and Afterlife in Ugarit and Israel." *Journal of the American Oriental Society* 108 (1988): 277-284.

1714. Starcky, J. "Psaumes aprocryphes de la grotte 4 de Qumran." *Revue Biblique* 73 (1966): 353-371.

On 4QPs^{f} columns vii to ix.

1715. Stummer, Friedrich. *Sumerisch-akkadische Parallelen zum Aufbau alttestamentlicher Psalmen.* Studien zur Geschichte und Kultur des Altertums II/1-2. Paderborn: Ferdinand Schöningh, 1922; reprinted New York: Johnson, 1968.

Observes similarities in form of composition between Babylonian and biblical psalms, and considers a direct influence of the former on the latter as possible. This is especially so with the Babylonian hymn literature. These Babylonian models were then filled with the Israelite spirit.

1716. Sweet, R. "A Pair of Double Acrostics in Akkadian." *Orientalia*, N.S., 38 (1969): 459-460.

1717. Toorn, Karel van der. "The Babylonian New Year Festival: New Insights from the Cuneiform Texts and Their

Bearing on Old Testament Study." In *Congress Volume. Leuven, 1989,* ed. J.A. Emerton. Supplements to Vetus Testamentum 43. 331-344. Leiden: E.J. Brill, 1991.

The Israelite Autumn Festival corresponds to the Babylonian New Year Festival in four aspects. (1) Both were originally agrarian feasts. (2) The Israelite festival came to be the setting for a solemn procession of the ark in Jerusalem. (3) The Old Testament interprets the return of the ark to the temple as a re-affirmation of Yahweh's kingship. (4) The Israelite or Judean king asserted the legitimacy of his rule by leading the procession of the ark. There is no basis for Mowinckel's idea of a dramatic cultic battle as part of these festivals.

1718. Tournay, R. "En marge d'une traduction des Psaumes." *Revue Biblique* 63 (1956): 161-181.

1719. Trafton, Joseph L. *The Syriac Version of the Psalms of Solomon: A Critical Evaluation.* Society of Biblical Literature SCS 11. Atlanta, GA: Scholars Press, 1985. xvi+276p.

Reviewed in *CBQ* 49 (1987): 653-655.

1720. ______. *The Psalms of Solomon: Syriac and Greek Texts.* Society of Biblical Literature SCS 11 Sup. Atlanta, GA: Scholars Press, 1985. 71p.

Reviewed in *CBQ* 49 (1987): 653-655.

1721. Urbina, Pedro Antonio. "Los Salmos de David en la 'Subida del Monte Carmela.'" *Scripta Theologica* 23 (1991): 939-959.

A study of the influence of the Psalms on the work of the Spanish lyric poet St. John of the Cross (1542-1591). Particular attention is given to his works *The Dark Night of the Soul* and *Ascent to Mount Carmel*.

1722. Virollaud, Ch. "Les assesseurs de la déesse-soleil à Ras Shamra." *Comptes Rendus du Groupe Linguistique d'Études Chamito-Sémitiques* 9 (1960-1963): 50-51.

1723. Wakeman, Mary K. *God's Battle with the Monster: A Study in Biblical Imagery*. Leiden: E.J. Brill, 1973. viii+151p.

Part 1 presents a comparative summary of Near Eastern myths relating to the battle. Part 2 presents the biblical materials. There was an earth-monster similar to the water-monster; the enemy is not permanently overcome, merely brought under the order of creation.

Reviewed by J.Z. Smith in *JBL* 94 (1975): 442-444.

1724. Walton, John H. *Israelite Literature in its Cultural Context: A Survey of Parallels Between Biblical and Ancient Near Eastern Texts*. Library of Biblical Interpretation. Grand Rapids, MI: Regency-Zondervan, 1989. 249p.

The parallels are grouped according to "genres": cosmology (creation stories and flood); personal archives and epics; laws; commandments and treaties; historical literature; hymns, prayers, and incantations; wisdom literature; prophetic and apocalyptic literature.

1725. Widengren, Geo. *The Accadian and Hebrew Psalms of Lamentation as Religious Documents: A Comparative*

Study. Diss. theol., University of Uppsala, 1936. Uppsala: Almqvist & Wiksell, 1936. 365p.

1726. ______. "Det sakrala kungadömet bland öst- och västsemiter." *Religion och Bibel* 2 (1943): 49-75.

1727. Wilhelm, Gernot. "Zur hurritischen Gebetsliteratur." In *Ernten was man sät. Festschrift für Klaus Koch zu seinem 65. Geburtstag,* ed. Dwight R. Daniels and Others. 37-47. Neukirchen-Vluyn: Neukirchener Verlag, 1991.

An analysis of a lengthy mid-15th century B.C. Hurrite intercessory prayer.

1728. Winter, P. "Magnificat and Benedictus -- Maccabean Psalms?" *Bulletin of the John Rylands Library* 37 (1954): 328-347.

1729. Worden, T. "The Literary Influence of the Ugaritic Fertility Myth on the Old Testament." *Vetus Testamentum* 3 (1953): 273-297.

1730. Wright, R.B. "The Psalms of Solomon, the Pharisees, and the Essenes." In *1972 Proceedings: International Organization for Septuagint and Cognate Studies and the Society of Biblical Literature Pseudepigrapha Seminar,* ed. R.A. Kraft. Septuagint and Cognate Studies 2. 136-147. Missoula, MT: Scholars Press, 1972.

Questions the assignment of the authorship to the Pharisees.

1731. _____. "Psalms of Solomon (First Century B.C.). A New Translation and Introduction." in *The Old Testament Pseudepigrapha, Volume 2: Expansions of the "Old Testament" and Legends, Wisdom and Philosophical Literature, Prayers, Psalms and Odes, Fragments of Lost Judeo-Hellenistic Works,* ed. James H. Charlesworth. 639-670. Garden City, NY: Doubleday and Co., 1985.

1732. Wyatt, N. "The Hollow Crown: Ambivalent Elements in West Semitic Royal Ideology." *Ugarit-Forschungen* 18 (1986): 421-436.

A myth about kings existed in the West Semitic area. It had five essential elements: 1) The king is a god. 2) He ascends the Mount of Assembly. 3) This mountain is the center of the world and paradise. 4) The king has a genuine grandeur, but this leads to hubris. The king claims he is El and this threatens the order in the cosmos. 5) The king is cast down from the height to which he aspires.

1733. Zandee, J. *Death as an Enemy according to Ancient Egyptian Conceptions.* Leiden: E.J. Brill, 1960.

1734. _____. "Hymnal Sayings addressed to the Sun-God by the High-Priest of Amün Nebwenenef, from his tomb in Thebes." *Jahrbericht van het Vooraziatisch-Egyptisch Gezelschap 'Ex Oriente Lux'* 18 (1964): 253-265.

1735. _____. *De Messias. Opvattingen aangaande het koningschap in de godsdiensten van het Oude Nabije Oosten.* Leiden: E.J. Brill, 1970. 44p.

1736. Zijl, P.J. van. *A Study of Texts in Connection with Baal in the Ugaritic Epics.* Alter Orient und Altes Testament 10. Neukirchen-Vluyn: Neukirchener Verlag, 1972.

1737. Zimmern, Heinrich. *Das babylonische Neujahrfest. Der alte Orient* 25/3. Leipzig: J.C. Hinrichs, 1926. 28p.

1738. Zobel, Hans-Jürgen. "Das Gebet um Abwendung der Not und seine Erhörung in den Klageliedern des Alten Testaments und in der Inschrift des Königs Zakir von Hamath." *Vetus Testamentum* 21 (1971): 91-99.

See also: 2570, 4292, 4741, 4764.

9. Theology and Themes

A. General Theology

1739. Allen, Leslie C. *Word Biblical Themes: Psalms.* Waco, TX: Word Books, 1987. 139p.

Organizes the theological content of the Psalter under seven subjects: function, praise, faith, blessing, salvation, hope, and scripture.

1740. Beaucamp, E. "La théologie des Psaumes: Un dialogue avec le Dieu vivant." *Études Franciscaines* 18 (1968): 103-136.

1741. Coates, Thomas. *The Psalms for Today.* St. Louis, MO: Concordia Publishing House, 1957. 118p.

1742. Frieling, Rudolf. *Die Psalmen.* Gesammelten Schriften zum Alten und Neuen Testament. Stuttgart: Urachhaus Johannes M. Mayer, 1985. 379p.

I. World View. II. The Way of Life. III. The New Song.

1743. Gunn, George S. *God in the Psalms.* Edinburgh: St. Andrew's Press, 1956. xii+216p.

1744. Haag, Ernst, and Frank-Lothar Hossfeld, eds. *Freude an der Weisung des Herrn. Beiträge zur Theologie der Psalmen. Festgabe zum 70. Geburtstag von Heinrich Groß.* Stuttgarter biblische Beiträge 13. Stuttgart: Katholisches Bibelwerk GmbH, 1986.

27 articles on various aspects of the psalms.
Reviewed in *CBQ* 50 (1988): 155-156.

1745. Kraus, Hans-Joachim. *Theologie der Psalmen.* Biblischer Kommentar zum Alten Testament, 15/3. Neukirchen-Vluyn: Neukirchener, 1979. 272p. Translated into English by Keith Crim and published as *Theology of the Psalms.* Minneapolis, MN: Augsburg, 1986. 235p.

The proper subject of a theology of the Psalms is "the testimony by which those who sing, pray, and speak point beyond themselves, the 'kerygmatic intention' of their praise and confession, their prayers and teachings." Consequently, the theology of the Psalms involves a constant effort to remain true to its subject matter -- God and Israel, God and the person in Israel, in their encounter and fellowship, established by God and brought to realization by God. It involves God's dealings with the person and the person's dealing with God.

1) The God of Israel. 2) The People of God. 3) The Sanctuary and Its Worship. 4) The King. 5) The Enemy Powers. 6) The Individual in the Presence of God. 7) The Psalms in the New Testament.

Review of the German edition by W. Brueggemann in *JBL* 101 (1982): 283-284; K.-H. Walkenhorst in *ZKT* 104 (1982): 25-47.

1746. Spieckermann, Hermann. *Heilsgegenwart: Eine Theologie der Psalmen.* Göttingen: Vandenhoeck & Ruprecht, 1989.

B. Royal Themes, Messianism, and Eschatology

1747. Ahlström, G.W. "Die Königsideologie in Israel. Ein Diskussionsbeitrag." *Theologische Zeitschrift* 18 (1962): 205-210.

1748. Ahuvah, A. "'Behold, A King will Reign in Righteousness' -- A Study of the Royal Ideal According to the Criterion of Reality." *Beth Mikra* 29 (1983/1984): 29-36. (Hebrew)

1749. Alexander, William. *The Witness of the Psalms to Christ and Christianity.* Eight Bampton Lectures (1876). London: John Murray, 1877.

1750. Alt, Albrecht. "Gedanken über das Königtum Jahwes." *Kleine Schriften zur Geschichte des Volkes Israel I.* 345-357. Munich: C.H. Beck, 1953.

1751. Amsler, Samuel. *David, roi et messie.* Neuchâtel: Delachaux & Niestle, 1963. 81p.

The main interest of the Old Testament writers revolves around the David who became the center of faith rather than the David of history.

Reviewed by J.M. Myers in *JBL* 83 (1964): 98-99.

1752. Asensio, Felix. "Salmos mesiánicos o salmos nacionales?" *Gregorianum* 33 (1952): 219-260, 566-611.

Psalms 1-72, especially Psalms 2, 16, 22, and 72.

1753. ______. "El *Yahweh mālak* de los 'Salmos del Reino' en la historia de la 'Salvación.'" *Estudios Biblicos* 25 (1966): 299-315.

1754. Barrois, Georges A. "The Mirror of the Psalms." Chap. in *The Face of Christ in the Old Testament.* 133-144. Crestwood, NY: St. Vladimir's Seminary Press, 1974.

This chapter is intended to lift the reader to an enlightened intimacy with Christ, who is seen as ready to burst forth from the psalms.

1755. Baumgärtel, Friedrich. "Zur Frage der theologischen Deutung der messianischen Psalmen." Beihefte zur Zeitschrift für die alttestamentliche Wissenschaft 42. 19-25. Berlin: Walter de Gruyter, 1967.

1756. Becker, Joachim. *Messiaserwartung im Alten Testament.* Stuttgarter Bibelstudien, no. 83. Stuttgart: Katholisches Bibelwerk, 1977. Translated into English by David E. Green and published as *Messianic Expectation in the Old Testament.* Philadelphia: Fortress Press, 1980; Edinburgh: T & T Clark, 1980. 96p.

Normative Yahwism was a strictly northern concern; Jerusalem-Judah and its royal ideology (the probable source of proto-messianic ideas) was outside the norm. Thus authentic Yahwism had no germs of messianism before the exile, or for that matter, after the exile. The demise of kingship brought about the transferral of the royal idea to the people as a whole. This finds expression in prophetic additions, redactional material, and the royal psalms (which are exilic and postexilic). No truly messianic figure appears in Jewish thought prior to the second century B.C. The "messianism" of the Old Testament consists in its character as *praeparatio evangelica.* It is something that has been grafted onto Old Testament doctrine.

Reviewed by D.J. McCarthy in *JBL* 101 (1982): 433-434.

1757. ______. "Die kollektive Deutung der Königspsalmen." *Theologie und Philosophie* 52 (1977): 561-578.

1758. Bentzen, Aage. *Det sakrale kongedomme. Bemaerkninger i en løbende diskussion om de gammeltestamentlige Salmer.* Copenhagen: Bianco Lunos Bogtrykkeri, 1945. 227p.

1759. ______. *Messias -- Moses redivivus -- Menschensohn.* Abhangungen zur Theolgie des Alten und Neuen Testaments 17. Zurich: Zwingli, 1948. 80p. English translation: *King and Messiah.* Lutterworth Studies in Church and Bible. London: Lutterworth Press, 1955.

1760. Bernhardt, K.-H. *Das Problem der altorientalischen Königs-Ideologie im Alten Testament, unter besonderer Berücksichtigung der Geschichte der Psalmenexegese dargestellt und kritisch gewürdigt.* Supplements to Vetus Testamentum 8. Leiden: E.J. Brill, 1961. 352p.

Rejects the "ritual pattern" theory and argues for a royal theology based on the historical rejection of the kingship and on the traditions of the nomadic period.

1761. Boer, P.A.H. de. "Vive le roi!" *Vetus Testamentum* 5 (1955): 225-231.

1762. Bonnes, Jean-Paul. *David et les Psaumes.* Paris: Editions du Seuil, 1957. 191p.

1763. Bonsirven, Joseph. *Le Règne de Dieu.* Théologie 37. Paris: Aubier, Édtions Montaigne, 1957. 230p.

1764. ______. "Le Règne de Dieu." In *Grands Thèmes bibliques,* ed. M.E. Boismard and Others. 167-177. Paris: Editions du Feu Nouveau, 1958.

1765. Brettler, Marc Zvi. *God is King: Understanding an Israelite Metaphor.* Journal for the Study of the Old Testament, Supplement Series 76. Sheffield: JSOT Press, 1989. 239p.

A study of the metaphor "God is King" and of royal appellations, royal qualities, royal trappings, royal involvement in society, and the process of becoming king, which seeks to discover which elements in each of these categories are metaphorically transferred to God and which are not, and why. The "enthronement psalms" did not celebrate God the king as newly enthroned; rather, the nations are here newly recognizing and celebrating the achievements of God who has always been enthroned.

Reviewed by W. Soll in *Interpretation* 45 (1991): 310-312; P.D. Miller in *Journal of Biblical Literature* 111 (1992): 120-122.

1766. Buber, Martin. *Königtum Gottes.* Das Kommende, Untersuchungen zur Entstehungsgeschichte des messianischen Glaubens I. Berlin: Schocken Verlag, 1932. xx+260p. 2nd ed., 1936. 3rd. ed., Heidelberg: L. Schneider, 1956. lxiv+220p. Translated into English by R. Smith and published as *Kingship of God.* New York: Harper and Row, 1967; London: SCM Press, 1967. 228p.

1767. Cazelles, Henri. *Le Messie de la Bible. Christologie de l'Ancien Testament.* Collection "Jésus et Jésus-Christ" 7. Paris: Desclée, 1978. 240p.

Examines the charisma of early leaders and the various ideas of Messiahship, kingship in the ancient East and the beginnings of the monarchy in Israel. Discusses the concept of Messiah in the prophets, psalms and other places, and concludes with an explanation of the title being applied to Jesus of Nazareth by the early church.

1768. Clines, D.J.A. "The Psalms and the King." *Themelios* 71 (1975): 1-6.

1769. Colunga, L. Alberto. "Jerusalén, la ciudad del Gran Rey. Exposición messiánica de algunos Salmos." *Estudios Biblicos* 14 (1955): 255-279.

Jerusalem, City of the Great King. A Messianic Exposition of Some Psalms (46ff, 87, 122, and 137).

1770. Cooke, G. "The Israelite King as Son of God." *Zeitschrift für die alttestamentliche Wissenschaft* 73 (1961): 202-225.

1771. Coppens, Joseph. *De Messiaanse Verwachting in het Psalmboek.* Mededelingen van de Koninklijke Vlaamse Academie voor Wetenschappen, Letteren en Schone Kunsten van België. Klasse der Letteren. Jaarg. 17, no. 5. Brussels: Academie voor Wetenschappen, Letteren en Schone Kunsten van België, 1955.

Surveys various messianic interpretations of the Psalms.

1772. ______. "La date des Psaumes de l'Intronisation et de la Royauté de Yahve." *Ephemerides Theologicae Lovanienses* 43 (1967): 192-197.

1773. _____. *Le messianisme royal: Les origines, son développement, son accomplissement.* Lectio Divina 54. Paris: Cerf, 1968. 228p.

A study of royal messianism and its apocalyptic development.

1774. _____. "La royauté de Yahvé dans le Psautier." *Ephemerides Theologicae Lovanienses* 53 (1977): 297-362.

The royalty of Yahweh in the Psalter. Psalms 1-89 (Book I: Psalms 5:1-12; 9-10; 24; 29; Book II: Psalms 44; 47; 48; 68; Book III: Psalms 74; 84; 89). The kingship of Yahweh appeared under very different aspects. Yahweh is proclaimed heavenly king, a cosmic king: master of the storm (29), cloud rider (68), creator and lord of the universe (74:13-17; 89:10-15; 24:1-2). His sovereignty on earth is revealed: (1) in war by his acting in favor of his chosen people; (2) but more directly on a moral and social plane in his role as protector and redeemer (Psalms 5; 9A; 9B); and (3) in the religious sphere in relation to his servants who minister in his sanctuary, or even to pagans (Psalm 47:7-10). There is also a future perspective that foreshadows the eschatological views of the prophets (Psalm 24:7-10 in its rereading; Psalms 9-10, with the addition of 9:7-8 and 10:16; and Psalm 48:9,15).

1775. _____. "La royauté de Yahvé dans le Psautier." *Ephemerides Theologicae Lovanienses* 54 (1978): 1-59.

The royalty of Yahweh in Books IV and V of the Psalter. Book IV is the major section in which Kingship psalms are found: Psalms 93, 97, 99 - the *Yahweh mālak* group; Psalms

95, 96, 98, where the formula is rare. The discussion on Book V includes Psalms 103 (put here because of its content), 145, 146, and 149. There are pre-exilic royal psalms in the Psalter (Psalms 29, 93, 47A, 68, 89:6-19). Psalms 5, 9A-B, 10 are individual prayers; some of them may be pre-exilic, but a post-exilic date is preferred. Psalm 24 in its present form (with additions) is post-exilic. Psalms 45 and 74 are exilic. Faith in Yahweh as king developed from a heavenly kingship (Psalms 29, 93), through God as creator of the earth, to God as a sovereign lawgiver of all the earth. This pattern is paralleled by the kingship psalms, which eventually broaden divine kingship to include all peoples. Since Psalms 103, 145, 146 foretell the kingdom of God, they speak more personally than other psalms do to Christians.

1776. ______. *La relève apocalyptique du messiasme royal. I. La royauté, le règne, le royaume de Dieu. Cadre de la relève apocalyptique.* Bibliotheca Ephemeridum Theologicarum Lovaniensium 50. Leuven: Leuven Université (Editions Peeters), 1979. 330p.

A study of the whole theme of divine reign. The "Yahweh malak" psalms are not taken as a homogeneous group; more psalms are considered post-exilic than is generally the case by other scholars. The re-use of some of these traditions in the New Testament is considered.

1777. Dahl, George. "The Messianic Expectation in the Psalter." *Journal of Biblical Literature* 57 (1938): 1-12.

1778. Delitzsch, Frans. *Mesianische Weissagungen in geschichtlicher Folge.* 1890. Reprinted with a *Geleitwort* by G. Maier. Giessen and Basel: Brunnen Verlag, 1992. 160p.

Traces the unfolding of Old Testament Messianism over the course of ten periods, beginning with the *Protoevangelium* of Genesis 3:15 and extending down through the prophets of the Restoration era.

1779. Descamps, A. "Le Royaume de Dieu." In *Grands thèmes bibliques*. Ed. M.E. Boismard and Others. 167-177. Paris: Éditions du Feu Nouveau, 1958.

1780. Didier, M. "Une lecture des Psaumes du règne de Yahwé." *Revue de Namur* 12 (1959): 457-470.

1781. Dietrich, Walter. "Gott als König. Zur Frage nach der theologischen und politischen Legitimität religiöser Begriffsbildung." *Zeitschrift für Theologie und Kirche* 77 (1980): 251-268.

An exploration of the theological and political legitimacy of religious terminology, tracing the history of the notion of "God as King" in ancient Israel, early Judaism, and Christianity. "God as King" plays a role only in a limited number of Old Testament passages.

1782. Durham, John I. "The King as 'Messiah' in the Psalms." *Review and Expositor* 81 (1984): 425-435.

The historical interpretation of the "messianic" psalms in order provides the right understanding of the distinctive messiahship of Jesus Christ.

1783. Dussaud, R. "Yahwé, fils de El." *Syria* 34 (1957): 232-242.

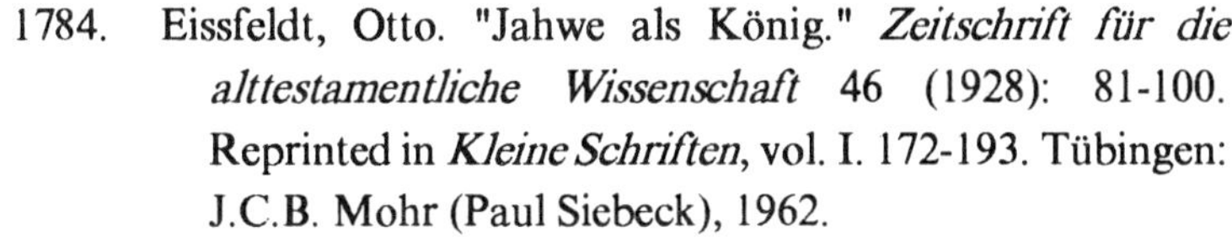

1784. Eissfeldt, Otto. "Jahwe als König." *Zeitschrift für die alttestamentliche Wissenschaft* 46 (1928): 81-100. Reprinted in *Kleine Schriften*, vol. I. 172-193. Tübingen: J.C.B. Mohr (Paul Siebeck), 1962.

1785. _____. "Malkiel (König ist El) und Malkija (König ist Jahwe): Gottesglaube und Namengebung in Israel." In *Atti dell'VIII Congresso Internazionale di Storia dell Religioni.* 261-263. Florence: Sansoni, 1956.

1786. _____. "Jahwes Königsprädizierung als Verklärung national-politischer Ansprüche Israels." In *Forschung zur Bibel. Wort, Lied und Gottesspruch. Beiträge zur Septuaginta. Festschrift für Joseph Ziegler*, ed. Rudolf Schnackenburg and Josef Schreiner. 2 vols. Vol. 2: 51-55. Würzburg: Echter Verlag, 1972.

Among other things, in at least four psalms (Psalms 2, 46, 47, and 82) where Yahweh's kingship and worldwide power are celebrated, what is really being expressed is the validity of the national and political claims of Israel under Davidic leadership. Thus these psalms were composed at a time when a Davidic descendant was actually on the throne.

1787. Feuillet, André. "Les psaumes eschatologiques du règne de Yahweh." *Nouvelle Revue Théologique.* 73 (1951): 244-260, 352-363.

A study of Psalms 47, 93, 96-99, which praise the eschatological triumph of the only true God, anticipating the person of the Messiah. Part one discusses their literary character, their eschatological meaning, and their origin. Part two places these psalms in the general context of Isaiah and Daniel. Part three points out similarities and differences with the New Testament.

1788. ______. "Les problèmes posés par l'exégèse des Psaumes. Quatre Psaumes royaux (II, XLV, LXXII, CX)." *Revue Thomiste* 85 (1985): 5-37.

I. The affect of Gunkel upon interpretation of the Psalms. II. The messianic interpretation of four royal psalms (2, 45, 72, and 110) and their connection with the New Testament.

1789. Ficker, Rudolf. "Kingship of God in the Psalms." *Bangalore Theological Forum* 12 (1980): 50-65.

1790. Fischer, Balth. "Le Christ dan les psaumes." *La Maison-Dieu* 27 (1951): 86-113. English summary in *Theological Digest* 1 (1953): 53-57; Spanish summary in A. Miller, "La visión cristiana de los salmos," *Kyrios* 1 (1958): 5-13.

1791. Fischer, James A. "Everyone a King: A Study of the Psalms." *The Bible Today* 97 (Oct., 1978): 1683-1689.

Liturgy functions as a current testimony to the growth of the community and the individual. Kingship psalms and laments have an affinity that is to be explained by the developed recognition of kingship as the possession of every Israelite.

1792. Fraine, J. de. *L'aspect religieux de la royauté israélite. L'institution monarchique dans l'Ancien Testament et dans les textes mésopotamiens.* Analecta Biblica 3. Rome: Pontifical Biblical Institute, 1954.

1793. Frisch, Amos. "Concerning Four Promises of Blessing for the King Respecting the Messiah (Ps 2; 72; Isa 11:)." *Beth Mikra* 47 (1971): 571-581. (Hebrew)

1794. Gray, John. "The Hebrew Conception of the Kingship of God: Its Origin and Development." *Vetus Testamentum* 6 (1956): 268-285.

1795. _____. "The Kingship of God in the Prophets and Psalms." *Vetus Testamentum* 11 (1961): 1-29.

1796. _____. *The Biblical Doctrine of the Reign of God.* Edinburgh: T & T Clark, 1979. xiii+401p.

This work supports and amplifies the work of Mowinckel, with the aid of Ugaritic evidence. "In the Enthronement Psalms we believe that we penetrate behind the Reign of God to the sacramental experience of it," specifically in the autumn festival.

1797. Gressmann, Hugo. *Der Ursprung der israelitisch-jüdischen Eschatologie.* Forschungen zur Religion und Literatur des Alten und Neuen Testaments 6. Göttingen: Vandenhoeck and Ruprecht, 1905.

1798. _____. *Der Messias.* Forschungen zur Religion und Literatur des Alten und Neuen Testaments 43. Göttingen: Vandenhoeck and Ruprecht, 1929.

1799. Grill, S. "Um die Theologie der Psalmen, ihre Messianität und ihre 'Christianisierung'." *Der Seelsorger* 27 (1956/57): 367-373.

1800. Gunkel, Hermann. "Die Endhoffnung der Psalmisten." In *Reden und Aufsätze.* 123-130. Göttingen: Vandenhoeck & Ruprecht, 1913.

1801. Hebert, A.G. "The Idea of Kingship in the OT." *The Reformed Theological Review* 18 (1959): 34-45.

1802. Herman, Wayne R. "The Kingship of Yahweh in the Hymnic Theophanies of the Old Testament." *Studia Biblica et Theologica* 16 (1988): 169-211.

A study of 10 Old Testament hymns which contain references to Yahweh's appearances and which explicitly or implicitly allude to Yahweh as "King": Judges 5:4-5; Deuteronomy 33:2-5,26-29; Psalms 29; 50:1-6; 97; Isaiah 30:27-33; Micah 1:2-7; Jeremiah 25:30-38; Habakkuk 3:3-15; and Zechariah 9:14-17.

1803. Howard, David M., Jr. "The Case for Kingship in the Old Testament Narrative Books and the Psalms." *Trinity Journal* 9 (1988): 19-35.

The idea of monarchy in Israel was favored by God from beginning to end. It was the centerpiece around which God accomplished the redemption of the world.

1804. Hunter, John. *Finding the Living Christ in the Psalms.* Grand Rapids, MN: Zondervan Publishing House, 1972.

Luke 24:44 means that all the psalms speak of Christ. Ten psalms are examined for their christological content.

1805. Isser, Stanley. "Studies of Ancient Jewish Messianism: Scholarship and Apologetics." *Journal of Ecumenical Studies* 25 (1988): 56-73.

A comparison and critique of Jewish and Christian approaches to messianism, with special attention to the writings of Joseph Klausner and Sigmund Mowinckel.

1806. Jeremias, Jörg. *Das Königtum Gottes in den Psalmen.* Forschungen zur Religion und Literatur des Alten und Neuen Testaments, 141. Göttingen: Vandenhoeck & Ruprecht, 1987.

Reviewed by Bernd Janowski in *Zeitschrift für Theologie und Kirche* 86 (1989): 389-454, and by Eckart Otto in "Mythos und Geschichte im Alten Testament -- Zur Diskussion einer neuen Arbeit von Jörg Jeremias." *Biblische Notizen* 42 (1988): 93-102.

1807. Johnson, Aubrey R. "The Role of the King in the Jerusalem Cultus." In *The Labyrinth. Further Studies in the Relation between Myth and Ritual in the Ancient World,* ed. S.H. Hooke. 71-111. London: Oxford University Press, 1935.

1808. _____. "Living Issues in Biblical Scholarship. Divine Kingship and the Old Testament." *The Expository Times* 62 (1950-51): 36-42.

1809. _____. *Sacral Kingship in Ancient Israel.* Cardiff: University of Wales Press, 1955.

1810. _____. "Hebrew Conceptions of Kingship." In *Myth, Ritual, and Kingship*, ed. S.H. Hooke. 204-235. London: Oxford University Press, 1958.

1811. Kapelrud, Arvid S. "Temple Building, A Task for Gods and Kings." *Orientalia*, N.S., 32 (1963): 56-62.

1812. _____. "Nochmals Jahwä mālāk." *Vetus Testamentum* 13 (1963): 229-231.

1813. Klausner, Joseph. *The Messianic Idea in Israel From Its Beginnings to the Completion of the Mishnah.* Translated from the 3rd Hebrew edition by W.F. Stinespring. New York: Macmillan Company, 1955. xv+543p.

Reviewed by M. Burrows in *JBL* 75 (1956): 150

1814. Köhler, Ludwig. "Syntactica III,IV. Jahwäh Mālāk." *Vetus Testamentum* 3 (1953): 188-189.

1815. Kraus, Hans-Joachim. *Die Königsherrschaft Gottes im Alten Testament: Untersuchungen zu den Liedern von Jahwes Thronbesteigung.* Beiträge zur historischen Theologie 13. Tübingen: J.C.B. Mohr, 1951.

Reviewed in *CBQ* 15 (1953): 107-110.

1816. Kreuzer, Siegfried. "Gottesherrschaft als Grundthema der alttestamentlichen Theologie." In *Zur Aktualität des Alten Testaments: Festschrift für Georg Sauer zum 65. Geburtstag*, ed. Siegfried Kruezer and Kurt Lüthi. 57-72. Frankfurt am Main: Lang, 1992.

The rule of God should be distinguished from the idea of kingship; the rule of God is a central theological theme.

1817. Łach, Stanisław, and Marian Filipiak, eds. *Mesjasz W Biblijnej Historii Zbawienia.* Lublin: Towarzystwo Naukowe Katolickiego Uniwersytetu Lubelskiego, 1964.

The Messiah in the History of Salvation of the Bible. Articles dealing with the Psalms include S. Łach on Messianism in contemporary Bible Studies, on Psalms 16, 45 and 72, M. Filipiak on Jeremiah 23:5, Psalms 2 and 110, and Qoheleth, J. Homerski on the beloved of God, the shepherd of Messianic Times, J. Kuc on Psalm 22. A résumé in French follows each article.

1818. Lang, Bernhard. "Messias und Messiaserwartung im alten Israel." *Bibel und Kirche* 33 (1978): 110-115.

The royal psalms and Isaiah (present messianism), post-exilic prophets (restoration messianism), Qumran (apocalyptic renaissance).

1819. Lipiński, Edward. "Les Psaumes de la royauté de Yahwé dans l'exégèse moderne." In *Le Psautier: Ses origines. Ses problèmes littérraires. Son influence,* ed. Robert de Langhe. Orientalia et Biblica Lovaniensia, IV. 133-272. Louvain: Publications Universitaires, 1962.

1820. _____. "Yāhweh mâlāk." *Biblica* 44 (1963): 405-460.

1821. _____. "Les Psaumes du règne. L'intronisation royale de Dieu." *Assemblées du Seigneur* 9 (1964): 7-22.

1822. _____. *La royauté de Yahwé dans la poésie et le culte de l'ancien Israël.* Verhandelingen van de Koninklijke Academie voor Wetenschappen, Letteren en Schone Kunsten van België, Klasse der Letteren XXVII/55. Brussells: Koninklijke Academie, 1965. 2nd, corrected edition, 1968. 560p.

The royalty of Yahweh in the poetry and cult of ancient Israel. Psalm 93 belongs to the "Songs of Zion"; it reflects the Davidic covenant and is dated to the time of Solomon or shortly thereafter. Psalm 97 is an "epiphany" psalm; vss. 2-5 may be pre-Davidic, but the psalm as a whole dates to 164 B.C. Psalm 99 is a "Song of Zion," containing amphictyonic and Near Eastern cultic traditions; it was composed during the time of Solomon. *Yahweh mālak* means "Yahweh has become king"; it is a liturgical proclamation, a cry of victory announcing the throne of Yahweh (cf. *Ba*^{c}*al Mālak*). Yahweh can be enthroned as king in the sense of warrior (Psalm 47); Yahweh is also a great king of the El type, who owns the land and makes a covenant. Yahweh's enthronement as king is associated with the procession of the ark during the Feast of Tabernacles. This is not a renewal of kingship, but celebrates its fact. The eschatological and apocalyptical writings continue these traditions.

Reviewed by L.R. Fisher in *JBL* 85 (1966): 498-499; reviewed also in *CBQ* 28 (1966): 77-79.

1823. Maag, V. "Jahwäs Heerscharen." *Schweizerische Theologische Umschau* 20 (1950): 27-52.

1824. _____. "*Malkut JHWH.*" *Congress Volume. Oxford 1959.* Supplements to Vetus Testamentum 7. 129-153. Leiden: E.J. Brill, 1960.

1825. McKenzie, J.L. "Royal Messianism." *Catholic Biblical Quarterly* 19 (1957): 27-52.

1826. Mays, James Luther. "The Language of the Reign of God." *Interpretation* 47 (1993): 117-126.

1827. Mettinger, Tryggve N.D. *King and Messiah. The Civil and Sacral Legitimation of the Israelite Kings.* Coniectanea Biblica, OT Series 8. Lund: CWK Gleerup, 1976.

Reviewed by B.O. Long in *JBL* 96 (1977): 585-586.

1828. Miller, A. "Gibt es direkt messianische Psalmen?" In *Miscellanea Biblica B. Ubach.* Ed. R.M. Díaz Carbonell. 201-209. Montserrat: Imprinta-escuela of Barcelona, 1953.

1829. _____. "Die Psalmen in christlicher Sicht." *Bibel und Liturgie* 24 (1956-1957): 134-140.

1830. Moenikes, A. "Messianismus im Alten Testament (vor-apokalyptische Zeit)." *Zeitschrift für Religions- und Geistesgeschichte* 40 (1988): 289-306.

"Present" messianism designates propaganda aimed at legitimating the existing of (Davidic) kingship; "future" messianism refers to the expectation of an ideal (Davidic) king.

1831. Mowinckel,Sigmund (1884-1965). *Urmensch und "Königsideologie".* Studia Theologica cura ordinum theologorum Scandinavorum edita 2 (1948): 71-89.

1832. ______. *Han som kommer: Messiasforventningen i Det Gamle Testament og pa Jesu tid.* Copenhagen: G.E.C. Gads Forlag, 1951. 417p. Translated into English by G.W. Anderson and published as *He That Cometh.* Nashville, TN: Abingdon, 1954; Oxford: B. Blackwell, 1956. xvi+528p.

Norwegian original reviewed by G.W. Anderson in *JBL* 70 (1951): 329-332. English version reviewed by J. Muilenburg in *JBL* 76 (1957): 243-246.

1833. Müller, Hans-Peter. *Ursprünge und Strukturen alttestamentlicher Eschatologie.* Beihefte zur Zeitschrift für alttestamentliche Wissenschaft 109. Berlin: Töpelmann, 1969. xii+232p.

(1) God's intervention in history and human affairs. This theme appears in hymns of praise and laments which speak of God's intervention or request it. It originates in the holy war; the Zion psalms reflect these same holy war and mythological traditions. The future and final intervention of God is expressed in terms of the day of Yahweh (holy war in origin), the deliverance of Zion, and the new exodus of Deutero-Isaiah. (2) The blessing and the curse. (3) The covenant as a present blessing and a future expectation (Sinai and Davidic).

Reviewed by J.H. Hayes in *JBL* 89 (1970): 95-96.

1834. North, Christopher R. "The Religious Aspect of Hebrew Kingship." *Zeitschrift für die alttestamentliche Wissenschaft* 50 (1932): 8-38.

1835. Noth, Martin. "Gott, König, Volk im Alten Testament." *Zeitschrift für Theologie und Kirche* 47 (1950): 157-191; reprinted in *Gesammelte Studien zum Alten Testament*, 188-229; Munich: Kaiser, 1957. Translated into English by D.R. Ap-Thomas and published as "God, King, Nation in the Old Testament." In *The Laws in the Pentateuch and Other Studies*. 145-178. Edinburgh: Oliver and Boyd, 1966; Philadelphia: Fortress Press, 1967.

We question the relevance of ancient Near Eastern sources for understanding the Old Testament, particularly the Myth and Ritual School's views on divine kingship in Israel, and reject the thesis that Israel shared a pre-established scheme of concepts and ideas with the whole ancient Near Eastern world.

1836. Ockinga, Boyo G. "The Inviolability of Zion -- A pre-Israelite Tradition?" *Biblische Notizen* 44 (1988): 54-60.

The Amarna letters reveal a special relationship between Jerusalem and the Pharaoh. This may have provided the model for the later Zion traditions.

1837. Ollenburger, Ben C. *Zion, The City of the Great King*. Journal for the Study of the Old Testament, Supplement Series 41. Sheffield: JSOT Press, 1987. 271p.

The central notion of Zion as symbol is the kingship of Yahweh, whose ritual setting is the celebration of Yahweh's kingship on Zion in the autumn festival in conjunction with the New Year. Yahweh comes as (1) creator and as conqueror of chaos, and as (2) founder of Zion, his royal residence. The symbol Zion must be distinguished from the symbol of Davidic kingship.

1838. Pelland, Gilles. "Le thème biblique du Régne chez saint Hilaire du Poitiers." *Gregorianum* 60 (1979): 639-674.

It is in Christ that the Kingdom exists. Psalm 2:7 is understood in the light of Acts 13:32-34.

1839. Phillips, O.E. *Exploring the Messianic Psalms.* Philadelphia: Hebrew Christian Fellowship, Inc. (Continental Press), 1967. 318p.

"Messianic Psalms" have to do with the Messiah, his life, reign, and such things in those Psalms which are predictions that have to do with Israel, and the world, that could not take place without the Messiah. More than 50 Psalms tell of first and second coming of the Messiah: Psalms 2, 8, 16-24, 40-48, 67-72, 85, 87, 89-91, 94-103, 107-113, 118, 122-126, and 132.

1840. Porteous, N.W. "Jerusalem -- Zion: The Growth of a Symbol." In *Verbannung und Heimkehr. Festschrift W. Rudolph,* ed. A. Kuschke. 235-252. Tübingen: J.C.B. Mohr (Paul Siebeck), 1961.

1841. Preez, Jannie du. "Three 'Enthronement Psalms' from an Ecological Perspective." *Missionalia* 19 (1991): 122-130.

1842. Rad, Gerhard von. "Das judäische Königsritual." *Theologische Literaturzeitung* 72 (1947): 211-216. Also published in *Gesammelte Studien.* Theologische Bücherei 8. 205-213. Munich: Chr. Kaiser Verlag, 1958. Translated into English by E.W. Trueman Dicken and published as

"The Royal Ritual in Judah." In *The Problem of the Hexateuch and Other Essays.* 222-231. New York: McGraw-Hill Book Co., 1966.

1843. Reich, Max Isaac. *The Messianic Hope of Israel.* Chicago: Moody Press, 1945.

1844. _____. *Studies in the Psalms of Israel.* Harrisburg, PA: Christian Publications, 1967.

1845. Rengstorf, K.H. "Old and New Testament Traces of a Formula of the Judaean Royal Ritual." *Novum Testamentum* 5 (1962): 229-244.

1846. Ridderbos, Jan. "Yahwäh Malak." *Vetus Testamentum* 4 (1954): 87-89.

1847. Ringgren, Helmer. "König und Messias." *Zeitschrift für die alttestamentliche Wissenschaft* 65 (1953): 120-147.

1848. _____. *The Messiah in the Old Testament.* Studies in Biblical Theology 18. London: SCM Press, 1956. 71p.

Israel took over a considerable part of its kingship ideology from the Canaanites. "The idea of the king doing penitence and atoning for the sins of his people leads the thought to one who is to come."

1849. Rosenberg, Roy A. "Yahweh Becomes King." *Journal of Biblical Literature* 85 (1966): 297-307.

Psalms 95-99 were composed in response to the prophet's teachings, and are directly dependent upon them. In addition, the seven "psalms of the days" (Psalms 24, 48, 82,

94, 81, 93, 92) celebrate the kingship of Yahweh in a way that reflects the character of the astral divinity associated with each day of the week in Babylonian astrological tradition.

1850. _____. "The Slain Messiah in the Old Testament." *Zeitschrift für die alttestamentliche Wissenschaft* 99 (1987): 259-261.

1851. Ross, James P. "Yahweh Seba᾽ot in Samuel and Psalms." *Vetus Testamentum* 17 (1967): 79-92.

By the time Israel took over this title, "it had become the name of a god whose principal attribute was royal majesty."

1852. Rost, L. "Königsherrschaft Jahwes in vorköniglicher Zeit?" *Theologische Literaturzeitung* 85 (1960): 721-724.

1853. Savignac, Jean de. "La Royauté en Israël." *Etudes Théologiques et Religieuses* 66 (1991): 413-417.

Compares and contrasts conceptions of monarchy in the ancient Near East and in Israel. In Israel the presence of God is not identified with royalty. In the royal psalms, however, there are some features common to the ancient Near East. This can be attributed to an idealized notion of a perfect king which ultimately contributed to the Messianic ideal.

1854. Scharbert, Josef. *Der Messias im Alten Testament.* Skripten des Lehrstuhls für Theologie des Alten Testaments, no. 7. Munich: Institut für Biblische Exegese der Universität München Altes Testament II, 1984. 140p.

1855. Schimanowski, Gottfried. *Weisheit und Messias.* Wissenschaftliche Untersuchungen zum NT 2,16. Tübingen: Mohr (Siebeck), 1985. xiii+410p.

1856. Schmidt, Hans (1877-1953). *Der Mythus vom wiederkehrenden König in Alter Testament. Festrede gehalten am 17. Januar 1925 zur Feier des Tages der Reichsgründung.* Schriften der Hessischen Hochschulen, Universität Giessen, Jahrg. 1925, Heft 1. Giessen: Alfred Töpelmann, 1925. 36p. 2nd ed., 1933. 32p.

1857. Schmidt, Werner H., and J. Becker. *Zukunft und Hoffnung.* Biblische Konfrontationen. Kohlhammer Taschenbücher 1014. Stuttgart: Kohlhammer, 1981. 202p.

1858. Schreiner, Josef. *Sion -- Jerusalem, Jahwes Königssitz. Theologie der Heiligen Stadt im Alten Testament.* Studien zum Alten und Neuen Testament 7. Munich: Koesel, 1963.

1859. Schunk, Klaus-Dietrich. "Die Attribute des eschatologischen Messias: Strukturlinien in der Ausprägung des alttestamentlichen Messiasbildes." *Theologische Literaturzeitung* 111 (1986): 642-651.

Traces the development of the portrait of the eschatological Messiah in the writings of the Old Testament.

1860. Selman, Martin J. "The Kingdom of God in the Old Testament." *Tyndale Bulletin* 40 (1989): 161-183.

Yahweh's kingdom is an important and distinct aspect of the broader theme of Yahweh's kingship. This kingdom manifests itself in two differing ways: a universal and cosmic reign and in Zion-centered Israel. The emphasis lies on "God's effective sovereignty rather than Israel's obedience to it." The emphasis is on the present.

1861. Smith, Gary V. "The Concept of God/the Gods as King in the Ancient Near East and the Bible." *Trinity Journal* 3 (1982): 13-38.

1862. Soggin, J. Alberto. "Gott als König in der biblischen Dichtung. Bemerkungen zu den *jhwh mlk*-Psalmen." *Proceedings of the Fifth World Congress of Jewish Studies 1969* (1971): 126-133.

1863. Tournay, Raymond J. "L'eschatologie individuelle dans les Psaumes." *Revue Biblique* 56 (1949): 481-506.

1864. Tuttle, Jeffrey P. "*Mashiah* as Davidic Ruler." *Calvary Baptist Theological Journal* 1 (1985): 44-60.

Upon the basic concept of *mashiah* as God's chosen and consecrated leader, there developed in the time of David a second concept of *mashiah* as the Davidic ruler. Upon these there is a third: *mashiah* as the coming Messiah.

1865. Ulrichsen, Jarl H. "JHWH MĀLAK: Einige Sprachliche Beobactungen." *Vetus Testamentum* 27 (1977): 361-374.

Michel (*VT* 6 [1956]: 40-68) does not clearly comprehend the active sense of the verb which he translates *mālak* to "function as a king, to rule." The verb *mālak* most likely stems from *melek* and is therefore denominative, having no nuance beyond the nominal sense. The accession of Yahweh speaks of the beginning of the new year, over which Yahweh rules as formerly.

1866. Vandenbroucke, F. "Le psautier, prophétie ou prière du Christ?" *Questions liturgiques et paroissiales* 33 (1952): 149-161, 201-213.

1867. _____. *Les Psaumes et le Christ.* Louvain: Centre Liturgique Abbaye du Mont César, 1955. 107p.

1868. Walter, Christopher. "Christological Themes in the Byzantine Marginal Psalters from the Ninth to the Eleventh Century." *Revue des Études Byzantines* 44 (1986): 269-287.

1869. Watts, J.D.W. "Yahweh Málak Psalms." *Theologische Zeitschrift* 21 (1965): 341-348.

1870. Welton, Peter. "Die Vernichtung des Todes und die Königsherrschaft Gottes." *Theologische Zeitschrift* 38 (1982): 129-146.

1871. _____. "Königsherrschaft Jahwes und Thronbesteigung." *Vetus Testamentum* 32 (1982): 297-310.

A survey of the history of the interpretation of the kingship and enthronement of Yahweh, concluding with a discussion of the dating and function of the Enthronement Psalms.

1872. Widengren, Geo. *Till det sakrala kungadömets historia i Israel.* Horae Soederblomianae I/3. Lund: G.W.K. Gleerup, 1947.

1873. _____. *Sakrales Königtum im Alten Testamentum und im Judentum. Franz Delitzsch-Vorlesungen, 1952.* Stuttgart: Kohlhammer, 1955.

Reviewed in *CBQ* 19 (1957): 142-146.

1874. ______. "King and Covenant." *Journal of Semitic Studies* 2 (1957): 1-32.

1875. Williams, W.G. "Liturgical Problems in Enthronement Psalms." *Journal of Bible and Religion* 25 (1957): 118-122.

1876. Wilson, T. Ernest. *The Messianic Psalms.* Neptune, NJ: Loizeaux Brothers, 1978. 188p.

Where there is a reference to the Messiah and it is applied to Christ and expounded in the New Testament, it is a Messianic psalm. In addition, there are three psalms which are obviously Messianic but are not quoted in the New Testament: Psalms 24, 72, and 89.

1877. Wurz, Heinrich. "Die Messiashoffnung des Alten Testaments." *Bibel und Liturgie* 53 (1980): 88-93.

See also: 1259, 1268, 1368, 1455, 1457, 1460, 1465, 1488, 1489, 1492, 1494, 1557, 1567, 1572, 1581, 1600, 1615, 1623, 1653, 1654, 1702, 1705, 1732, 1735, 2267, 4475, 4482.

C. The "I" of the Psalms

1878. Balla, Emil. *Das Ich der Psalmen.* Forschungen zur Religion und Literature des Alten und Neuen Testaments 16. Göttingen: Vandenhoeck und Ruprecht, 1912. 155p.

The I-Psalms in the Psalter and in the remaining books of the Old Testament are all to be understood in an individual sense, except for those in which express statements make necessary another understanding of the "I."

1879. Bardtke, H. "Das Ich des Meisters in den *Hodajoth* von Qumrân." *Wissenschaftlichee Zeitschrift der Karl-Marx-Universität Leipzig* 6 (1956/1957): 93-104.

1880. Beer, Georg (1865-1946). *Individual- und Gemeindepsalmen. Ein Beitrag zur Erklärung des Psalters.* Marburg: N.G. Elwert, 1894. ci+92p.

Opposes Smend.

1881. Coblenz, Felix. *Über das betende Ich in den Psalmen. Ein beitrag zur erklärung des Psalters.* Frankfurt am Main: J. Kauffmann, 1897. iv+191p.

Opposes Smend.

1882. Croft, Steven J.L. *The Identity of the Individual in the Psalms.* Journal for the Study of the Old Testament Supplement Series 44. Sheffield: JSOT Press, 1987. 218p.

The problem is a complex one and demands an equally complex solution. The "wicked" are defined primarily in relation to God's judgment rather than by race. They are all who offend against Yahweh's laws. The "enemies," or "antagonists" are defined in relation to the subject to whom they are hostile; on its own, it denotes no particular group of people, inside or outside of Israel. They are not described in stereotyped patterns. The "poor" can be placed on a continuum along two axes, one describing the condition (afflicted, destitute, in need, righteous, empty metaphor), the other describing the speaker (individual, king = I; king = C; community).

Reviewed by J.L. Mays in *Interpretation* 43 (1989): 312-314.

1883. Duin, Cornelius van. *"Zal het stof u loven?": Weerlegging van de individualistische uitleg van woorden voor dood en onderwereld in de psalmen.* The Hague: CIP-Gegevens kominklijke bibliotheek, 1989. xvii+385p.

"Shall the dust praise thee:" A Refutation of the Individualistic Reading of the Terms for Death and the Nether World in the Psalms. The psalms of the Old Testament, including the so-called "I-Psalms," are not expressions of individual religiosity, but documents of the nation.

1884. Gamberoni, Johann. "Der Einzelne in den Psalmen." In *Freude an der Weisung des Herrn. Beiträge zur Theologie der Psalmen. Festgabe zum 70. Geburtstag von Heinrich Gross,* ed. Ernst Haag and Frank-Lothar Hossfeld. Stuttgarter biblische Beiträge 13. 107-123. Stuttgart: Katholisches Bibelwerk, 1986.

The personal belongs to the fundamental and symbolic, but not to the forms and proclamations of the personal experience.

1885. Gerleman, Gillis. "Der 'Einzelne' der Klage- und Dankpsalmen." *Vetus Testamentum* 32 (1982): 33-49.

The Individual Laments and Thanksgiving Psalms written by anonymous authors were intended by their stylistic patterns to reflect experiences in the life of David.

1886. Johnson, Aubrey R. "The Hebrew Conception of Corporate Personality." In *Werden und Wesen des Alten Testaments,* ed. P. Volz, F. Stummer and J. Hempel. Beihefte zur Zeitschrift für die alttestamentliche Wissenschaft 66. 49ff. Berlin: A. Töpelmann, 1936.

1887. _____. *The Vitality of the Individual in the Thought of Ancient Israel.* Cardiff: University of Wales Press, 1949. 2nd ed., 1964. 154p.

1888. Leimdörfer, D. *Das Psalter-Ego in den Ich-Psalmen.* Hamburg: G. Fritzsche, 1898.

The "I" refers to an individual.

1889. Mowinckel, Sigmund. "Traditionalism and Personality in the Psalms." *Hebrew Union College Annual* 23 (1950/1951): 205-231.

1890. Robinson, H. Wheeler. "The Hebrew Conception of Corporate Personality." In *Werden und Wesen des Alten Testaments.* Ed. F. Stummer and J. Hempel. Beihefte zur Zeitschrift für die alttestamentliche Wissenschaft 66. 49-62. Berlin: A. Töpelmann, 1936.

1891. _____. *Corporate Personality in Ancient Israel.* Facet Books -- Biblical Series 11. Philadelphia: Fortress Press, 1964. Revised edition, with an introduction to the first edition by John Reumann and an introduction to the revised edition by C.S. Rodd. Edinburgh: T & T Clark, 1981. 64p.

1892. Scharbert, Jose. "Das 'Wir' der Psalmen auf dem Hintergrund altorientalischen Betens." In *Freude an der*

Weisung des Herrn. Beiträge zur Theologie der Psalmen. Festgabe zum 70. Geburtstag von Heinrich Gross, ed. Ernst Haag and Frank-Lothar Hossfeld. Stuttgarter biblische Beiträge 13. 297-324. Stuttgart: Katholisches Bibelwerk, 1986.

The abundance of "I" prayers in the psalter and the almost complete absence of the "we" in Mesopotamia lets us surmise that the people did not have an active role in the liturgy. In the second Temple a stronger "community" was able to express itself than was the case before the exile or among neighboring peoples. It is only following the bitter experiences of 597 that a "national We" is clearly recognizable.

1893. Schneider, Severin. "Das Denken in Bildern als Voraussetzung für das persönliche Psalmenbeten." *Bibel und Kirche* 35 (1980): 47-54.

1894. Schuurmanns-Stekhoven, J.Z. "Ueber das Ich der Psalmen." *Zeitschrift für die alttestamentliche Wissenschaft* 9 (1889): 131-135.

The "I" refers to an individual.

1895. Smend, Rudolph. "Über das Ich der Psalmen." *Zeitschrift für die alttestamentliche Wissenschaft* 8 (1888): 49-147.

The Psalter is the songbook of the Second Temple. As such, the subject in the individual psalms is the community. Almost all the I-Psalms are songs of the community. At most, the "I" in Psalms 3, 4, 62 and 73 could be understood as an actual individual, but ultimately probably not even these songs refer to an individual.

D. The Poor

1896. Bächli, O. "Die Erwählung der Geringen im Alten Testament." *Theologische Zeitschrift* 22 (1966): 385-395.

1897. Berghe, Paul von der. "*Ani* et *Anaw* dans les psaumes." In *Le Psautier. Ses origines. Ses problèmes littéraires. Son influence*, ed. by Robert De Langhe. Orientalia et Biblica Lovaniensia 4. 273-298. Louvain: Publications Universitaires, 1962.

A survey and evaluation of the various approaches to studying the relationship of *Ani* and *Anaw*.

1898. Birkeland, Harris. *ᶜAni und ᶜanaw in den Psalmen*. Skrifter utgitt av Det Norske Videnskaps-Akademi i Oslo, II. Historisk-filosofisk Klasse 1932, No.4. Translated into German from the Norwegian manuscript by Eugen Ludwig Rapp. Oslo: Jacob Dybwad, 1933. 118p.

A study of the verb ענה II, including the words עָנִי and עָנָו, with special attention to Psalms 88, 22, 102, 69, 25, 86, 34, 70, 109, 9-10, 35, 140, 37, 74, 72, 82, 76, 12, 147, and 149. 1) If עָנָו is a Hebrew word, then it means exactly the same as עָנִי; most likely, however, Hebrew knew only the last word (the former is only a corruption of the latter); 2) in no place do these words designate a party; 3) the "I" is predominantly a private individual (the interpretation of these words as designations for parties is what necessitated the collective explanation of the "I" of the psalms); 4) to be sure, these words can have a religious meaning, but this has its cause in a natural development of the word itself and not in its application to the nation or to a part of the nation; 5) these words speak of actual suffering and poverty and are to be taken in their most natural (non-allegorical) meaning.

1899. Causse, Antonin. *Les "pauvres" d'Israël. Prophètes, Psalmistes. Messianistes.* Études d'histoire ed de philosophie religieuses 3. Paris: Librairie Istra, 1922. 172p.

1900. Cortese, E. "Poveri e umili nei Salmi." *Rivista Biblica* 35 (1987): 299-306.

In the Psalter the terms *ʿānāw(îm)* and *ʿānî* have quite distinct referents. The former describes the religious stance of the "humble"; the latter refers to the "poor." Yahweh "helps" or "saves" the poor, but "exalts" the humble.

1901. Donald, T. "The Semantic Field 'Rich and Poor' in Hebrew and Accadian Literature." *Oriens Antiquus* 3 (1964): 27-41.

1902. Drijvers, Pius. "A Cry for Need or a Spiritual Song?" *Schrift* 32 (1974): 58-60.

1903. Gelin, Albert. *Les pauvres de Yahvé.* Paris: Les éditions du Cerf, 1953. 182p. Translated into English by Kathryn Sullivan and published as *The Poor of Yahweh.* Collegeville, MN: Liturgical Press, 1964. 125p.

English translation reviewed in *CBQ* 27 (1965): 192.

1904. Gillingham, Sue. "The Poor in the Psalms." *The Expository Times* 100 (1988): 15-19.

Generally, *dal* and *ᵓebyôn* are used to describe the various states of material deprivation, while *ᶜānî* and *ᶜānāw* depict different conditions of spiritual need. Physical and spiritual poverty are two sides of the same coin.

1905. Loeb, Isidore. *La littérature des Pauvres dan la Bible.* Preface by Théodore Reinach. Paris: Librairie Léopold Cerf, 1892. xv+280p.

At the time of the return from Babylonian captivity, there was a class of persons, not necessarily organized into one compact body, but made up of the pious, just, holy, pure, and humble persons who constituted the choicest element of the returned captives. This class of persons, though modest and retiring, was yet quite active in literary work. Their work is found mainly in the Psalms and in Second Isaiah. The composition of the Psalms took place between 589 and 167 B.C. No psalm existed before the exile, and none was as late as the Hasmonean period. There is no historical background to these poems; they are a history of the Jewish soul at the time of the Second Temple; they are not liturgical compositions intended for temple service.

1906. Lohfink, Norbert. "Von der 'Anawim-Partei' zur 'Kirche der Armen.'" *Biblica* 67 (1986): 153-176.

Since 1880 a certain number of theories have been promoted concerning the biblical *'ănāwîm* either as a group or as a movement or as a form of spirituality in ancient Israel. They come from (1) the intellectual pietists of the 19th century, (2) those popular around the time of the Second Vatican Council, and (3) those now associated with "liberation theology."

1907. _____. *Lobgesänge der Armen: Studien zum Magnifikat, den Hodajot von Qumran und einigen späten Psalmen.* Stuttgarter Bibelstudien 143. Stuttgart: Katholisches Bibelwerk, 1990. 138p.

The idea of the poor in the Magnificat, the Qumran Hodayot, and in Psalms 140, 146, 147, and 149.
Reviewed by E. Schuller in *JBL* 111 (1992): 710-712.

1908. Martin-Achard, R. "Yahwe et les *Anawim.*" *Theologische Zeitschrift* 21 (1965): 349-357.

1909. Ploeg, Johannes van der. "Les pauvres d'Israel et leur piété." *Oudtestamentische Studiën* 7 (1950): 236-270.

1910. Rahlfs, A. *'Ani und 'anaw in den Psalmen.* Göttingen: Vandenhoeck & Ruprecht, 1892.

1911. Schwantes, M. *Das Recht der Armen.* Beiträge zur Biblischen Exegese und Theologie 4. Frankfurt and Berne: P. Lang, 1977. 312p.

A discussion of the four main terms for "poor" -- *rš, dll, ᶜny, ᵓbywn. The poor do have rights; in God's people they are more than a scandal, they are a power.*

1912. Stamm, Johann Jakob. *Die Leiden des Unschuldigen in Babylon und Israel.* Abhandlungen zur Theologie des Alten und Neuen Testaments 10. Zürich: Zwingli-Verlag, 1946. 83p.

See also: 499, 554, 1464, 1745.

E. The Evil-Doers and the Enemies

1913. Anderson, George W. "Enemies and Evildoers in the Book of Psalms." *Bulletin of the John Rylands Library* 48 (1965): 18-29.

1914. Birkeland, Harris. *Die Feinde des Individuums in der israelitischen Psalmenliteratur.* Oslo: Gröndahl, 1933. vii+388p.

For the most part the enemies are foreigners, enemies in war or alien rulers and the suffering is caused by defeat in war, impending war, or alien occupation or domination. The accusers are political rivals who are attempting to create mischief between the king and his overlord. The "I" then is a king, leader of the armed forces, or (in the post-exilic period) a governor of Jewish blood or a high priest. For the most part, it is the Israelites or Jews as a whole who are the "afflicted" or "humble." These "righteous" are opposed to the nation's enemies, who are the "evildoers" and the "wicked." There is little reference in these psalms to physical illness; where this happens, the enemies are fellow Israelites or Jews whose actions are part of court intrigue.

1915. ______. *The Evildoers in the Book of Psalms.* Avhandlinger Utgitt av Det Norske Videnskaps-Akademi, II. Historisk-Filosofisk Klasse, 1952, No. 2. Oslo: Jacob Dybwad, 1955. 96p.

A revision of *Die Feinde des Individuums in der israelitischen Psalmenliteratur.* We can no longer admit that certain psalms are genuinely individual; rather, all of the enemies are gentiles either outside Israel and in a state of war or within Israel and representatives of the occupying power. "We have to interpret the text as it is, or confess that we cannot interpret it." The psalms reflect a nationalism in which the kingdom of Yahweh means rule over the entire world. This is reflected in the ideology of the New Year's festival with its celebration of the enthronement of the heavenly king who comes to rule the world and to overcome all enemies or evildoers who are working against this. The enemy's strength is military might or words filled with powerful magic. They are directed against the king or a national leader, who is the "I" in these psalms. Practically all individual psalms are royal psalms. Where references to physical illness appear (and these are few), the enemies are gentiles who are visiting the sick king.

Reviewed by M. Tsevat in *JBL* 76 (1957): 162-164.

1916. Böcher, O. *Dämonenfurcht und Dämonenabwehr.* Beiträge zur Wissenschaft von Alten und Neuen Testament 90. Stuttgart: Kohlhammer, 1970.

1917. Brongers, Hendrik Antonie. "De chasidim in het boek der psalmen." *Nederlands Theologisch Tijdschrift* 8 (1954): 279-297.

1918. Cherian, C.M. "Attitude to Enemies in the Psalms." *Biblebhashyam* 8 (1982): 104-117.

It is wrong to suppose that the psalmists have a markedly different spirit from that of the New Testament writers.

1919. Fraine, Jean de. "Les nations païennes dans les Psaumes." In *Studi sull'Oriente e la Bibbia offerti al P. Giovanni Rinaldi.* 285-292. Genova: Editrice Studio e Vita, 1967.

There was a gradual change of outlook in the way the psalmists looked at their non-Yahwist neighbors, beginning with hope for complete destruction and moving toward a concerned interest in the conversion and shared interests of these *goyyim*.

1920. Gelander, S. "The Language of the Wicked in the Psalms." In *Proceedings of the Tenth World Congress of Jewish Studies; Division A: The Bible and Its World.* 37-42. Jerusalem: World Union of Jewish Studies, 1990. (Hebrew)

1921. Hauret, Charles. "Les ennemis-sorciers dans les supplications individualles." *Recherches Bibliques* 8 (Paris, 1967): 129-137.

1922. Hjelt, A. "Sjukdomslidandet och fienderna i psalmerna (Ett bidgragtil bedömande af S. Mowinckels teori)." In *Studier tilegrede Prof. F. Buhl.* 64-74. Copenhagen: V. Pios Boghandel, 1925.

There is no evidence to support Mowinckel's claim that the psalmists looked upon the evildoers as the cause of their illness.

1923. Hobbs, T.R., and P.K. Jackson. "The Enemy in the Psalms." *Biblical Theology Bulletin* 21 (1991): 22-29.

The enemy profile includes the alien, aggressor, and desecrator. Enemies are characteristically described with stereotyped animal and deviant imagery. This reveals a broad cultural pattern. This Middle Eastern cultural process must be diffused before the psalms can serve elsewhere as useful guides in prayer.

1924. Illman, Karl-Johan. "Vän och fiende i bönepsalmerna." *Svensk Exegetisk Aarsbok* 54 (1989): 90-100.

Friends and Enemies in the Prayer-Psalms.

1925. Keel-Leu, Othmar. *Feinde und Gottesleugner. Studien zum Image der Widersacher in den Individualpsalmen.* Stuttgarter biblischer Monographien 7. Stuttgart: Katholisches Bibelwerk, 1969.

1926. ______. "Der bedrängte Beter. Wer sind die Feinde in den Psalmen." *Bibel und Kirche* 26 (1971): 103-107.

1927. Lamp, Erich. "Öffentlichkeit als Bedrohung - Ein Beitrag zur Deutung des 'Feindes' im Klagepsalm des Einzelnen." *Biblische Notizen* 50 (1989): 46-57.

According to social psychological theory, the individual sometimes perceives those outside of himself as threats. In the psalms, such individuals call their enemies godless, sacrilegious, and foreigners.

1928. Langton, Edward. *Essentials of Demonology. A Study of Jewish and Christian Doctrine, Its Origin and Development.* London: Epworth Press, 1949. xxii+234p.

1929. Mowinckel, Sigmund. "Fiendene i de individuelle Klagesalmer." *Norsk Teologisk Tidsskrift* 34 (1934): 1-39.

1930. Puukko, Antti Filemon. "Der Feind in den alttestamentlichen Psalmen." *Oudtestamentische Studiën* 8 (1950): 47-65.

1931. Ridderbos, Nicolaas Hermann. *De "Werkers der Ongerechtighed" in de individueele Psalmen. Een beoordeeling van Mowinckels opvatting.* Kampen: J.H. Kok, 1939. 350p.

Mainly a polemic against Mowinckel's magic theory. The evildoers represent a collective body; there are at least 7 different groups of enemies.

1932. Ruppert, L. *Der leidende Gerechte und seine Feinde: eine Wortfelduntersuchung.* Würzburg: Echter Verlag, 1973.

1933. Sauer, Georg. *Die strafende Vergeltung Gottes in den Psalmen. Eine frömmigkeitsgeschichtliche Untersuchung.* Erlangen: 1961.

1934. _____. "I nemici nei Salmi." *Protestantesimo* 13 (1958): 201-207.

The problem of the Old Testament cursing psalms and the New Testament love of enemies.

1935. Sauer, Groth. *Die strafende Gerechtigkeit Gottes in den Psalmen. Eine frömmigkeitsgeschichtliche Untersuchung.* Halle: Max Niemeyer Verlag, 1956.

1936. Schmid, R. "Die Fluchpsalmen im christlichen Gebet." In *Theologie im Wandel. Festschrift zum 150 jährigen Bestehen der Katholisch-Theologischen Fakultät an der Universität Tübingen, 1817-1967.* Munich-Freiburg: Wewel, 1967.

1937. Sheppard, Gerald T. "'Enemies' and the Politics of Prayer in the Book of Psalms." In *The Bible and the Politics of*

Exegesis. Essays in Honor of Norman K. Gottwald on His Sixty-Fifth Birthday, ed. David Jobling, Peggy L. Day, and Gerald T. Sheppard. 61-82. Cleveland, OH: Pilgrim Press, 1991.

Gottwald's socio-literary approach suggests that "enemies" most commonly designates rulers and oppressors, and provides a safe means of exposing wrongdoers to shame. Child's canonical approach reveals how the enemy psalms have been appropriated by various religious communities.

1938. Ubbelohde, Herbert. *Fluchpsalmen und alttestamentliche Sittlichkeit.* Breslau: Nischkowsky, 1938. xv+213p.

1939. Vos, J.G. "The Ethical Problem of the Imprecating Psalms." *Westminster Theological Journal* 4/2 (1942): 123-138.

See also: 75, 531, 554, 619, 1242, 1357, 1383, 1384, 1406, 1464, 1625, 1745, 2261

F. Miscellaneous Themes

1940. Adams, Daniel J. "The Psalms and Korean Theology." *Taiwan Journal of Theology* 8 (1986): 157-169.

1941. Albertz, Rainer. *Weltschöpfung und Menschenschöpfung. Untersucht bei Deuterojesaja, Hiob und in den Psalmen.* Stuttgart: Calwer Verlag, 1974.

1942. Alexander, T.D. "The Psalms and the Afterlife." *Irish Biblical Studies* 9 (1987): 2-17.

Some Psalms do speak clearly of a life after death: Psalms 49, 73, and possibly 16.

1943. Allgeier, Arthur. "Grundsätzliches zu einer Psalmenerklärung für das Leben." *Theologische Revue* 35 (1936): 1-7.

1944. Alonso Schökel, Luis. "The Experience of the Psalmists." *The Way* 17 (1977): 186-195.

1945. Amirtham, S. "To be near and to be far away from Yahweh: the Witness of the Individual Psalms of Lament to the Concept of the Presence of God." *Bangalore Theological Forum* 2 (1968): 31-55.

1946. Anderson, Bernhard W. *Creation Versus Chaos. The Reinterpretation of Mythical Symbolism in the Bible.* New York: Association Press, 1967. 192p.

1947. Arc, Jeanne d'. "'Sacrifice de louange.' Sur une expression des psaumes." *Christus* 102 (1979): 195-201.

1948. Bailey, L.R., Sr. *Biblical Perspectives on Death.* Overtures to Biblical Theology. Philadelphia: Fortress Press, 1979. xvi+159p.

1949. Balentine, Samuel E. *The Hidden Good. The Hiding of the Face of God in the Old Testament.* Oxford Theological Monographs. Oxford: University Press, 1983. xiii+202p.

1950. _____. "Enthroned on the Praises and Laments of Israel." *The Princeton Seminary Bulletin* Supplementary Issue 2 (1992): 20-35.

1951. Barth, Christoph. *Die Errettung vom Tode in den individuellen Klage- und Dankliedern des Alten Testaments.* Zollikon b. Zürich: Evangelischer Verlag, 1947. 168p.

1952. Barucq, A. "La lode divina nei Salmi[The Praise of God in the Psalms]." *Bibbia e Oriente* 1 (1959): 66-77.

1953. Bauer, Johannes B. "Theologie der Psalmen." *Bibel und Liturgie*20 (1952-1953): 99-103 (Psalm 119[118]), 183-189 (Prayer), 208-210 (The Width of the Heart), 225-227 (The Spirit of God), 257-260 (Priests), 289-292 (Human Existence), 321-327 (The Way), 353-359 (The Human).

1954. _____. "Theologie der Psalmen." *Bibel und Liturgie* 21 (1953-1954): 3-6 (The Hand of God), 34-35 (Poverty), 91-94 (Hope), 99-105 (The Idea of the Return of the Heathen), 130-133 (The Basis of the Piety in the Psalter), 163-166 (Sin), 195-198 (Forgiveness of Sins), 242-245 (Stillness), 276-278 (Cup).

1955. _____. "Theologie der Psalmen." *Bibel und Liturgie* 22 (1954-1955): 42-45 (Trust).

1956. _____. "Der Psalm ein Spiegel." *Bibel und Liturgie* 22 (1954-1955): 264-266.

1957. Beaucamp, Évode. "Le présent du salut dans le livre des Psaumes." In *Studia Hierosolymitana III*, ed. Giovanni Claudio Bottini. Studium Biblicum Franciscanum

Collectio Maior N. 30. Jerusalem: Franciscan Printing Press, 1982.

1958. ______. "Le psautier et la quête du salut." *Lumière et Vie* 40 (1991): 93-105.

The psalmist, and through his voice the people of Israel, does not cease crying to God for salvation. The believer may call on God with great confidence based on the memory of the liberating experience of the covenant. This appeal itself turns into thanksgiving and results in the announcement of salvation for the pagan nations.

1959. Beauchamp, Paul. "Plainte de louange dans les Psaumes." *Christus* 13 (1967): 65-82.

1960. Becker, Joachim. *Gottesfurcht im Alten Testament.* Analecta Biblica 25. Rome: Pontifical Biblical Institute, 1965. xix+303p.

Reviewed by E. Achtemeier in *JBL* 85 (1966): 518.

1961. Bell, Robert D. "Righteousness in the Psalms: Subtheme in a Book." *Biblical Viewpoint* 25 (1991): 47-52.

Righteousness includes more than moral conformity; it includes covenantal, social, and legal standards.

1962. Bentzen, Aage. "Der Tod des Beters in den Psalmen. Randbemerkungen zur Diskussion zwischen Mowinckel und Widengren." In Gottes ist der Orient. Festschrift für Prof. D. Dr. Otto *Eissfeldt DD zu seinem 70. Geburtstag am 1. September 1957.* 57-60. Berlin: Evangelische Verlaganstalt, 1959.

1963. Berchat, M. "La vie de foi du Psalmiste." *Cahiers Universités Catholiques* (1958): 212-224.

1964. Bernimont, E. "De l'inégale valeur des Psaumes." *Nouvelle Revue Théologique* 84 (1962): 843-852.

1965. Bernini, Giuseppe. "Alcuni aspetti dell'antropologia del Salterio." In *L'uomo nella Bibbia...* 147-152. Brescia: Paideia Editrice, 1975.

1966. Bishop, E.F.F. "Islam in the Psalter." *Muslim World* 55 (1965): 19-27.

1967. Blenkinsopp, J. "Can We Pray the Cursing Psalms?" *Clergy Review* 50 (1965): 534-538.

1968. Blidstein, G.J. "Nature in Psalms." *Judaism* 13 (1964): 29-36.

1969. Bollegui, J.M. *Los Salmos. Oraciones inventadas por Dios para los hombres.* Barcelona: Consejo Superior de Investigaciones Cientificas, 1967.

1970. Bomberg, Bernhard. "Die Vergeltungslehre in den Psalmen." *Neue Kirchliche Zeitschrift* 41 (1930): 539-566.

1971. Bout, Hendrik. *Het zondebeset in het Book der Psalmen. Een exegetisch-theologische studie.* Leiden: Luctor et Emergo, 1952. 189p.

1972. Brongers, H.A. "De *chasidim* in het boek der psalmen." *Norsk Teologisk Tidsskrift* 8 (1954): 279-297.

1973. ______. "Die Rache- und Fluchpsalmen im Alten Testament." *Oudtestamentische Studiën* 13 (1963): 21-42.

(1) Israel, like Yahweh, was responsible for justice and righteousness in this world, and (2) Israelite faith did not affirm a life beyond this one. Thus punishment for sin had to take place in this life. Anyone who disturbed the shalom had to be dealt with.

1974. Brzegowy, Tadeusz. *Miasto Boze w Psalmach [The City of God in the Psalter].* Cracow: Polskie Towarzystwo Teologiczne, 1989. 287p.

The psalms reflect Israel's adaptation of terminology and images from Canaanite religion to express its belief in God. The Canaanite cult of the God of the Most High was the vehicle for Israel's adoption of the common Semitic theology of God as king. This theology was accommodated to the ancient Israelite tradition of Yahweh Sabaoth who brought Israel out of Egypt. David introduced this theology to Jerusalem when he brought the Ark of the Covenant to the city. The psalms refer to Jerusalem as "the city of God" because of its Temple. The belief that God dwelled in Jerusalem gave Israel confidence, yet also created problems for the Israelite idea of God.

1975. Buber, Martin. *Recht und Unrecht. Deutung einiger Psalmen. Sammlung Klosterberg, Europäische Reihe. Basel: B. Schwabe, 1952. 75p.* Translated into English by Ronald Gregor Smith and published as *Right and Wrong: An Interpretation of Some Psalms.* London: SCM Press Ltd., 1952.

1976. Bückers, H. "Die Sündenvergebung in den Psalmen." *Divus Thomas Freiblatter* 29 (1951): 188-210.

1977. Butler, Trent C. "Piety in the Psalms." *Review and Expositor* 81 (1984): 385-394.

1978. Casalis, Mateus. "Angústia versus esperança: uma leitura ontológico-dialética de Alguns Salmos." *Estudos Teologicos (Brazil)* 25 (1985): 281-288.

1979. Clark, D.L., and B.A. Mastin. " *Venite exultemus Domino:* Some Reflections on the Interpretation of the Psalter." *Church Quarterly Review* 167 (1966): 413-424.

1980. Collins, Terence. "The Physiology of Tears in the Old Testament." *Catholic Biblical Quarterly* 33 (1971): 18-38, 185-197.

Part II covers Psalms 22, 31, 38, 69.

1981. Coppens, Joseph. "Les psaumes des *Hasîdîm.*" In *Mélanges bibliques rédigés en l'honneur de André Robert.* Travaux d l'Institut Catholique de Paris 4. 214-224. Paris: Bloud & Gay, 1957.

There are various shades of meanings in the use of *ḥāsîd,* corresponding to the categories of the psalms in which the word appears: pietist, sapiential, national, and professional.

1982. ______. *Le Psautier et ses problèmes.* Analecta Lovanienses Biblica et Orientalia III/19. Louvain: Publications universitaires de Louvain, 1960.

1983. ______. "Les Saints *(qedôšîm)* dans le Psautier." *Ephemerides Theologicae Lovanienses* 39 (1963): 485-500.

1984. _____. "Le *Saddîq* (= juste) dans le Psautier." In *De la Tôrah au Messie. Études d'exégèse et d'herméneutique bibliques offertes à Henri Cazelles pour ses 25 années d'enseignement à l'Institut Catholique de Paris (Octobre 1979).* 299-306. Paris: Desclée, 1981.

1985. Crollins, A.A. Robert. "Derek in the Psalms." *Biblical Theology Bulletin* 4 (1974): 312-317.

1986. Dawes, Stephen B. "*ᶜănāwâ* in Translation and Tradition." *Vetus Testamentum* 41 (1991): 38-48.

ᶜănāwâ means "humility" in all cases.

1987. Deissler, Alfons. "Der anthropologische Charakter des Psalms 33(32)." In *Mélanges Bibliques rédigés en l'honneur de A. Robert,* ed. Henri Cazelles. 225-233. Paris: Bloud & Gay, 1956.

1988. _____. "Das lobpreisende Gottesvolk in den Psalmen." In *Sentire Ecclesiam. Festschrift Hugo Rahner,* ed. J. Daniélou and H. Vorglimmler. 17-49. Freiburg im Breisgau: Herder, 1961.

1) General questions. 2) The religious consciousness of Israel rests not on the creator God but on the historical actions of the covenant God. 3) The covenant people praise the covenant God for the grand beginning of their history. 4) The people of God praise the God who helps in the present. 5) The community of Yahweh sing to the God who governs the cosmos. 6) The people of Yahweh praise their covenant God as the king of the endtime. 7) The community of Yahweh praise God's gracious and saving rule on Zion.

1989. _____. "Das Israel der Psalmen als Gottesvolk der Hoffenden." In *Die Zeit Jesu. Festschrift Heinrich Schlier,* ed. G. Bornkamm and K. Rahner. 15-37. Freiburg im Breisgau: Herder, 1970.

1990. Duhaime, Jean. "La souffrance dans les psaumes 3-41." *Science et esprit* 41 (1989): 33-48.

The teaching of Psalms 3-41 on suffering. The psalms furnish less of a *testimony* on the way by which certain individuals have overcome their suffering, than *models* which will allow one to think and react appropriately in similar situations.

1991. Eichhorn, Dieter. *Gott als Fels, Burg und Zuflucht. Eine Untersuchung zum Gebet des Mittlers in den Psalmen.* Bern: Herbert Land; Frankfurt am Main: Peter Land, 1972. 146p.

1992. Eissfeldt, Otto. "'Mein Gott' im Alten Testament." *Zeitschrift für die alttestamentliche Wissenschaft* 61 (1945/48): 3-16. Reprinted in *Kleine Schriften III.* 35-47. Tübingen: J.C.B. Mohr, 1966.

1993. _____. "Gott und das Meer in der Bibel." In *Studia Orientalia Ioanni Pedersen...dicata* 76-84. Helsinki: Finnish Oriental Society, 1953.

1994. Emden, Cecil S. "The Psalmist's Emphasis on God's Kindness." *Church Quarterly Review* 156 (1955): 233-235.

1995. Ewbank, Walter Frederick. "Spiritual Interpretation of the Psalms." *Church Quarterly Review* 165 (1964): 429-436.

1996. Fischer, B. "Zum Problem einer christlichen Interpretation der Psalmen." *Theologische Revue* 61 (1971): 5-12.

1997. Forrester, W.F. "Sin and Repentance in the Psalms." *Clergy Review* 41 (1956): 663-674.

1998. Fraine, J. de. "Die Heiden in den Psalmen." *Das Heilige Land* 8/4 (1955): 51-54.

1999. _____. "'Entmythologisierung' dans les Psaumes." In *Le Psautier: Ses origines. Ses problèmes littérraires. Son influence*, ed. Robert de Langhe. Orientalia et Biblica Lovaniensia, IV. 89-106. Louvain: Publications Universitaires, 1962.

By employing Bultmann's "demythologizing" approach to the psalms we find that certain traits of Canaanite myth are preserved, but their intention is changed to express a new Yahwistic view of reality. Special attention is given to Psalms 48, 82, and 91.

2000. Franken, H.J. *The Mystical Communion with Jhwh in the Book of Psalms.* Leiden: E.J. Brill, 1954. 97p.

The scope of this study is not a description of the psychological side of the attitude of the pious; rather it is a description of the religious aspect, namely the mystical aspects of the relationship with God, as they are found in the Psalms. The mystical aspect seems to be related to the magical. The magical tends to restrict the freedom of the individual; the mystical comes as a liberation into the direction of the world of God. The difference between the two thus lies in the direction in which they work and in the result they create in the life of the pious. The magical element remained a need of the psalmists; its presence was a problem to the "holy" that induced them to refer to it as "vanity," "nothingness" and symbols denoting emptiness or sudden break and end. Whoever is in its grasp, experiencing its power, realizes that he is going to non-existence. "Silence" is opposite to praise. In the Psalms, all true seeking after the immediate presence of the Lord has to follow the path of righteousness, applying oneself to the pattern of life revealed in the covenant. These findings are applied to Psalms 16, 18, 25, 27, 31, 36, and 63.

2001. Frost, S.B. "The Christian Interpretation of the Psalms." *Canadian Journal of Theology* 5 (1959): 25-34.

2002. Fuhs, H.F. *Sehen und Schauen. Die Wurzel hzh im alten Orient und im Alten Testament. Ein Beitrag zum prophetischen Offenbarungsempfang.* Forschung zur Bibel 32. Würzburg: Echter Verlag, 1978. xiv+378.

1) The seer tradition. 2) Seeing God and God's works (Based in large part on the Psalms).

2003. Gelinder, Shammai. "Justice and the Order of Creation. On the Relationship Between Understandings of the World and Structural Principles in Biblical Poetry." *Beth Mikra* 29 (1983/1984): 158-179. (Hebrew)

In the Psalms, nature helps the righteous or harms the wicked, who are often compared to various plants. Justice was created as an integral part of the world. Both Ecclesiastes and Job rebel against this idea.

2004. Gemser, Berend. "Gesinnungsethik im Psalter." *Oudtestamentische Studiën* 13 (1963): 1-20.

The intentional ethical ideals of the psalms are often superior to the ideals discoverable in contemporary literature outside of Israel, particularly those of Sumer, Akkad and Babylonia.

2005. Gesché, Adolphe. *La christologie du Commentaire sur les Psaumes découvert à Toura.* Universitas catholica Lovaniensis. Dissertationes ad gradum magistri in Facultate Theologica vel in Facultate Iuris Canonici consequendum conscriptae. Ser. III/7. Gembloux: Duculot, 1962. xxxi+448p.

2006. Gibert, Pierre. "Nature et histoire dans le Genèse et les Psaumes." *Lumière et Vie* 161 (1983): 5-14.

The cosmos is not an entity that can be contemplated independently of human action, whether the latter be one of sovereign mastery of or laborious submission: it can never be detached from a history.

2007. Gierlich, Augustinus M. *Der Lichtgedanke in den Psalmen.* Freiburger Theologische Studien 56. Freiburg im Breisgau: Herder, 1940. viii+206p.

2008. Goeke, H. *Das Menschenbild der individuellen Klagelieder. Ein Beitrag zur alttestamentlichen Anthropologie.* Bonn: University of Bonn, 1971.

2009. ______. "Die Anthropologie der individuellen Klagelieder." *Bibel und Leben* 14 (1973): 13-29, 112-137.

2010. Good, James. "Depression in the Psalms." *The Bible Today* 27 (1989): 113-115.

The psalter contains hymns of every variety but few that really convey depression - Psalm 88 is a true exception. Psalms 6, 22, and 31 speak from the pits, but the depression is relative because trust in Yahweh remains present.

2011. Goodman, A.E. "חסד and תורה in the Linguistic Tradition of the Psalter." In *Words and Meanings: Essays Presented to David Winton Thomas on his retirement from the Regius Professorship of Hebrew in the University of Cambridge, 1968*, ed. Peter R. Ackroyd and Barnabas Lindars. 105-115. Cambridge: At the University Press, 1968.

2012. Gross, Heinrich. "'Bei Ihm is Erlösung in Fülle.' Befreiung in den Psalmen." *Bibel und Kirche* 42 (1987): 104-108.

The Hebrew verbs for liberation are *gāʾal* and *pādāh.* They have their origin in the commercial and social life of Israel, but also include the religious.

2013. Gruenthaner, Michael J. "The Future Life in the Psalms." *Catholic Biblical Quarterly* 2 (1940): 57-63.

The psalms contain numerous references both to a blessed future life and to bodily resurrection.

2014. Hall, Bernard. "The Problem of Retribution in the Psalms." *Scriptura* 7/3 (1955): 84-92.

2015. Hamp, Vinzenz. "Das Ethos der Psalmen." 1965. Reprinted in *Weisheit und Gottesfurcht. Aufsätze zur alttestamentlichen Einleitung, Exegese und Theologie*, ed. Georg Schmuttermayr. 217-232. St. Ottilien: EOS, 1990.

2016. Huppenbauer, H.W. "God and Nature in the Psalms." *Ghana Bulletin of Theology* 3 (1969): 19-32.

2017. Inch, Morris A. *Psychology in the Psalms: A Portrait of Man in God's World.* Waco, TX: Word Books, 1969.

A commentary on selected Psalms that are correlated with selected readings. The topics covered include pain, corporate personality, life, prayer, history, hope, etc.

2018. Jones, E. "Suffering in the Psalter." *Congregational Quarterly* 34 (1956): 53-63.

2019. Kellerhals, Emanuel. *Vier Psalmen. Was sie damals bedeuteten; was sie heute hoch sagen.* Basel: Verlag Friedrich Reinhardt, 1955. 54p.

2020. Kilpp, Nelson. "Os Salmos Como Expressão de Espiritualidade." *Estudos Teológicos* 23 (1983): 141-153.

Christian theologians have rightly joined spirituality with the Holy Spirit, as can be seen by reference to various psalms of praise and supplication.

2021. Kim, Ee Kon. "'Outcry,' Its Context in Biblical Theology." *Interpretation* 42 (1988): 229-239.

2022. Kloppers, M.H.O. "'n Verkenning van die wijse waarop die 'vreeddeling' (*gēr*) as teologiese term binnen die ketubim funksioneer, met besondere verwijsing na die psalms." *Nederduits Gereformeerde Teologiese Tydskrif* 28 (1987): 130-141.

An Introduction of the Theological Function of the Term 'stranger,' (*gēr*) in the Writings, with Special Attention to the Psalms.

2023. Koch, Klaus. "Gibt es eine Vergeltungsdogma im Alten Testament?" *Zeitschrift für Theologie und Kirche*(1955): 1-42.

2024. ______. "Denn seine Güte währet ewiglich." *Evangelische Theologie* 21 (1961): 537-544.

The meaning of God's steadfast love enduring forever (Psalms 100, 106, 107, 118, and 136).

2025. Kratz, Reinhard Gregor. "Die Gnade des täglichen Brots: späte Psalmen auf dem Weg zum Vaterunser." *Zeitschrift für Theologie und Kirche* 89 (1992): 1-40.

2026. Kraus, Hans-Joachim. "Von Leben und Tod in Psalmen." In *Biblisch-theologische Aufsätze.* 258-277. Neukirchen-Vluyn: Neukirchener Verlag, 1972.

2027. Krings, H. *Der Mensch vor Gott. Die Daseinserfahrung in den Psalmen.* Würzburg: Echter Verlag, 1952.

2028. Kugel, James L. "Topics in the History of the Spirituality of the Psalms." In *Jewish Spirituality from the Bible Through the Middle Ages*, ed. A. Green. 113-144. New York: The Crossroad Publishing Co., 1987.

2029. Kühlewein, Johannes. *Geschichte in den Psalmen.* Calwer Theologische Monographien, Series A, no. 2. Stuttgart: Calwer Verlag, 1973.

Our faith lives as a result of history and prayer lives upon history. It was God's interventions in the remote and near past that gave the Israelites reason for faith; consciously or unconsciously, they related to what had happened. There was no situation in the life of the faithful Israelite when this was not the case. The psalms are examined for their historical bases and references.

2030. Kuntz, J.K. "The Retribution Motif in Psalmic Wisdom." *Zeitschrift für die alttestamentliche Wissenschaft* 89 (1977): 223-233.

2031. Łach, Jósef. "Hasid/im w świetle Psalmów." In *Grzech. odkupienie, miłość. Studia z biblistyki III*, ed. Jan Łz h. 346-366. Warsaw: Akademia Teologii Katolickiej, 1983.

2032. Łach, S. "Le sens d l'attribut de Dieu *hannun* à la lumière des Psaumes." *Folia Orientalia* 21 (1980): 93-102.

2033. Lauha, A. "'Dominus benefecit.' Die Wortwurzel GML und die Psalmenfrömmigkeit." *Annual of the Swedish Theological Institute* 11 (1977-1978): 57-62.

The root *gml* has the general meaning of "to complete, to accomplish a deed." God's deeds are always good; it is not necessary that humankind find them to be agreeable or pleasant. Psalm 13:6b should be translated, "I will sing to the Lord, for he has accomplished his deed in my regard."

2034. Levine, Herbert. "The Symbolic *sukkah* in Psalms." *Prooftexts: A Journal of Jewish Literary History* 7 (1987): 259-267.

In the narrative books of the Hebrew Bible, the term *sukkah* refers to a small hut or booth, which was built during harvest time and during its commemorative holiday, Sukkoth. In the poetic books, however, each use of the covering sukkah is figurative. In the psalms, particularly in the psalms of lament, the sukkah motif characterizes the poets ambivalent relationship to a hidden, but sheltering God.

2035. L'Heureux, C.E. "Dis-ease and Healing in the Psalms." Chap. in *Life Journey and the Old Testament: An Experiential Approach to the Bible and Personal Transformation.* Mahwah, NJ: Paulist Press, 1986.

2036. Louf, André. "A l'école des Psaumes." *Christus* 96 (1977): 419-431.

2037. McGovern, John J. "The Waters of Death." *Catholic Biblical Quarterly* 21 (1959): 350-358.

A discussion of the "waters which are under the earth" as a picture of Sheol.

2038. McKeating, Henry. "Divine Forgiveness in the Psalms." *Scottish Journal of Theology* 18 (1965): 69-83.

2039. Marböck, Johannes. "Dimensionen des Menschseins in den Psalmen. Zur Bedeutung des Psalmengebetes." *Theologisch-Praktische Quartalschrift* 127 (1979): 7-14.

2040. March, W. Eugene. "'Father' as a Metaphor for God in the Psalms." *Austin Seminary Bulletin* 97 (1981): 5-12.

2041. Martin-Achard, Robert. *La mort en face selon la Bible hébräique.* Essais bibliques 15. Geneva: Labor et Fides, 1988. 136p.

1) The Old Testament conception of human life, including views of death and afterlife among the Egyptians and Mesopotamians. 2) Image(s) of death in the Old Testament. 3) Expressions of hope for future life in the Old Testament.

2042. Mathias, Dietmar. "Das 'Gottesvolk' in der Sicht der Geschichtssummarien des Psalters." In *Gottesvolk: Beiträge zu einem Thema biblischer Theologie. Festschrift S. Wagner*, ed. Arndt Meinhold and Rüdiger Lux. 193-208. Berlin: Evangelische Verlagsanstalt, 1991.

Five psalms (78, 105, 106, 135, and 136) portray God's relation to God's people by means of historical summaries.

2043. Mays, James Luther. "A Question of Identity: The Threefold Hermeneutic of Psalmody." *Asbury Theological Journal* 46 (1991): 87-94.

2044. Menezes, Rui de. "From Dust to Glory -- the Anthropology of the Psalms." *Jeevadhara* 16 (1986): 105-120.

Humanity is at once both transient and transcendent, made of dust but destined for glory.

2045. Miller, Athanasius. "Das Ideal der Gottverbundenheit nach der Lehre der Psalmen." *Benediktinische Monatschrift* 19 (1937): 153-173.

2046. ______. "Fluchpsalmen und israelitisches Recht." *Angelicum* 20 (1943): 92-101.

2047. ______. "The Psalms from a Christian Viewpoint." *Worship* 31 (1957): 334-345.

2048. Mindling, Joseph A. "Hope for a Felicitous Afterlife in Psalms 16, 49, and 73." *Laurentianum* 32 (1991): 305-369.

2049. Möller, Margarete. "Gebet und Kerygma in den Psalmen." *Theolgische Versuche* 3 (1971): 11-29.

2050. Monloubou, Louis. *L'âme des psalmistes ou la spiritualité dur psautier.* Collationes "Paroles de vie." 1968.

2051. Murphy, Roland.E. "The Faith of the Psalmists." *Interpretation* 34 (1980): 229-239.

2052. Murray, Robert. "The Psalms in Their Original World and in Tradition." *Priests and People* 2 (1988): 274-280.

2053. Osswald, E. "Glaubenszuversicht und Glaubensanfechtung im Alten Testament unter besonderer Berücksichtigung der Psalmen." *Theologische Literaturzeitung* 104 (1979): 705-712.

2054. Papagiannopoulos, Johannes. "Cursing in the Psalms." *Ecclesia* 64 (1987): 577-580, 612-615. Greek.

Some curses are uttered against the sinner; others are uttered against personal enemies.

2055. Parsons, I.R.M. "Suffering in the Psalms." *Australian Biblical Review* 20 (1972): 49-53.

2056. Paulsen, Sabine. "Schöpfungsverständnis im 'Psalm des Volkes' (Ps 104) und im 'Psalm der Theologen' (Ps 8)." *Ministerial Formation* 53 (1991): 27-30, 41.

2057. Pax, E. "Studien zum Vergeltungsproblem der Psalmen." *Liber Annuus* 11 (1960-1961): 56-112.

2058. Peifer, Claude J. "Sing for us the songs of Zion." *The Bible Today* 97 (Oct., 1978): 1690-1696.

The historical and mythological background of the Songs of Zion and the implications of the theology of these psalms for the Old and New Testaments.

2059. Petersen, C. *Mythos im Alten Testament. Bestimmung des Mythosbegriffs und Untersuchung der mythischen Elemente in den Psalmen.* Beihefte zur Zeitschrift für die alttestamentliche Wissenschaft 157. Berlin: Walter de Gruyter, 1982. xviii+280p.

A discussion of the concept "myth" and the appropriateness of its use for Old Testament material, including a study of Psalms 8, 19A, 24A, 33, 65A, 74, 75, 78, 89A, 95A, 96, 102:26-28, 103, 104, 115, 119, 121, 124, 134, 136, 146, 148. "Myth" refers to the portrayal of events which lie outside historical time and involve the action of the deity. The Old Testament uses mythic elements often and to good purpose. God is not simply a god of history, and those who do not recognize the mythic elements will miss much of importance for Old Testament theology.

Reviewed in *CBQ* 46 (1984): 555-556.

2060. Pezhumkattil, Abraham. "Israel's Faith Reflected in the Psalms." *Bible Bhashyam* 16 (1990): 156-172.

The Psalms contain the entire narration of Israel's salvation history.

2061. Podella, Thomas. "Grundzüge alttestamentlicher Jenseitsvorstellungen שאול." *Biblische Notizen* 43 (1988): 70-89.

The concept of the netherworld as found in the Old Testament. God's presence and power do not extend to it. The idea of the netherworld does not imply a belief in immortality.

2062. Preuss, Horst-Dietrich. "Erfahrungen im betenden Umgang mit Psalmen." In *Erfahrung -- Glaube -- Theologie. Beiträge zu Bedeutung und Ort religiöser Erfahrung,* ed. H.D. Preuss. 43-64. Stuttgart: Calwer Verlag, 1983.

2063. Prinsloo, W.S. "Enkele riglyne uit die Ou Testament: Die houding teenoor siekte en siekes." *Nederduits Gereformeerde Teologiese Tydskrif* 23 (1982): 18-28.

The Old Testament attitude towards sickness and healing; God is considered to be the cause of both.

2064. Rad, Gerhard von. "'Gerechtigkeit' und 'Leben' in der Kultsprache der Psalmen." In *Festschrift Alfred Bertholet zum 80. Geburtstag,* ed. by W. Baumgartner and Others. 418-437. Tübingen: J.C.B. Mohr (Paul Siebeck), 1950. Reprinted in *Gesammelte Studien zum Alten Testament.* Theologische Bücherei 8. 225-247. Munich: Chr. Kaiser Verlag, 1958. Translated into English and published as "'Righteousness' and 'Life' in the Cultic Language of the Psalms," in *The Problem of the Hexateuch and Other Essays.* Translated by E.W. Trueman Dicken. 242-266.

New York: McGraw-Hill, 1966; London: Oliver and Boyd, 1966.

2065. _____. "Das theologische Problem des alttestamentlichen Schöpfungsglaubens." In *Werden und Wesen des Alten Testaments*. Beihefte zur Zeitschrift für die alttestamentliche Wissenschaft 66. 138-147. Berlin: Alfred Töpelmann, 1936; reprinted in *Gesammelte Studien zum Alten Testament*, Theologische Bücherei 8. Munich: Chr. Kaiser Verlag, 1958; translated into English by E. W. Trueman Dicken and published as "The Theological Problem of the Old Testament Doctrine of Creation," in *The Problem of the Hexateuch and Other Essays*, 131-143; New York: McGraw-Hill, 1966; London: Oliver and Boyd, 1966; reprinted in *Creation in the Old Testament*, ed. Bernhard W. Anderson. Issues in Religion and Theology, no. 6. 53-64. Philadelphia: Fortress Press, 1984; London: SPCK, 1984. 178p.

2066. _____. *Der Heilige Krieg im alten Israel*. Abhandlungen zur Theologie des Alten und Neuen Testament 20. Zürich: Zwingli-Verlag, 1951. Translated into English and edited by Marva J. Dawn and John Howard Yoder and published as *Holy War in Ancient Israel*. Introduction by Ben C. Ollenburger. Annotated Bibliography by Judith E. Sanderson. Grand Rapids, MI: William B. Eerdmans, 1991. vi+170p.

2067. Raja, B.J. "Eco-Spirituality in the Psalms." *Vidyajyoti* 53 (1989): 637-650.

Modern ecological concerns have stirred world-wide responses. Psalms such as 8, 19, 33, 100, 104, 145, and 148, can be regarded as creation songs. Wherever there is life, there is God's blessing for which Israel thanks God. Eco-spirituality, too, is ordered toward seeing God through God's creation. Human beings have sinned in violating the earth, and in so doing have harmed themselves.

2068. Ramaroson, Léonard. "Immortalité et résurrrection dans les Psaumes." *Science et Esprit* 36 (1984): 287-295. Published in English as "Immortality and Resurrection in the Psalms." *Theology Digest* 32 (1985): 235-238.

Three Psalms speak of a life of perfect and eternal happiness in the presence of God destined for the just: Psalms 16, 49 and 73.

2069. Rao, T.J. Raja. "Agony and Anguish: The Psalmist in His Suffering." *Jeevadhara* 17 (1988): 94-100.

2070. Rayan, Samuel. "The Earth is the Lord's." *Vidyajyoti* 54 (1990): 113-132.

A biblical reflection on ecological issues with reference to other non-biblical traditions. The earth is the Lord's (Psalm 24). The earth is also ours (Psalm 115).

2071. Rayner, Frank A. "The Doctrine of Redemption in the Acrostic Scriptures." *The Evangelical Quarterly* 23 (1951): 139-140.

Psalms 25, 34, 37, 111-112, 119, 145.

2072. Reinelt, Heinz. "Gottes Herrschaftbereich nach den Aussagen der Psalmen." In *Freude an der Weisung des Herrn. Beiträge zur Theologie der Psalmen. Festgabe zum 70. Geburtstag von H. Groß,* ed. E. Haag and F.L.

Hossfeld. Stuttgarter biblische Beiträge 13. 265-274. Stuttgart: Katholisches Bibelwerk, 1986.

Heaven and earth belong to God's realm of power, because they were created by God.

2073. Ridderbos, Nic. H. "De betuigingen van 'onschuld, rechtvaardigheid' in de psalmen." *Gereformeerd Theologisch Tidschrift* 50 (1950): 86-104. Reprinted in *Psalmenstudie. Prof. Nic. H. Ridderbos en het boek der Psalmen. Opstellen van prof. dr. Nic. H. Ridderbos,* ed. C. Van Ginkel and P.J. van Midden. 51-66. Kampen: Kok, 1991.

2074. Rinaldi, Giuseppe. "L'Universo nei Salmi." *Bibbia e Oriente* 15 (1973): 229-238.

The entire universe was viewed as the theophanous seat of God; the lower world was looked upon as the place prepared for humankind by God.

2075. _____. "Il mondo per l'uomo nei Salmo." *Bibbia e Oriente* 16 (1974): 163-176.

2076. Ringgren, Helmer. "Quelques traits essentiels de la piété des Psaumes." In *Mélanges Bibliques rédigés en l'honneur de André Robert.* Travaux de l'Institut Catholique de Paris 4. 205-213. Paris, Bloud & Gay, 1957.

2077. Robinson, H. Wheeler. "The Inner Life of the Psalmists." In *The Psalmists: Essays on their religious experience and teaching, their social background, and their place in the development of Hebrew Psalmody,* edited with an

Introduction by D.C. Simpson. 45-65. London: Oxford University Press (Humphrey Milford), 1926.

2078. ______. "The Social Life of the Psalmists." In *The Psalmists: Essays on their religious experience and teaching, their social background, and their place in the development of Hebrew Psalmody*, edited with an Introduction by D.C. Simpson. 67-86. London: Oxford University Press (Humphrey Milford), 1926. 197p.

2079. Robinson, Theodore H. "The God of the Psalmists." In *The Psalmists: Essays on their religious experience and teaching, their social background, and their place in the development of Hebrew Psalmody*, edited with an Introduction by D.C. Simpson. 23-44. London: Oxford University Press (Humphrey Milford), 1926. 197p.

2080. Rochettes, Jacqueline des. "Psaumes et Communication." *Bulletin de littérature ecclésiastique* 91 (1990): 101-111.

The use of dialogue in the Davidic psalms. It is difficult to answer whether any communication between God and humankind takes place in the psalms. It does seem, however, that a kind of evolution in relationship is produced in human hearts by prayer.

2081. Römer, Thomas. "La redécouverte d'un mythe dans l'Ancien Testament: la création comme combat." *Etudes Théologiques et Religieuses* 64 (1989): 561-573.

Exilic discourse about God the Creator took two main directions. A conservative group that did not go into Exile spoke of God in traditional terms as warrior against chaos. A liberal priestly group in Exile spoke of God as distant, unique, mysterious, and presented divine creative activity in a more "abstract" fashion.

2082. Rosłon, Jósef Wiesław. "Zbawienie Jako Życie w Oparciu o Księgę Psalmów." *Ruch Biblijny i Liturgiczny* 39 (1986): 177-197.

The meaning of the term "salvation" in the book of Psalms. The psalms understood salvation as the support which is necessary for life.

2083. Schenker, Adrian. "Das Gebet im Lichte der psalmen." *Bibel und Kirche* 35 (1980): 37-41.

2084. Scheuner, Dora. "Die politische Glaubenshaltung in den Psalmen." In *Theologische Aufsätze Karl Barth zum 50. Geburtstag*. Ed. E. Wolf. 136-145. Munich: Chr. Kaiser, 1936.

2085. Schreiner, J. "Gottes Verfügen durch 'Geben' und 'Nehmen' in der Sicht der Psalmen." In *Ein Gott -- Eine Offenbarung. Beiträge zur biblischen Exegese, Theologie und Spiritualität. Festschrift Notker Füglister*, ed. F.V. Reiterer. 307-331. Würzburg: Echter Verlag, 1991.

2086. Schuttermayr, Georg. "Vom Gott unter Göttern zum einzigen Gott. Zu den Spuren der Geschichte des Jahweglaubens in den Psalmen." In *Freude an der Weisung des Herrn. Beiträge zur Theologie der Psalmen. Festgabe zum 70. Geburtstag von H. Groß*, ed. E. Haag and F.L. Hossfeld. Stuttgarter biblische Beiträge 13. 349-374. Stuttgart: Katholisches Bibelwerk, 1986.

An attempt is made to locate a few psalms at their appropriate place within the development of the Yahweh faith. Psalm 31 does not yet recognize a Yahweh monolatry. The offensive promotion of Yahweh as a personal God in Psalm 91 points more to the typical pre-exilic situation between Yahweh and other gods than to an exclusive honoring of Yahweh. In Psalms 135 and 136 Yahweh is addressed as a national god and proclaimed simply as "God of Gods."

2087. Scott, Robert Balgarnie Young. *The Psalms as Christian Praise.* New York: Association Press, 1959. 88p.

What is the Book of Psalms? What does it contain? How did it come to us? Jewish Psalms in the Christian Bible? The Psalms as a Christian text.

2088. Segalla, Giuseppe. "'Quaerere Deum' nei Salmi." *Quaerere Deum. Atti della XXV Settimana Biblica Italiana, Brescia* (1980): 191-212.

2089. Sheppard, Gerald T. "Theology and the Book of Psalms." *Interpretation* 46 (1992): 143-155.

While the Psalter imparts instruction to the faithful on the ways of God, also teaches them to pray. Simply put, prayer is the effort to ask something of God and to anticipate a divine response in word, deed, or presence. The textual warrants for a Christian interpretation of the Psalms are examined.

2090. Smal, P.J.N. *Die Universalisme in die Psalms.* Doctoral diss., University of Amsterdam, 1956. Kampen: Kok, 1956.

2091. Smick, Elmer B. "Mythopoetic Language in the Psalms." *Westminster Theological Journal* 44 (1982): 88-98.

The Old Testament writers were not committed to a mythical view of the universe or of God; however, they used contemporary mythology to illustrate their theology.

2092. Smith, Billy K. "The Nature of the Hebrew Psalms." *Biblical Illustrator* 15 (4,1989): 14-16.

2093. Smith, Mark S. "'Seeing God' in the Psalms: The Background to the Beatific Vision in the Hebrew Bible." *Catholic Biblical Quarterly* 50 (1988): 171-183.

Dahood has suggested that passages like Psalms 11:7; 17:15; 27:4,13 and others point to an Israelite belief in beholding God externally in the afterlife. Not so. "Seeing God" refers to some sort of "culminating experience in the temple" resembling a prophetic vision.

2094. ______. *Psalms: The Divine Journey.* Mahwah, NJ: Paulist Press, 1987.

2095. ______. "The Psalms as a Book for Pilgrims." *Interpretation* 46 (1992): 156-166.

Through their psalms, the pilgrims of ancient Israel created a view of the world and of God that today remains central to the faith and life of the church.

2096. Smitten, Wilhelm in der. "Sprechender Glaube. Einige Gedanken zu den Psalmen." *Dienender Glaube* 48 (1972): 217-219.

2097. Soll, William Michael. "The Israelite Lament: Faith Seeking Understanding." *Quarterly Review (Methodist)* 8 (Fall, 1988): 77-88.

2098. Sorg, Rembert. *Hesed and Hasid in the Psalms.* St. Louis, MO: Pio Decimo Press, 1953. 63p.

The Psalms provide us with the material for true contemplative prayer.

Reviewed in *CBQ* 17 (1955): 520.

2099. Spieckermann, Hermann. "'Die ganze Erde is seiner Herrlichkeit voll' Pantheismus im Alten Testament?" *Zeitschrift für Theologie und Kirche* 87 (1990): 415-436.

The nature and development of pantheistic ideas behind Old Testament statements about the presence of God's glory in the earth.

2100. Stadelmann, Luís I.J. "As maldições nos Salmos." *Perspectiva Teológica* 20 (52,1988): 317-338.

Three suggestions are made for assimilating the Psalms' maledictory language and including it in our prayers: literary, theological, and hermeneutical.

2101. Steck, Odil Hannes. *Friedensvorstellungen im alten Jerusalem: Psalmen, Jesaja, Deuterojesaja.* Theologische Studien 111. Zürich: Theologischer Verlag, 1972.

The whole cosmos was first established in peace by its Creator, and Jerusalem became the ideal and channel of peace in the psalms, Isaiah, and Second Isaiah.

2102. Stoop, F. "Le sens de Dieu dans les Psaumes." *Schweizerische Zeitschrift für Geschichte* 19 (1969): 32ff.

2103. Strange, Marcian. "The Worldliness of the Psalms." *Worship* 36 (1962): 566-573.

2104. Stuhlmueller, Carroll. "Jacob's Well [The Resurrection of the Body in the Old Testament]." *The Bible Today* 29 (1991): 150-151.

The Old Testament does not support belief in the resurrection of the body from the dead. Psalms 6, 30, 88, and 113 clearly deny any personal survival after death. Only in Daniel is there a reference to a resurrection.

2105. Surburg, Raymond F. "Interpretation of the Imprecatory Psalms." *The Springfielder* 39 (1975): 88-102.

2106. Terrien, Samuel L. "Creation, Cultus, and Faith in the Psalter." *Theological Education* 2 (1966): 116-128.

2107. Thordarson, Thorir Kr. "The Mythic Dimension. Hermeneutical Remarks on the Language of the Psalter." *Vetus Testamentum* 24 (1974): 212-240.

2108. Thuruthumaly, J. "The Joy of the Psalmist." *Bible Bhashyam* 13 (1987): 100-104.

2109. Tromp, Nicholas J. *Primitive Conceptions of Death and the Netherworld in the Old Testament.* Biblica et Orientalia 21. Rome: Pontifical Biblical Institute, 1969. xxiv+241p.

The conceptions of death and the netherworld in the Ugaritic mythological texts are also found in the Old

Testament, particularly in the poetic literature, in a far richer and more pervasive way than has been recognized.

Reviewed by G.M. Landes in *JBL* 89 (1970): 473-474.

2110. Trublet, Jacques. "Le motif de la création dans les Psaumes." *Foi et Vie* 87 (1988): 23-48.

2111. ______. "Violence et prière. Essai sur les Psaumes d'imprécation." *Christus* 27 (1980): 220-224.

2112. Uffenheimer, Binyamin. "The Religious Experience of the Psalmists and the Prophetic Mind." *Immanuel* 21 (Summer, 1987): 7-27.

2113. Ungern-Sternberg, R. "Das Wohnen im Hause Gottes; eine terminologische Psalmenstudie." *Kerygma und Dogma* 17 (1971): 209-223.

2114. Vawter, Bruce. "Intimations of Immortality in the Old Testament." *Journal of Biblical Literature* 91 (1972): 158-171.

Dahood has argued that the Psalms testify rather extensively to an Israelite faith in resurrection and immortality. He has not properly understood the relevant passages, because he makes a mistake in reading these passages "according to the philologically possible rather than according to the theologically probable."

2115. Veit, M. "Die Psalmen und Wir." *Der Evangelische Erzieher* 32 (1980): 467-482.

2116. Vonck, P. "L'expression de confiance dans le Psautier." *Publications de L'université Lovanium de Kishasa* (1969): 1-51.

2117. Vosbergh, L. *Studien zum Reden vom Schöpfer in den Psalmen.* Munich: Chr. Kaiser Verlag, 1975.

Reviewed in *CBQ* 39 (1977): 136-137.

2118. Wächter, Ludwig. *Der Tod im Alten Testament.* Arbeiten zur Theologie 2/8. Stuttgart: Calwer Verlag, 1967. 233p.

2119. Wagner, N.E. "רנה in the Psalter." *Vetus Testamentum* 10 (1960): 435-441.

2120. Wanke, Gunther. *Die Zionstheologie der Korachiten.* Beihefte zur Zeitschrift für die alttestamentliche Wissenschaft 97. 1966. Berlin: Töpelmann, 1966. v+120p.

The Korahite theology originated in the exile or later; thus there is no basis for recognizing a pre-exilic Zion theology or a tradition of Zion songs.

Reviewed by M. Buss in *JBL* 86 (1967): 358-359; reviewed also in *CBQ* 29 (1967): 185.

2121. Weijden, Athanasius Henricus van der. *Die 'Gerechtigkeit' in den Psalmen.* Nijmegen: Janssen, 1952. xvi+251p.

Reviewed in *CBQ* 15 (1953): 505-507.

2122. Westermann, Claus. "Anthropologische und theologische Aspekte des Gebets in den Psalmen." *Liturgisches Jahrbuch* 23 (1973): 83-96. Reprinted in *Zur Neueren*

Psalmenforschung, ed. Peter H.A. Neumann, 452-468; Darmstadt: Wissenschaftliche Buchgesellschaft, 1976.

2123. Wolverton, Wallace I. "The Psalmist's Belief in God's Presence." *Canadian Journal of Theology* 9 (1963): 82-94.

2124. ______. "The Meaning of the Psalms." *Anglican Theological Review* 47 (1965): 16-33.

2125. Zenger, Erich. "Was wird anders beim kanonischer Psalmenauslegung?" In *Ein Gott -- Eine Offenbarung. Beiträge zur biblischen Exegese, Theologie und Spiritualität. Festschrift Notker Füglister*, ed. F.V. Reiterer. 397-413. Würzburg: Echter Verlag, 1991.

2126. Zolli, Eugenio. *I Salmi. Documenti di Vita Vissuta.* Milan: Edizione Viola, 1953. 178p.

Examines the psychology of the Psalter.
Reviewed in *CBQ* 16 (1954): 487-488.

See also: 1247.

10. Public Worship and Private Devotion

A. Worship and Devotion

2127. Aeschbacher, G. "Bemerkungen zur rhythmische Gestalt des Huguenotten Psalters." In *Festschrift Arnold Geering.* 11. Berne, 1972.

2128. Aymard, P. *Prier avec les Psaumes. Présentation et choix de textes.* Brussels: Desclée De Brouwer, 1977. 152p.

The Psalms are arranged according to themes. Certain Psalms are modified by substituting quotations from other Psalms for seemingly irrelevant passages.

2129. Baldermann, Ingo. *Wer hört mein Weinen? Kinder entdecken sich selbst in den Psalmen.* Wege des Lernens 4. Neukirchen-Vluyn: Neukirchener Verlag, 1986. 133p.

2130. ______. *Ich werde nicht sterben, sondern leben. Psalmen als Gebrauchtexte.* Wegen des Lernen 7. Neukirchen-Vluyn: Neukirchener Verlag, 1990. 146p.

2131. Barmann, Lawrence. "Newman on the Psalms as Christian Prayer." *Worship* 38 (1964): 207-214.

2132. *Bay Psalm Book, The.* A facsimile reprint of the first edition of 1640. Chicago: University of Chicago Press (1956).

2133. Beaucamp, Évode. "Le Psautier: Répertoire des chants liturgiques d'Israël." *Science et Esprit* 23 (1971): 153-166, 343-366.

2134. ______. *Israël en prière. Des Psaumes au Notre Père.* Lire la Bible 69. Paris: Éditions du Cerf, 1985. 263p.

2135. Beauchamp, Paul. *Psaumes Nuit et Jour.* Paris: Éditions du Seuil, 1980. 254p. German edition: *Ich rufe zu dir bei Tag und bei Nacht. Die Psalmen als Gebete der Christen.* Düsseldorf: Patmos Verlag, 1983. 229p.

1) The Psalms and Us. 2) Supplication. 3) Praise. 4) Promise. 5) The Psalms and the World: Psalms 8, 19, 104, and 139 refer to "creation at hand"; Psalms 74, 89, and 136 refer to "remote creation"; Psalms 93-98 refer to "creation to come." An exposition of Psalm 22 serves as a recapitulation. Reviewed in *CBQ* 43 (1981): 436-437.

2136. Bence, Barry. "The Psalms in Ministry." *Word and World* 5 (1985): 188-191.

2137. Berger, H. *Untersuchungen zu den Psalmdifferenzen.* Regensburg: Pustet, 1966.

2138. Berrigan, Daniel. *Uncommon Prayer: A Book of Psalms.* Illustrations by Robert McGovern. New York: A Crossroad Book (Seabury Press), 1978. xii+145p.

2139. Blanchard, P. "Le Psautier dans la liturgie." In *Richesses et déficiences des anciens Psautier latins,* ed. D.R. Weber. Collectanea Biblica Latina 13. 231-248. Rome: Abbaye Saint Jérôme, 1959.

2140. Blenkinsopp, Joseph. "Can We Pray the Cursing Psalms?" In *A Sketchbook of Biblical Theology.* 83-87. New York: Herder and Herder, 1968.

2141. Bonhoeffer, Dietrich. *Das Gebetbuch der Bibel: Eine Einführung in die Psalmen. Mit einem Einblick in Bonhoeffers Leben und Schaffen von Eberhard Bethge.* Bad Salzuflen: Verlag für Missions- und Bibel-Kunde, 1940; reprint, 1953; reprinted in *Gesammelte Schriften* IV, ed. E. Bethge; 544-569; Munich: Chr. Kaiser Verlag, 1965; 9th ed., Neuhausen-Stuttgart: Hänssler-Verlag, 1978. 47p. Translated from the 8th German edition of 1966 by James H. Burtness and published in English as *Psalms: The Prayer Book of the Bible*, with a sketch on the life of Dietrich Bonhoeffer by Eberhard Bethge. Minneapolis, MN: Augsburg Publishing House, 1970; reprint, 1983. 86p. New German edition: *Das Gebetbuch der Bibel: Eine Einfuhrung in die Psalmen, Dietrich Bonhoeffer Werke 5*, ed. Gerhard L. Muller and Albrecht Schönherr; Munich: Chr. Kaiser Verlag, 1987. Translated into English by James H. Burtness and published as *The Prayerbook of the Bible: An Introduction to the Psalms*, ed. Geffrey B. Kelly in conjunction with Muller and Schönherr. Minneapolis, MN: Fortress Press, 1992.

The role of the psalms within the prayer life of the church. Just as Jesus Christ taught us to pray the words of the Lord's Prayer, so "the prayer book of the Bible" contains in greater fullness and richness the words which God wants us to speak to God in the name of Jesus Christ. The Psalms are given to us in order that we may learn to pray in the name of Jesus Christ. David is a prototype of Jesus Christ, so that whatever happens to him happens for the sake of Jesus Christ, who is in him and shall go out of him.

The following themes are represented in the Psalms: creation, law, holy history, Messiah, church, life, suffering, guilt, the enemies, and the end time. It would not be difficult to arrange all of these as parts of the Lord's Prayer and to show how the Psalter can be taken up completely into the prayer of Jesus.

Reviewed by Geffrey B. Kelly in *Weavings: A Journal of the Christian Spiritual Life* VI/5 (1991): 36-41; Roland E. Murphy, *Catholic Biblical Quarterly* 32 (1970): 598-599.

2142. ______. *Meditating on the Word.* Translated from selected works in *Gesammelte Schriften* (Ed. Eberhard Bethge; Munich: Chr. Kaiser Verlag, 1958f) and edited by David McI. Gracie. Afterword by John Vannorsdall. Nashville, TN: The Upper Room, 1986. 154p.

2143. Botz, P. "Praying the Psalms." *Worship* 46 (1972): 204-213.

2144. Breit, H. "Die Psalmen in der christlichen Kirche." *Klerus Blatt* 45 (1965): 379-384.

2145. Brillet, Gaston. *365 Méditations sur la Bible -- Les Psaumes.* Les Editions Montaigne, 1958. English version: *The Psalms -- Meditations on the Old Testament.* Translated by Jane Wynne Saul. New York: Desclee Company, 1960. 243p.

2146. Brownlow, Leroy. *A Psalm in My Heart: Daily Devotionals from the Book of Psalms.* Fort Worth, TX: Brownlow Publishing Co., 1989. 367p.

2147. Brueggemann, Walter. "Psalms and the Life of Faith." *Journal for the Study of the Old Testament* 17 (1980): 3-32.

2148. ______. "Reservoirs of Unreason." *Reformed Liturgy and Music* 17 (1983): 99-104.

Liturgy and the lament psalms.

2149. ______. "The Psalms as Prayer." *Reformed Liturgy and Music* 23 (Winter, 1989): 13-26.

2150. Candole, H. de. *The Christian Use of the Psalms.* London: Oxford University Press, 1955.

2151. Coddaire, Louis, and Louis Weil. "The Use of the Psalter in Worship." *Worship* 52 (1978): 342-348.

2152. Collins, Donald E. *Like Trees That Grow Beside a Stream: Praying Through the Psalms.* Nashville, TN: The Upper Room, 1991. 214p.

2153. Collins, Mary. "Glorious Praise: The ICEL Liturgical Psalter." *Worship* 66 (1992): 290-310.

2154. Council, Raymond. "Out of the Depths: Pastoral Care to the Severely Depressed." *Pastoral Psychology* 31 (Fall, 1982): 58-64.

2155. Cullinan, Thomas. "Opening Words on the Psalms." *Clergy Review* 63 (1978): 205-207.

The staying-power of the Psalms as Christian and Jewish prayer derives from their beginning with people where they are, not necessarily where they ought to be.

2156. Cunningham, Lawrence S. "Praying the Psalms." *Theology Today* 46 (1989): 39-44.

2157. Davidson, Robert. *Wisdom and Worship.* London: SCM Press, 1990; Philadelphia: Trinity Press International, 1990. xi+148p.

2158. Dawson, Gerrit S. "Praying the Difficult Psalms." *Weavings: A Journal of the Christian Spiritual Life* VI/5 (1991): 28-35.

2159. Dearman, J. Andrew. "The Psalms as Prayers." *Austin Seminary Bulletin* 101 (1985): 25-30.

2160. Dunlop, Lawrence. *Patterns of Prayer in the Psalms.* New York, 1982.

2161. Dunnam, Maxie. *Living the Psalms: A Confidence for All Seasons.* Nashville, TN: The Upper Room, 1991. 157p.

A study book prepared with both individuals and groups in mind. 2 vol. videocassette available.

2162. Elbogen, Ismar (1874-1943). *Der jüdische Gottesdienst in seiner geschichtlichen Entwicklung.* Leipzig and Berlin: G. Fock, 1913. 2nd ed., Frankfurt am Main: J. Kaufmann, 1924. 3rd ed., 1931. xv+635p. Reprinted, Hildesheim: Olms, 1962. Translated into English by Raymond P. Scheindlin and Published as *Jewish Liturgy: A Comprehensive History.* Philadelphia: Jewish Publication Society; New York: Jewish Theological Seminary of America, 1993.

2163. Emery, Pierre-Yves. *La méditation de l'Écriture, et, Les psaumes, prière pur l'Église.* 4th ed., Taizé: Les Presses de Taizé, 1967. 78p.

2164. Fischer, Balthasar. "How to Pray the Psalms." *Orates Fratres: A Review Concerned with the Problems of Liturgical Renewal* 25 (1950-1951): 10-20.

2165. ______. "Gemeinschaftsgebet in den christlichen Gemeinden und in der christlichen Familie in der alten Christenheit." *Liturgisches Jahrbuch* 24 (1974): 92-109.

The transition from primitive Christian hymns to the use of the complete Psalter was slow and met with some resistance. It is remarkable that psalmody found its way into the homes of early Christians.

2166. Fischer, K. *Die Psalmkompositionen in Rom in ausgehenden 16. und beginnenden 17. Jahrhundert.* Diss., University of Cologne, 1970; rev. Regensburg: Pustet, 1979.

2167. Füglister, Notker. *Das Psalmengebet.* Munich: Kösel-Verlag, 1965; French version: *Les Psaumes, prière poétique*, 1967.

German version reviewed in *CBQ* 28 (1966): 355.

2168. Garrone, G. *How to Pray the Psalms.* Notre Dame, IN: Fides Publishers Inc., 1965.

2169. Gasnier, Michael. *Les Psaumes, école de spiritualité.* Paris: Éditions Salvator-Mulhouse, 1957. 214p. Translated into English by Aldhelm Dean and published as *The Psalms: School of Spirituality.* St. Louis, MO: B. Herder, 1961; London: Challoner, 1962. v+160p.

English version reviewed in *CBQ* 24 (1962): 476.

2170. Gelin, Albert. *The Psalms Are Our Prayers.* Translated by Michael J. Bell. Collegeville, MN: Liturgical Press, 1964. 61p.

Reviewed in *CBQ* 27 (1965): 192.

2171. Gelston, Anthony. "Psalms at the Daily Services." *Churchman: Journal of Anglican Theology* 89 (1975): 267-275.

2172. George, Augustin. *Prier les Psaumes.* Supplément à *Équipes enseignantes.* Paris, 1960. English version: *Praying the Psalms: A Guide for Using the Psalms as Christian Prayer.* Translated from the French by Richard X. Redmond. Scripture Study Series. Notre Dame, IN: Fides Publishers, Inc., 1964.

Second edition of French version reviewed in *CBQ* 24 (1962): 477.

2173. Grün, Synkletika. *Psalmengebet im Lichte des NT.* Regensburg: Friedrich Pustet, 1959. 482p.

2174. Heiler, Friedrich (1892-1967). *Das Gebet. Eine religionsgeschichtliche und religionspsychologische Untersuchung.* 2nd ed. Munich: E. Reinhardt, 1920. xix+558p. 5th ed., 1923. Reprint, 1969. Translated into English by Samuel McComb with the assistance of J. Edgar Park and published as *Prayer. A Study in the History and Psychology of Religion.* New York: Oxford University Press, 1932. 2nd ed., 1958.

2175. Heinen, Karl. "Die Psalmen -- Gebete für Christen?" *Bibel und Liturgie* 51 (1978): 232-235.

2176. Himbaugh, M. Cecilia. *The Psalms in Modern Life.* Chicago: Regnery, 1960. xi+259p.

Intended as a companion to the Breviary.
Reviewed in *CBQ* 24 (1962): 351-352.

2177. Hinricher, Gemma. "Die Fluch- und Vergeltungspsalmen im Stundengebet." *Bibel und Kirche* 35 (1980): 55-59.

2178. Hustad, Donald P. "The Psalms as Worship Expression: Personal and Congregational." *Review and Expositor: A Baptist Theological Journal* 81 (1984): 407-424.

2179. Jacob, Edmond. "Prier avec les Psaumes." *Foi et Vie* 84 (1985): 58-66.

2180. Janecko, Benedict. *The Psalms. Heartbeat of Life and Worship.* St. Meinrad, IN: Abbey Press, 1986. 83p.

2181. Jungmann, Joseph A. *The Mass of the Roman Rite, Its Origins and Development.* Translated by Francis A. Brunner. 2 vols. New York: Benziger Brothers, Inc., 1951, 1955.

2182. Kaniarakath, G. "Praying the Psalms as an Experience of Prophetic Solidarity." *Jeevadhara* 19 (1989): 105-117.

2183. Kessler, Colette. "Les psaumes dans la liturgie juive." *Lumière et Vie* 40 (1991): 13-24.

2184. Knockaert, André. "Intérioriser les psaumes." *Lumen Vitae* 38 (1983): 51-61.

2185. Knox, Ronald A. *The Book of Psalms in Latin and English with the Canticles Used in the Divine Office.* New York: Sheed & Ward, 1948. xi+451p.

2186. Lacan, M.-F. "Les Psaumes, prière de l'Église." *La Vie Spirituelle* 112 (1965): 519-530.

2187. Lamb, John Alexander. *The Psalms in Christian Worship.* London: Faith Press, 1962.

Surveys the use of the psalms in various rites and denominations.

2188. Lamparter, Helmut. *Das Psalmengebet in der Christengemeinde. Eine Einführung in das Gebetbuch der Bibel.* Calwer Hefte 75. Stuttgart: Calwer Verlag, 1965. 44p.

2189. Landau, Rudolf. "'...der hoch in der Höhe thront -- der tief in die Tiefe sieht.' Einige Aspekte zur Bedeutung des Psalters für die Praxis der Kirche." In *Werden und Wirken des Alten Testaments. Festschrift für Claus Westermann zum 70. Geburtstag,* ed. R. Albertz, R. Müller, H.-P. Wolff, and W. Zimmerli. 334-354. Göttingen: Vandenhoeck & Ruprecht, 1980; Neukirchen-Vluyn: Neukirchener Verlag, 1980.

2190. Leafblad, Bruce H. "The Psalms in Christian Worship." *Southwestern Journal of Theology* 27 (1984): 40-53.

2191. Limburg, James. "The Autumn Leaves: Pages from the Psalter for Late Pentecost." *Word and World* 12 (1992): 272-277.

2192. McCandless, J. Bardarah. "Enfleshing the Psalms." *Religious Education* 81 (1986): 372-390.

2193. Martini, Carlo Maria. *What Am I That You Care for Me? Praying with the Psalms.* Collegeville, MN: Liturgical Press, 1992. 138p.

Part I is a devotional study of six psalms. Part II, "The School of the Word," includes New Testament-inspired reflections on Psalm 51.

2194. Meyer, Stephen G. "The Psalms and Personal Counseling." *Journal of Psychology and Theology* 2 (1974): 26-30.

2195. Miller, Patrick D., Jr. "The Psalms and Pastoral Care." *Reformed Liturgy Music* 24 (1990): 647-655.

2196. Miriam, Vincent. "Choral Speaking with the Psalms." *Worship* 33 (1959): 171-174.

2197. Mohrmann, Ch. "A propos des collectes du psautier." *Vigiliae christianae: A Review of Early Christian Life and Language* 6 (1952): 1-19.

While Wilmart and Brou are correct in assigning the collects from the first two series in their book to Africa and Spain, it is better to think of the third series (Roman) as having its place of origin in the Calabrian *Closter Vivarium* with Cassiodorus as the suggested editor. The custom of ending the reading of the Psalm with an oration is attested for the first time by Cassianus with regard to the Egyptian monks. It is here that a Christian *relecture* of the Psalter takes place.

2198. Morgan, Dewi. *Arising from the Psalms.* New York: Morehouse-Barlow Co., 1966.

2199. Morse, Merrill. *Psalms for Troubled Times.* Collegeville, MN: The Liturgical Press, 1991. 192p.

While often dark, the psalms of lamentation can be an intensely personal and rewarding way to address life's stresses and sorrows.

2200. Motte, Dominique. "L'homme des psaumes." *Lumière et Vie* 40 (1991): 123-140.

How is one to join the person or speaker who prays in the psalms?

2201. Mowbray, Thomas L. "The Function in Ministry of Psalms Dealing with Anger: The Angry Psalmist." *Journal of Pastoral Counseling* 21 (1986): 34-39.

2202. Müller, Augustin R. "Altes Testament und Liturgie." *Archiv für Liturgie Wissenschaft* 26 (1984): 361-375.

Summary of the literature.

2203. Negoitsa, Athanase. "The Psalter in the Orthodox Church." *Svensk Exegetisk Årsbok* 32 (1967): 56-68.

2204. Newell, Herbert. "The Psalter in the Parish Worship of the Church of England." *The Expository Times* 66 (1955): 323-325.

2205. Old, Hughes Oliphant. "The Psalms of Praise in the Worship of the New Testament Church." *Interpretation* 39 (1985): 20-33.

2206. Otto, Echart. "Sigmund Mowinckels Bedeutung für die gegenwärtige Liturgiedebatte: Ein Beitrag zur Applikationsproblematik biblischer Überlieferung." *Jahrbuch für Liturgie und Hymnologie* 19 (1975): 19-36.

2207. Owens, John Joseph and Mary Frances Owens. "Teaching the Psalms." *Review and Expositor* 81 (1984): 461-466.

2208. Peifer, Claude. "The Psalms as Christian Prayer." *The Bible Today* 65 (1973): 1100-1106.

2209. Pereira, Theodore. "The Psalms as Prayer for Today." *Vidyajyoti* (1975): 242-251.

2210. Peterson, Eugene H. *A Year with the Psalms: 365 Meditations and Prayers.* Waco, TX: Word Books, 1979.

2211. ______. *Answering God. The Psalms as Tools for Prayer.* San Francisco: Harper & Row, 1989. vii+151p.

2212. Pinell, J. *Liber Orationum Psalmographicus. Colectas de Salmos de antiquo Rito Hispanico. Rec. y edition critica.* Monumenta Hispaniae Sacra. Serie Liturgica 9. Barcelona-Madrid: Consejo Superior de Investigaciones Científicas, Instituto F. Enrique Flórez, 1972.

The *Psalmenorationes* of the old Spanish liturgy.

2213. *Psalms of Hope. Psalms of Joy. Psalms of Love. Psalms of Praise. Psalms of Thanksgiving.* Videographed and edited by Gerard Pottebaum. 30 minutes each. Loveland, OH: Treehaus Communications, 1986. Videocassette.

A Series of 30-minute video meditations with music on the Psalms. Hope: Psalms 139, 62, 16, 27, 65, 23, 121. Joy: Psalms 100, 104, 96, and 8. Love: Psalms 147, 91, 19, 34, and 63. Praise: Psalms 145, 103, 67, 146, and 148. Thanksgiving: Psalms 84, 111, 107, and 29.

2214. *Psalms of Mercy, Psalms of Joy, Psalms of Gratitude, Psalms of Peace.* Collegeville, MN: The Liturgical Press, 1993. 64p each.

Reflections and prayers on various psalms.

2215. *Psalms of Tenderness, Psalms of Trust, Psalms of Friendship, Psalms of Suffering.* Collegeville, MN: The Liturgical Press, 1991. 64p each.

2216. *Psalter, The: Part I. A Selection of the Most Frequently Appointed Psalms.* Prayer Book Studies 23. New York: The Church Hymnal Corporation, 1970.

2217. Quesson, Noël. *50 Psaumes pour tous les jours.* Limoges, France: Droguet & Ardant. Translated into English and edited by Marie-France Curtin and published as *The Spirit of the Psalms.* Mahwah, NJ: Paulist Press, 1991. 272p.

50 psalms are looked at "with Israel," "with Jesus," and "with our time."

2218. Rabinowitz, L.J. "The Psalms in Jewish Liturgy." *Historia Judaica* 6 (1944): 109-122.

2219. Richardson, Robert D. "The Psalms as Christian Prayer and Praises." *Anglican Theological Review* 42 (1960): 326-346.

2220. Salmon, P. "De l'interpretation des psaumes dans la liturgie aux origenes de l'office divin." In *L'office divin*, ed. P. Salmon. Lex Orandi 27. 100-134. Paris: Édtions du Cerf, 1955. English version: "The Interpretation of the Psalms during the Formative Period of the Office." In *The Breviary through the Centuries*. Translated by D.M. Hanley. 42-61. Collegeville, MN: Liturgical Press, 1962.

2221. Schattauer, Thomas H. "The Koinonicon of the Byzantine Liturgy: An Historical Study." *Orientalia Christiana Periodica* 49 (1983): 91-129.

2222. Schilling, Othmar. *Israels Lieder -- Gebete der Kirche. Vergegenwärtigung der Psalmen.* Stuttgart: Katholisches Bibelwerk, 1966. 163p.

2223. Schneider, H. "Psalmenfrömmigkeit einst und heute." *Geist und Leben* 33 (1960): 359-369.

2224. Schneider, Severin. "Das Denken in Bildern als Voraussetzung für das persönliche Psalmenbeten." *Bibel und Kirche* 35 (1980): 47-54.

The personal application of the Psalms takes place not by "accommodation" but by entering into the imagery of the Psalter in order to perceive the underlying thought.

2225. Shepherd, Massey H., Jr. *The Psalms in Christian Worship. A Practical Guide.* Minneapolis, MN: Augsburg

Publishing House, 1976; Collegeville, MN: The Liturgical Press, 1976. 128p.

2226. ______. *A Liturgical Psalter for the Christian Year.* Minneapolis, MN: Augsburg Press, 1976; Collegeville, MN: The Liturgical Press, 1976. 125p.

2227. Simundson, Daniel J. "Mental Health in the Bible." *Word & World* 9 (1989): 140-146.

2228. Strandling, Leslie E. *Praying the Psalms.* Foreword by George E. Sweazey. London: SPCK, 1977; Philadelphia: Fortress Press, 1977. 119p.

2229. Ströle, Benedikta. "Psalmen -- Lieder der Verfolgten." *Bibel und Kirche* 35 (1980): 42-47.

The contemporary relevance of those psalms which are cries for help.

2230. Stuhlmueller, Carroll. "Reality of Presence and Praise in the Psalms." In *Biblical Studies in Contemporary Thought*, ed. Miriam Ward. 77-87. Somerville, MA: Greeno, Hadden and Co., 1975.

2231. Taylor, Charles L. *A Layman's Guide to 70 Psalms -- For Devotion and Study.* Nashville, TN: Abingdon Press, 1973. 128p.

2232. Troeger, Thomas H. *Rage! Reflect! Rejoice! Praying with the Psalmists.* Philadelphia: Westminster Press, 1977. 96p.

An attempt to capture the real emotions linked to prayer in ten psalms.

2233. Vanek, Elizabeth Anne. "The Psalms: Praying from where one is." *Emmanuel* 96 (1990): 434-437, 447-448.

2234. Verbraken, Patrick. *Oraisons sur les Cent Cinquante Psaumes.* Lex Orandi 42. Paris: Les Éditions du Cerf, 1967.

The *Psalmenorationes.* The orientation is liturgical and the psalms are viewed as pointing toward Christ. The prayers are in Latin, with French translation.

2235. Vogel, Dwight W. *The Psalms for Worship Today.* St. Louis, MO: Concordia Publishing House, 1974.

A booklet for use in community prayer, using *The Psalms for Modern Man.*

2236. V-Skij, P. "The Meaning and Structure of the Hexapsalmion." *The Journal of the Moscow Patriarchate* 10 (1968): 62-68.

Liturgical explanation of the six repeating psalms of the matin (Psalms 3, 37, 62, 87, 102, 142 [LXX]). A brief history of Russian Psalm translation is included.

2237. Wahl, Thomas Peter. "Praying Israel's Psalms Responsibly as Christians: An Exercise in Hermeneutic." *Worship* 54 (1980): 386-396.

2238. _____. "Psalms in Christian Prayer." *Worship* 63 (1989): 143-148.

2239. _____. "The Lord's Song in a Foreign Land." *Worship* 66 (1992): 66-80, 171-176, 339-352, 427-448.

The Psalms in liturgy.

2240. Wallwork, Norman. "The Psalter and the Divine Office." *Studia Liturgica* 12 (1977): 46-64.

2241. Wilmart, A., and L. Brou. *The Psalter Collects from V-VI century sources.* Henry Bradshaw Society 83. London: Henry Bradshaw Society, 1949.

This collection of the *Psalmenorationes* contains three series: African, Spanish, and Roman.

2242. Wolfenden, Graham. "The Psalms in Jewish and Early Christian Worship." *Priests and People* 4 (1990): 309-313.

2243. Worden, Thomas. *The Psalms Are Christian Prayer.* New York: Sheed and Ward, 1961.

Reviewed in *CBQ* 25 (1963): 500-501.

2244. Wyrtzen, Don. *A Musician Looks at the Psalms: A Journal of Daily Meditations.* Foreword by Charles R. Swindoll. Grand Rapids, MI: Daybreak Books (Zondervan Publishing House), 1988. 416p.

2245. Yancey, Philip D. "How I Learned to Stop Hating and Start Loving the Psalms." *Christianity Today* 33 (October 6, 1989): 28-29, 30-32.

2246. Zyl, D.C. van. "Psalmhermeneuse en psalmberyming." *Nederduits Gereformeerde Teologiese Tydskrif* 29 (1988): 61-65.

Reflections concerning the principles that should underlie the production of metrical versions of the Psalms for Christian liturgical use.

B. Preaching and Sermons

2247. Achtemeier, Elizabeth. "Preaching from the Psalms." *Review and Expositor* 81 (1984): 437-449.

2248. Birch, Bruce C. "Homiletical Resources: The Psalter as Preaching Text." *Quarterly Review (Methodist)* 1 (Winter, 1981): 61-93.

2249. Bosley, Harold A. *Sermons on the Psalms.* New York: Harper and Brothers, 1956. 208p.

Psalms 1, 14, 16, 19, 27:1-14, 30:1-12, 60:1-4 and 61:1-8, 62, 73:1-28, 74:1-12, 74:1-23, 77:1-15, 78:1-8, 118:1-9,19-24,29, 121:1-8 and 127:1, 137, 139:1-18, 147:1-20, 149:1-5 and 150:1-6.

2250. Briscoe, Stuart. *What Works When Life Doesn't.* Foreword by Hudson T. Armerding. Wheaton, IL: Victor Books (SP Publications), 1976.

Twelve selected psalms show how the psalms speak to our deepest emotions -- those of death, depression, and fear.

2251. Calvin, John (1509-1564). *Der Psalter auf der Kanzel Calvins. Bisher unbekannte Psalmenpredigten.* Edited with an Introduction by Erwin Mülhaupt. Neukirchen: Neukirchener Verlag der Buchhandlung des Erziehungsvereins, 1959. 134p.

2252. ______. *Psalmpredigten; Passions-, Oster und Pfingstpredigten Johannes Calvin.* Ed. Erwin Mülhaupt. Supplementa Calviniana, Sermons inédits 7. Neukirchen: Neukirchener Verlag der Buchhandlung des Erziehungsvereins, 1981. liv+184p.

2253. Chappell, Clovis G. *Sermons from the Psalms.* Nashville, TN: Cokesbury Press, 1931. 215p.

Psalms 119:71, 23:1, 103:2, 22:1, 1:3, 119:59, 73:2, 56:9, 66:16, 8:6, 39:1, 30:5, 27:13, 42:1, 40:3, 34:3, 85:6.

2254. Donne, John (1573-1631). *Sermons on the Psalms and Gospels. With a Selection of Prayers and Meditations.* Edited with an Introduction by Evelyn M. Simpson. Berkeley: University of California Press, 1963. Reprint, 1974. 244p.

2255. Dotts, Ted J., Jr. "Recognizing the Tone: Preaching from the Psalms During Pentecost." *Quarterly Review (Methodist)* 8 (1988): 71-88.

2256. Drennan, Hugh H. *Aids to the Psalms. Exploring the Message, Cycle C.* Lima, OH: C.S.S. Publishing Co., 1991. 152p.

2257. ______. *Aids to the Psalms: Exploring the Message, Cycle A.* Lima, OH: C.S.S. Publishing Co., 1992. 152p.

2258. Earles, Brent D. *Psalms for Graduates.* Grand Rapids,MI: Baker Book House, 1984. 152p.

A collection of 31 meditations for graduates based on the Psalm.

2259. Ebeling, Gerhard. *Psalmenmeditationen.* Tübingen: J.C.B. Mohr, 1968. 176p.

2260. Gaiser, Frederick J. "'Come and See What God Has Done': The Psalms of Easter." *Word and World* 7 (1987): 207-214.

2261. Gerstenberger, Erhard S. "Enemies and Evildoers in the Psalms: A Challenge to Christian Preaching." *Horizons in Biblical Theology* 5 (1983): 61-77.

2262. Guardini,Romano. *Universitätspredigten.* 1955. Translated into French by Madelaine Cé and published as *Psaumes et Fêtes: Sermons Universitaires.* Paris: Éditions du Cerf, 1961. 274p.

Eight of the thirteen sermons are on the Psalms, covering Psalms 1, (23(22), 91(90), 139(138), 114-115(113), 148, and 104(103).

Reviewed in *CBQ* 23 (1961): 388.

2263. Hamilton, Stephen A. "Violent Vengeance in the Psalms: Can It Possibly Preach?" *Journal for Preachers* 14 (3, 1991): 16-22.

2264. Herntrich, Volkmar. *Das Loblied der Gemeinde. Psalmenpredigten.* Theologische Existenz Heute 73. Munich: Evangelische Verlag, 1940.

2265. Howell, James C. "Jerome's Homilies on the Psalter in Bethlehem." In *The Listening Heart: Essays in Wisdom and the Psalms in Honor of Roland E. Murphy.* Ed. K.G. Hoglund and Others. Journal for the Study of the Old

Testament Supplement Series 58. 181-197. Sheffield: JSOT Press, 1987.

2266. Hull, William E. "Preaching on the Psalms." *Review and Expositor* 81 (1984): 451-456.

2267. Jacobson, Delmar L. "The Royal Psalms and Jesus Messiah: Preparing to Preach on a Royal Psalm." *Word and World* 5 (1985): 192-198.

2268. Kameeta, Zephania. *Why, O Lord: Psalms and Sermons from Namibia.* Geneva: World Council of Churches, 1986. x+62p.

2269. Kraus, Hans-Joachim, and J. Tibbe. *Psalmenpredigten.* Alttestamentliche Predigten 3. Neukirchen Kreis Moers: Neukirchener Verlag, 1958. 113p.

2270. Laestadius, Lars Levi (1800-1861). *Evangeliepostilla. Nytt urval av hans baesta predikningar i oeversaettning fraan finska spraaeket, aemnesrubriker, psalmfoerslag, kort levnadsteckning med illustrationer samt ordfoerklaringar av Per Boreman....* Stockholm: Svenska Kyrkans Diakonistyrelses Bokfoerlag, 1957. 416p.

2271. McEachern, Alton E. "Preaching from the Psalms." *Review and Expositor* 81 (1984): 457-460.

2272. McKay, D.P. "Cotton Mather's Unpublished Singing Sermon [with text]." *New England Quarterly* 48 (1975): 410-422.

2273. Mischke, Bernard C. *Meditations on the Psalms.* New York: Sheed and Ward, 1963. ix+298p.

Reviewed in *CBQ* 25 (1963): 516.

2274. Neumann, F. *Where do we Stand? A Selective Homiletical Commentary on the Old Testament. Vol. III. Escape from Futility. The Psalms and Wisdom Literature.* With introductions by James Muilenburg and Donald E. Gowan. Brooklyn, NY: Theo. Gaus, 1979. xii+298p.

Fifty-three sermons, forty-one of which are on the Psalms.

2275. Ogilvie, Lloyd John. *Falling into Greatness.* Nashville, TN: Thomas Nelson, 1984. 218p.

Psalms 1, 8, 17, 23, 27, 42, 46, 55, 62, 73, 84, 90 and 91, 95, 100, 103, 116, 121, 139, 145.

2276. Parsons, Greg W. "Guidelines for Understanding and Proclaiming the Psalms." *Bibliotheca Sacra* 147 (1990): 169-187.

2277. Perron, Ernest. *Meditations sur dix psaumes.* Beatenberg: École Biblioque, 1960. 51p.

2278. Redding, David A. *Psalms of David.* Westwood, NJ: Fleming H. Revell, 1963. xvii+171p.

2279. Rothuizen, G.Th. *Landschap. Een bundel gedachten over de Psalmen.* Kampen: Kok, 1965. Translated into English by John F. Jansen and published as *Landscape: A Bundle of Thoughts about the Psalms (1-50).* Richmond, VA: John Knox Press, 1971.

2280. Routley, Erik. *Ascent to the Cross. St. Giles' Lectures for Holy Week, 1961.* London: SCM Press, 1962; Nashville, TN: Abingdon, 1962. 94p.

Primarily a devotion. I. He will keep your life (Psalms 120, 121, 122); II. Their anger was kindled (Psalms 123, 124, 125); III. Around your table (Psalms 126, 127, 128); IV. Out of the deep (Psalms 129, 130, 131); V. Together in Unity (Psalms 132, 133, 134).

2281. Scammon, John H. "The Minister and the Psalms." *Andover Newton Quarterly* 1 (1960): 28-38.

2282. *Sermon Bible, The.* Vols. II: 240-520; III: 1-255. New York: Funk and Wagnalls Co. (c1890).

A collection of sermonic outlines from a variety of authors and sources.

2283. Smith, Robert Ora. *Meditations on the Psalms. Meditations on the Themes of Evil, God, Good, Life, Nationalism, Prayer, Suffering, and Universalism.* New York: William Frederick Press, 1956. 45p.

2284. Snowden, Rita F. *Psalms in the Midst of Life.* Philadelphia: Fortress Press, 1963. Also published under the title *Sung in our Hearts,* London: Epworth Press, 1963. 124p.

A collection of 29 meditations based on the Psalms.

2285. Sundstroem, Erland. *Oss foeljer ju herden. Meditationer kring tjugotredje psalmen.* Stockholm: Missionsfoerbundets foerlag, 1965. 55p.

2286. Throntveit, Mark A. "The Penitential Psalms and Lenten Discipline." *Lutheran Quarterly,* N.S., 1 (1987): 495-512.

Psalms 6, 32, 38, 51, 102, 130, 143.

2287. Toombs, Lawrence E. "The Psalter." Chap. in *The Old Testament in Christian Preaching.* 166-186. Philadelphia: Westminister Press, 1961.

2288. Watkinson, R.L., W. Forsyth, Joseph S. Exell, and William Jones. *The Preacher's Complete Homiletic Commentary on the Book of Psalms.* Vol. I. New York: Funk & Wagnalls, n.d.

2289. Wesley, John (1703-1791). *The Works of John Wesley.* Vols. 1-4: *Sermons.* Bicentennial Edition. Ed. Albert C. Outler. Nashville, TN: Abingdon Press, 1984, 1985, 1986, 1987.

Includes "The Reformation of Manners" (Psalm 94:16; 2: 300-324), "On Eternity" (Psalm 90:2; 2:358-372), "A Call to Backsliders" (Psalm 77:7-8; 3:210-226), "What Is Man?" (Psalm 8:3-4; 3:454-463), "On the Death of John Fletcher" (Psalm 37:37; 3:610-629), "What Is Man?" (Psalm 8:4; 4:19-27), "Human Life a Dream" (Psalm 73:20; 4:108-119), "The Danger of Increasing Riches" (Psalm 62:10; 4:177-186), and "On Guardian Angels" (Psalm 91:11; 4:224-235).

2290. Whyte, Robert B. *Personalities behind the Psalms: Sermons on Twelve Psalms and Their Authors.* Nashville, TN: Abingdon-Cokesbury, 1942. 191p.

Psalms 22, 29, 43, 50, 72, 73, 88, 89, 90, 100, 108, 119.

2291. Wolverton, Wallace I. "Sermons in the Psalms [Psalms 78, 103, 106]." *Canadian Journal of Theology* 10 (1964): 166-176.

2292. Yates, Kyle M. *Preaching from the Psalms.* Nashville, TN: Broadman Press, 1948. 203p.

Psalms 1, 2, 15, 23, 32, 34, 40, 42-43, 46, 51, 57, 73, 84, 100, 103, 107, 110, 116, 130, and 139.

C. Music and Songs

2293. Alison, Richard (fl. 1588-1606). *The Psalmes of David in Meter. 1599.* Ed. Ian Harwood. English Lute Songs (Menston, Yorkshire) 1. Menston, England: Scolar Press, 1968. 150p.

2294. ______. *Psalms of David. The Four-part Settings in Allison's Companion 1599 to the London Edition of the English Metrical Psalter.* Ed. Robert Illing. Adelaide: R. Illing, 1985. 103p.

2295. Appel, R.G. *The Music of the Bay Psalm Book, 9th Edition (1698).* Cambridge, MA: Harvard University Press, 1975.

2296. Avenary, H. "A Genizah Find of Saadya's Psalm-preface and its Musical Aspects." *Hebrew Union College Annual* 39 (1968): 145-162.

2297. Badalì, Enrico. "La musica presso gli ittiti: un aspetto particolare del culto in onore di divinità." *Bibbia e Oriente* 28 (1986): 55-64.

The Hittites used the standard types of instruments in their cult: strings, percussion, winds.

2298. Bailey, Terence. "Accentual and Cursive Cadences in Gregorian Psalmody." *American Musicological Society Journal* 29 (1976): 463-471.

2299. Ball, M. *Singing to the Lord. The Psalms as Hymns.* London: Bible Reading Fellowship, 1979. 78p.

An account of how the Biblical psalms have been rendered in English by Christian hymn-writers.

2300. Bäumlin, Klaus. "Die Zumutung der Genfer Psalmen: Notizen über ein vergessenes reformiertes Erbe." *Reformation* 35 (1986): 272-280.

2301. Benedictines of Solesmes, ed. *Paléographie musicale.* 17 vols. Berne: Lang, 1889-.

Facsimiles and studies of plainsong Manuscripts.

2302. _____. *Graduale Romanum.* Tournai, Belgium: Desclée & Co., 1974. 918p.

2303. Bermingham, Ronald P. "Les Psaumes mesurés de Jean-Anoine de Baïf: la poétique païenne au service de la Contre-Réforme." *Renaissance and Reformation,* N.S., 11 (1987): 41-57.

2304. Brueggemann, Walter. "Praise and the Psalms: A Politics of Glad Abandonment." *The Hymn* 43 (1992): 14-19.

2305. Cabaniss, Allen. "The Background of Metrical Psalmody." *Calvin Theological Journal* 20 (1985): 191-206.

2306. Calvin, Jean (1509-1564). *Calvin's First Psalter: 1539. With Critical Notes, and Modal Harmonies to the Melodies.* Ed. Richard R. Terry. London: E. Benn, 1932. xiii+112p.

2307. Casetti, P. "Funktionen der Musik in der Bibel." *Freiburger Zeitschrift für Philosophie und Theologie* 24 (1977): 366-389.

2308. Chambers, Joseph D. *The Psalter, or, Seven Ordinary Hours of Prayer, According to the Use of the Illustrious & Excellent Church of Sarum; and the hymns, antiphons, & orisons or collects, for the principal festivals and seasons; with the appropriate musical intonations and melodies; together with hymns and other devotions from ancient English sources, and the more important variations of the York and Hereford uses; also, the litany & vigils of the dead. Translated and arranged for private or coenobial uses, with explanatory notes and comments.* London: Printed and Sold by Joseph Masters, 1852. 442p.

2309. *Christian Music Directories, The: Printed Music 1992-1993.* San Jose, CA: Resource Publications, 1993. 1083p.

Formerly called *The Music Locator,* this resource indexes printed music from over 500 publishers.

2310. *Christian Music Directories, The: Recorded Music 1992.* San Jose, CA: Resource Publications, 1992. 1015p.

This resource indexes recorded music from over 500 music companies.

2311. Conomos, Dimitri. "Psalmody and the Communion Cycle; Communion Hymns." *St. Vladimir's Theological Quarterly* 25 (1981): 35-62, 95-122.

Liturgical cycle of Byzantine Koinonika.

2312. Crawford, Richard. *Andrew Law, American Psalmodist.* Evanston, IL: Northwestern University Press, 1968. xix+424p.

2313. _____, ed. *The Core Repertory of Early American Psalmody.* Recent Researches in American Music 11-12. Madison, WI: University of Wisconsin, 1984.

2314. _____. "Psalmody." In *The New Grove Dictionary of American Music,* ed. H. Wiley Hitchcock and Stanley Sadie. III: 635-643. New York: Macmillan, 1986.

1. Early psalm books, congregations, and singing-schools. 2. The rise of choirs and elaborate psalmody. 3. Musical style. 4. Reform.

2315. Cuchesne-Guillemin, Marcelle. "A Hurrian Musical Score from Ugarit: The Discovery of Mesopotamian Music." *Sources from the Ancient Near East* 2 (1984): 65-94.

2316. Davie, D. "Psalmody as Translation." *Modern Language Review* 85 (1990): 817-828.

2317. Douglas, Winfred. *Church Music in History and Practice. Studies in the Praise of God.* New York: Charles Scribner's, 1937. xvi+311p. Revised with Additonal Material by Leonard Ellinwood. New York: Scribner's, 1962. xxii+263p.

History and background on Anglican liturgy.

2318. Dovaras, John. *Choral Settings of the Scriptures with English Texts.* Dayton, OH: Roger Dean Publishing (Lorenz Publishing Co.), 1988. 62p.

2319. Draffkorn Kilmer, A. "The Cult Song with Music from Ancient Ugarit." *Revue d'assyriologie et d'archéologie orientale* 68 (1974): 69-82.

2320. Dyer, Joseph. "The Singing of the Psalms in the Early-Medieval Office." *Speculum* 64 (1989): 535-578.

2321. Dyk, P.J. van. "Music in Old Testament Times." *Old Testament Essays* 4 (1991): 373-380.

2322. Eaton, J.H. "Music's Place in Worship: A Contribution from the Psalms." In *Prophets, Worship and Theodicy: Studies in Prophetism, Biblical Theology and Structural Rhetorical Analysis and on the Place of Music in Worship. Papers Read at the Joint British-Dutch Old Testament Conference held at Woudschoten 1982*, ed. A.S. van der Woude. *Oudtestamentische Studiën* 23. Leiden: E.J. Brill, 1984.

2323. Ellinwood, L. "Tallis' Tunes and Tudor Psalmody." *Musica Disciplina* 2 (1948): 189ff.

2324. Elsky, M. "Polyphonic Psalm Settings and the Voice of George Herbert's The Temple." *Modern Language Quarterly* 42 (1981): 227-246.

2325. Ende, Richard C. von. *Church Music: An International Bibliography.* Metuchen, NJ: Scarecrow Press, 1980. 473p.

2326. Evetts-Secker, J. "An Elizabethan Experiment in Psalmody: Ralph Buckland's *Seaven Sparkes of the Enkindled Soule.*" *Sixteenth Century Journal* 15 (1984): 311-326.

2327. Ferguson, Everett. "Psalm-singing at the Eucharist: Liturgical Controversy in the 4th Century." *Austin Seminary Bulletin* 98 (1983): 52-77.

Coptic, Greek, Latin, Syriac, Armenian versions of *Visio Pauli.*

2328. Finesinger, S.B. "Musical Instruments in the Old Testament." *Hebrew Union College Annual* 3 (1926): 21-76.

2329. Finney, T.M. "Psalmody Controversy: A Catalogue." *Perspectives* 9 (1968): 286-296.

2330. Finscher, Ludwig. "Zur Cantus-Firmus-Behandlung in der Psalm-Motette der Josquinzeit." In *Hans Albrecht in Memoriam.* 55ff. Kassel: Barenbreiter, 1962.

2331. Frost, Maurice. *English and Scottish Psalm and Hymn Tunes, c. 1543-1677.* London: Oxford University Press, 1953. 531p.

2332. Galpin, F.W. *The Music of the Sumerians.* London: Cambridge University Press, 1937. Reprint, Westport, CT: Greenwood Press, 1970.

2333. Gelineau, Joseph. *The Grail/Gelineau Psalter. 150 Psalms and 18 Canticles.* Text: The Grail (England). Psalmody: Joseph Gelineau. Compiled and edited by J. Robert Carroll. Chicago, IL: G.I.A. Publications, Inc., 1972. 249p.

2334. Gerstenberger, Erhard S. "Singing a New Song: On Old Testament and Latin American Psalmody." *Word and World* 5 (1985): 155-167.

2335. Gradenwirtz, P. *The Music of Israel: Its Rise and Growth Through 5000 Years.* New York: Norton, 1949.

2336. Gressmann, Hugo. *Musik und Musikinstrumente im Alten Testament.* Religiongeschichtlichc Versuche und Vorarbeiten 2/1/ Giessen: J. Ricker, 1903. 32p.

2337. _____. "The Development of Hebrew Psalmody." In *The Psalmists: Essays on their religious experience and teaching, their social background, and their place in the development of Hebrew Psalmody*, edited with an Introduction by D.C. Simpson. 1-21. London: Oxford University Press (Humphrey Milford), 1926.

2338. Groom, Lester H. *Accompanying Harmonies for the Plainsong Psalter.* New York: The H.W. Gray Co., Inc., 1933.

2339. Grözinger, K.E. *Musik und Gesang in der Theologie der frühen jüdischen Literatur. Talmud, Midrasch, Mystik.* Texte und Studien zum Antiken Judentum 3. Tübingen: J.C.B. Mohr (Paul Siebeck), 1982. xiv+373p.

2340. Haïk-Vantoura, Suzanne. *La musique de la Bible révélée: une notation millénaire décryptée.* Paris: Robert Dumas, 1976. 2nd. edition, Paris: Dessain et Tolra, 1978. Translated from the 2nd French edition of 1978 by Dennis Weber and edited by John Wheeler, and published as The Music of the Bible Revealed: The Deciphering of a Millinary Notation. Berkeley, CA: BIBAL Press, 1991. 576p.

Claims to have reconstructed the original melodies for the Psalms. The Tiberian signs have been misunderstood; a new "key" to deciphering their original musical meaning is offered. Here, chironomy, a system of hand gestures that convey musical meaning, becomes important for passing on the original musical melodies; each sign represents a pitch on a scale. Recordings are available.

Appreciative reviews and summaries given by John Wheeler, "Music of the Temple," *Archaeology and Biblical Research* 2/1 (Winter, 1989): 12-20; "The Music of the Temple," *Archaeology and Biblical Research* 2/4 (Autumn, 1989): 113-122; "Biblical Songs for Modern Harpers," *Folk Harp Journal* 71 (Winter, 1990): 54. Critical review by P. Jeffrey in *Biblical Archaeology Review* 18/4 (July/August, 1992): 6.

2341. ______. *The 150 Psalms in their Ancient Melodies.* 2 vols. Paris: Fondation Roi David, 1985. 852p.

2342. Harper, John. *Forms and Orders of Western Liturgy from the 10th to the 18th Century. A Historical Introduction and Guide for Students and Musicians.* Oxford: Clarendon Press (Oxford University Press), 1991. 337p.

2343. Hermany, D. "Anthems based on Psalms." *Journal of Church Music* 9 (Nov, 1967): 12; 10 (Feb, 1968): 12; 10 (March, 1968): 12; 11 (March, 1969): 11.

2344. Holbert, John, S. T. Kimbrough, Jr., and Carlton R. Young. *Psalms for Praise and Worship: A Complete Liturgical Psalter.* Nashville, TN: Abingdon Press, 1992.

2345. Holm-Nielsen, Svend. "The Importance of Late Jewish Psalmody for the Understanding of the Old Testament Psalmody Tradition." *Studia Theologica* 14 (1960): 1-53.

2346. Hood, George. *A History of Music in New England. With Biographical Sketches of Reformers and Psalmists.* Boston: Wilkins & Carter, 1846. vii+252p. Reprint, 1970.

2347. Howard, Julie. *Sing for Joy: Psalm Settings for God's Children.* Collegeville, MN: The Liturgical Press, 1991. Songbook, 48p; Accompaniment Book, 64p. Cassette.

2348. Idelsohn, A.Z. *Thesaurus of Hebrew Oriental Melodies.* 10 vols. Leipzig-New York-Jerusalem, 1914-1932. Reprint, New York: KTAV, 1973.

2349. ______. *Jewish Music in its Historical Development.* New York: H. Holt and Co., 1929. 2nd ed., 1944. Reprint, New York: Schocken Books, 1965. xi+535p.

2350. Illing, Robert. *Est-Barley-Ravenscroft and the English Metrical Psalter.* Adelaide: R. Illing, 1969.

2351. Jacobi, J.C. *Psalmodia Germanica, or, The German Psalmody. Translated from the High Dutch; together with their proper tunes and thorough bass. London: G.*

Smith, 1722-25. 2nd ed., 1732. viii+212p. 3rd ed., corrected and very much enlarged, London: Re-printed and sold by H. Gaine, at the Bible & Crown, in Queen-Street, 1756. vi+279p. Supplement added by J. Haberkorn, 1765.

2352. Julian, John, ed. *A Dictionary of Hymnology.* 2 vols. Second Revised Edition with New Supplement. London: John Murray, 1907; reprint, New York: Dover Publications, 1957.

2353. Kelly, Thomas Forrest. *The Beneventan Chant.* New York: Cambridge University Press, 1989. 424p.

The Beneventan Chant was the Latin church music of Southern Italy as it existed before the spread of Gregorian chant.

2354. Kilmer, A.D., R.L. Crocker, and R.R. Brown. *Sounds from Silence. Recent Discoveries in Ancient Near Eastern Music.* Berkeley, CA: Bit Enki Publications, 1976. (Booklet and stereo record.)

2355. Kraeling Carl H., and Lucetta Mowry. "Music in the Bible." *The New Oxford History of Music*, ed. J. A. Westrop and Others. 11 vols. Vol. 1: *Ancient and Oriental Music,* ed. Egon Wellesz. 283-312. London: Oxford University Press, 1957.

2356. Laster, James. *Catalogue of Choral Music Arranged in Biblical Order.* Metuchen, NJ: Scarecrow Press, 1983. 269p.

2357. _____. *Catalogue of Vocal Solos and Duets Arranged in Biblical Order.* Metuchen, NJ: Scarecrow Press, 1984. 212p.

2358. Leaver, Robin A. *Goostly Psalmes and Spiritual Songes. English and Dutch Metrical Psalms from Coverdale to Utehove, 1535-1566. Oxford Studies in British Church Music.* New York: Oxford University Press, 1991. xvii+344p.

1) The Reformation, Liturgical Change, and Hymnody. 2) Early Beginnings of Hymnody in English. 3) Early Beginnings of Hymnody in Dutch. 4) Liturgical Necessity in the English Church. 5) Liturgical Necessity in the Dutch Stranger Church. 6) Strangers and Exiles Abroad. 7) Return to England. 8) Conclusion.

2359. _____. "Isaac Watt's Hermeneutical Principles and the Decline of English Metrical Psalmody." *Churchman: A Journal of Anglican Theology* 92 (1978): 56-60.

2360. _____. "Psalm Singing and Organ Regulations in a London Church *c* 1700." *The Hymn* 35 (1984): 29-35.

2361. Leeb, Helmut. *Die Psalmodie bei Ambrosius.* Wiener Beiträge zur Theologie 18. Vienna: Herder, 1967. 115p.

2362. *Liber Usualis with Introduction and Rubrics in English, The.* Edited by the Benedictines of Solesmes. Tournai, Belgium: Desclée & Co., 1934; reprint, New York, 1952. 1912p.

2363. Litton, James, ed. *The Plainsong Psalter.* New York: The Church Hymnal Corporation, 1988. xv+324p.

2364. Lobwasser, Ambrosius (1515-1585). *Das Düsseldorfer Gesangbuch von 1612.* Ed. Evangelische Kirchengemeinden Düsseldorf. Facsimile reproduction. Schriftenreihe des Vereins für Rheinische Kirchengeschichte 72. Cologne: Rheinland-Verlag, 1983; Bonn: R. Habelt Verlag, 1983. 774p.

2365. Macdougall, H.C. *Early New England Psalmody: An Historical Appreciation, 1620-1820.* Brattleboro, VT: Stephen Daye Press, 1940. Reprint, 1969. 179p.

2366. McKinnon, James W. "Musical Instruments in Medieval Psalm Commentaries and Psalters." *Journal of the American Musicological Society* 21 (1968): 3-20.

2367. ______. *Music in Early Christian Literature.* Cambridge Readings in the Literature of Music. New York: Cambridge University Press, 1987. 192p.

2368. MacLean, Ewen A. "Gaelic Psalm-singing and the Lowland Connection." *Liturgical Review* 3/2 (1973): 54.-62.

2369. Mahrenholz, Christhard, and Oskar Sühngen, in collaboration with Otto Schliske, eds. *Handbuch zum evangelischen Kirchengesangbuch.* Band I-III (5 vols.). Göttingen: Vandenhoeck & Ruprecht, 1956-1970.

Information related to the German Lutheran Hymnal. Of particular interest is Band II/2, *Die biblischen Quellen der Lieder [The Biblical Sources of the Songs],* by Rudolf Köhler (1957).

2370. Metcalf, Frank Johnson. *American Psalmody; or titles of books containing tunes printed in America from 1721 to*

1820. New introduction by Harry Eskew. New York: Da Capo Press, 1968.

An unabridged republication of the first edition published in New York in 1917. Reviewed by R.A. Crawford in *Notes* 26 (1969): 42-43.

2371. Miller, Patrick D., Jr. "The Psalms as Praise and Poetry." *The Hymn* 40 (1989): 12-16.

2372. Miller, Terry E. "Oral Tradition Psalmody Surviving in England and Scotland." *The Hymn* 35 (1984): 29-35.

2373. Müller, Norbert. *Die liturgische Vergegenwärtigung der Psalmen. Untersuchungen zur hermeneutischen Problematik der lutherischen Propriumpsalmodie.* Forschungen zur Geschichte und Lehre des Protestantismus, 10. Reihe, Band 21. Munich: Chr. Kaiser Verlag, 1961.

2374. ______. "Luthers Psalmlieder und die Mitte seiner Theologie." *Theologische Literaturzeitung* 108 (1983): 481-492.

2375. Naumbourg, S. *Zemiroth Yisrael. 3 vols.* Leipzig: Kaufmann, (1864). Reprint as Out of Print Classics Series of Synagogue Music 13-14. New York: Sacred Music Press (Bloch Publishing Co.), 1954.

2376. Ortigue, Joseph Louis d'. *Dictionnaire liturgique, historique et théorique de plain-chant et de musique d'église, au moyen âge et dans les temps modernes.* Paris: J.P. Migne, 1853. Reprint, New York: Da Capo, 1971. 1563p.

2377. Owen, Barbara. "The Bay Psalm Book and Its Era." *The Hymn* 41 (1990): 12-19.

2378. *Oxford American Psalter, The.* Pointed and Set to Anglican Chants by Ray F. Brown. New York: Oxford University Press, 1949.

2379. *Oxford Psalter, The. Containing The Psalms, together with The Canticles and Hymns, The Litany (1544) and Proper Psalms for Certain Days.* Newly Pointed for Chanting and Edited by Henry G. Ley, E. Stanley Roper, and C. Hylton Stewart. London: Oxford University Press, 1929. 2nd ed., 1936.

2380. Patrick, Millar. *Four Centuries of Scottish Psalmody.* London: Geoffrey Cumberlege (Oxford University Press), 1949. 234p.

2381. Perry, David W. *Hymns and Tunes Indexed by First Lines, Tune Names, and Metres Compiled from Current English Hymnbooks.* Croydon, England: Hymn Society of Great Britain & Ireland, Royal School of Church Music, 1980. 310p.

2382. Peter, Jeffery. "The Introduction of Psalmody into the Roman Mass by Pope Celestine I (422-432): Reinterpreting a Passage in the *Liber Pontificalis.*" *Archiv für Liturgie Wissenschaft* 26 (1984): 147-165.

2383. Pidoux, P. *Le psautier huguenot du XVIe siècle. Mélodies et documents.* 2 vols. Basel: Édition Bärenreiter, 1962.

2384. Pierik, Marie. *The Psalter in the Temple and the Church.* Washington, D.C.: The Catholic University of America Press, 1957. xi+101p.

Reviewed in *CBQ* 19 (1957): 408-409.

2385. Pratt, Waldo S. *The Music of the Pilgrims.* Boston: Oliver Ditson Co., 1921. Reprint, 1971.

2386. ______. *The Music of the French Psalter of 1562. A Historical Survey and Analysis. With the Music in Modern Notation.* New York: Columbia University Press, 1939; Oxford: Oxford University Press, 1939.

2387. *Presbyterian Hymnal, The: Hymns, Psalms, and Spiritual Songs.* Louisville, KY: Westminster/John Knox Press, 1990.

2388. *Psalter Hymnal 1987, The.* Grand Rapids, MI: CRC Publications, 1987.

2389. Quasten, Johannes. *Musik und Gesang in den Kulten der heidnischen Antike und christlichen Frühzeit.* Münster (Westfalen): Aschendorff, 1930. Reprint, 1973. Translated into English by Boniface Ramsey and published as *Music & Worship in Pagan & Christian Antiquity.* Washington, D.C.: National Association of Pastoral Musicians, 1983.

2390. Ramseth, Betty Ann. *Making Happy Noises: Psalms in Melody and Motion for Children.* Minneapolis, MN: Augsburg Fortress, 1974.

2391. Randel, D. *The Responsorial Psalm Tones for the Mozarabic Office.* Princeton, NJ: Princeton University Press, 1969.

2392. Reid, W.S. "Battle Hymns of the Lord: Calvinist Psalmody of the Sixteenth Century." *Sixteenth Century Journal* 2 (1971): 36-54.

2393. Ritchie, James. *FolkPsalms: A Musical Story Based on the Book of Psalms.* Arr. John Erickson. 20 minutes. Nashville, TN: Cokesbury, 1993.

2394. Rupprecht, Oliver C. "Timeless Treasure: Luther's Psalm Hymns." *Concordia Theological Quarterly* 47 (1983): 131-146.

2395. Sachs, Curt. *The Rise of Music in the Ancient World, East and West.* New York: W.W. Norton & Co., 1943. 324p.

2396. Sadie, Stanley, ed. *The New Grove Dictionary of Musical Instruments.* 3 vols. London: Macmillan Press Limited, 1984.

2397. Salevic, M. *Die Vertonung der Psalmen Davids im 20 Jahrhundert; Studien im deutschen Sprachbereich.* Regensburg: Pustet, 1976.

2398. Schalk, Carl. "Improvisatory Psalm Singing: Some Techniques and Suggestions." *The Hymn* 33 (1982): 84-88.

2399. Schneider, Severin. "Loben und Singen in den Psalmen." *Dienender Glaube* 55 (1979): 214-220.

2400. Schütz, Heinrich (1585-1672). *Psalmen Davids, op. 2.* Stuttgarter Schützausgabe in Kooperation mit dem Hänssler Musik-Verlag. Stuttgart, Germany: Carus-Verlag, 1991.

2401. *Scottish Psalter, 1929. Metrical Version and Scripture Paraphrases, with Tunes, The.* London: Oxford University Press, 1929.

2402. Seebass, Tilman. *Musikdarstellung und Psalterillustration im früheren Mittelalter: Studien ausgehend von einer Ikonologie der Handschrift Paris, Bibliothèque Nationale, Fonds Latin 1118.* 2 vols. Berne: Francke, 1973.

2403. Seidel, Hans. "Untersuchungen zur Aufführungspraxis der Psalmen in altisraelitischen Gottesdienst." *Vetus Testamentum* 33 (1983): 503-509.

2404. ______. *Musik in Altisrael: Untersuchungen zur Musikgeschichte und Musikpraxis Altisraels anhand biblischer und ausserbiblischer Texte.* Beiträge zur Erforschung des Alten Testaments und des Antiken Judentums 12. Frankfurt am Main/Bern/New York: Lang, 1989. ii+352p.

2405. Sendrey, Alfred. *Bibliography of Jewish Music.* New York: Columbia University Press, 1951. Reprint, New York: Kraus Reprint Co., 1969. 404p.

2406. ______. *Music in Ancient Israel.* New York: Philosophical Library, 1969.

Reviewed by E. Werner in *Journal of the American Musicological Society* 23 (1970): 529.

2407. _____, and Mildred Norton. *David's Harp. The Story of Music in Biblical Times.* New York: New American Library, 1964.

2408. Singer, Samuel. *Die religiöse Lyrik des Mittelalters. Das Nachleben der Psalmen.* Bern: Francke, 1933. 142p.

2409. Smith, C.-S., ed. *Early Psalmody in 17th Century America.* New York: New York Public Library, 1938-.

2410. Smith, J.A. "The Ancient Synagogue, the Early Church and Singing." *Music and Letters* 65 (1984): 1-16.

2411. _____. "Which Psalms Were Sung in the Temple?" *Music and Letters* 71 (1990): 167-186.

2412. Spencer, Donald Amos. *Hymn and Scripture Selection Guide: A cross reference of scripture and hymns with over 12,000 references for 380 hymns and gospel songs.* Valley Forge, PA: Judson Press, 1977. 176p.

2413. Steiner, Ruth. "Psalter, Liturgical." In *The New Grove Dictionary of Music and Musicians* (20 vols.), ed. Stanley Sadie. London: Macmillan Publishers Limited, 1980.

2414. Szövërffy, Joseph. *A Guide to Byzantine Hymnography: A Classified Bibliography of Texts and Studies.* 2 vols. Brookline, MA: Classical Foila Editions, 1978; Leiden: E.J. Brill, 1978.

2415. Temperley, Nicholas. "John Playford and the Metrical Psalms." *Journal of the American Musicological Society* 25 (1972): 331-378.

2416. ______. "Middleburg Psalms." *Studies in Bibliography* 30 (1977): 162-179.

2417. ______, Howard Slenk, Margaret Munck, and John M. Barkley. "Psalms, metrical." In *The New Grove Dictionary of Music and Musicians* (20 vols.), ed. Stanley Sadie. London: Macmillan Publishers Limited, 1980.

2418. Thalben-Ball, G.T., ed. *The Choral Psalter*. London: Ernest Benn, Ltd., 1957.

2419. Thuner, O.E. *Dansk Salme-Leksikon: Haandbog i dansk Salmesang. En hymnologisk Sammenstilling af Ord og Toner med historiske og bibliografiske Oplysninger.* Copenhagen: O. Lohse, 1930. 592p.

Lists 1108 Danish psalm settings with detailed information concerning sources. Indexed by melody groups, personal names, and first line of text.

2420. Turner, E.R. "Earwitnesses to Resonance in Space: An Interpretation of Puritan Psalmody in Early 18th-Century New England." *American Studies* 25 (1984): 25-47.

2421. Vogel, Dwight W. *Singing the Psalms. Singing the Psalms and Canticles in the United Methodist Hymnal.* Your Ministry of Series. Nashville, TN: Discipleship Resources, 1991. 40p.

2422. Warrington, James. *Short Titles of Books Relating to the History of Psalmody in the United States, 1620-1820.* Philadelphia: Private Printing, 1898.

2423. Watts, Isaac (1674-1748). *The Psalms, Hymns and Spiritual Songs of the Rev. Isaac Watts, D.D.: To Which are added, Select Hymns, from other authors; and directions for musical expression by Samuel M. Worcester, D.D.* Edited by Samuel M. Worcester. New Edition. Boston: Crocker & Brewster, 1867.

2424. Webber, Christopher L. *A New Metrical Psalter.* New York: The Church Hymnal Corporation, 1986. 240p.

2425. Wegener, Max. *Die Musikinstrumente des Alten Orients.* Orbis Antiquus 2. Münster in Westfalen: Aschendorff, 1950. 73p.

2426. Wellesz, E. *Byzantine Music and Hymnography.* Oxford: Oxford University Press, 1949.

2427. Werner, Eric. "Preliminary Notes for a Comparative Study of Catholic and Jewish Musical Punctuation." *Hebrew Union College Annual* 15 (1940): 335-360.

2428. ______. "The Origin of the Eight Modes of Music (Octoechos)." *Hebrew Union College Annual* 21 (1948): 211-255.

2429. ______. "The Origins of Psalmody." *Hebrew Union College Annual* 25 (1954): 327-345.

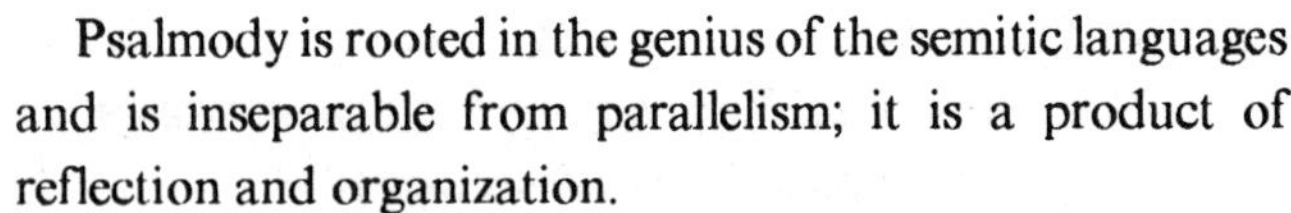
Psalmody is rooted in the genius of the semitic languages and is inseparable from parallelism; it is a product of reflection and organization.

2430. ______. "The Music of Post-Biblical Judaism." In *The New Oxford History of Music*, ed. J.A. Westrup and Others. 11 vols. Vol. 1: *Ancient and Oriental Music*, ed. Egon Wellesz. 313-335. London: Oxford University Press, 1957.

2431. ______. *The Sacred Bridge: The Interdependence of Liturgy and Music in Synagogue and Church During the First Millennium.* 2 vols. Vol. 1: London and New York: Columbia University Press, 1959; reprint 1970; Vol. 2: New York: KTAV Publishing House, 1984. xviii+271p.

2432. ______, Bruno Stäblein, and Ludwig Finscher. "Psalm." In *Die Musik in Geschichte und Gegenwart: Allgemeine Enzyklopädie der Musik,* ed. Friedrich Blume. Vol. 10: 1668-1713. Kassel, Germany: Bärenreiter Verlag, 1962.

A. Pre-Christian and early Christian Psalms (Werner). B. Latin Psalm Singing in the Middle Ages (Stäblein). C. Polyphonic Psalm Composition (Finscher).

2433. ______, Thomas H. Connolly, Paul Doe, and Malcolm Boyd. "Psalm." In *The New Grove Dictionary of Music and Musicians* (20 vols.), ed. Stanley Sadie. London: Macmillan Publishers Limited, 1980.

I. Antiquity and early Christianity. II. Latin monophonic psalmody. III. Polyphonic psalms.

2434. _____ and I. Sonne. "The Philosophy and Theory of Music in Judaeo-Arabic Literature." *Hebrew Union College Annual* 16 (1941): 251-319; 17 (1943): 511-572.

2435. *Worship: A Hymnal and Service Book for Roman Catholics.* 3rd ed. Chicago, IL: G.I.A. Publications, 1986. 1213+p.

2436. Wyton, Alec, ed. *The Anglican Chant Psalter.* New York: The Church Hymnal Corporation, 1987. xii+342p.

2437. Young, Thomas. *The Metrical Psalms and Paraphrases. A Short Sketch of Their History with Biographical Notes of Their Authors.* London: A. & C. Black: Edinburgh: R & R. Clark, 1909. x+199p.

2438. Zahn, Johannes., ed. *Die Melodien der deutschen evangelischen Kirchenlieder aus den Quellen geschopft und mitgeteilt.* 6 vols. Gütersloh: Bertelsmann, 1889-1893; reprint, Hildesheim: Georg Olms, 1963.

Presents 8806 melodies, derived from the earliest sources, for the German Protestant Liturgy. Classified according to metrical form. Also includes biographical notices of 463 chorale composers or editors or chorale collections. Index of composers and of first-line of text.

2439. Zak, R.A. "Dialogue and Discourse in Stravinsky's Symphony of Psalms." *Criticism* 22 (1980): 357-375.

2440. Zimmermann, Heinz Werner. *Psalmkonzert.* For SSATB choir, unison children's choir, baritone soloist, three trumpets, vibraphone, and string bass. Berlin: Verlag Merseburger, 1965. English edition by Audrey Davidson and Marian Johns. St. Louis, MO: Concordia Publishing House, 1967.

See also: 4932.